# WHO IS THE DOCTOR 2

# WHO IS THE DOCTOR 2

## THE UNOFFICIAL GUIDE TO DOCTOR WHO

### THE MODERN SERIES

GRAEME BURK & ROBERT SMITH?

Published by ECW Press
665 Gerrard Street East
Toronto, Ontario, Canada M4M 1Y2
416-694-3348 / info@ecwpress.com

Cover design and illustration: Natalie Racz
Author photo: Heather Murray

LIBRARY AND ARCHIVES CANADA CATALOGUING IN PUBLICATION

Title: Who is the doctor : the unofficial guide to Doctor Who. 2,
the modern series / Graeme Burk & Robert Smith?

Names: Burk, Graeme, 1969– author. | Smith?, Robert, 1972
October 28– author.

Identifiers: Canadiana (print) 20190230622
Canadiana (ebook) 20190230630

ISBN 978-1-77041-415-0 (softcover)
ISBN 978-1-77305-471-1 (PDF)
ISBN 978-1-77305-470-4 (EPUB)

Subjects: LCSH: Doctor Who (Television program : 2005– )

Classification: LCC PN1992.77.D63 B88 2020
DDC 791.45/72—dc23

The publication of *Who Is The Doctor 2* has been funded in part by the Government of Canada. *Ce livre est financé en partie par le gouvernement
du Canada*. We also acknowledge the contribution of the Government of Ontario through the Ontario Book Publishing Tax Credit, and through
Ontario Creates for the marketing of this book.

. . . . . . . . . . . . . . . . . . . . . . . . . . . . . . . . . . . . . . . . . . . . . . . . . . . . . . . . .

*For Shannon Dohar and Joy Piedmont:*
*the best of friends and the best of fans*
*— GB*

*For Gina, for friendship and support when I needed it most*
*— RS?*

# Contents

## SERIES ELEVEN (2018)

## APPENDICES

# Introduction

"We are here today because *Doctor Who* is the greatest show on television. We really mean this, by the way. That's not hyperbole."

That was the opening line of the first volume of our *Doctor Who* episode guide — *Who Is The Doctor* — which was published way back in 2012. Eight years later, we're back for a second volume, and . . . yep. We still mean that.

*Doctor Who* has now been on for 37 seasons across 56 years. (That's 26 seasons of the Classic Series from 1963 to 1989 and 11 seasons of the Modern Series that began in 2005) and has broadcast (at the time of writing) 313 stories. You would think with a show this long-lived that you would need a book just to understand what's going on . . .

Nah.

This is all you need to know about *Doctor Who*: it's about someone called the Doctor, who travels in a time machine disguised as a blue telephone box and battles monsters.

The rest of it — the Doctor's ability to regenerate their form into someone new (male or female), the Doctor's home planet, the Doctor's companions — that's stuff that goes into *Doctor Who* for sure, but you don't need to know about those things to enjoy it.

Because that's the thing about *Doctor Who*: it's fun. Pure, unadulterated fun. The kind of fun that comes from travelling through time and space in a machine that's bigger on the inside than the outside. Fun television shouldn't require a Ph.D. or even an entrance exam. You shouldn't need a book like ours to understand *Doctor Who*.

But we think this book can make watching *Doctor Who* even more fun for you.

## Who We Are

This book is a co-authored affair, written by two friends with very different ideas about *Doctor Who*, television drama and, indeed, life. If you haven't met us before, this is who we are. (If you have, welcome back.)

Here are six facts about us . . . one of them is a lie. (You can find the answers in the Acknowledgements.)

### Graeme Burk (GB)

1. I've been watching *Doctor Who* since I was a 14-year-old entranced by the killer mummies in "Pyramids of Mars."
2. I've written a number of books about *Doctor Who*, edited a fanzine about *Doctor Who* and currently co-host a podcast about *Doctor Who* called *Reality Bomb*.
3. I once told Sophie Aldred that Ace was tied with Leela as my favourite *Doctor Who* companion.
4. I hosted a game show on public access cable TV as a teenager.
5. I contributed to the memoir of *Doctor Who*'s creator, Sydney Newman, and even found new evidence that Newman came up with the original idea of *Doctor Who*.
6. Colin Baker once kissed me on the mouth on my birthday.

### Robert Smith? (RS?)

1. I've been watching *Doctor Who* since I was a five-year-old entranced by the giant fly in "The Green Death."
2. I've written and edited a number of books about *Doctor Who*, *Star Trek*, *Buffy the Vampire Slayer* and zombies.
3. I share a birthday and am exactly the same age as one of actors who played the Doctor.
4. I've been attacked by pirates in the Gulf of Guinea, got kidnapped in Senegal and was bitten by a lion in South Africa.
5. I once accidentally created an entire academic subdiscipline and in doing so won a Guinness World Record.
6. Colin Baker once told me he loved me.

## About the Book

We review 66 stories (including three mini-episodes) that comprise Series Seven through Eleven of the modern version of *Doctor Who*. Each of them has a guide entry, which includes the following categories:

**The Big Idea** What the story is about in 45 words or less.

**Roots and References** These are the things in literature or pop culture that might have influenced the writing, design or production of the story, along with references directly cited by characters in the episode.

**Adventures in Time and Space** *Doctor Who* has been around since 1963; you're bound to find a reference or two (or 13) to past *Doctor Who* continuity in a story. We cover everything from the Atraxi to the Zygons.

**The Story Arc Effect** Series Seven to Ten of the Modern Series are each driven by an ongoing story arc — from a repeated meme to the development of a story. We'll explain how a particular episode fits into that series' arc.

**Unfinished Business** During Series Eleven, there was no story arc, so we track instead the ongoing character developments within the ensemble cast.

**The Doctor and the Companion** A statement on the progress of the relationship between the Doctor and the central companions.

**Monster of the Week** *Doctor Who* is all about the monsters. We talk about who or what they are.

**Stand Up and Cheer** The great moment in the story . . .

**Roll Your Eyes** . . . and the one that made you cringe.

**You're Not Making Sense** That moment in the story that made you go, "WTF?!"

**Interesting Trivia** Intriguing bits of behind-the-scenes information, facts about the *Doctor Who* universe and queries about the story. Or stuff that we found fascinating and think you will too.

**Cool?/Don't Be Stupid?/Aw, Brilliant?** The bottom-line critique by one of the authors.

**Second Opinion** The co-author contributes their own critique. Sometimes there's blessed agreement. Sometimes there's an unholy brawl.

## The Psychic Papers

This book also includes histories of various elements of the series, including its mythos, monsters and production. These entries will offer complete histories and may include spoilers for Classic *Doctor Who* stories and mild spoilers of other Modern Series stories. If you're reading this guide while watching the episodes for the first time, consider yourself warned.

## Oh My God, It's Back! It's the Unbelievably Geeky Part

We include this section in the introduction for all our books. If you're not a hardcore fan, don't worry about any of this stuff; you can skip to the end of the introduction. If you are hardcore, we're happy to argue with you, oh serious nerd. (We speak as one of you.)

We get that there are all kinds of intricate debates about matters pertaining to *Doctor Who*. (Here's one: was Sara Kingdom a companion?) Ultimately, this guide reflects the thinking of its authors. (Our answer to the above is yes.) Moreover, there are some things we had to make a call on for the sake of consistency. Here's a list of things to keep in mind.

- We continue with the stance from *Who Is The Doctor* that the post-2005 version of *Doctor Who* is effectively a new TV series, albeit one linked by continuity and heritage to the 1963–89 Classic version. Thus we call the 2014 season of *Doctor Who* "Series Eight," not "Season 34." This is pretty much how it is seen by most fans, the press and the BBC's own official home video boxsets. (We also follow the British convention of calling a season a "series" in this context.)

- We tend to include anything that has been broadcast on BBC1, which is why we're including the mini-episode "Friend from the Future." Anything that didn't air on BBC1 initially is included in an appendix.
- We didn't include the majority of online-only mini-episodes. You'll have to go someplace else to read a review of the school-class-written "Good as Gold." (It's trippy as hell.)
- In terms of the season placement of Christmas episodes, we tend to follow the lead of the BBC's own boxsets; thus "Last Christmas" is in Series Nine.
- The incarnation of the central character played by John Hurt does not call himself "the Doctor." He specifically renounces that name, in fact. We therefore do not use the "War Doctor" name BBC uses for him in its branding and choose to instead call him "the Warrior."
- We mostly follow the convention used by the producers of *Doctor Who* for episode numbering, whereby episode one is the first episode of the season proper. Thus Christmas specials are usually numbered as "0." Occasionally, if there's more than one episode before the first episode, we also use the designation "X."
- With the 2013 specials, we use the term "2013" instead of a season designation because they were made separately, as opposed to part of a season of *Doctor Who*.
- We've elected to call the post-2005 show the "Modern Series" as opposed to the "New Series" on the very reasonable grounds that it's been back for 15 years!

## Finally . . .

And we're back.

Like we said at the start, we're not writing these books because you need to consult them as a codex to a holy text. We're writing these books because *Doctor Who* is the most fun show on TV. And we think we can help you to have more fun.

We closed our introduction in the original *Who Is The Doctor* by saying, "We hope that *Who Is The Doctor* expands your understanding of *Doctor Who*, that it gives you something to laugh at, think about and argue with." We still want you to do that.

And now . . . here's the greatest show on television.

# SERIES SEVEN (2012—13)

**Starring**
Matt Smith as the Doctor
Karen Gillan as Amy Pond (7.01–7.05)
Arthur Darvill as Rory Williams (7.01–7.05)
Jenna-Louise Coleman as Clara Oswald
(7.01, 7.06–7.14)

**Executive Producers**
Steven Moffat
Piers Wenger and Beth Willis (7.00)
Caroline Skinner (7.01–7.14)

**Producers**
Marcus Wilson (7.00–7.07, 7.10–7.12)
Denise Paul (7.08–7.09, 7.13–7.14)

# 7.00 The Doctor, the Widow and the Wardrobe

**Written by** Steven Moffat **Directed by** Farren Blackburn

**Original airdate** December 25, 2011

**The Big Idea** The Doctor returns a favour to a recently widowed mother and her children at Christmas. But one of the Doctor's Christmas presents is a portal to a sentient forest on another planet in the future.

**Roots and References** *The Lion, the Witch and the Wardrobe* by C.S. Lewis (the title of the story, the children, the World War II setting and the magic box opening into a snow-covered forest); the BBC comedy series *Outnumbered* (Claire Skinner was best known for playing the mother in this sitcom, which was still running when this episode aired, and her casting seems to be influenced by it); Ursula K. Le Guin's *The Word for World Is Forest* (an invading force destroying the ecosystem); John Christopher's novels and the TV adaptation of *The Tripods* (the walker); the *Bones* episode "Spaceman in a Crater" (the Doctor's initial fall); J.R.R. Tolkien's *The Lord of the Rings* (the tree people resemble the Ents from *The Two Towers*). The Doctor with his backwards spacesuit looks like a 1940s robot or spaceman as seen in countless pulp science-fiction magazines of the era.

**Adventures in Time and Space** The soldiers are from the planet Androzani Major, which featured in the fifth Doctor's final story, 1984's "The Caves of Androzani." The Doctor mentions a tree from the Forest of Cheem that once fancied him, referring to Jabe in 2005's "The End of the World."

**Who Is the Doctor?** This episode begins a sequence of stories where the Doctor tries to make himself as anonymous as possible in the wake of having erased himself from history. Here, the Doctor poses as the Caretaker, only barely introducing himself as the Doctor. He does this out of gratitude to Madge for helping him after crashing to Earth, telling her he'll help her when she makes a wish for him. She does so three years later and he helps give her children a magical Christmas to remember.

**The Doctor and Amy** Having spent the adventure witnessing the bonds of family, the Doctor goes to visit Amy and Rory at the end of the story. They're already aware (thanks to a conversation with River in 2011's "The Wedding of River Song") that he isn't dead, but it's been two years since they've seen him. Nevertheless, they set a place for him every Christmas, just in case.

**Monster of the Week** The Wooden King and Queen start life as statues made of wood, but they're activated when Cyril sits on the throne. They're mute but can communicate by speaking through the voice of someone with whom they're in physical contact. They return to wooden form after Madge saves the life force of the trees.

**Stand Up and Cheer** The "interrogation" by the Androzani soldiers is hilarious. They won't interrogate Madge while she's crying, then one of them starts tearing up because he has mother issues. Another lowers her gun because pointing it at an unarmed, crying woman would be a "bad visual" (understanding public relations is apparently part of Androzani military training!). When the others agree to lower their guns out of respect for Madge as a woman, she manages to take control of the situation, a lovely moment of the show poking fun at overly sensitive attitudes.

**Roll Your Eyes** We could quite safely live without ever seeing another "woman driver" joke in *Doctor Who* ever again, thanks very much.

**You're Not Making Any Sense** Reg's plane is a Lancaster bomber, but those didn't come into use until 1942, a year after this story is set. And what happened to the other two crew members, including the one that was badly injured?

**Interesting Trivia** This episode was designed to be the most Christmassy of all the Christmas episodes. Which is slightly odd, as it's also a clear homage to C.S. Lewis's *The Lion, the Witch and the Wardrobe* (with the contrivance that the TARDIS is the Doctor's wardrobe, painted to look like a police box). All the snow in Narnia notwithstanding, that book isn't particularly Christmassy, despite the brief appearance of Father Christmas in one chapter. But merging the two styles together produces something quite visually striking, with walking Christmas trees, baubles that hatch and giant presents you can crawl through.

With this story, co-executive producers Piers Wenger and Beth Willis departed *Doctor Who*. As a parting gift, Moffat named Ven-Garr and Billis after his colleagues.

A "prequel" to the story appeared on the BBC's website a couple of weeks before "The Doctor, the Widow and the Wardrobe" was broadcast. It was not actually a prequel (the BBC website has a funny way of titling these things, as we'll see) but rather a scene set before the start of the story: the Doctor tries to call Amy from the TARDIS just before the spaceship begins to blow up. Even before he leaves the message, he knows she left the TARDIS a long time ago, and we realize he's calling her because he wanted a chat before blowing up. This leads directly into the opening scene in the spaceship.

**The TARDIS Chronometer** England, Christmas 1938 and Christmas 1941. The forest scenes take place in 5345.

**Cool? (RS?)** If Series Six was all about fathers and the difficult relationships they had with their children, "The Doctor, the Widow and the Wardrobe" is about a mother. It's no coincidence that Claire Skinner is the only guest star with "companion" billing in the credits during the entire Amy Pond era. Madge Arwell is the clear star of the show, grieving her lost husband but determined to carry on with a stiff upper lip in order to give her children one last happy Christmas before she has to break the terrible news to them.

For child actors, Maurice Cole and Holly Earl are pretty good as Cyril and Lily, with a decent amount of character that never gets cloying. The comedy cameos by the Androzani soldiers are fun, and the Wooden King and Queen are scary, even though they don't need to be. The Doctor's opening scenes, from the all-action destruction of the ship through to the comedy of the backwards helmet of his spacesuit, are also really fun.

I also can't praise the visuals enough. Everything here sparkles with Christmas magic and sheer wonder. Modern *Doctor Who* hasn't been one for majestic worldbuilding and amazement. Moments like the stunning garden in "The Girl Who Waited" have been few and far between. So the journey from the sitting room through the box into the forest is just incredible.

The whistle-stop tour of the house is also fabulous; the additions are so perfectly Doctorish. No, scratch that: they're so perfectly eleventh Doctorish. With taps that run lemonade, chairs that spin and a child's bedroom to end all bedrooms, the house perfectly encapsulates the childlike eleventh Doctor. Matt Smith is utterly adorable here, exclaiming, "I know!" at every new marvel and doing some fun pratfall comedy. You can't help but be charmed by him.

But this is a story about a grieving mother learning to live again. From her initial mistrust of the Doctor to her turning the tables on the Androzani soldiers to ascending to the throne by being strong enough, Madge goes through a cycle of growth, becoming whole once more . . .

. . . which makes it a little odd that there's a happy ending tacked on. After all this character growth, with Madge surviving and then thriving in a new world, the episode ends with something of a cod resolution, with her husband having survived. You can see why they did it: having a dead father on Christmas probably isn't a good visual, to quote the Androzani soldier, but the story has been actively dealing with a dead father the entire time, so the meat of it is already there, even if the eventual outcome flip-flops due to some timey-wimeyness.

The one thing I will note is that the producers are clearly aware of this because they go to great lengths to make it feel earned. The trip through the vortex is much longer than it probably would have been otherwise, leading us to a conclusion we could likely predict but can't help cheering anyway, despite being pretty saccharine. It's smile-worthy on the first viewing, even if it is the source of some significant eye-rolling subsequently.

I'm of two minds about the final scene with Amy. On the one hand, it's lovely and gives the episode more weight than it would otherwise have. On the other, it does kind of undercut the whole point. After the arc-heavy stories of Series Six, this episode was a breath of fresh air, with the Doctor going by a different name and just having an adventure, with all the wonder and magic that entails. Bringing Amy and Rory in at the end, as sweet as it is, kind of ruins that.

"The Doctor, the Widow and the Wardrobe" isn't the most perfect episode of *Doctor Who* ever made, but I can't help loving it. The (mostly) standalone nature of the story gives it a chance to do something different, and the visuals are astonishing. The focus on character is a great decision, and there's some truly hilarious comedy. It's best viewed with a large helping of pudding, some bon-bons and wrapping paper strewn everywhere. Incidentally, a happy Christmas to all of you at home!

**Second Opinion (GB)** Here's the thing with most *Doctor Who* Christmas specials: whatever I think about them while I watch them, I'll have forgotten most of them by the time I'm midway through the next season. That's not to say there aren't some exceptions to this rule — and there are some exceptions still to come — but most often, they honestly could be written by the Silence for all I'll remember them in future.

"The Doctor, the Widow and the Wardrobe" is a case in point. When it was first broadcast, it would be the only *Doctor Who* for another nine months. It carried a lot of weight. But by the time we made it to the middle of Series Seven, it was about as substantial as vapour.

Don't get me wrong, it features a great pre-credits sequence and buckets of charm everywhere you look, from the Doctor's crazy changes to the house (and Farren Blackburn's direction does a nice job of keeping that going) to, well, practically everything Claire Skinner does. But . . . beyond that, there's not a lot to this story.

The plot is slight. The menace isn't particularly scary. The PR-obsessed comedy soldiers are lame (and as someone who loves Bill Bailey, that's painful for me to say). And I don't know what planet my co-author is on: Matt Smith is doing children's TV presenting rather than acting — waggling his arms and shouting far too much. But where it really fails badly is the ending, which my esteemed partner lets off too easily. Even by Moffat-era standards, this is a way-too-sloppy use of the reset button.

There's one scene that really hits home: when Madge and the Doctor talk about the fact that once Christmas is done, Madge has to tell her children their father is dead. It's a moment of bitter honesty, beautifully acted by Claire Skinner and a briefly come-to-his-senses Matt Smith . . .

. . . and it's a moment completely invalidated by the ending because, wh-hey, it's Christmas, let's just do crazy magic and reset everything.

It's not that I have a problem with happy endings. I just believe "The Doctor, the Widow and the Wardrobe" would be more memorable and more substantial as a drama had it kept in the uncomfortable truth that every holiday can be happiness suffused with duty, guilt and sadness and that even jolly adventures can end in harsh reality.

Which is to say, I think you could have still had that sombre message on Christmas Day. It just takes courage. And effort. But that is not a choice made by "The Doctor, the Widow and the Wardrobe." It would rather wallow in its whimsy and in a few episodes it will . . .

Oh, sorry. What were we talking about?

- - - - - - - - - - - - - - - - - - - - - - - - - - - - - - - - - - - - - - - - - - - -

## Matt Smith

The youngest actor ever to play the role of the Doctor, Matt Smith was only 26 years old when he was cast in late 2008. Executive producer Steven Moffat had been planning to cast someone in their forties, and he was completely taken by surprise by the young actor. Smith had only just turned to theatre: he had trained to become a professional footballer, but an injury led him to take up acting. He was a rising star on the West End, receiving acclaim for his work in plays like *Swimming with Sharks* with Christian Slater (and his future *Doctor Who* co-star Arthur Darvill) and had received good notices for his early TV work, which included the 2007 BBC series *Party Animals*. He made films during and after his time as the eleventh Doctor, starring in Ryan Gosling's 2014 directorial debut *Lost River* and having a small but critical role in 2015's *Terminator: Genisys*, which would have expanded into a major role had the planned sequels happened. His greatest post–*Doctor Who* success was his portrayal of Prince Philip in the first two seasons of the 2016 Netflix series *The Crown*, for which he was twice nominated for an Emmy. He continues to work in film, playing a key role in *Star Wars: The Rise of Skywalker* and Marvel and Sony's planned adaptation of *Morbius, the Living Vampire*.

- - - - - - - - - - - - - - - - - - - - - - - - - - - - - - - - - - - - - - - - - - - -

## 7.01 Asylum of the Daleks

**Written by** Steven Moffat **Directed by** Nick Hurran
**Original airdate** September 1, 2012

**The Big Idea** The Doctor, Rory and Amy are given an impossible mission by the Daleks: stop the creature who threatens the asylum for insane Daleks. That creature's name is Oswin Oswald.

**Roots and References** Arkham Asylum from *Batman* comics (the asylum); the 1955 film *Night of the Hunter* (Amy's modelling stint sees her with "love" and "hate" written on her hands, similar to Robert Mitchum's character). Georges Bizet's 1875 opera *Carmen* features throughout both in terms of its soundtrack (the Doctor claims to have played the triangle in the recording Oswin plays) and visual references (Oswin's red costume, the flower in her hair). Rudimental's song "Feel the Love" is used during Amy's modelling session.

**Adventures in Time and Space** The Doctor is still believed to be dead following the events of "The Wedding of River Song" (2011). He meets with Darla von Karlsen in the ruins of Skaro, the Dalek homeworld (previously believed to be destroyed in 1988's "Remembrance of the Daleks" and featuring architecture first seen in 1963's "The Daleks"). The human Daleks are an update of the Robomen used by the Daleks in 1964's "The Dalek Invasion of Earth." The nanocloud that converts humans uses nanogene technology (2005's "The Empty Child"/"The Doctor Dances"). Amy is continuing her modelling career, which was established in 2011's "Closing Time."

Rory mentions his stint guarding Amy for 2,000 years in 2010's "The Pandorica Opens"/"The Big Bang" (continuing the confusing tradition of a human Rory remembering a life lived as an Auton duplicate). Amy can't have children as a result of her complicated pregnancy while imprisoned at Demon's Run (2012's "A Good Man Goes to War").

There are a *lot* of different Daleks on display: the New Paradigm Daleks from 2010's "Victory of the Daleks" have been pushed to a more managerial role, while the bronze Modern Series Daleks are back in force. The asylum has two 1960s models of Daleks (one with blue-and-grey livery, the other with a black top in the style of a throne room Dalek from 1967's "Evil of the Daleks"), a black Dalek from 1984's "Resurrection of the Daleks," a silver Dalek from 1974's "Death to the Daleks" and a white Imperial Dalek and the special weapons Dalek from "Remembrance of the Daleks."

Oswin says the Daleks in intensive care came from "Spiridon, Kembel, Aridius, Vulcan, Exxilon." The Doctor explains they were all in skirmishes with him, referring to 1973's "Planet of the Daleks," 1965's "The Daleks' Master Plan" and "The Chase," 1966's "The Power of the Daleks" and 1974's "Death to the Daleks." The Doctor reminds the Daleks he's known as the Oncoming Storm to them, a moniker given to him in 2005's "Bad Wolf"/"The Parting of the Ways." At the end of the episode, the Doctor dances around the console repeating "Doctor who?" again and again, echoing Dorium in "The Wedding of River Song."

**The Impossible Girl Effect** We won't know why for a while, but there is something very wrong about the presence of Oswin Oswald, entertainer from the starship *Alaska* and captive of the Daleks — and it's not just because she survived a year making soufflés without eggs and milk. Her presence in "Asylum of the Daleks" is setting up a mystery that will be explored in the second half of Series Seven. Her last words will become very important: "Run you clever boy, and remember."

**Who Is the Doctor?** The Doctor is known by the Daleks as their predator. He's surprised to discover the Daleks have a concept of beauty. This story continues a sequence of stories where the Doctor becomes more anonymous; here, his identity is erased from the Daleks' hive mind.

**The Doctor and Amy** Amy knows the Doctor so well, she's figured out his thought processes about how he'll defend them from the Daleks and that he's noticed from their body language that Amy and Rory have split up. But Amy isn't always one step ahead; the Doctor engineers a situation where Rory and Amy are able to talk and reconcile.

**Monster of the Week** The Daleks are back, deadlier than ever. No, really. We're taken to their asylum, which is a dumping ground for the Daleks who are irrevocably damaged or insane. The Daleks do this instead of exterminating them because they consider hatred beautiful. The Daleks have also developed a way to convert humans (both living and dead) into Daleks. They look and act like humans (and can retain their memories), but Dalek implements, like eye stalks or guns, can pop out of them.

**Stand Up and Cheer** The climax is genuinely heart-stopping as we cut from Oswin talking to the Doctor to a Dalek intoning the exact same dialogue. And it becomes clear the Doctor had figured out that Oswin was a Dalek ages ago. All the pieces were there for the viewer as well: the eggs and the milk for the soufflés, as well as Oswin's ability to survive in the Dalek asylum for a year. Plus the viewer had additional clues, like the Daleks' heads-up displays being in English and Oswin's quarters looking, somewhat, like the inside of a Dalek.

**Roll Your Eyes** Amy having turfed Rory because she can't have kids suddenly reminds the viewer that this show hasn't had a woman write for it in quite a while. And goodness does it show.

**You're Not Making Any Sense** The Daleks sending their predator to take care of a problem in their asylum? We're on board for that. But the Daleks researching which particular Doctor they're getting and then finding the right companions seems a bit far-fetched. And executing that plan right down to installing human Dalek agents to infiltrate where they are? Not to mention knowing what modelling shoot Amy was doing and what bus Rory was taking and doing all this instead of, you know, teleporting them. What you're telling us is that the Daleks are obsessive *Doctor Who* fans.

**Interesting Trivia** Prior to the season beginning, fans had several webisodes to set the stage: there was another incorrectly termed "prequel" where the Doctor is given a psychic message to meet Darla von Karlsen on Skaro. The more substantive work was Pond Life, a series of webisodes written by Chris Chibnall where we see how the Doctor keeps affecting Amy and Rory's married life and which ends with a scene indicating that Amy and Rory have decided to part ways. Most of these webisodes can still be found on YouTube or as extras on the DVD or Blu-ray sets, but the TV stories are constructed in such a way that nothing is lost if you haven't seen them.

When we last saw the Daleks in "Victory of the Daleks," the New Paradigm Daleks were set to take over from the original ones, and that was the case in comics and videogames and books (and the only appearance we had of a Dalek on TV in Series Six, at the start of "The Wedding of River Song"). But here we're back to the familiar bronze versions we've known since 2005, with the New Paradigm Daleks in the background acting as managerial figures. So what happened? First, the props were much harder for the operators to move: while the original Dalek construction since 1963 required the operators to simply sit and move around using their feet, the New Paradigm Daleks were taller, so moving them required the operators to stand and push up on them with their shoulders, which proved not only uncomfortable but a potential health-and-safety issue. And second . . . the new Daleks were *incredibly* unpopular with fans, who derided them online and elsewhere. Consequently, the new Daleks were sidelined. They're mostly stationary here and not very involved. We'll see even less of them in future.

While her casting as companion Clara Oswald had already been announced and her episodes were being shot, Jenna Coleman's presence in "Asylum of the Daleks" was a well-kept secret. When the episode was screened in New York and Toronto in advance of the season (your humble authors were at the latter screening), there was a video from writer and executive producer Steven Moffat asking fans to not spoil this detail. Fortunately, the fans didn't disappoint.

Most of the past Daleks were fan-made replicas: the only original prop from the Classic Series was the special weapons Dalek from "Remembrance of the Daleks." While many of them were made to look like they belonged to a specific era of the program, some of them were borrowed because they were a Dalek and they needed a lot of them to fill a room. One such replica Dalek was borrowed from former showrunner Russell T Davies, who had a Dalek in the entrance of his home even before he brought *Doctor Who* back to TV.

**The TARDIS Chronometer** Present-day Earth (circa 2012) and the Daleks' asylum planet, presumably sometime in the future.

**Cool? (GB)** In the season of *Doctor Who* that preceded this, Steven Moffat limited the Daleks to a single brief appearance (of a dying Dalek, no less, in the pre-credits sequence of the series finale). Word was out that Moffat felt the Doctor's arch-enemies were, in a word, overused. "There's a problem with the Daleks. They are the most famous of the Doctor's adversaries and the most frequent, which means they are the most reliably defeatable enemies in the universe," Moffat said in a BBC interview.

With "Asylum of the Daleks," Moffat claimed he wanted to make the Daleks scarier than ever. They were. But . . .

The Daleks kill *no one* in this episode.

Think about it. Amy, Rory and the Doctor are practically the only characters in the story (aside from Oswin), and their survival is kind of, sort of guaranteed. The supporting characters — like Darla and the victims of the *Alaska* and all the other human Dalek agents — are already dead before the story happens. There's literally no one in the story for the Daleks to kill.

The trick employed here is rather grand. The viewer already knows how dangerous a Dalek can be. "Asylum of the Daleks" turns that against us. The tension, jeopardy and horror is created from how dangerous the viewer imagines the situation to be. We don't need to see Rory exterminated to know how dangerous the scene is when he's in a room with Daleks stuttering into life, any more than we need to see someone mauled to death when we see them stumble into a cave of hibernating bears.

And boy does Steven Moffat get the most out of that trick. Again and again, we're faced with Daleks that are addled and can't shoot straight — but we know they're capable of becoming something far worse. That's what causes the tension while watching this, and that's why "Asylum of the Daleks" works. As much as you might think Daleks are rubbish, the truth is there's a part of every fan that wants to believe they are the scariest things ever.

If invoking fear was the only thing "Asylum of the Daleks" did, that would be impressive enough. But it does far more than that. Moffat intersperses his Dalek change-up with two other mysteries to solve: who Oswin Oswald is, and how Amy and Rory split up. The first mystery is more deftly handled. The Doctor knows what has happened more or less from the start, so the fun for the viewer is in keeping up and seeing if they pick up the clues both overt (the soufflés) and subtle (the design of Oswin's quarters).

Oswin is wonderful, by the way. By *Doctor Who*'s seventh season, we know that Steven Moffat has a certain capacity for writing female characters who are sassy, flirty, smart and enigmatic. It's a glorious tradition that started with Nancy in "The Empty Child"/"The Doctor Dances" and continues with Reinette, Sally Sparrow, River Song and so on. But Oswin Oswald might be my favourite iteration of this character type. Jenna Coleman belongs in some kind of hall of fame for flirting alone. But she's even better doing the being-a-genius bit. It's an incredible feat, impossible even, but it will cast a long shadow over Coleman's future work on the series.

The less successfully handled mystery is the Ponds' breakup, which is resolved clunkily and is entirely predicated on — gasp! — Amy not being able to have children and also not being able to have an actual adult conversation about it with her spouse.

I must also admit I do resent a little how easily the Daleks have gone from being a small remnant rebuilding themselves to how they were before the Time War: a veritable empire that has not only subjugated whole planets but seems to have retained all past versions dating back to the Classic Series . . . even though their whole race was destroyed. That the Doctor has no apparent emotional issue with that whatsoever makes it even more wince-worthy. It makes little sense in the overall narrative since the series came back, but wh-hey, there's a grey-and-blue Dalek from 1964! Who cares?! That said, I'm here to praise "Asylum of the Daleks," not bury it. I'm fairly sure it will stand the test of time as one of the best modern *Doctor Who* stories, because it manages to take us inside an allegedly defeatable race and remind us of what makes them scary — and they barely fire a single shot. That's undefinable magic.

**Second Opinion (RS?)** My co-author has pegged all the many wonderful things about this story. But I do want to disagree with him on one point: the Ponds' breakup.

Okay, predicating it on Amy's inability to have children is not just a roll-your-eyes cliché but actively dumb. Worse, it undercuts the fact that they already have a daughter — and also draws attention to the fact that they didn't seem so bothered by said daughter's kidnapping last year, so why would we expect them to be more invested parents now?

That aside though, I think Graeme's flat-out wrong. The set-up is marvellous: arguing about who loves each other more is exactly the kind of thing that real couples do in the middle of a fight. And the Doctor straightening his bowtie is an absolutely sublime moment.

However, it's not just a moment. For me, the reason this works is because having them almost break up and reconcile injects some much-needed life into the characters. Ever since "The God Complex," there's been no earthly reason why we needed to see these characters again. They ended their adventure with the Doctor, survived and went on to wedded, middle-class bliss. What on Gallifrey are they doing appearing in "The Doctor, the Widow and the Wardrobe," for instance?

Here, though, their inclusion feels welcome, because the story has a direction for them to go in. Having the Daleks recruit them for the mission — rather than the Doctor stalking them from history, say — because they know he needs his companions is a great move. Giving them marital troubles reminds us why we like them. (And how much more shocking would it have been if we'd had an actual break from them until this story?) Having the Doctor engineer their reconciliation is stupendous. As is the rest of this story.

## 7.02 Dinosaurs on a Spaceship

**Written by** Chris Chibnall **Directed by** Saul Metzstein

**Original airdate** September 8, 2012

**The Big Idea** Pretty much the title. Also, throw in a Victorian big-game hunter, Queen Nefertiti, Rory's dad and an intergalactic scavenger for good measure.

**Roots and References** Michael Crichton's 1990 novel *Jurassic Park* and its 1993 film adaptation (the dinosaurs in a technological setting); the 1988 animated film *The Land before Time* (Tricey the stegosaurus); H. Rider Haggard's character Allan Quartermain (Riddell); Edgar Rice Burroughs's *John Carter of Mars* series (there are echoes of Dejah Thoris in Nefertiti's portrayal); *2001: A Space Odyssey* (the Robots sing "Daisy Bell" when deactivated). The Doctor calls Solomon's operation "Argos for the universe," referring to the chain of catalogue retailers in the U.K.; Brian mentions the science fiction of Arthur C. Clarke and quotes from *Blake's 7* ("Teleport now!"); Solomon plays Franz Schubert's "Fantasia in F Minor for Piano Four Hands" (for the second episode in a row, the Doctor claims to be on a recording of classical music; this time he's hands three and four).

The episode title, of course, is derived from Charles Dickens's 1850 novel *David Copperfield*. (Okay, fine. It's from the 2006 film *Snakes on a Plane*.)

**Adventures in Time and Space** Solomon has commandeered a Silurian ark. Its chief scientist is from the same gene pool as Malohkeh from 2010's "The Hungry Earth"/"Cold Blood" (and, naturally, played by the same actor), while the Doctor's identity is still unknown after his erasure at the end of 2011's "The Wedding of River Song."

**Who Is the Doctor?** The Doctor tests the idea of a gang of people with whom to have adventures. He claims he still keeps a Christmas list. He impulsively snogs

Rory when he comes up with the solution the Doctor is looking for (which is problematic — not because Rory's a man, but kissing someone without consent is wrong). The Doctor describes himself as a "very emotive man." We see his cold fury as he leaves Solomon to his fate with the missiles as retribution for his genocide of the Silurians.

**The Doctor and Amy** It's been ten months since the Doctor last saw Amy and Rory, which leaves Amy to wonder aloud if the Doctor is trying to wean them off him. The Doctor promises he's not. (It would seem the Doctor and the Ponds have an arrangement about their adventuring together.) Even so, in spite of both sides' protestations to the contrary, Amy is worried a time is coming soon when the Doctor won't show up.

**Monster of the Week** Um . . . well, there are dinosaurs in this story for sure (namely *Pterodactylus*, *Triceratops* and *Tyrannosaurus*), but they don't actually qualify as monsters. The closest thing we get are two very large, very red and very camp robots.

**Stand Up and Cheer** Brian sitting in the front entrance of the TARDIS, excitedly eating a packed lunch sandwich and looking out over the Earth from orbit is probably the sweetest thing ever.

**Roll Your Eyes** Amy says to Queen Nefertiti and Riddell, "Please don't start flirting. I will not have flirting companions." Which is either, depending on your point of view, the least self-aware thing Amy has ever said or the most hypocritical.

**You're Not Making Any Sense** Solomon doesn't try to teleport or jettison the beacon because . . . well, just because, okay?

**Interesting Trivia** There's something interesting going on with the opening credits to each story this season. The time vortex is getting darker, with more lightning, and the *Doctor Who* logo changes texture for each story: here it has scales (like the titular reptiles); for "Asylum of the Daleks," it had bumps like on the Daleks. In "A Town Called Mercy," it's wood (like the architecture in the Western town); "The Power of Three" is similar to the black boxes; and in "The Angels Take Manhattan," the logo is weathered bronze like the Statue of Liberty.

This story continues what has been an honourable tradition in *Doctor Who*: stunt-casting comedians in quirky roles. Here, we have David Mitchell and Robert Webb of *That Mitchell and Webb Look* and *Peep Show* doing the voices of the robots. Over the years, the Classic Series saw Hale and Pace playing store clerks in 1989's "Survival," Ken Dodd as an intergalactic toll collector in 1987's "Delta and the Bannermen" and John Cleese as an art critic in 1979's "City of Death." Even third Doctor Jon Pertwee was best known prior to *Doctor Who* for his radio comedy work.

**The TARDIS Chronometer** Primarily on a spaceship in 2367, with side trips to Amy and Rory's home in the present day, the African plains of 1902 and Egypt in 1334 BCE.

**Cool? (GB)** "Dinosaurs on a Spaceship" is fun. Frothy, undemanding fun. Okay, I'm done. Get question-mark boy in here to argue back, and we can call it a day for this one.

Except . . .

It's actually more than that.

I mean, don't get me wrong, "frothy fun" isn't so much a mission statement for "Dinosaurs on a Spaceship" as it is a tattoo it proudly wears and is happy to show off when it's in a flirty mood. But there are a lot of lovely, smart and downright radical things it does as well.

Let's start with Brian. Remember when families were a regular part of *Doctor Who*'s DNA? When companions weren't just isolated characters but part of a world that the Doctor's travels actually influenced? I remember that time fondly. It departed when Russell T Davies left and Steven Moffat arrived. (Just as a side note: Davies talks about his family upbringing quite fondly; Moffat hardly at all — the difference in approach may be as simple, and as complicated, as that.) Up until now, the only parents we've seen for companions in the Matt Smith era have been Amy's spurious (and slightly Dickensian) ones and Rory mentioning that his mum loved Dusty Springfield in "The Rebel Flesh"/"The Almost People."

Brian's arrival makes me wish time travel was for real, because I would have made sure that he was a character who existed in Series Five and Six — he's that brilliant. I just adore how ordinary and, well, Dad-like he is. He's so very similar to Rory (they have the same quirky sense of humour, the same awkwardness), but, like many fathers, he's caught up in what he pictured his child being (and how they failed to do that) rather than seeing them for what they are. And all that is thrown on its head by travelling with the Doctor, which is charming and sweet.

Let's talk about Nefertiti for a minute. She's a character who could have been disastrously handled, but Chris Chibnall has it covered. She has genuine agency; she chooses what she does and doesn't do, whom she's with and not with. She travels with the Doctor not just to flirt but out of a sense of honour. She's smart, and she can also kick ass. Every time I watch this story, I'm bracing myself to loathe her, but every time I end up cheering for her.

Then there's the Doctor. I should be annoyed by him, because it's Matt Smith in full waggling-his-arms-and-talking-loudly children's presenter mode, but this time Smith is playing with the audience. The Doctor is all gosh-gee-whiz about dinosaurs and having a Christmas list . . . but with Solomon he shows a steelier side, and we're reminded that the Doctor is a darker, more complicated figure than he makes himself out to be. I don't think that side of him gets used enough at this point in Matt Smith's tenure. And that's not entirely down to Matt Smith, I'd argue.

There are aggravating bits in this story, to be sure. The dinosaurs aren't scary, for one thing. It tries to do the same trick as the previous episode, where we perceive the threat rather than see it carried out, only here it falls flat, which honestly it didn't need to. Like *Jurassic Park*, all it needs is a few characters to act as dino-fodder. Instead, bewilderingly, we have Riddell, a big-game hunter who is crying out to be killed off but instead stays alive so we can have the "what the hell?" moment of Nefertiti taking him as a lover at the end.

"Dinosaurs on a Spaceship" remains frothy fun, but that is something of an illusion. It's fun, it's dramatically engaging, it's funny, and it's more than the sum of its parts.

I guess what I'm saying is that "Dinosaurs on a Spaceship" is . . . *Doctor Who*. **Second Opinion (RS?)** Yes, yes, "Dinosaurs on a Spaceship" is frothy, fun and non-stop enjoyable from start to finish. Oh, I'm not talking about the episode; I'm talking about the title.

Ever since "Let's Kill Hitler," the show has been on a bit of a mission to raise the high-concept stakes. So we've had "The Girl Who Waited" and "The Wedding of River Song," with "The Angels Take Manhattan" and "The Name of the Doctor" coming up. All big, bold titles intended to shake us out of our complacency. And the one thing they have in common is that they're all fakes.

"The Wedding of River Song" promises the long-awaited marriage, but it turns out to be with a robot replica of the Doctor; "The Girl Who Waited" isn't about young Amelia Pond after all; "The Name of the Doctor" will resolutely fail to reveal the Doctor's name; and — spoiler alert — the Angels will only take a single apartment complex in Battery Park.

"Dinosaurs on a Spaceship" fits perfectly well with these big teases. Yes, there are dinosaurs, and they do actually exist on a spaceship. But they're barely in it — and everything else is a lot less fun. Instead, there's a bunch of pseudo-companions who are absolutely critically important this one time and never again; Solomon, who is way too nasty for the level of froth that this title promises; and Rory's dad, here only by chance and yet pivotal to the climax.

There are, as my co-author points out, a lot of things to like about this episode. One can even do so without taking random potshots at Matt Smith (who is wonderful). But the most unambiguous success it has is its title. The rest might be somewhat downhill from there, although I will admit it's a pretty high elevation to start with. Dinosaurs! On a freaking spaceship!

## Karen Gillan

The character of Amy Pond in *Doctor Who* was Karen Gillan's breakout role. Born in 1987 in Inverness, Scotland, Gillan dropped out of drama school to work as a model before she landed a role in the ensemble sketch-comedy series *The Kevin Bishop Show*. Occasional roles followed, including the Soothsayer in the 2008 *Doctor Who* episode "The Fires of Pompeii" (alongside future Doctor Peter Capaldi). She had auditioned on video for the role of Amy, but Steven Moffat dismissed her as being "too wee" before he was convinced to let her audition in person. She has had one of the best post–*Doctor Who* careers of any actor in the Modern Series, featuring in the 2012 TV film *We'll Take Manhattan* (where she played model Jean Shrimpton), playing the lead in the 2014 film *Oculus* and starring in the 2014 TV comedy *Selfie*. She played Nebula in four Marvel Cinematic Universe films, starting with *Guardians of the Galaxy* (2014), and Martha in 2017's *Jumanji: Welcome to the Jungle* and its sequel. In 2018, Gillan wrote and directed her first independent film, *The Party's Only Just Beginning*.

## 7.03 A Town Called Mercy

**Written by** Toby Whithouse **Directed by** Saul Metzstein
**Original airdate** September 15, 2012

**The Big Idea** In a sleepy little town in the Old West, a cybernetic gunslinger is chasing an alien war criminal.

**Roots and References** The story derives its setting from any number of Westerns, particularly the 1952 film *High Noon* (the wait for the Gunslinger and the exploration of differences in morality); *Star Trek*, especially the *Deep Space Nine* episode "Duet" (the morality play with an alien war criminal).

**Adventures in Time and Space** The Doctor references both the Master and the Daleks when mentioning the victims of war criminals who have survived because of his own mercy. This is the first out-and-out *Doctor Who* Western since 1966's "The Gunfighters."

**Who Is the Doctor?** Faced with a war criminal, the Doctor reaches his limit here, deciding to toss Jex out of the town limits so that he can be executed by the Gunslinger. He physically hauls Jex out of the safety of the jail and throws him bodily into the wilderness. He even picks up a gun and points it at Jex to prevent him returning. When Jex challenges him, saying he wouldn't use it, the Doctor states that he genuinely doesn't know whether he would or not. He says he'd rather face a Dalek than frightened people.

**The Doctor and Amy** She functions as the Doctor's conscience, saying, "This is not how we roll, and you know it" when the Doctor goes too far. She asks him where he's drawing the line, if he'll hunt down everyone who ever made a bomb or a bullet and execute them. Once again, she and Rory choose to go back home after their adventure rather than continuing on travelling, pointing out that they have friends at home for the first time.

**Monster of the Week** The Gunslinger, a cybernetic soldier that resulted from experimentation during an alien war. His programming was damaged in the conflict, at which point he decided to hunt down the scientists who had experimented on him. However, he can't bring himself to harm innocent people.

**Stand Up and Cheer** The Doctor speaking for a male horse called Susan — who wants its owner to respect its life choices — is comedy gold. It's exactly the kind of improv scenario that Matt Smith excels at.

**Roll Your Eyes** "Everyone who isn't an American, drop your gun." Puh-lease. Neither of us is American and we're not especially fond of guns either, but do we have to milk the same timeworn old clichés every single time the TARDIS visits the U.S.?

**You're Not Making Any Sense** Why doesn't the Doctor take Jex away in his TARDIS, thus solving the entire problem in one fell swoop?

**Interesting Trivia** This episode was filmed in Spain, as that was thought to be cheaper than constructing a Western set on location in the U.K. It helped that there were ready-made Western mock-ups available in the form of Fort Bravo and Oasys, two Spanish theme parks. They get used so often for Westerns that the former is known as Texas Hollywood and the latter as Mini Hollywood. Classic Westerns such as *The Good, the Bad and the Ugly* and *For a Few Dollars More* were filmed there.

There was a short mini-episode called "The Making of the Gunslinger" that aired as a prequel to this story. It showed some of the background to the war and the creation of the cybernetic soldiers. It's available on the DVD release or on YouTube.

**The TARDIS Chronometer** The town of Mercy, 1870. It's never directly specified, but Mercy is likely located in Nevada, as there's a poster in Isaac's office issued by the governor of that state. The geography also tracks, as the southern part of Nevada is 200 miles from the Mexican border, which is where the TARDIS was originally headed.

**Cool? (RS?)** There's always been an issue when it comes to the Doctor and guns. Ever since the previous time *Doctor Who* tried to do a Western, in the William Hartnell story "The Gunfighters," the title character has been defined by his avoidance of direct weapons. Especially human-made guns.

Sometimes this gets used as a psych-out, as in the cliffhanger to "The Time of Angels," where he fires a gun, but at a gravity globe. Sometimes his hatred of guns is ramped up to 11 for no particular reason, as in "The Sontaran Stratagem." While the Doctor might not be firing the guns, often his companions are happy to, as Davros mentions in "Journey's End." In the Classic Series, he fired a gun a few times, but a) never human guns and b) only at monsters. It's not a coincidence that it's the Doctor holding the gun in "Dalek," which shows how broken he is.

If you're going to have the Doctor point a pistol at a man, you'd better do a damn fine job of making it convincing.

And this is where "A Town Called Mercy" falls down. The Doctor picking up a gun should be a shocking moment, simultaneously weighed down by the sheer depth of argument-building happening before, during and after it. Instead, it's all a bit arbitrary.

On paper, it makes sense that Isaac would be protecting Jex (because he cured cholera and installed electric lighting), while Jex's crimes are too large for the Doctor to ignore. But it's not given enough depth. The Doctor dithers for a bit and mentions some unnamed victims from some unspecified other episodes. On this basis, he throws Jex out of town and points a gun at him . . . until Amy effectively says, "Nah," so he relents and then pledges to protect Jex at all costs, even warding off a lynch mob of teenagers. That sound you just heard was my neck snapping from the whiplash.

And without the careful structure to keep this scene in place, the whole thing falls apart. The Doctor loses all moral authority and doesn't earn it back; instead, the episode becomes about Jex, which is complicated because it's never clear what we're meant to make of him. Is he a reformed Mengele? A coward? Someone who was caught up in the horrors of war to whom peacetime rules don't apply? An ultimately brave hero? All of the above at different points? There's mileage in making your guest character ambiguous, but the episode doesn't attempt to make anything from that either.

Instead, what we're left with is a series of images: the Doctor in the Wild West; the Gunslinger looming over the town; Susan the horse; the Doctor flinging Jex out into the wilderness; the teenagers being talked out of violence; the people praying in church; Jex committing suicide. Some of these are quite powerful, but they don't hang together at all.

The plot has to be really contrived to make it all work: why doesn't the Gunslinger just march through the town until he finds Jex? After all, he'd be skilled enough to avoid killing any innocents along the way. Instead, most of the episode feels forced, essentially biding its time until — gasp! — the Gunslinger . . . marches through the town looking for Jex.

There's also the fact that Amy and Rory have almost nothing to do. The joke of the entire saloon being shocked into silence when the Doctor says his name hinges upon the unlikely idea that the townspeople don't recognize Jex, who's been living with them for weeks and saving them from cholera and the like. The script ties itself in knots for the sake of this one joke, which isn't particularly great in the first place. Indeed, aside from Isaac, the townspeople are extremely underdeveloped. The confrontation between the Doctor and the lynch mob has the Doctor lecturing a teenager in the abstract with words like "Violence doesn't end violence, it only extends it," which is the sort of thing your dad would say and would elicit an eye roll from any actual teenager. It's supposed to be profound, but it just feels like scolding. Why Walter doesn't shoot him on the spot for that speech alone, I have no idea.

Also, neither the Gunslinger nor the Doctor seem all that bothered by Isaac's death, when it was a direct result of the very issue with which each had been grappling. The Gunslinger shoots an innocent man and essentially shrugs, because shoot happens. The Doctor's amoral near-execution of one man got another killed, but he's more interested in taking over the marshal's job than he is in thinking through the consequences of his actions.

Then there's the fact that after pointing a pistol at Jex, getting Isaac killed and being called out by his best friend for violating his core principles, the Doctor *still* carries a gun. When the preacher tells him to put on the gun belt, he simply does. How much cooler would it have been for the Doctor to face an armed lynch mob with only his words as weapons? I don't know about you, but that feels like the kind of TV show I'd rather be watching. If only someone would make something like that for us . . .

That's the problem with "A Town Called Mercy" in a nutshell. It wants to be deep and profound, but it drops the ball in almost every meaningful way. In a half season that manages the surprise feat of multiple excellent Chris Chibnall scripts and Steven Moffat monster retreads firing on all cylinders, the failure of this story to make an impact might be the biggest surprise of all.

**Second Opinion (GB)** Readers of our past work will know this already — and if you're new, don't worry, you'll pick up on it rather quickly — but I'm usually quite besotted with Toby Whithouse as a writer on *Doctor Who* (not to mention *Being Human* and *The Game*). I love the way Whithouse pulls *Doctor Who* out of its comfort zone and forces the drama into new territory — and adds a boatload of zingers to make it funny as well. It's usually why you see me as the main reviewer on Whithouse's stories.

I took a hard pass on lead-reviewing "A Town Called Mercy" because it's the one massive exception to my Whithouse love. It's a dreary, by-the-numbers story with cheap emotional trickery and a humdrum examination of the banality of evil, justice and redemption. Worse, it has only one good joke — and yes, it's Susan the horse.

This story can be summed up by the scene made of 100% pure bullshit: where the Doctor forces Jex out of town so he can face the Gunslinger's justice. Why? Apparently, he touched a nerve in the Doctor. We can guess what, but nothing is made clear. Then the Doctor exchanges a few fluffy bon mots with Amy, and he changes his mind. As the kids today say, WTF?

And don't get me started about how all this is stopped by cute banter instead of . . . oh, I don't know, a real dramatic confrontation between Amy and the Doctor?

I've complained previously that Steven Moffat's vision for *Doctor Who* at this point is similar to *Seinfeld*'s: no hugging, no learning. "A Town Called Mercy" should be a story about the painful reality of atonement, but no one's bothering. Jex goes on a journey from lying to avoidance to noble sacrifice, not because he's learned from the Doctor or the townsfolk but because . . . reasons.

This is the cautionary tale of what happens when everyone — writer, stars, producers and director — completely coast instead of doing their jobs. Better luck next time, Toby.

## 7.04 The Power of Three

**Written by** Chris Chibnall **Directed by** Douglas MacKinnon
**Original airdate** September 22, 2012

**The Big Idea** Amy and Rory are faced with a choice between their time-travelling life and the one at home on Earth. Meanwhile, the Doctor has to stay on the planet for over a year to investigate tiny black boxes . . . provided he doesn't get bored.
**Roots and References** *Star Trek* (Brian does his own version of the Captain's Log); *Thunderbirds* ("Glasses" from the UNIT scientific team looks a lot like Brains); *The Man Who Came to Dinner* (the Doctor being stranded on Earth with Amy and Rory, disrupting their lives); *Saturday Night Fever* (the Doctor adopts John Travolta's famous disco pose when he gets one of his hearts to restart). The

boxes are featured on the U.K. version of *The Apprentice* (the reality show's star, Lord Alan Sugar, is seen criticizing a candidate's performance on a task involving the cubes in a sequence shot on *The Apprentice* set).

**Adventures in Time and Space** Kate Stewart (she'll go by Kate Lethbridge-Stewart in later episodes) is the daughter of Brigadier Alistair Gordon Lethbridge-Stewart, who was head of the United Nations Intelligence Taskforce (later the Unified Intelligence Taskforce) during the third Doctor's era. The Brigadier's offscreen death in 2011's "The Wedding of River Song" is also mentioned. The call sign "Trap One" is used all the time in UNIT stories from the 1970s. UNIT's headquarters is still based in the Tower of London, which was established in 2005's "The Christmas Invasion." In 1890, the Doctor is said to have foiled an (offscreen) infiltration of the Savoy Hotel by the Zygons, the first reference to these Classic Series monsters (from 1975's "Terror of the Zygons") in the Modern Series. The Doctor, Amy and Rory partake of fish fingers and custard, a . . . delicacy the Doctor developed in 2010's "The Eleventh Hour." The Doctor admits to Brian that, when it comes to companions, "some leave me" (*most*, actually, starting with Susan in 1964's "The Dalek Invasion of Earth"), "some got left behind" (like Rose in 2006's "Doomsday") and "some . . . not many, but . . . some died" (most notably Katarina and Sara Kingdom in 1966's "The Daleks' Master Plan" and Adric in 1982's "Earthshock").

**Who Is the Doctor?** Given how awkward the Doctor has been in the past towards military figures and UNIT (see 2008's "The Sontaran Stratagem"/"The Poison Sky," for example), it's interesting to note he salutes Kate, which is a sign of the respect he has for Kate and her family. The Doctor is unbelievably bored at first, being stuck on Earth, but seems to gradually get the hang of it.

**The Doctor and Amy** The Doctor knows Amy and Rory will eventually stop travelling, but he keeps coming back to see Amy because she was the first face his current incarnation saw, and she is thus seared onto his hearts. Meanwhile, Amy — who now has a job as a travel writer — and Rory — who is becoming highly regarded at the hospital where he works — are pondering whether they can travel with the Doctor much longer.

**Monster of the Week** The Shakri are cosmic pest exterminators who are convinced that humans are a plague that will eventually infest the galaxy. They release small black cubes all over the Earth, which act as "slug pellets" to entice humans and eventually kill them. The Shakri have android orderlies who look humanoid except they don't have noses or mouths.

**Stand Up and Cheer** Matt Smith gives his best speech in the role (and he's had a lot of great ones) when he says, "I'm not running away. But this is one corner of one country in one continent on one planet that's a corner of a galaxy that's a corner of a universe that is forever growing and shrinking and creating and destroying and never remaining the same for a single millisecond. And there is so much, so much to see, Amy. Because it goes so fast. I'm not running away from things, I am running to them before they flare and fade forever." Which says so much about what we love about the Doctor, and the eleventh Doctor in particular.

**Roll Your Eyes** The episode closes on Amy saying in voiceover, "It was also when we realized something the Shakri never understood. What cubed actually means. *The power of three!*" And it's said to really emphasize the story title. Which makes you thankful they hadn't done it for any of the other stories this season: "But in the end I learned how to love, thanks to going to the *asylum of the Daleks!*" or "But the Doctor really learned what it meant to care when he went to *a town called Mercy!*"

**You're Not Making Any Sense** One co-author's (okay, it's Graeme's) notes say, "Ending is *rubbish*!!!" And it's true. It's not only that the Doctor solves it by whipping out his sonic screwdriver — it's that the Doctor, Amy and Rory just take off *without worrying about any of the other people lying on the other beds in the room around them.*

**Interesting Trivia** Kate Lethbridge-Stewart holds the distinction of being the first character on *Doctor Who* the TV series originally created as part of the unlicensed spinoff videos made about *Doctor Who* during the 15-year gap before the Modern Series began. These videos were unlicensed by the BBC but used characters from *Doctor Who* through agreement with the writers of the original Classic Series stories (the BBC shares copyright with these writers on characters created by them). The videos were cheaply made, often brought back a *Doctor Who* monster and had a ready audience of fans starved for content while the series was off the air. One of these videos was called *Downtime*. It was made in 1995 by Reeltime Pictures and featured the Brigadier and the Yeti alongside other Classic Series characters. In this production, Kate was played by Beverly Cressman and had a son, Gordon. Cressman resurfaced as Kate in other unlicensed *Doctor Who* videos made by Reeltime. That said, it's not known if Kate is meant to be the same character from *Downtime* or if indeed the character was bought or licensed from Reeltime. (Writer Chris Chibnall says he created the character independently, which is credible, though it could be that others connected Chibnall's creation to a character already in existence.) If it is the *Downtime* Kate Lethbridge-Stewart, we have yet to find out if her son exists within the TV series, though she does later mention being a mother of two.

Amy supposes that she's been travelling with the Doctor for ten years. Which means that there have been a *lot* of untelevised adventures, particularly since the Doctor left Amy and Rory behind in "The God Complex." Though it's unclear if she's counting the two-year gap at the end of "The Eleventh Hour."

If the end of the story seems like it's missing a scene or two, that's because a lot of the ending had to be edited during production. There was supposed to have been a sequence where the Shakri, who was not a hologram, was taken down by Amy and Rory, and the Doctor then used the Shakri's weaponry to repeal the cubes. But actor Steven Berkoff became ill, and the ending was rejigged using only the three leads. There was more rejigging of scenes: the "slow invasion" happens later in the original version, which begins with the trip to Henry VIII's court and the engagement party (which doesn't lead to Amy being asked to be a bridesmaid because she flakes out so much).

Chris Chibnall took his inspiration for the cubes from the shipwreck of the *MSC Napoli* off the Devon coast where he lived. The *Napoli* was a container ship, and, as a result of the damage and subsequent breaking up of the ship, merchandise from the ship washed onto shore, and people gathered to scavenge it. Chibnall thought the mania people have for collecting free things might make a good idea for a story.

**The TARDIS Chronometer** Over the course of a year in present-day London, with side trips to 1890 and the court of Henry VIII.

**Cool? (GB)** The first 32 minutes of "The Power of Three" are brilliant. In fact, I'd go so far as to say that if "The Power of Three" was only those first 32 minutes, we'd be hailing it as a classic of the eleventh Doctor's era.

Unfortunately for "The Power of Three," it's not 32 minutes long.

But what works in this episode is outstanding. The companions positing "Which life do we choose?" is great. The opening sequence, which juxtaposes fast-paced clips of adventures with a humdrum regular life of complaining you're out of dishwasher tablets, is genius. And I love the fact that this is, essentially, a story of how Amy and Rory grapple with their addiction to life with the Doctor. Moreover, the Doctor is struggling with his addiction to Amy and Rory. The genius of the "before they flare and fade forever" speech is that the Doctor is also talking about why he's travelling with Amy and Rory and how important they've become to him. He's still bewildered they have jobs.

This is the Moffat-era story that most feels like it belongs in the Russell T Davies era. There's a weird occurrence happening on contemporary Earth with lots of clips of BBC newsreaders describing what's happening while the threat also ends up being integrated into popular culture. It not only has the trappings of the RTD years, it has the ethos of it, as the relationship with the Doctor's companions is played off against the companions' friends, families and lives.

It's nice to see the lived-in state of Amy and Rory's marriage. I adore the

Doctor's reaction to Amy exasperatingly telling Rory his scrubs are in the lounge where he left them. It's a side of their marriage not usually shown, and it's wonderful to watch them just being a couple. I sometimes give Karen Gillan a hard time, but she and Arthur Darvill hit exactly the right notes with this. Gillan is also great in her scenes alone with Matt Smith.

Brian also once again immediately endears himself to the audience. The scene where he runs through every possible permutation of what the cubes could be is charming and funny. (The Doctor's reaction — "Very thorough, Brian" — is priceless!) And Brian's devotion to the single-minded boredom of watching the cubes also adds real warmth. Chris Chibnall clearly has a handle on supporting characters; you can see that this is the writer about to launch *Broadchurch* in a matter of months.

That sense of character even extends to UNIT's return. While UNIT was only occasionally well serviced in the Davies years, here UNIT is rebooted and now led by a civilian scientist, in a lovely fine-tuning of UNIT's premise that will serve the show well in the future. And Jemma Redgrave is brilliant from the moment she awkwardly walks in to Amy and Rory's house, hands in her pockets, slouched and apologizing for the bad behaviour of the soldiers.

I found the way the slow invasion unfolds to be genius, as the cubes go from being a pop-culture sensation to commonplace paperweights and only then become massive threats. Matt Smith gets a killer speech and is on top of his game . . .

Then we get to the thirty-third minute, and it all goes to pieces.

The full story of why the climax of "The Power of Three" finds the three leads standing around talking while the Doctor magics everything right with the sonic screwdriver probably hasn't been written yet. But it completely undoes all the jeopardy that had been built up in the first two-thirds of the story as the Shakri finally unleash their plan with the cubes. It kills the story — and all the goodwill for the plotline that sees us stuck on Earth for a year — dead.

But the worst thing is that with the story having worked to the conclusion that maybe, just maybe, Amy and Rory are ready to live a life without the Doctor, we have Brian of all people suddenly giving them permission to just go on doing their thing. Given everything we've been through, that feels dishonest. In this story, Rory and Amy experience growth, agree to commitments, put down roots and live a life — and the Doctor comes to terms with that. Only it's a lie, apparently. We're back to a central problem in this era of *Doctor Who*: there isn't growth, only the illusion of it.

But I have to say, for 32 minutes, "The Power of Three" was glorious.

**Second Opinion (RS?)** Let's not go overboard here. Even without the hot mess of the ending, "The Power of Three" is . . . okay. Some of it is quite lovely. But, unlike my co-author, I just don't see it as the über-prize of the late Matt Smith era. It's not even Chris Chibnall's best story of this season, and it doesn't hold a candle to the season opener.

Broadly speaking, this is "The Lodger" but with less comedy and more traction, since it features previously established characters rather than a one-off companion created for the story. As a threat, the cubes are . . . serviceable. The domestic set-up is . . . passable. The established family member is great, as my co-author points out, but there's no kitchen-sink realism to it. Where's the rest of Rory's family? Where's Amy's? Where are their friends? I don't mean showing a few random extras; I mean characters with depth, like Donna's friend Nerys or Jackie's lover Tony, who feel like real people despite being barely seen. Instead, what we have is yet another Russell T Davies–lite story that proves why nobody should do Russell T Davies stories who aren't named Russell T Davies.

I'm also not nearly as in love with the speech as Graeme is. There's nothing wrong with it, but it doesn't particularly grab me either. Which is my problem with the episode in a nutshell.

I will agree with Graeme about Kate Stewart being an amazing addition. Especially for a long-time viewer, having the daughter of Brigadier Lethbridge-Stewart now running UNIT is heartwarmingly lovely. The revelation about who she is comes along perfectly, with the Doctor having figured it out around the same time that we do.

"The Power of Three" definitely has some good parts. But I don't think I'd be hailing it as a classic, even if it was only the first 32 minutes. I'm happy for Graeme that his cube sang to him. But mine just kind of sat there.

. . . . . . . . . . . . . . . . . . . . . . . . . . . . . . . . . . . . . . . . . . . . . . . . . . . . . . .

## Arthur Darvill

Like his co-star Karen Gillan, Arthur Darvill's first major TV role was on *Doctor Who*. He was working mostly in theatre prior to *Doctor Who*, not just as an actor but also as a musician and composer (he had scored two musical plays by the time he was 27). Within a year of leaving *Doctor Who*, Darvill was performing on Broadway as the lead in the musical *Once* (which he then took to the West End). On television, he played the Reverend Paul Coates in all three seasons of Chris Chibnall's 2013 series *Broadchurch* (opposite past and future Doctors David Tennant and Jodie Whittaker). He's best known outside *Doctor Who* for playing time traveller Rip Hunter in the first three seasons of the 2016 DC Comics TV adaptation *Legends of Tomorrow*.

. . . . . . . . . . . . . . . . . . . . . . . . . . . . . . . . . . . . . . . . . . . . . . . . . . . . . . .

# 7.05 The Angels Take Manhattan

**Written by** Steven Moffat **Directed by** Nick Hurran

**Original airdate** September 29, 2012

**The Big Idea** Statues comes to life in New York as the Weeping Angels run a battery farm that will have severe consequences for Amy and Rory.

**Roots and References** Dashiell Hammett's 1930s crime novels *The Maltese Falcon* and *The Thin Man* (the hard-boiled detective genre setting; Grayle is a stand-in for *The Maltese Falcon*'s villain Guttman, while the banter between the Doctor and River is an homage to *The Thin Man*); the 2005 *Doctor Who* story "Dalek" (the injured Angel being kept in chains by a collector echoes Van Statten very clearly). The title is derived from the 1984 Muppets film *The Muppets Take Manhattan*. Sting's song "Englishman in New York" plays over establishing shots of New York.

**Adventures in Time and Space** The fact that the Doctor erased himself from history in 2011's "The Wedding of River Song" means that River was pardoned for the sentence we've seen her serving since 2010's "The Time of Angels"/"Flesh and Stone." Amy's afterword references a number of her adventures with the Doctor, such as fighting pirates at sea (2012's "The Curse of the Black Spot"), saving a whale in outer space (2010's "The Beast Below"), inspiring the greatest painter who ever lived (2010's "Vincent and the Doctor") and falling in love with a man who would wait 2,000 years for her (2010's "The Big Bang"). River's still travelling through time and space using a vortex manipulator like those we've seen since 2005's "The Empty Child"/"The Doctor Dances." The Doctor warns Amy that she is creating a "fixed time," referring to the "fixed points in time" principle that was established in 2008's "The Fires of Pompeii." When the Doctor returned Amy and Rory home at the end of 2011's "The God Complex," he said, "And what's the alternative? Me standing over your grave?" which comes to pass here. The episode ends with a callback to Amelia in the garden in 2010's "The Eleventh Hour."

**Who Is the Doctor?** Much of this story is an exploration of the fact that the Doctor doesn't like endings — whether that be of a book or with his friends. Here he talks to River as though he's part of a married couple. (He fancies Melody Malone after reading about her, not realizing she's River!) He flips River's coded messages to him from the past with a "Yowzah!" in Chinese and even gives River some of his regeneration energy to heal her broken hand.

**The Doctor and Amy** After Rory is thrown back in time, Amy chooses to leave the Doctor in order to be with her husband. They're locked in the past in fixed time where the Doctor can't reach them. They grow old together and die in New York, with Rory living until 82 and Amy (taking the name Amelia Williams) until 87. She writes an afterword to the Melody Malone book, explaining to the Doctor that they both loved him and asking him not to travel alone.

**Monster of the Week** The Weeping Angels have moved on from being creatures that turned to stone and look like statues to being able to take over existing statues. And they don't need to be made of stone either, as the Statue of Liberty is made of copper. Apparently they can also look at each other down a corridor with no consequences as well, but that's another issue . . .

**Stand Up and Cheer** The farewell scene between the Doctor and Amy is very emotional. It comes down to two people having their last conversation, with Amy making a final, definitive choice between her two boys. The afterword that follows is a lovely touch, giving us the closure we need in a timey-wimey way.

**Roll Your Eyes** If the story starts with Melody seeing the Skinny Guy, why is "The Skinny Guy" the title of chapter 7 and not, say, chapter 2? Did Melody Malone really spend six chapters establishing tedious background details? (The episode itself spends about six minutes on this.) If so, how on earth did she become a bestselling novelist?

**You're Not Making Any Sense** The Statue of Liberty set piece is a grand idea. The statue stomping around New York is slightly less grand. The statue stomping around a city we're explicitly told never sleeps without anyone noticing is quite a bit less grand . . .

**Interesting Trivia** There was an additional scene (written by Chris Chibnall) detailing Rory's father, Brian, meeting with Amy and Rory's son as an old man. The scene was entitled "P.S." and released on the BBC *Doctor Who* website and DVD in storyboard form, with a voiceover by Arthur Darvill. It wasn't a cut scene; it was always intended to be filmed and released as a DVD extra, but Mark Williams's filming commitments meant it was never made. It's a lovely coda to this story, though, so check it out on YouTube.

Another DVD extra that ties into this story and the half season is "The Inforarium," which sees the Doctor erasing information about himself from a database of illicit information. Technically, he doesn't erase it but rather memory-proofs it, so that any information about him is forgotten seconds after it is learned. It's a trick he learned from the Silence . . .

Previous *Doctor Who* stories filmed in New York (such as 2007's "Daleks in Manhattan") relied on a few establishing shots and minimal cast. For this story, the principal cast were flown to New York to film scenes in Central Park (although the Angels and the TARDIS weren't; they were added in post-production). While there, Matt Smith and Steven Moffat made an impromptu visit to the Way Station, a *Doctor Who*–themed bar in Brooklyn, surprising the attendees of a fan gathering who had come to watch the previous season's finale.

Karen Gillan insisted on being the one to read Amy's afterword to Matt Smith herself, so that his reactions would be real. A crowd of American fans turned out to watch this scene being filmed, which the actors weren't expecting, so Gillan had to speak very quietly, while Smith held the book at an incorrect page in case photos of its contents were leaked. Gillan discovered she only had one page of the script, so she improvised the rest of it. The two were extremely emotional during the filming of their farewell in the cemetery scene. And you can tell. (Not that we're complaining.)

**The TARDIS Chronometer** New York, 2012; the Chin Dynasty, 221 BCE; New York, 1938.

**Cool? (RS?)** Steven Moffat must be the sort of person who goes to a fine restaurant and samples the food, saying, "Yes, this mushroom tortellini is superb, but wouldn't it be so much better if you added some hummus? And fries? And a glass of red wine? And a cheesecake? All those things are delicious, so just imagine how amazing this meal is going to be with all of them at once!" Here we have a story that seems to have it all: Weeping Angels, River Song, time-travel malarkey, emotional moments and a clever meta-narrative. It's like "Blink," only with three times as much stuff packed in.

This sees the final wrap-up of Amy and Rory's story. Which is odd, because their story was wrapped up perfectly well in "The God Complex" — and nothing that happened since, with the possible exception of the fifth "Pond Life" mini-episode, has in any way changed that. They moved from regulars to nostalgic recurring characters who recurred every episode (even pointlessly, like in the "The Doctor, the Widow and the Wardrobe") simply because they and their daughter appear to be the only people the eleventh Doctor actually knows.

I'm actually a pretty big fan of Steven Moffat, especially his writing. I liked Series Six more than most (it was an actual arc, for about the first time in *Doctor Who* ever, and it hung together pretty well, if you ignore the three-month gap in the middle), and I think some of his individual episodes rival the best that *Doctor Who* has ever produced. But, at the same time, some of his showrunning decisions seem designed wholly to make you miss Russell T Davies. Having Amy and Rory linger far beyond their sell-by date is the most obvious example.

The same isn't true of River, even though it should be. Her story is one that was also completely wrapped up in Series Six, but the character is given a new lease on life thanks to her pardon. That allows her to become a free agent, and so we get to see her relationship with the Doctor in full bloom. The fact that the pardon comes from the Doctor erasing himself from history is just delightful:

it's a really great way of moving both the story and the character forward that doesn't feel at all forced.

The biggest problem with this story is the Angels themselves. They're a great concept and have a great design, but the rules seem to change every time we meet them — and not in a way that adds to their mystique. Last time we saw them, their central premise was even absent (sending people back in time), although that's thankfully restored here. But now, rather than looking like statues, it appears they can "take over" statues for reasons that make no — hey, everyone, it's the Statue of Liberty!

The Angels also look directly at each other several times, such as in the corridor of the apartment building, and somehow that entirely fails to neutralize the threat, even though we know that was enough to do so in "Blink." Not being able to look at each other wasn't just a throwaway element — it was the climax of the entire story. One repeatedly voted up there with the best of *Doctor Who* ever, so it's not as though nobody noticed.

However, there are some fun moments in this episode. Having a battery farm in Battery Park is quite clever, as is the Doctor saying, "Once we know it's coming, it's written in stone," followed by a segue to Rory's grave. River's line "When one's in love with an ageless god who insists on the face of a 12-year-old, one does one's best to hide the damage" might be the perfect manifesto for the character. And having the paradox created by Rory dying twice is an amusing take on the character's biggest flaw. The Chin Dynasty visit is a bit under-cooked, though.

The story twists itself into knots trying to find a way to separate the Doctor and Amy forever. New York in 1938 is inaccessible by the TARDIS, which is all well and good . . . so long as Amy and Rory don't take a train to Pennsylvania and meet the Doctor there or anything like that. The Doctor does later say that Amy is creating fixed time, which, by *Doctor Who* language, is a better way of locking them in to their destiny, although it still doesn't preclude him seeing them again.

A better solution might have been to have the Doctor go back with them, spend 65 years living with them, and step out from behind a gravestone in 2012, moments after his younger self left. Then you have a cast-iron reason for the Doctor not being able to go back and see them: because he'd cross his own timeline. Ah well.

How the final scene works is anyone's guess. Amy tells the Doctor to go visit young Amelia the night he left and won't see her again for 12 years. Apparently he does so and outlines her entire future to her, something we're told in this very episode is a big no-no. Double-you . . . tee . . . eff? Doesn't this contradict just about *everything*?

"The Angels Take Manhattan" is a perfectly good mini-season finale. It has so much going on that you'll almost certainly find something to like, although equally there's probably something else that's going to annoy you. It wraps up Amy and Rory's story in an emotionally satisfying way, even if the tortured logic of doing so will have you pulling out your hair for days. It opens a new avenue for River, which is quite welcome. And it continues to make a mockery of the best monster created for the New Series. Yep, it's a Steven Moffat script all right. Come back, Russell T Davies, all is forgiven!

All that said, I can't wait for the sequel. Now, what shall we call it? "The Great Angel Caper," "Angel Treasure Island," "Angels Most Wanted," "It's a Very Merry Angel Christmas Movie" . . .

**Second Opinion (GB)** Hello, Doctor. I'm here along with a few of your friends. Well, fans, actually. We're here because we've noticed something. We're concerned about something important going on with you right now.

You see, it's time we had an intervention.

We need to talk . . . about this, um, obsession of yours with Amy.

Look, it's sweet that you met this girl when she was young and came back into her life when she was older. My co-author thinks "The Eleventh Hour" is the perfect gateway story, and that's one of the reasons I can see why.

And I love your relationship with Amy. It's a romance with your best friend. It's platonic and romantic at the same time. I get how compelling it is for you and that it's what drives you when it comes to her.

But . . . dude. You've become a bit creepy about it.

And no it's not the "You're the first face this face saw" business (but while we're at it . . . *eww*). It's that you just can't let her go. She gets married, you keep travelling together. And that's cool. But then you realize it's not, so you have her move out, give her a house and a chance for a life on her own. Except you don't. You keep coming back into her and Rory's lives, never giving them a chance to find a life of their own other than crazy time-and-space travelling. And even when it looks like they're ready to stay put, you keep indulging them.

And when Amy has to choose — has to *really* choose — you can't do the understanding thing. The decent thing. The thing that a Time Lord who has lived for over a thousand years should understand. Hell, you did a great speech about that an episode ago. You should want Amy to make the most of those precious moments with her husband.

Instead, you have a tantrum. Three of them, actually. And your response is she should spend that precious time with you.

Let go, Doctor.

Really. I mean, man, you couldn't even bother to remember that River lost her mum. Dude, that's just *cold*.

Amy may have been your best friend and a romance all rolled up in one, but you blocked her and Rory from being grown-ups time and again. And she had to do the grown-up thing. You didn't.

That's not cool. It's time to evaluate your life choices before you go on to — oh. Hmmm.

Let me start again . . .

## 7.06 The Snowmen

**Written by** Steven Moffat **Directed by** Saul Metzstein

**Original airdate** December 25, 2012

**The Big Idea** Creatures made of snow are terrorizing Victorian London. But where has the Doctor gone?

**Roots and References** Sherlock Holmes (Simeon suggests that Conan Doyle is basing Holmes on Vastra, while the Doctor later pretends, badly, to be the great detective and Murray Gold does a pastiche of *Sherlock*'s incidental music); Raymond Briggs's *The Snowman* (the title and the sentient snowmen); *Batman: The Dark Knight Returns* (the Doctor's realization he put on a bowtie without knowing it echoes a scene where a retired Bruce Wayne realizes he's shaved his moustache). The Doctor plays with a Mr. Punch puppet, which the Ice Governess later mirrors.

**Adventures in Time and Space** This is a prequel to 1968's "The Web of Fear," which featured the Great Intelligence using the robotic Yeti (previously seen in 1967's "The Abominable Snowmen") to invade London's Underground. After the Great Intelligence is created here, the Doctor inadvertently gives it the idea to invade the London Underground thanks to his lunch tin. Victorian Clara shows a fondness for soufflés, just as Oswin did in "Asylum of the Daleks." We see a return of Madame Vastra and Jenny from 2010's "A Good Man Goes to War," this time with Strax, the Sontaran nurse from the same story, resurrected from the dead and now working for Vastra. Strax has trouble determining human gender, which is an extension of a joke first started in 1973's "The Time Warrior."

**The Impossible Girl Effect** The Doctor meets Clara Oswin Oswald, a second version of Oswin Oswald from "Asylum of the Daleks," although until she says, "Run, you clever boy, and remember," he doesn't realize she's the soufflé girl from the Dalek asylum. Clara, like Oswin, is killed, giving rise to her "impossible" nature. At the end of the story, we see a third Clara in modern times (whom we meet properly in the next story).

**Who Is the Doctor?** He's deeply traumatized after the loss of Amy and Rory. As a result, he's retired from saving the world, even giving up his beloved bowtie. His experience with Clara causes him to re-engage once again. He seems to only vaguely recall the events of "The Web of Fear." To be fair, it was a long time ago and bits of it may be missing . . .

**The Doctor and Clara** The Doctor and Clara flirt outrageously, even kissing. He gives her a key to the TARDIS almost instantaneously. She initially cuts through his shell, and he makes a bargain with the universe to save the world if she lives. (She doesn't, but he saves the world anyway.) Later, the mystery of who she is empowers him to return to adventuring.

**Monster of the Week** The Snowmen are made from malevolent snow, powered by the fears and anger of Walter Simeon, as channelled by the Great Intelligence, a disembodied entity that is created from Simeon's dreams. Natch.

**Stand Up and Cheer** The sequence where Clara follows the Doctor up an invisible staircase to find the TARDIS on a cloud is quite magical. This childlike wonder is exactly the kind of thing that the show does so well and so beautifully.

**Roll Your Eyes** The resolution depends on the rain turning salty, becoming the tears of a whole family, as filtered through the magical properties of the snow. We were thankfully spared the mystical properties of the snow turning the viewers' response to this cheese into yellow chunks hurling down from above.

**You're Not Making Any Sense** The spiral staircase is beautiful but confusing. For the most part, it spirals up clockwise. But at the top of the cloud, it spirals up counter clockwise. So does Clara have to do a little jog inside the cloud as she encounters the awkward bit?

**Interesting Trivia** There were not one, not two, but three extra features associated with this story. The first was "The Great Detective," which was released during the BBC Children in Need telethon in November 2012. It establishes the members of the Paternoster Gang (including the fact that the Doctor is technically a member of it) and that the Doctor has retired. The webisode "The Battle of Demons Run: Two Days Later" features the crucial linking material that explained how Strax survived the battle from "A Good Man Goes to War" and why he's now living with Madame Vastra and Jenny, although it wasn't released until after this episode aired. Finally, "Vastra Investigates" explains some of Madame Vastra's origins and shows how she was awoken by an extension to the London Underground (mentioned in "A Good Man Goes to War"). In fact, there was technically a fourth extra feature: the novella *Devil in the Smoke: An*

*Adventure for the Great Detective* was released a few weeks before Christmas, making "The Snowmen" the first *Doctor Who* story to have a prose prequel.

Series Seven was broken into two segments: "Series 7a," five episodes broadcast in September 2012, and "Series 7b," broadcast six months later in the spring of 2013. Set between these two points, "The Snowmen" saw a major production overhaul of the series, with a new title sequence (which includes, for the first time in the Modern Series, a glimpse of the Doctor's face), a new TARDIS interior and a one-off costume for the eleventh Doctor. When one factors in the new companion, many fans commented that this was effectively a new season. However, the BBC maintains that it's all part of the Seventh Series and released it as such on home video, so that's good enough for us.

The Doctor retiring was a rejected storyline that Douglas Adams had proposed in the 1970s, but nobody could get the idea to work without fundamentally breaking the series. It's a testament to how far television has moved on that the show can support this idea in 2012. With the ability to have recurring characters, ongoing storylines and emotional consequences to events from previous episodes, this episode takes a difficult concept from four decades earlier and slides it into the ongoing story arc without breaking a sweat.

In many respects, this whole story exists to be the punchline for a joke nobody would get for another ten months. The reveal at the end is that the story is a prequel to "The Web of Fear," a 1967 story that was — at time of transmission — largely missing from the archives. So we see the creation of the Great Intelligence, a bunch of (abominable) snowmen and a lunch tin with a map of the London Underground from 1967 on it. It's all a direct lead-in to the fact that most of the story had actually been recovered in Jos, Nigeria, and would be released to the public in October 2013. Steven Moffat was undoubtedly aware of this at time of writing, and he likely wrote the episode as an enormous tease for a long-game joke that wouldn't pay off for ages. Totes worth it.

**The TARDIS Chronometer** London, 1842, 1892 and 2012.

**Cool? (RS?)** Pop quiz. What's wrong with "The Snowmen"?

Is it the Doctor's absence from much of the story? Not at all. It's necessary time he needs to grieve after tragically losing Amy and Rory. It shows us that, unlike the Classic Series, where the Doctor just moved on after his beloved companions left, the Modern Series is interested in dealing with the emotional ramifications of how loss affects even the Doctor. Having him retreat to a cloud is actually kind of magnificent.

Is it the fact that we got the wrong Clara? The original plan was that this Clara would have been the new companion, giving us the first historical companion of the Modern Series. And, it must be said, Victorian Clara is downright awesome. The fact that she's hiding her class roots (even despite the fact that Jenna-Louise Coleman can't do the London accent) is a great character note. She's much flirtier with the Doctor than modern-day Clara will be. But were they wrong to kill this one off and replace her with a modern-day counterpart? I'd argue not. As a fan, I love the idea of mixing up the companions the way they did in the '60s and the '80s. Australian companions, American companions, companions in pyjamas . . . I love them all. (Well, maybe not the one in the pyjamas, but at least he had that nifty gold star for mathematical excellence.) But I still don't think it makes marketing sense for the Modern Series to do anything other than have a present-day girl as a lead-in for all the many, many millions of viewers who aren't as hardcore as I am. Take that away and you've likely halved the audience in one fell swoop.

Is it the set-up to the "Web of Fear" joke that pays off only for continuity-obsessed nerds? Without knowing about the return of the missing episodes, the punchline of the Great Intelligence and the map of the London Underground was funny only to a very small subset of the audience. But it's a throwaway gag that probably flew over the heads of most viewers, so I don't see the problem.

Is it the two child actors, who might have become pseudo-companions? Had the Victorian Clara joined the TARDIS, it's likely that her charges would have featured in the series or on board the TARDIS as recurring characters. Child actors can be notoriously dodgy. But we got lucky here: the Darcey-Aldens are actually quite good, especially Ellie. Not necessarily crying out to become the next Jackie and Rory, but they work for this story.

Is it the fact that Vastra, Jenny and Strax are reintroduced with no explanation? Almost, but not quite. It's disconcerting that there's no explanation for why Strax isn't dead, given that we saw him die in "A Good Man Goes to War." There isn't even a line of dialogue or any use of the fact that he's from a clone race. Instead, he's just onscreen, and the Paternoster Gang are apparently the Doctor's substitute family now, no questions asked. (Fortunately, there is an answer to this, although you have to go hunting for it. The webisode "The Battle of Demons Run: Two Days Later" has the details. Though it took me ages to find out it existed, and I'm a rabid fan, so what hope does anyone else have?)

Is it the fact that they redesign everything from the TARDIS interior to the credits to the Doctor's costume, despite this not being a) a new Doctor, b) a new production team or c) a new season? Answer: yes. It's madness. Series Seven got split across two years for reasons nobody's clear on, but, instead of providing unity across the episodes, the production team act as though the show is being rebooted. And, as it turns out, it'll have to be rebooted again half a season later. So what was the point?

Is it the fact that this is the grimmest episode yet of the Modern Series? No, it isn't. In case you hadn't noticed, I already answered the quiz in the previous paragraph. This is an episode that sees the Doctor in a depressed slump, losing every single battle he tries to fight, bargaining with the universe and failing — and where the only victory (Simeon's death) is entirely reversed in the next episode.

But all that doesn't matter one jot. Because "The Snowmen" is basically *The Empire Strikes Back* of *Doctor Who* episodes: our heroes keep losing, and badly, but it doesn't matter in the slightest when the quality is this good. Even poor marketing decisions can't keep a good (snow)man down.

**Second Opinion (GB)** It's the staircase that gets me every time. It's the stunning, gobsmacking imaginative visual of this ladder leading to a staircase leading into the clouds . . . to the TARDIS. To say I adore it is an understatement.

But I think the genius of the staircase is that it's servicing something else entirely. "The Snowmen" looks like it's trying to be a pilot for a new phase of *Doctor Who*, with a remote, retired Doctor living in his TARDIS-in-the-sky in Victorian London. There he meets a companion who brings him back to travelling in time and space with the Paternoster Gang to act as the home base.

And maybe that was the plan until they changed their mind and decided not to have the next companion be from Victorian England. But rather than scrapping the would-be pilot for the next phase of *Doctor Who*, Steven Moffat kept it going . . .

And then killed off the would-be companion just as she was given the TARDIS key.

The effect of that is incredible. Because you have the careful build of the new set-up: the mystery Clara brings (why is she both barmaid and governess?), the frisson of instant romance with the Doctor (and my co-author is absolutely correct about how incredible Victorian Clara is) and the demonstration of her worthiness (the scene with the umbrella is wonderful). All this is built up beautifully — and then the rug is pulled out from under us all as Clara is thrown out of the TARDIS.

In some ways, the ending of "The Snowmen" is kind of ridiculous: the Doctor engages in a futile duel with fate (yeah, that usually works out for him) and then decides to travel again to solve a mystery to do with Clara (setting in motion the idea that she's a mystery to solve rather than a character). But in other ways, it has real weight. We have the careful set-up of "Rose" or "Smith and Jones" or "The Eleventh Hour" and . . . it just doesn't work out. And that's the power of "The Snowmen": anyone can capture the Doctor's fancy and prove themselves worthy for companion-hood, but not all can survive it.

In the end, it's all about the staircase. It's magical, impossible and beautiful. But it also leads to a disturbing fall from grace. That's not easy drama for Christmas Day, but, like the strongest *Doctor Who* Christmas specials, it's at its best when it acknowledges the melancholy under the holiday veneer.

## The Psychic Papers: The Great Intelligence

It sounds pretty formidable: a disembodied intelligence that can plot against the Doctor, using robotic servants to wreak havoc in the real world while existing in an astral plane. And yet the Great Intelligence appeared in only two Classic *Doctor Who* stories in the '60s: 1967's "The Abominable Snowmen" and, a mere five months later, 1968's "The Web of Fear." Both of these six-part stories were penned by the writing duo of Mervyn Haisman and Henry Lincoln.

The first story saw the Intelligence take over the mind of a Tibetan monk, using robots that looked like Yeti to attack a monastery (though a real Yeti does appear briefly at the end). The Yeti were robots operated by control spheres that did the bidding of the Great Intelligence. The latter story saw the Yeti invade the London Underground, with the Intelligence attempting to take over the Doctor's mind. In both cases, the disembodied Intelligence was mostly in the background, acting out its plans through possessed humans or furry robots.

At the end of that adventure, the Doctor was foiled in his attempt to drain the Great Intelligence, the implication being that the Great Intelligence and the Yeti would be back for a rematch. And, originally, there were plans for more Yeti adventures. (One of them was a potential story that might have written out the second Doctor's companion Jamie, set in a 19th-century Scottish castle.) Unfortunately, a dispute between the writers and the production staff over rewrites on what became 1967's "The Dominators" (as well as a protracted dispute over compensation from licensing their characters the Quarks for the *Doctor Who* comic strip) prevented any more appearances from the Great Intelligence. It's a shame, because the Yeti were immensely popular in their day. So much so that Patrick Troughton recorded a special introduction to their second story to warn children who'd found them cuddly in their first appearance that they were scarier in the second.

Until 2013, the two 1960s stories both had most of their episodes missing. Before then, the sum total of Yeti appearances was the equivalent of three episodes. (They had a brief cameo appearance in a single scene in 1983's "The Five Doctors.") It's a testament to their effectiveness that they maintained an appeal for all this time.

But what is the Great Intelligence? A Tibetan monk who became possessed by it claimed that it was formless in space and that he astral-travelled to make contact with it, whereupon it took over his body, wishing for one of its own. It possessed him for 300 years, so the astral-travel thing may have involved time travel. The Doctor later describes it as a shapeless thing floating about in space like a cloud of mist. That's all we knew . . . until "The Snowmen." The Great Intelligence will become something of a recurring villain over the next half season, with appearances by a possessed Dr. Simeon in several episodes.

It's clear that the Great Intelligence and the Yeti were memorable villains, despite their paucity of material. Jon Pertwee famously defended the Earthbound nature of many of his stories by claiming that there was nothing scarier than a Yeti in the loo in Tooting Bec. (Presumably he never went to the loo in Glasgow.) Curiously, the Yeti's roar was actually devised from a slowed-down toilet flush! Is that a coincidence on Pertwee's part? Or does it speak to his great intelligence?

## 7.07 The Bells of Saint John

**Written by** Steven Moffat **Directed by** Colm McCarthy
**Original airdate** March 30, 2013

**The Big Idea** Human souls are being uploaded and harvested through wifi networks, including that of Clara Oswald, the latest version of the impossible girl the Doctor keeps meeting.

**Roots and References** *The Matrix* (human minds connected to a computer network); *Saturday Night Fever* (the Doctor does the disco pose again); *Star Trek IV: The Voyage Home* (the Doctor's line "I can't tell the future; I just work there" is a variant on Kirk's line "I'm from Iowa; I only work in outer space"). There's mention of the London riots of 2011 (the corporation claims to have started at least one of them) and the actual police box that exists in Earl's Court. The title is derived from the Saint John's Ambulance badge on the TARDIS's police box exterior (and its phone).

**Adventures in Time and Space** The Great Intelligence, having now taken on the likeness of Dr. Simeon from "The Snowmen," returns, as does UNIT (last seen in "The Power of Three"). The Doctor has taken to wearing Amy's reading glasses (from "The Angels Take Manhattan"). The Doctor leaves some Jammie Dodgers for Clara (2010's "Victory of the Daleks"). The symbols for the wifi used by the Great Intelligence are reminiscent of the Exillon language from 1974's "Death to the Daleks." Artie is reading *Summer Falls*, a novel by Amelia Williams, which gives us a hint of what Amy has been up to since we last saw her . . .

**The Impossible Girl Effect** The Doctor is reconnected (through mysterious means) to a new version of Clara, one that lives in the 21st century with echoes of the Victorian version's life (she's taking care of children, much like the governess of "The Snowmen"). A number of aspects of Oswin Oswald and Victorian Clara seem to originate with this version: "Run you clever boy and remember" is Clara's mnemonic for remembering the Maitland family's wifi password ("rycbar123") and "Oswin" is a login that Clara derives from "Oswald, for the win."

**Who Is the Doctor?** The death of Victorian Clara in "The Snowmen" has caused the Doctor to retreat again (literally, to one of the monastic kind), but hearing from Clara in the present day rouses him to action. He now wears a modified outfit, with a purple tweed morning coat and a waistcoat (but still keeps the bowtie). He apparently competed in the Antigrav Olympics. He's ridiculously pleased with being called "Doctor Who?"

**The Doctor and Clara** The Doctor has become obsessed with Clara: he's in the process of making a painting of her when he's summoned to answer the TARDIS phone, and when he discovers the version living in the 21st century, he doesn't distinguish her from the person he got to know in "The Snowmen." (Clara is a little creeped out by the emotional intensity of someone who is, to her, a perfect stranger.) The Doctor is immediately deeply loyal to Clara. He guards her while she's sleeping and leaves a message to Kizlet that she is "under my protection." Clara reads the Doctor's intentions romantically (she calls the TARDIS a "snog box"); the Doctor blushes when he finds his intentions are seen as less than honourable.

**Monster of the Week** The mysterious corporation harvesting human minds for the Great Intelligence uses mobile base stations (called "Spoonheads"), robots that can walk and transmit wifi signals. They generate basic camouflage using the subconscious of their victims (with Clara they use a character in the *Summer Falls* book she read).

**Stand Up and Cheer** The Doctor motorcycles up the Shard, only to reveal it's not the Doctor at all; in fact, the Doctor is telecommuting his victory from a coffee shop using a laptop. There's something wonderful and uniquely *Doctor Who* about that.

**Roll Your Eyes** We liked Clara's mysterious call to the Doctor thinking she's calling a helpdesk. We loved the payoff to the scene where the Doctor resorts to acting like a bored IT guy (from the year 1207, no less!) but . . . did it have to use the gendered trope that a girl can't understand computer stuff?

**You're Not Making Any Sense** The premise sounds cool — "human minds are stolen through the wifi" — but, um, how does it work, exactly? Wifi is basically a mode of broadcasting within a network of computers. It's about as sophisticated as radio. There's the handwaving that the alien language of the networks chosen indicate higher technology and that the base stations do the actual mind sucking, but, even by the standards of *Doctor Who*, it's still ridiculously vague.

**Interesting Trivia** There are a number of mysteries left for the viewer in this story, but perhaps the most tantalizing one is who gave Clara the Doctor's phone number. Clara describes her as a "woman in a shop" who tells her it's the number "to the best helpline in the universe." At this point, the likeliest suspect is River Song. Or is it? We will see . . .

The Shard is a neo-futurist tower (that looks like, um, a shard of glass) that had been under construction for a few years when the episode was made. By the time "The Bells of Saint John" was transmitted, it had been open for only a couple of months; it opened in February 2013. This isn't the first time *Doctor Who* has capitalized on a new feature in the London skyline as a plot point. The still relatively recent Canary Wharf tower — opened only a decade prior — was Torchwood's headquarters and the source of a Cybermen and Dalek invasion in 2006's "Army of Ghosts"/"Doomsday." The London Eye (a.k.a. the Millennium Wheel, opened in 2000) was the antennae transmitting signals from the Nestene in 2005's "Rose."

As with *The Angel's Kiss* — the novel by River Song (as "Melody Malone") in "The Angels Take Manhattan" that was adapted into a real novella (written by Justin Richards) — BBC Books also adapted *Summer Falls* into a novella, with author James Goss ghostwriting for Amy Pond. Both featured in the 2013 collection *Summer Falls and Other Stories*.

At one point, Mahler mentions that their effort to track the TARDIS was embarrassingly foiled at Earl's Court. This is a reference to the only bona fide police box that still exists in London, just outside the Earl's Court Underground station. This is not an original police box from the 1930s to the 1960s — those were all destroyed — but a replica that was constructed in 1996 with CCTV cameras along with the traditional phone to contact police. The new police box was intended as a pilot project, though some more cynically inclined think it was built so that the Metropolitan Police could still claim rights to the police box image. The same year the Earl's Court box was constructed, the BBC filed for a trademark on the police box design. In spite of the Met's objections, the U.K. patent office gave the BBC the trademark in 2002. The Earl's Court box had its phone and cameras disabled by the early 2000s and had fallen into disrepair. The Metropolitan Police eventually agreed to maintain the box, given its tourist appeal, especially with *Doctor Who* back on TV. For a while, during the series' fiftieth anniversary, Google Earth's Street View function allowed the user to go "inside" the Earl's Court police box into a street-view representation of the TARDIS set!

**The TARDIS Chronometer** Cumbria in 1207, and suburban London in the present day.

**Cool? (GB)** Every so often, if you're lucky, you get a *Doctor Who* story like "The Bells of Saint John." A story full of invention, excitement, laughs and great fun. If I could only use one word to describe "The Bells of Saint John," it would be "joyous." If I could use another word, it would be "exuberant." And if I got a third, I'd throw in "confident."

The Doctor and Clara stopping a crashing airplane is one of the best scenes this season and indeed all of modern *Doctor Who*. If "The Bells of Saint John" was this scene alone, I would be happy. Some TV shows would make this a major point of jeopardy. Here we get it as part of an exposition scene where the new companion discovers what the TARDIS is, done as if it's a continuous take. (It's not.) Not only is it hugely exciting but it brilliantly introduces the TARDIS to a new companion in the context of an action scene. It has huge dollops of ridiculousness (Clara never lets go of her coffee cup the entire time, which is an amazing little touch) and, before the sequence can outstay its welcome, it has the beautiful sight gag of Clara almost finally getting a swig of coffee — before she's yanked away.

There's just so much charm in this story. Clara's conversation with the Doctor outside her window is lovely. And all that pivots in a delightfully unexpected direction as Clara (reasonably) thinks the Doctor's intentions are lascivious, while the Doctor is adorably shocked by this. I love this angle to bits.

Have I mentioned how great Clara is out of the starting gate? So much is established about her here. The book *101 Places to See* — with Clara listing her age in the front, from nine to 24 — says so much about who she is and what she wants. But it's the wonderfully mature way she declares she wants a relationship with the Doctor on her own terms: she won't just pack up and leave for time and space like every companion in the Modern Series since Rose Tyler; instead, the Doctor has to schedule a time to come over — like most friendships, actually.

The charm isn't solely given to the heroes. Celia Imrie's Ms. Kizlet is such a great villain; you have to love a character who gives an employee their earned vacation days before terminating them, literally.

Of course, parts of this story are ridiculous (wifi can harvest souls!), and it's hugely derivative (it's basically a rehash of 2006's "The Idiot's Lantern," only using wifi instead of television), and, yes, it has its obvious flaws (it's a story about the internet, so let's have a ton of scenes with the Doctor or Clara furiously typing as though coding is some kind of magical incantation). But you have Clara's elegant little hack that figures out the bad guys' base of operations, because she knows how people think. And, as bonkers as the premise is, it also has the most chilling teaser *Doctor Who* has had in ages.

I guess that's why I love "The Bells of Saint John." It's flagrantly ridiculous, but it makes its ridiculousness a virtue. It's a *Doctor Who* story that posits that wifi can be used to steal people's conscious minds as part of a plan conducted by an office populated with employees with hacked personalities but who still keep Facebook accounts. A story where obstacles like a plane crash are mere trifles and the Doctor can get a help desk call while in the Middle Ages.

No other television show on Earth can do this. "The Bells of Saint John" is everything I love about *Doctor Who*.

**Second Opinion (RS?)** I hate to be so curmudgeonly, given my co-author's good mood, but that plane scene really bugs me.

Imagine you're an airline pilot in 2013. You wake up in your cockpit, mid-flight, to find that two strangers have broken into the cockpit and are wrestling with the controls. Do you a) react as though the plane has been hijacked and do anything possible to neutralize said hijackers, b) take a measure of last resort and immediately plunge the plane into the ground in order to thwart what is clearly a terrorist attack in progress, or c) shrug and look goofy and otherwise pay no attention to the two lunatics currently in a restricted area flying your plane into near-total darkness?

I don't mind *Doctor Who* being goofy fun. In fact, that's one of the greatest things about it. And Graeme rightly identifies so many of the fun parts of this episode. But when things like this happen, it's the writing equivalent of a boom mike wandering into shot: you realize that what you're doing is watching a television program that's been contrived by a writer somewhere.

So the Doctor can, and should, be as goofy as he wants to be. The companion can join in. But when you drop the ball on having ancillary characters act believably, the whole thing comes crashing down like a studio set of a plane piloted by actors wearing costumes and reading lines in a TV show.

Happily, that's only a few seconds of misfiring in an episode that's otherwise exactly what my co-author claims it is. I'd like to make special mention of the utterly stupendous reveal that it's the mobile base station that has travelled to the Shard, rather than the Doctor himself, which may be one of Steven Moffat's finest twists. For me, that's the equivalent of the plot figuratively grabbing the controls in the episode's cockpit and narrowly avoiding disaster. And, okay fine, now I'm cheering along with an episode that radiates, well, joyous, exuberant confidence. Damn you, co-author . . .

## Jenna Coleman

By the time Jenna Coleman was cast in *Doctor Who*, she had already won a most popular newcomer award at the National Television Awards for her portrayal of Jasmine Thomas in the British soap *Emmerdale* (which she was in from 2005 to 2009). Born in 1986, Coleman went to *Emmerdale* instead of drama school. She translated her success from that soap into an acclaimed role on the 2009 BBC drama *Waterloo Road*. *Doctor Who* was her grandmother's favourite show, so she was thrilled when she was asked to audition for the role of Clara. During her time on the series, Coleman shortened her stage name from "Jenna-Louise" to "Jenna." Less than a year after she finally left *Doctor Who* in 2015 (after nearly doing so in 2014 — twice!), Coleman took on the role of Queen Victoria in the BBC/PBS series *Victoria*. That series has been hugely popular, and Coleman is arguably now better known for *Victoria* than *Doctor Who*. She continues to act in other television programs, including the 2018 BBC drama *The Cry*.

# 7.08 The Rings of Akhaten

**Written by** Neil Cross **Directed by** Ferren Blackburn
**Original airdate** April 6, 2013

**The Big Idea** The Doctor takes Clara to see a religious ceremony on the Rings of Akhaten. Only things don't go according to plan when the Old God wakes up.

**Roots and References** The 1997 film *The Fifth Element* and the comics of Jean Girard, better known as Moebius (the aliens and alien society); Frank Herbert's 1968 novel *Dune* (the Old God). The Doctor is reading the 1981 *Beano Summer Special* while watching Dave and Ellie meet. The Doctor quotes the Lewis Carroll poem "The Walrus and the Carpenter."

**Adventures in Time and Space** The Doctor mentions his granddaughter (Susan, who travelled with the first Doctor). The pressed leaf that Clara described as "Page One" in "The Bells of Saint John" is revealed to be the leaf that nearly killed her father and brought her parents together. The Doctor offers up memories of the Time War and his race's passing (first mentioned in 2005's "The End of the World"). The Doctor obliquely references the Victorian Clara from "The Snowmen."

**The Impossible Girl Effect** The Doctor stalks Clara and her family in the past to see how her parents came together and how she grew up but does not come any closer to finding out who she really is.

**Who Is the Doctor?** The Doctor reminds Clara that he never walks away from trouble. He's willing to sacrifice the sum total of all his memories to stop Akhaten.

**The Doctor and Clara** The Doctor takes Clara to Akhaten purely to impress her. She sacrifices her most precious object — the leaf that brought her parents together — for the Doctor. She comes to realize, though, that the Doctor has been spying on her throughout her life and calls him on it. He refuses to admit it's because of her duplicates but says she reminds him of someone. Clara tells him that he can visit her again, not as a stand-in for someone else, "but as me."

**Monster of the Week** Akhaten, the Old God, is a star-sized parasite that feeds off memories and stories of sentient beings.

**Stand Up and Cheer** When Merry Gejelh is taken by Akhaten, Clara accuses the Doctor of walking away. The Doctor tells her, "Listen, there's one thing you need to know about travelling with me. Well, one thing apart from the blue box and the two hearts. We don't walk away."

**Roll Your Eyes** The Doctor's sacrificial stand against Akhaten should be dramatic and stirring. But it seems strident and whiny. The jamboree sing-song in the background doesn't help much.

**You're Not Making Any Sense** You're travelling with an alien through time and space to all kinds of dangerous places, and you bring your most precious and fragile possession with you? Who does this?

**Interesting Trivia** The writers for Series Seven were unusual in that they were almost all showrunners (head writer and executive producer) on other television series: Chris Chibnall was, at the time, coming off *Law & Order: U.K.* and was just starting pre-production on *Broadchurch*; Toby Whithouse was showrunning *Being Human*; and Mark Gatiss showran *Sherlock* with Steven Moffat. "The Rings of Akhaten" was written by Neil Cross, whose hiring was quite a coup, coming off the hugely popular BBC crime series *Luther*. Using other showrunners made it easier for Steven Moffat, as they tended to understand the budgetary and production demands a show like *Doctor Who* faced. Of this season's writers, the only ones who weren't producing TV series were Neil Gaiman (a wildly successful novelist who eventually turned to producing TV with 2019's *Good Omens*) and Steve Thompson (yes, um, we'll talk about him in a couple of episodes . . . ).

In spite of being an acclaimed writer, Neil Cross did have to perform major rewrites. Cross's original ending had the Doctor defeating Akhaten using his memories after his dramatic speech. Steven Moffat pointed out that the Doctor did this rather a lot and suggested it would be better if Clara saved the day instead. That led to Cross changing the start of his episode from a more mundane scene in the Maitlands' kitchen to the Doctor's investigation of Clara's past, which led to the invention of the all-important leaf. Moffat then seeded that leaf (pardon the pun) by including it in the previous episode.

It would seem that the TARDIS isn't translating everything for Clara. While the Doctor can understand Dor'een, Clara can't. Given that the TARDIS also refuses to let her in, it would seem the TARDIS is becoming actively hostile towards Ms. Oswald. We will return to this very soon . . .

Clara's mother, Ellie Oswald, died on March 5, 2005. According to Rose Tyler's missing person poster in 2005's "Aliens of London," Rose was last seen on March 6, 2005. If Rose called Jackie in the early hours of March 6 at the end of "Rose," this might mean that Ellie was killed in the Auton attack the night before. That does seem to be a wee bit of a stretch; leaving aside the conditions listed above, Clara never indicates that her mother is a victim of violence. But for fans who like to connect events in the *Doctor Who* universe, have fun.

**The TARDIS Chronometer** The Doctor follows the events of Clara's life, from her parents' meeting in the early 1980s until her mother's death in 2005. The Doctor takes Clara to the inhabited rings that surround the planet Akhaten in an unspecified era.

**Cool? (GB)** In its portrayal of alien societies since 2005, *Doctor Who* has basically repeated "The End of the World" over and over again: the creatures look different, but it's broadly, comfortably the same people you'd meet on a bus. (Remember "The End of the World" gave us space plumbers!) What I love about "The Rings of Akhaten" is that it tries to do a genuinely alien society with different ideals and ideas. Here, we have a society governed by the preciousness of memories and a religious service to sing lullabies to a living god to keep him asleep. It feels different right from the start.

And the jeopardy in the story unspools differently too. The beast in the cage thought to be a god isn't; it's a guard. The god is the size of a sun, and the Doctor's heroic gambit to stop it — which any other week would have been enough — utterly fails. Everyone is saved because Clara uses the most precious object she owns against it, and it works because of its potential, which is a lovely idea: what could be is more powerful than what was.

But it's not just the alien setting that I love about "The Rings of Akhaten" — it's Clara. There is an assumption among some fans about Clara that, because she has these doppelgängers roaming time and space, she's merely defined by the mystery about her. The thing is, in this very episode, Clara rejects the Doctor for doing that to her. So should we fans resist writing off Clara as just "the impossible girl"? After all, "The Rings of Akhaten" does a glorious job of defining Clara by who she is and not who she happens to look like. The Doctor fusses over who Clara is supposed to be, but we learn who she *is*: someone who, at this point, has suffered a significant loss and has to let go of what she has left of her mother to save a little girl and her new best friend. That climactic scene is all the more poignant — and the idea of the potential the leaf holds all the sweeter — because we saw Clara's mum live and die in a sequence that left us none the wiser about the season's mystery but taught us what motivates Clara.

It's not that I don't see the flaws in the story: Akhaten is supposed to be this terrifying menace but looks like a demented jack-o'-lantern. The line between cool ideas and vague, fuzzy silliness does become permeable at points. Merry Gejelh is a rare exception to the rule that kids in *Doctor Who* ruin things, but only just.

What "The Rings of Akhaten" does right, though, far outweighs what it fails to do. The universe it creates, and the heroine named Clara Oswald, makes it the most important leaf in the coming seasons of *Doctor Who*.

**Second Opinion (RS?)** Dear Diary,

The Doctor is a hero! It's been seven minutes since he left, departing our world after having destroyed the Old God. I was sitting in the amphitheatre, and I saw the whole thing. Our sun came to life, looking terrifying and eating memories.

But then the Doctor came to the rescue, utterly heroically. It was magnificent. He talked and talked and talked. Okay, maybe he talked a bit too much, and it didn't really do anything, but it was still pretty amazing. And then Clara joined in and gave the Old God a leaf, because it had potential. Which was pretty impressive. I mean, it's not like there aren't things around here that also have potential, like this candlelight I'm using to write by, on account of there being no sunlight anymore. So yeah, maybe we should have thought of that. But still. It was the kind of thing heroes do.

Anyhow, having turned the sun off, the Doctor and Clara promptly left. Job well done and all. Only . . . it's a bit dark now. And cold. Quite cold, in fact. And getting colder. But I'm sure the Doctor will be back any moment now to fix it. After all, he's a hero! A sun-killing hero. He wouldn't have destroyed our source of heat and light and left us to a miserable, freezing death mere minutes later would he?

Would he?

Doctor?

# 7.09 Cold War

**Written by** Mark Gatiss **Directed by** Douglas Mackinnon

**Original airdate** April 13, 2013

**The Big Idea** An Ice Warrior runs amok on board a nuclear-capable Russian submarine at the height of the Cold War.

**Roots and References** The 1981 German film *Das Boot* (tense drama in the confined space of a submarine); the Able Archer 83 military exercise (misleading Russians into almost starting a nuclear war); Tom Clancy's 1984 novel and the 1991 film adaptation *The Hunt for Red October* (the nuclear-capable Russian submarine); *Alien* (Skaldak stalking the ship). The Doctor quotes the Elvis Presley hit "Viva Las Vegas" while wearing glasses similar to those Elvis wore, while Grisenko sings Ultravox's "Vienna" and gets Clara to sing Duran Duran's "Hungry Like the Wolf."

**Adventures in Time and Space** The Ice Warriors have previously appeared in four stories, featuring the second and third Doctors. The Hostile Action Displacement System that displaces the TARDIS was last seen in 1968's "The Krotons." This is only its second appearance. The Doctor pretended to be an Earth ambassador in "The Curse of Peladon." The TARDIS's translation facility (established in the Modern Series in 2005's "The End of the World") gets explained to Clara. The malleability of history is also discussed, which has been a feature of the series since 1975's "Pyramids of Mars."

**Who Is the Doctor?** For once, he introduces himself directly as a time traveller, rather than using the psychic paper or lying about who he is. He carries a Barbie doll and a ball of yarn in his pockets.

**The Doctor and Clara** The Doctor isn't happy about Clara going in alone to talk to Skaldak but relents because she's not a soldier. He tells her it wasn't a test but concedes that she did great. Once the threat is over, she gives the Doctor a long, intense hug and says, "Saved the world, then? . . . That's what we do."

**Monster of the Week** The Ice Warriors — a proud, militaristic race seen several times in the Classic Series — make their first onscreen appearance without their armour, revealing their reptilian look, as well as the fact that their armour can function independently.

**Stand Up and Cheer** The Doctor's idle offer to kiss Professor Grisenko being accepted is utterly hilarious.

**Roll Your Eyes** The idea of showing us the Ice Warrior's true form has potential. So long as you make that huge revelation meaningful and amazing. Rather than, say, bog-standard CGI.

**You're Not Making Any Sense** We're told that an Ice Warrior leaving its shell is the gravest dishonour. Skaldak leaves his because he's been chained up. Except that the armour later breaks free of the shackles anyway. So why does he submit himself to this entirely unnecessary dishonour?

**Interesting Trivia** The Ice Warriors are the first returning monster from the Classic Series not to be given a major design overhaul. The suit of armour is streamlined slightly, losing the tufts of fur that stuck out from the joints, but overall the design is remarkably similar to what we saw 40-plus years earlier. Ironically, Steven Moffat was originally reluctant to bring back the Ice Warriors on the grounds that he thought they looked like the kind of generic green monsters that people used to make fun of *Doctor Who* for including. He was convinced to do so only when Mark Gatiss proposed revealing their true form. This is the first story to establish that the Ice Warriors' armour is actually cybernetic and not organic.

Even though the Ice Warriors' appearance was much the same, voice artist Nicholas Briggs had a harder time with Skaldak's voice. Skaldak was voiced in an ADR (alternative dialogue recording) session with a different director present, who was not in favour of Briggs's interpretation of Skaldak's voice, even though it was the voice the Ice Warriors used in the '60s and '70s. Briggs was ultimately able to win the day on this.

Back in the mid-1990s when they were casting what eventually became the 1996 TV Movie, Liam Cunningham, who plays Zhukov here (and is best known for playing Ser Davos Seaworth on *Game of Thrones*), was then–executive producer Philip Segal's first choice to play the Doctor.

To answer Grisenko's burning question: Ultravox disbanded in 1988. Billy Currie would briefly reform the band (without any original members) in the 1990s before the band reformed with former members Currie, Midge Ure, Chris Cross and Warren Cann in 2008. The band finally folded in 2017.

**The TARDIS Chronometer** On board a Russian submarine, 1983.

**Cool? (RS?)** I'm really not a fan of Mark Gatiss scripts. I can see why others like them (my co-author included), but they just bug me. I think it's the masses of potential that never get converted into kinetic energy: he always sets up great scenarios with some delicious premises, and then does very little of interest after that.

Look at "Victory of the Daleks," which has an awesome opening (Daleks serving Churchill!) and then terrible follow-through (New Paradigm Daleks, Spitfires in space). Or "The Unquiet Dead," with its great set-up (the dead come back to life and go to the theatre!) and its boring result (rape humour, gas monsters with no nuance at all).

"Cold War" has many of the same problems as every Gatiss script: it's an Ice Warrior on a Russian sub at the height of nuclear tension! Brilliant. And then … it's a straightforward base-under-siege story. So many interesting directions this could have gone; so few of them actually taken. There's an attempt to link this into the "one minute to midnight" feel of the nerve-racking American–Soviet standoff that enveloped the time, but it barely connects. One of the soldiers proposes an alliance, which could have been fascinating, but better to kill him off in case that plotline threatened to be gripping or something.

Instead, the story is far more interested in having a rogue CGI monster stalking the confines of a claustrophobic environment — and it succeeds rather well at that. One of the things Gatiss does well is build atmosphere: "Night Terrors," for example, might have been rubbish, but it was scary rubbish. "Cold War" doesn't really care about anything other than making Skaldak as terrifying as possible — this is why he's the greatest of the Martian heroes, why he leaves his suit at all, why the suit starts walking on its own, et cetera — but, on those terms at least, it works.

It also has David Warner and Liam Cunningham being superb, for which I'll forgive a lot of plot faults. It's a shame that Warner is too old to play the captain, as he'd probably have excelled at it, but his role as the '80s-music-loving professor is charming and quirky. It's genuinely terrifying when he's threatened with beheading, largely because Warner is just so likeable. Cunningham does a great job as Zhukov, adding gravitas and a convincing Russian look to the proceedings.

Then there's Skaldak, who's clearly so badass because he's the fusion of three entirely different cultures and species. His outer shell is pure upgraded Classic Series Ice Warrior. Cool. His inner self is from an entirely different species, one that patently doesn't need the shell in the first place and whose hands never fit those gloves. Okay. And his spaceship is plainly from a third civilization altogether. Um.

Also, what's with the weird loss of the TARDIS? It vanishes pretty much entirely because the whole plot would be solved in 30 seconds if it were present. Okay, fine, that's true of lots of *Doctor Who* stories. So Gatiss has it disappear due to the HADS, because he's the type of writer who's never missed a chance for some continuity porn, and he's not about to start now. But the explanation is a) delayed until the end, b) extremely unsatisfying, and c) told, not shown. So is a crucial, nuclear-armed Soviet submarine really going to take a cruise to the other side of the planet while the world is at war, no matter how grateful the crew is for the Doctor's help? Soviet high command is going to authorize this little joyride? I don't think so.

Unfortunately, that's the Gatiss style in a nutshell. It's a cool idea if you don't think about it, and it collapses under the weight of its own inanity when you do. So it's something of a minor miracle that "Cold War" succeeds as well as it does. Turn your brain off, and it's a thrilling, claustrophobic scare story with a fun title. Turn your brain on and . . . nah, let's not go there. Better to relocate your brain to the South Pole for the duration and not ask too many questions.

**Second Opinion (GB)** I've never completely agreed with my co-author about Mark Gatiss. His stories are in the middle of the pack — and sometimes the absolute *middle* of the middle of the pack — but his stories are, with some exceptions, highly entertaining. "Cold War" is no exception. I thought it pulled off its central conceit — an alien stalking a Russian sub — with considerable aplomb.

Could it have worked better without an old monster? Perhaps, but they went somewhere original with Skaldak abandoning his armour. Could the ending have done more with the at-the-brink-of-nuclear-war 1980s setting? Possibly, but it stayed in its lane and let the ghost-train thrill ride play out instead.

Question-mark boy has hit new places of ludicrousness, though, when he can claim a spaceship seen in the last two minutes wouldn't be the one used by the Ice Warriors. I also disagree that Skaldak as designed didn't need the armour (and I could see how his hands would fit the gloves). I think one of the coolest things about this story is that the costume isn't just limited to the 1960s design but actual armour.

My main problem with "Cold War" is with Douglas MacKinnon's direction, which takes the intriguing possibilities of a story set on a submarine and shoots it all in wide shot and (pardon the pun) floodlights it. This story is crying out for a more claustrophobic approach, using source lighting and shadows and hand-held camera to sell the chaos. The result is a story completely without ambience that frequently feels like it's on a set.

The acting, as Robert points out, is great (though I can't see any reason for Grisenko being there other than Gatiss wanting to give his friend David Warner a part). The real standout performance belongs to Jenna Coleman as Clara, who finally has to face down a monster. Coleman is amazing in the scene where she starts singing "Hungry Like the Wolf" and puts all her terror into the song. But the capper is when Clara says, "That's what we do," having come out from the other end of things.

"Cold War" doesn't have much more ambition than an entertaining thrill ride in a submarine. Unlike my co-author, I don't think that's a bad thing. There's a lot worse than being in the middle.

## The Psychic Papers: The Ice Warriors

Like any television production, *Doctor Who* is a collaboration of different artists and tradespeople, and what each of them brings can radically change the direction of a *Doctor Who* story. Take the 1967 serial "The Ice Warriors," where the second Doctor finds a group of scientists in the future staving off a second Ice Age when they find a large humanoid frozen thousands of years earlier. If another designer had been assigned to that story, we might well know of this as the story that featured cyborg Space Vikings. That's what writer Brian Hayles had in mind.

Hayles was inspired by reading about a woolly mammoth that was perfectly preserved in the ice. He thought this could be extrapolated to a humanoid and settled on one that looked like a Viking with a helmet/mask that obscured its eyes. Indeed, Jamie says to the second Doctor, "It looks like a Viking warrior. Look at the helmet." However, "The Ice Warriors" was designed by Martin Baugh, who was more taken by a comment made in the outline that the Warrior came from Mars and had a sort of reptilian look under the helmet.

The result was that Space Vikings were out, large reptilian aliens were in.

If any complaints were made by Brian Hayles or the producers, none made a difference. Baugh's vision of the Ice Warriors was instantly successful, partially because they were so large and looming and partially because of an innovation to use only minimal makeup on the mouth, allowing the monsters to be seen speaking (in a hissing, snake-like voice), though most of the dialogue was actually pre-recorded and played live for the actors to mime in studio.

The titular creatures in "The Ice Warriors" dated from prior to human civilization, but they claimed that Martian society still continued. In 1969's "The Seeds of Death," the Ice Warriors returned in a plot to turn the Earth of the mid-21st century into Martian-like conditions using the network of teleporting T-Mat devices all over the Earth. "The Seeds of Death" added an Ice Lord, who led the Ice Warriors. The Ice Lords were not encumbered by the bulky armour and instead wore a more ceremonially royal costume with a cape. (They still wore helmets, albeit of a different design.)

In 1971, in preparation for Jon Pertwee's third year as the Doctor, the producers decided they should use more past monsters and asked Brian Hayles to have the Ice Warriors fight the third Doctor. Hayles had a story set on Peladon, a still-barbaric, pre-technological society about to join the Galactic Federation (it was a metaphor for the U.K. joining the European Economic Community). However, to avoid a predictable plotline, Hayles came up with an incredible twist: what if the Ice Warriors weren't the villains after all? In "The Curse of Peladon," the Doctor discovers they're honourable and completely blameless. It was a game-changing move. In a stroke, it gave the Ice Warriors new subtleties and changed the paradigm of *Doctor Who* monsters; they could now have more nuanced motivations and didn't have to be the villain.

Of course, it was reversed in 1974's "The Monster of Peladon" (the sequel to "The Curse of Peladon"), where the Ice Warriors were revealed to be behind unrest among Peladon's miners (this time they were homaging the 1974 U.K. miner's strike). But, even here, the Ice Lord Azaxyr is revealed to be working with a faction from Galaxy Five and is not representative of the rest of his species.

In the 1980s, when bringing back past monsters was something *Doctor Who* was keen to do, there were two attempts to bring back the Ice Warriors, both times foiled by cancellations or near-cancellation. The first of these — a story by Philip Martin called "Mission to Magnus," which would also have featured Sil from 1985's "Vengeance on Varos" — was scuppered by the cancellation of the series in 1985 (which became an 18-month hiatus). There were preliminary talks about having the Ice Warriors in the Classic Series' 27th season in 1990, but *Doctor Who*'s cancellation in 1989, this time final, prevented this from being realized. It took the Modern Series of *Doctor Who* seven seasons to bring back the Ice Warriors, with a design closer to the original than most other returning monsters. The Ice Warriors' most recent appearance in "Empress of Mars" aired in the fiftieth anniversary year of their creation, something we might not have seen had Martin Baugh decided to go with cyborg Space Vikings.

## 7.10 Hide

**Written by** Neil Cross **Directed by** Jamie Payne
**Original airdate** April 20, 2013

**The Big Idea** The Doctor and Clara join up with psychic ghost hunters to track down a mysterious figure who keeps appearing in the same place throughout all of time.

**Roots and References** Nigel Kneale's 1954 British TV serial *The Quatermass Experiment* and its sequels (tense investigation of an alien menace); Sherlock Holmes, especially "The Adventure of the Crooked Man" (the Crooked Man); the 1979–82 British TV series *Sapphire and Steel* (paranormal investigators in a spooky house); the 1972 British TV play *The Stone Tape* (the house capturing an image), also by Nigel Kneale. The Doctor recites lyrics from the Cole Porter song "Let's Do It, Let's Fall in Love." The Doctor and Clara claim they're Ghostbusters (from the 1984 film of the same name).

**Adventures in Time and Space** The crystals from Metebelis III played a crucial role during the third Doctor's era. His desire to go to that planet was a recurring theme in the Classic Series' tenth season; when he eventually made it, in

1973's "The Green Death," he took one of the crystals and gave it to departing companion Jo Grant. Subsequently, she sent it back to the Doctor, whose third regeneration occurred as a result of the spider beings who ruled the planet wanting it back in 1974's "Planet of the Spiders." The Eye of Harmony was first seen in 1977's "The Deadly Assassin." The disastrous effect of entropy was something seen in the fourth Doctor's final story, 1981's "Logopolis." The Cloister Bell that rings here (portending doom) was first heard in that story. Apparently it's the week to be reminding the Doctor of things that killed him.

The Doctor's habit of air-kissing both cheeks, first seen in 2010's "The Lodger," resumes here. The orange spacesuits from the 42nd century, first seen in 2006's "The Impossible Planet"/"The Satan Pit," are used once again. Hila's disappearance is a fixed point in time (2008's "The Fires of Pompeii"). The TARDIS's emergency holographic interface from 2011's "Let's Kill Hitler" returns.

**The Impossible Girl Effect** When asked whether he sees humans as either ghosts or nothing, the Doctor says that Clara is the only mystery worth solving. The reason the Doctor came to Caliburn House in the first place is because he wanted to use Emma's psychic abilities to discover Clara's true nature. However, Emma tells him that Clara is a perfectly ordinary girl, nothing more.

**Who Is the Doctor?** Emma counsels Clara not to trust the Doctor, saying, "There's a sliver of ice in his heart." When facing the creature in the pocket universe, the Doctor admits to being afraid. It's a rare admission from him, exemplified by the fact that he announces, "I am the Doctor, and I am afraid."

**The Doctor and Clara** Clara won't go investigating until the Doctor literally dares her. Clara has trouble facing the realities of time travel, such as watching the entire life cycle of the Earth pass by in a few minutes or the idea that she's dead in the future. She finds it disconcerting that the Doctor is okay with this.

**Monster of the Week** The Crooked Man (not identified in the episode but named as such in the credits) is a creature trapped in a pocket universe. It looks like a skull on a thick twisted neck with a scorpion-like body. The creatures are clearly a diploid species, since it has a mate.

**Stand Up and Cheer** The moment you realize that this isn't a ghost story after all but is instead a beautiful and touching love story about two hideous creatures. Yes, that moment: "Hold hands. That's what you're meant to do. Keep doing that and don't let go. That's the secret." The Doctor consciously realizing he has his arm around Clara's shoulder as he says it is just delightful.

**Roll Your Eyes** Usually when you put two women in a scene, the biggest TV trope is having two women talk about a man. But here, left in a scene together, Emma first talks about her feelings for Palmer and then hands off to Clara for her to talk about the Doctor. It's a double rainbow of Bechdel test failures.

**You're Not Making Any Sense** The Doctor and Palmer use negatives to make slides for the projector. However, that isn't what a slide projector does: it enlarges 35mm slides, which aren't the same thing as film negatives at all.

**Interesting Trivia** Originally, the Doctor was going to meet Bernard Quatermass, the fictional scientist from *The Quatermass Experiment* and its sequels. The Quatermass serials were a sort of predecessor to *Doctor Who*; it first aired in 1953 — and was broadcast live — with sequels airing in 1955, 1958 and 1979. A remake of *The Quatermass Experiment*, featuring David Tennant, was broadcast live in 2005, soon after Tennant was cast in *Doctor Who*. It's notable for bringing science fiction and horror to British television screens for the first time and treating it as adult subject matter. It's long been implied that Quatermass exists in the *Doctor Who* universe, with a reference to Bernard and the British Rocket Group in 1988's "Remembrance of the Daleks," as well as Bernard being a unit of measurement in 2009's "Planet of the Dead." Neil Cross wanted Quatermass to appear in the story as a guest star. However, this was dropped when the rights were unable to be secured. There's more than a passing resemblance to the character of Palmer, however.

Cross and his family flew to Cardiff to watch the filming, whereupon his children were promptly appointed "monster consultants" to determine whether the monster was scary enough. This was Cross's first face-to-face meeting with the production team, as he lived in New Zealand; he'd known executive producer Caroline Skinner, who had worked around his schedule during the scripting process. Steven Moffat was so pleased with the script for "Hide" that he asked Cross for another, which resulted in "The Rings of Akhaten."

There's a running theme here of the TARDIS not liking Clara. It's unclear whether this is because she's the impossible girl or just because the TARDIS is being petty. This develops from "The Rings of Akhaten" and was also the subject of a short DVD extra called "Clara and the TARDIS." In that one, Clara's attempt to find her deleted bedroom on board the TARDIS resulted in multiple versions of her appearing in the console room and the TARDIS taunting her with pictures of previous companions.

Unusually, the eleventh Doctor isn't wearing his bowtie when he's hiding from the monster in the pocket universe. Maybe that vulnerability is why he's willing to admit he's afraid?

"Metebelis" should be "Met-a-BEE-lis" not "Meh-TAB-a-lis." And yet Matt Smith does it not once, but twice. Here's the thing. In television, there's a read-through, rehearsal, filming and even after filming there's ADR (when new or changed dialogue is recorded). Given all these stages, why did no one flag that

Matt Smith pronounced the word incorrectly? And why didn't they fix it for the DVD release?

**The TARDIS Chronometer** Caliburn House, November 25, 1974, and various time zones from six billion years ago to the far future; Hila Tacorian and the monster are in a collapsing pocket universe.

**Cool? (RS?)** "Hide" does two things really well. The first is the premise: it takes the idea of a ghost in a house — one of the most standard stories there is — and makes it work. Really work. It amps up the atmosphere and the tension, it gives us appropriate scares (like the Doctor not being the one holding Clara's hand), and it even uses non-televisual tricks like having a cold spot, which is quite impressive.

Most of the story is powered from this. It's all stock stuff — candelabra, psychics, professors and haunted houses — but the way the elements are assembled is excellent. The lights are kept low, the characters discover things as we do, and the horror is kept offscreen. This forces "Hide" to do it old school, with mysterious noises and offstage movement that lets the viewer fill in the gaps, rather than giving us everything on a platter.

Even when it relocates to the pocket universe, it's still incredibly tense and claustrophobic. The Crooked Man is utterly terrifying, both in its looks and movement (cleverly filmed backwards to give it a more unearthly quality). The Doctor admitting that he's afraid could have been hokey, but it works because the story's earned it.

In fact, almost every aspect is working in tandem here. The setting of the 1970s, with its clunky technology and remnants of post-war trauma, fits surprisingly well. It evokes Classic *Who* without being a slave to it, giving us the best of both worlds. Professor Palmer is exactly the sort of character we'd have met in the Jon Pertwee era.

But it's Jessica Raine's Emma who steals the show. Having a psychic along for the ride is another bog-standard storytelling element that is here turned into something wonderful. Raine really sells us on Emma as the central character in this drama, one who's called the Lantern, because she can bridge the two worlds, while the rest of them (the Doctor included) are just along for the ride. The fact that the Doctor was there for Emma all along, not the monster, is just delicious.

The only bum note is the lack of any real material given to Hila Tacorian. She's set up as the centrepiece of the story, but when we finally meet her, she barely has a line. Even when later revelations occur (such as her being a descendent of Emma and Alec), it's only happening around her, not to her. And her ultimate fate is left hanging. As a MacGuffin, she's excellent; as a character, she's nonexistent. Well, we wouldn't want to take lines away from all the white folks, would we?

However, it's the second thing that "Hide" does well that really makes it something special: namely, the genre switch at the end. It turns a ghost story into a love story, which is an amazing way to pull the rug out from under our feet. The fact that it happens late in the day isn't a problem in the slightest, because it retroactively informs so much of what we'd seen. Having not one but two monsters all along was very clever, as is the fact that the most hideous and terrifying creature imaginable turns out to be the pocket-universe equivalent of a lovesick teenager writing, "Will you hold my hand? Circle yes or no."

What's more, it ties into the other themes of the episode remarkably well. It echoes not only the low-key romance between the two guest characters but also the low-key romance between the Doctor and Clara. Turning the tables on the "companion"/"assistant" dichotomy (something that's been a running thread in the New Series going all the way back to "Rose") is a cute joke at the opening . . . and turns out to be a clever foreshadowing of the twist, via a clever pun. That's just awesome.

What's especially great here is that, until this moment, "Hide" is following the standard *Doctor Who* formula to a T: an initially weird/supernatural aspect that provides lots of scares/tension turns out to be an alien/time traveller, thus giving us a rational/technobabble explanation for everything; there's a hideous/ terrifying monster that must be defeated; and it all comes down to the human spirit/childlike mechanics to rescue the Doctor/companion. Up until this moment, "Hide" is an almost perfectly formed *Doctor Who* story, and there's no shame in that.

But the genre switch at the end turns it all upside down. We're not expecting it in the slightest, because *Doctor Who* is fundamentally a genre-switching show already. Almost every episode starts out as one kind of story and turns into another. "The Doctor, the Widow and the Wardrobe" starts as a Christmas fairy tale and ends as an environmental parable. "A Town Called Mercy" starts as a Western and ends as a Nuremberg trial. "The Rings of Akhaten" starts as a pantheon of aliens and ends in a terrible tragedy with the freezing death of everyone involved because nobody thought about the consequences of removing the sun from a planetary system.

So where "Hide" excels is in turning the *Doctor Who* formula up to 11. By sticking so resolutely to the tried-and-true formula, it allows the show to do what it does best: scare the willies out of children, thanks to a 1970s haunted house that can be realized on a BBC budget. And then it spins all our heads around when we discover that there are no monsters here at all, only lonely souls. Scaring you into paying attention, then forcing you to think once you are. Oh, how I love this show!

People have complained about the title not really being representative, but I think they're wrong. Sure, the monster isn't hiding anywhere and the Doctor/Hila Tacorian are running rather than hiding, but it's not really about them. I think it's more about the fact that this is a charming love story disguised as a terrifying ghost story. The fact that the one can be confused for the other just goes to show how good the production team is when they have something really clever . . . to hide.

**Second Opinion (GB)** What he said. Though I'm still annoyed about the Bechdel test failure and Matt Smith mispronouncing "Metebelis."

## 7.11 Journey to the Centre of the TARDIS

**Written by** Stephen Thompson **Directed by** Mat King

**Original airdate** April 27, 2013

**The Big Idea** When a salvage crew get a hold of the badly damaged TARDIS with Clara trapped inside, the Doctor has to force the crew to rescue Clara. But the TARDIS has other ideas.

**Roots and References** The 1962–74 BBC sitcom *Steptoe and Son* (the bickering family of rag-and-bone salvagers); the 1969 film *Butch Cassidy and the Sundance Kid* (the jump off the cliff). The title is a homage to Jules Verne's 1864 novel, *Journey to the Centre of the Earth*. The salvage crew play "Fire Woman" by the Cult when they pull in the TARDIS.

**Adventures in Time and Space** We hear the TARDIS Cloister Bell threatening disaster throughout (1981's "Logopolis" and onward). The Doctor's crib from 2011's "A Good Man Goes to War" makes an appearance, as do Amy's papier mâché TARDIS models (from 2010's "The Eleventh Hour"). Among the TARDIS rooms is a swimming pool (a feature that dates back to 1978's "The Invasion of Time"), while the TARDIS library (also first mentioned in the same story) features the book *The History of the Time War* (mentioned throughout the Modern Series). The observatory features a telescope that looks like the moonlight-focusing device from Torchwood House in 2006's "Tooth and Claw." Among the TARDIS's features that the Doctor tries to use as selling points are the conceptual geometer (1979's "The Horns of Nimon") and the dynomorphic generator (as seen in 1982's "Time-Flight"; that story also established the TARDIS's ability to adjust the attitude of its control room). Architectural reconfiguration was a facility introduced in 1982's "Castrovalva," while the "echo" room was established in 2011's "The Doctor's Wife."

Several voices from the past are heard talking about the TARDIS as it is "leaking," including Susan and Ian (from 1963's "An Unearthly Child"), the third Doctor and Jo Grant (1971's "Colony in Space"), the eleventh Doctor and Idris (2011's "The Doctor's Wife"), the fourth Doctor (1977's "Robots of Death"), the ninth Doctor (2005's "Rose"), Martha (2007's "Smith and Jones") and the fifth Doctor (2007's "Time Crash"). The climax takes place in the Eye of Harmony, established as part of the TARDIS in the 1996 TV Movie. The Doctor faking a self-destruct countdown is something he did in 1985's "Attack of the Cybermen," while locking people in the TARDIS dates all the way back to "An Unearthly Child."

**The Impossible Girl Effect** The TARDIS continues to not like Clara. When the Doctor thinks they're finished, he confronts Clara, demanding she tell him the secret of her duplicates, but she knows nothing about them.

**Who Is the Doctor?** The Doctor is, on the surface, willing to bargain the TARDIS for Clara's life. Fortunately, he wasn't required to. Clara learns the Doctor's name and his involvement in the Time War, though she quickly forgets both things.

**The Doctor and Clara** Having found out his name, Clara begins to doubt the Doctor as he tries to shelter her from learning the nature of the Time Zombies, and the Doctor starts to question the veracity of her very existence. The two reconcile when it becomes quite clear that she knows nothing about her duplicates in time and space. (They both forget the whole incident when everything resets.)

**Monster of the Week** Time Zombies are the future echoes of the salvage crew after the Eye of Harmony has destroyed their bodies on a cellular level.

**Stand Up and Cheer** The Doctor facing down the brothers and forcing them to assist in helping find Clara is downright cold, particularly the Doctor changing the countdown from an hour to 30 minutes. The change in the Doctor's manner when he reveals it was all a bluff is equally charming.

**Roll Your Eyes** How stupid is the entire Van Baalen family?! They're facing a ship that uses technology far beyond their knowledge and are warned repeatedly of the dangers facing them, yet they never listen and ultimately die.

**You're Not Making Any Sense** Just how dumb is Tricky to be fooled into thinking he was an android? Think of the hundreds of ways you're reminded every day you're human. How do you not stub your toe or cut yourself shaving or really have to go pee in the middle of the night and not realize you're actually human? Then again, see above . . .

**Interesting Trivia** Actor Ashley Walters got into trouble on his first day when he tweeted a photo of himself in costume in his dressing room and said, "Space." Security on the *Doctor Who* set is immense (as we'll see in a couple of episodes' time). Suffice it to say, Walters received a visit from executives reminding him of all the No Tweeting signs on set.

Who wrote *The History of the Time War*? And when was it written? Generally speaking, histories are written after the outcome of a conflict. If the book was written after the war, then the only person left to write such an account would be the Doctor, which might explain the inclusion of his name. That said, it may have been written by the Time Lords at a particular juncture during the war when victory seemed assured (or there was a lull) or by another race not involved (though how would they know the Doctor's true name?).

**The TARDIS Chronometer** An unspecified point in the future (close enough to play popular music from the late 1980s), though much of the story takes place within the TARDIS, which is technically outside time.

**Cool? (GB)** Hell no, it isn't. Nothing in this story is cool at all. And I am most definitely not cool with this story.

The closest it comes to cool are the visuals. The Doctor and Clara standing in the heart of the TARDIS while it explodes, all the fragments perfectly still, is a stunning image. But even that image makes no sense: a bunch of fragmented metal in a white void? It's almost a metaphor for this whole story: a nice idea, but nothing is any damn good.

Part of the problem is the TARDIS has only been explored a few times in *Doctor Who*'s history. It's not the *Enterprise*. It's not a spaceship. It's a mythical vessel that travels through space and time and was created by god-like creatures. To explore it takes a genius or a poet or someone at least really clever.

Nah . . . let's get the writer of "Curse of the Black Spot" ("Possibly the stupidest *Doctor Who* story, ever" — Graeme Burk, *Who Is The Doctor*) to do it instead.

And everything goes to stupid town.

Poetic imagery (the architectural configuration tree) is undermined by stupid people doing stupid things. Gregor steals an orb and bullies the TARDIS to give him back the door. It's a scene that diminishes both the TARDIS and Gregor. The TARDIS can't be salvaged by a bunch of guys, even if damaged. The whole thing is a flawed premise.

And these guys . . . if only they had any glimmerings of sentience, if only they demonstrated the intelligence of, say, Clara or Palmer from "Hide" — or *anyone*, really. Had that been the case, I might have found some way to empathize with these characters.

But. They. Are. So. Unbelievably. Stupid. And cruel.

I have no sympathy for Tricky when he's revealed to be a human. First of all, it's pretty obvious he's not an android. Second, he'd have to be an idiot not to realize it. Third, what family of ratfuckers would do that to someone? Congratulations: you've alienated me from every character that's not the Doctor or Clara. Which is a submoronic move in a story with only five speaking parts.

But it's worse than that. The Van Baalen clan are the first major role for Black actors since Nefertiti. And all of them are duplicitous and stupid. This is first story with an completely non-white guest cast — and they're playing glorified car-jackers. This is rock bottom for portrayal of race in modern *Doctor Who*. It's appalling.

At this point, the series was barely casting characters of colour. (And often only because it was required in the script, like Rita in "The God Complex.") In a season, we'll have a Black supporting character, and in three seasons we'll have people of colour as companions across two Doctors. But right now . . . this is *Doctor Who*'s come-to-Jesus moment.

And the exploration of the TARDIS does nothing that is interesting or compelling. "The Doctor's Wife" had the brilliant idea that doors would open through images in your mind. "Journey" travels through tons of fan service and gives us a timey-wimey menace and solution that feels like a retread of a retread of a retread and adds insult to injury by literally pressing the reset button on what little character development happened in the story.

"Journey to the Centre of the TARDIS" should have been the slam-dunk story of the fiftieth-anniversary season. Instead, it left me hoping that from now on we'll stay outside the TARDIS.

Definitely not cool.

**Second Opinion (RS?)** Journey to the Centre of Your Memory with this fruity homage to someone's approximation of quality. Aromas of rich, vibrant visuals, with more than a hint of racism. Medium-bodied and jaunty but risqué acidity will have you wondering where it all went wrong. Like walking in on an act of fellatio: awkward and uncomfortable, but don't tell anyone how much you enjoyed it.

Have you ever wanted to unlock the full power of memory? Access those dark, hidden recesses of the brain that dare not let horrific memories out into the light? Well, now you can. Drink this Encyclopedia Gallifreyica wine, and you too will briefly know the Doctor's name and — even more spectacularly — remember the events of the episode "Journey to the Centre of the TARDIS." For a brief time only.

## The Psychic Papers: What's Inside the TARDIS?

The most obvious answer to this question is the console room. For viewers of *Doctor Who*, it's the very heart of the TARDIS, with the controls, time rotor and usually some decorations (hat stands, chairs, et cetera). It's been remodelled many times over the years, from the "classic desktop theme" of a white room with "roundels" that featured throughout the 20th century to the organic look of the Eccleston and Tennant TARDIS to the metallic styles and Victorian flourishes found in the Smith and Capaldi TARDIS.

In the Modern Series, viewers have barely had more than glimpses of the TARDIS beyond the console room. In "The Christmas Invasion," we saw the TARDIS wardrobe, as the Doctor chose his new outfit. (Similar rooms appeared in the Classic Series when the sixth and seventh Doctor chose their new outfits in 1984's "The Twin Dilemma" and 1987's "Time and the Rani," respectively.) In "The Doctor's Wife," we mostly saw corridors. It's not until "Journey to the Centre of the TARDIS," in the seventh season of the modern show, that we spend any extensive time inside, with our first look at rooms such as the library, the architectural reconfiguration system and so forth.

It wasn't always like this. In its earliest appearances, the TARDIS was more than just a control room. The third story, 1964's "The Edge of Destruction," was set wholly inside the TARDIS and showed us various sleeping quarters (with space-age beds), as well as a food machine (press a button and you get a whole meal in a pill, in the best kind of 1960s futurism) and the fault locator. The latter was a machine that was supposed to locate any problems with the TARDIS, but it was quickly phased out, presumably because it would undercut drama.

During the first three Doctors' eras, glimpses of what lay beyond the interior door were limited to bedrooms and corridors or the power room (located just off the console room, seen only in 1968's "The Mind Robber"). But the fourth Doctor's time saw a lot more exploration of what was inside this infinitely large space. In 1976's "The Masque of Mandragora," we not only saw an enormous cupboard full of boots (just because), but we learned that there was a secondary control room. Or, more accurately, we learned that the control room we were used to was in fact the secondary one. The "original" only appeared for one season but looked backwards, being all brass and wood and Victorian steampunk, rather than the futuristic white one with roundels we were used to.

In 1978's "The Invasion of Time," the Doctor was chased through the TARDIS by Sontarans, which meant we got to see a lot more of it. There's a swimming pool (which the Doctor calls the bathroom), sickbay and rooms full of art and plants. The fourth Doctor's final story, 1981's "Logopolis," saw yet more exploration of the TARDIS interior, with a cloister room featuring benches, crumbling pillars and yet more plants.

The fifth Doctor's opening story, 1981's "Castrovalva," showcased the zero room, a place of tranquility to calm the unstable period following a regeneration. It was ultimately destroyed when the architecture was deleted so the TARDIS could escape a hydrogen inrush. It's been subsequently established that the Doctor has occasionally deleted a number of companion bedrooms and even the swimming pool (because it started to leak).

The later period of the Classic era moved the action out of the TARDIS again, so we only saw the console room and the occasional companion room. The 1996 TV movie showed only two interior TARDIS sets, but they were certainly spectacular. The console room had a massive set (viewers only saw a limited part of it), which took its cues from the Victorian secondary control room from Season 14 of the Classic Series. There was an antique-looking wooden console at the centre of a massive oak-panelled room, a library and a ceiling that showed gigantic holographic images. The other set was the cloister room, only this time it was huge and cavernous and housed an interface to the Eye of Harmony, the TARDIS's source of power.

After the sleeping quarters of the early stories, for a long time there was no real mention of where the companions slept, though the console room did have a bed that came out of the wall in 1973's "Planet of the Daleks." Lalla Ward's Romana was the first companion we saw have a room of her own (in 1980's "Full Circle"). It wasn't installed as a regular feature until Peter Davison was cast as the Doctor and producer John Nathan-Turner, keen to show that there was "no hanky-panky in the TARDIS" among his young cast, made sure the female companions' room was shown onscreen. In the Modern Series, the only companions to speak about having a room were Amy and Rory (in "The Doctor's Wife," where they complained the Doctor had configured the room to have bunk beds).

The Modern Series has kept the TARDIS action mostly confined to the console room. It makes sense, because this is a showpiece set, the thing that everyone associates with the TARDIS interior, and it keeps the rest of the action outside, where it probably should be anyway. That said, occasionally it's nice to see that there's more to this infinite space, that it's somewhere people actually spend time and not just a ferry from one adventure to the next. After all, the TARDIS is bigger on the inside. A lot bigger.

# 7.12 The Crimson Horror

**Written by** Mark Gatiss **Directed by** Saul Metzstein
**Original airdate** May 4, 2013

**The Big Idea** While investigating a grisly murder in Yorkshire, Madame Vastra and the Paternoster Gang face the Crimson Horror, a mysterious cause of death in which victims turn bright red — and its latest victim is the Doctor.

**Roots and References** Sherlock Holmes (Madame Vastra); Jules Verne's 1902 novel *Les Frères Kip* (the Victorian interest in optography — viewing the last image a dead person saw captured on their eye); the 1959 film *House of Wax* (the process and people being made into waxwork tableaux); the 1930 film version of *Frankenstein* and its successors (the Doctor's look and walk after the process, and his relationship with blind Ada); the 1980 film *The Elephant Man* (keeping Ada behind a partition during Mrs. Gillyflower's lecture for Victorian shock value); the 1961–69 TV series *The Avengers* (the loudspeakers simulating a factory and Jenny's outfit emulating Emma Peel's leather catsuit — appropriately enough in an episode where Diana Rigg guest stars). Mrs. Gillyflower sings "Blake's Jerusalem," while the flashback sequences emulate early films from the late 19th century. Young Thomas Thomas with his unerring ability to give good directions is a play on the British GPS system TomTom.

**Adventures in Time and Space** The Doctor mentions his struggles to get Tegan back to Heathrow airport, which was a running theme during the 1982 season of the Classic Series. (The Doctor follows on by saying "brave heart," his particular catchphrase to Tegan.) The Paternoster Gang, last seen in "The Snowmen," recognize Clara. Artie and Angie have photos of the Doctor and Clara from "Hide," "Cold War" and "The Snowmen."

**The Impossible Girl Effect** When asked by an amazed Jenny how Clara can still be alive after the events of "The Snowmen," the Doctor's answer is, "It's complicated." Madame Vastra is quite smug that she correctly divined that the Doctor and Clara had "unfinished business." Artie and Angie's photos to blackmail Clara include one of the Victorian governess from "The Snowmen," which she naturally doesn't recognize, but she doesn't comment on it.

**Who Is the Doctor?** When the process fails on the Doctor, he's regarded as a monster by Ada but treated kindly. The Doctor is very tender with Ada after the process is reversed and empathic to her plight. He can also do a pretty convincing Yorkshire accent.

**The Doctor and Clara** The pair are quite affectionate — she calls him clever clogs and he kisses her on the forehead — but they're still only seeing each other on Tuesdays (provided the Doctor can steer the TARDIS correctly).

**Monster of the Week** Mr. Sweet is a tiny, leech-like creature that has symbiotically attached itself to Mrs. Gillyflower. Madame Vastra recognizes it as a plague carrier from prehistoric Earth; its venom can destroy all life on Earth.

**Stand Up and Cheer** Having been denigrated repeatedly and made to look foolish (though, let's be honest, he often actually is), Strax finally gets to save the day.

**Roll Your Eyes** Jenny is quite right to slap the Doctor. It's really, really not cool to jump someone and kiss them without their consent.

**You're Not Making Any Sense** When Clara's trapped in the glass tableau, isn't there a man in the tableau with her being preserved? What happened to him?

**Interesting Trivia** Steven Moffat originally wanted to write a story from the Paternoster Gang's point of view, where their case would eventually intersect with the Doctor. Moffat eventually handed off the story to Mark Gatiss, who was at the time performing in the play *The Recruiting Officer* with actress Rachael Stirling and her mother, Dame Diana Rigg (whom Gatiss also knew). Gatiss learned that mother and daughter had never appeared on television together, so he fashioned the parts of Mrs. Gillyflower and Ada for Rigg and Stirling.

Mrs. Gillyflower and her organization spoof the social-hygiene movement, which was popular in the late 19th and early 20th centuries. The movement attempted to curb venereal diseases and to fight prostitution and poverty, but it also branched off into eugenics, with the aim of improving human genetics and quality of life. On the one hand, the movement favoured scientific methodology and followed Charles Darwin's theories of evolution and led to improvements in public health and family planning. On the other hand, being a product of 19th-century values, the paradigm supported white people, and the movement was known to support practices such as forced sterilization, often along racial lines.

Sweetville is based on the model communities built by industrialists in the late 19th century for factory workers, where housing in a planned community was offered to employees. These were borne out of the social-hygiene movement but also that of good business — the theory being that healthy employees with better living conditions meant an efficient workforce. In Britain, the most famous of these was the Bournville estate — a community for Cadbury's workers — which was first built in Birmingham in 1898. The name "Sweetville" is also a nod to radio presenter and author Matthew Sweet, who assisted Mark Gatiss with the Victorian history in the episode.

Artie apparently managed to find a photo of Clara and the Doctor on a Soviet nuclear submarine in the school library. Presumably in *The Big Book of Miraculously Declassified Soviet-Era Top Secret Documents about Near-Nuclear Incidents Involving Aliens.*

**The TARDIS Chronometer** Yorkshire and London, 1893.

**Cool? (GB)** One of the great things about *Doctor Who* is that certain stories improve with age. "The Crimson Horror" is for me a shining example of this. I didn't dislike this story on first viewing; it's simply that, except for the delightful structure, which I adored and still do, I treated the rest of it the way Robert treated, say, "Cold War": as a middling story, worthy of middling attention.

But away from the hype of the upcoming fiftieth anniversary, I found "The Crimson Horror" much better than the dismissal I had given it five years earlier.

In fact, I'd even go so far as to offer the perhaps-surprising opinion that this is one of the best stories of Series Seven.

What stood out for me rewatching "The Crimson Horror" was that it captured the lurid aspect of Victorian life: it was an era full of grotesquerie. "The Crimson Horror" doubles down on this with the freakish victims, the sleazy morgue attendant, people kept under glass, Ada on display like a freakshow — and the horrific leech suckling on Mrs. Gillyflower, who indulgently drops a little salt on her bosom for it when no one is looking.

Mrs. Gillyflower is a whole subcategory of this grotesqueness, and Diana Rigg's performance is probably my favourite thing about this episode. Rigg plays the role as though Mrs. Gillyflower has zero fucks to give. She doesn't care that her plan is flawed and will destroy the world. She doesn't care about her own daughter, except to use her as a hostage (and not just to escape the Doctor). She doesn't even care that there's a hideous thing hanging off her, taking snacks from her. Rigg plays Gillyflower as selfishness incarnate, and there's something delightfully, sadistically gleeful about her that I find satisfying — and I wonder if perhaps that resonates more in the years since "The Crimson Horror" was first broadcast.

Rachael Stirling is wonderful here too. Her scenes with Matt Smith showcase a wonderful empathy between the characters, first as she cares for him as a monster and then when he cares for her after her mother's cruelty is revealed. And the scene where Ada kills Mr. Sweet is a disgusting yet satisfying moment, with the character finding her way again.

About the only thing I'm still somewhat cool towards is the Paternoster Gang's presence. Madame Vastra has surprisingly little to do here, nothing beyond directing Jenny's line of inquiry. I don't know why she didn't stay in London. Strax finally succeeding is a great moment, but it does point out how ridiculous he's become. Back in the '70s, Sontarans were jingoistic, but at least they were threatening. Dan Starkey plays Strax too broadly — and, worse, the writing indulges that. (I get that Strax is probably meant to play more to the younger side of the audience — which is why his victory here is so charming — but I feel there are ways of doing that without annoying everyone else.) The only person really required was Jenny, and, honestly, I would have been quite happy watching Catrin Stewart kicking more ass. Because the Paternoster Gang is present, Clara doesn't get much to do either, but the exchange between the Doctor and Clara about the use of a chair versus a sonic screwdriver is witty and delightful, so I'm grateful for what little we have.

Sometimes *Doctor Who* stories get better with age. I'm glad this is one of them. "The Crimson Horror" is full of surprises; in fact, it's downright bonkers. In a good way.

**Second Opinion (RS?)** I've long been on the record as an enthusiastic proponent of a female Doctor. Much as I love Matt Smith, I think we were already overdue for somebody other than yet another white guy to play the Doctor. Of all the (mostly nonsensical) arguments against having a female Doctor, only one ever struck a chord with me: the Doctor is one of the few role models for boys who isn't a macho, gun-toting military hero.

There's a lot of mileage in that. Growing up, the Doctor made it okay to be a feminized guy who genuinely liked and respected women. That's pretty powerful. We don't live in quite as straitjacketed a world as the one I grew up in (thank goodness), so there are other role models to be found that subvert the hypermasculinity expectation for boys, but the Doctor is still a pretty powerful voice.

And then something like "The Crimson Horror" comes along and ruins it.

The Doctor's forced kiss with Jenny is at best cringeworthy and at worst downright wrong. What message is *Doctor Who* sending to young boys of this generation? That it's perfectly fine to kiss a woman whom you know for a fact does not welcome it? I appreciate that Jenny slaps him afterwards for it, but it's not good enough. This is sexual assault, and it's awful. (And no, the Doctor doing the same thing to Rory in "Dinosaurs on a Spaceship" does not make it better. It's still wrong.)

I agree with my co-author that "The Crimson Horror" has its good points, and it does break the Mark Gatiss curse in that sense. But that kiss is a monumental failure.

And it proves something else too: that we shouldn't just have a female Doctor, we should have women writing, directing and managing the show. I mostly adore the Moffat era for its inventiveness and wit, but the sausage party it's been thus far — with not a single word out of Matt Smith's mouth being written by a woman — shows exactly how this kind of mistake happens. If this is what a male Doctor brings to the role, then a female Doctor can't come quickly enough. Let's tattoo this on someone's forehead: the Doctor never forces himself sexually on someone ever again.

## 7.13 Nightmare in Silver

**Written by** Neil Gaiman **Directed by** Stephen Woolfenden
**Original airdate** May 11, 2013

**The Big Idea** The TARDIS lands in an abandoned amusement park. But there are Cybermen here — and they're evolving.

**Roots and References** The Turk, a famous chess-playing machine from the 18th century (the chess-playing Cyberman); Douglas Adams's 1978 radio series and successors *The Hitchhiker's Guide to the Galaxy* (the subether communicator); Ursula K. Le Guin's 1966 novel *Rocannon's World* (ansible transmission); the 1993 film *Jurassic Park* (the theme park under siege); the 1964 Roald Dahl novel *Charlie and the Chocolate Factory* (the golden ticket); *Star Trek: The Next Generation* (the Cybermen originally inspired the Borg, but now it seems the Borg have inspired the Cybermen).

**Adventures in Time and Space** This story decommissions the "Cybus" Cybermen who made their first appearance in 2006's "Rise of the Cybermen"/"The Age of Steel" (the musical theme for the Cybermen from that story returns). The Cyberplanner previously appeared in 1968's "The Wheel in Space" and 1968's "The Invasion," although it was a stationary machine then. The chess-playing Cyberman is said to be the 699th wonder of the universe, a reference to 1974's "Death to the Daleks," where the destruction of the City of the Exxilons reduced the number from 700 to 699. The Doctor notes that early versions of the Cyber operating system could be scrambled by cleaning fluid or gold; the former is a reference to 1967's "The Moonbase," while the latter was a stable of the Classic Series from 1975's "Revenge of the Cybermen" onwards. The Cybermen emerging from their tombs echoes similar scenes in 1967's "Tomb of the Cybermen."

Mr. Clever notes that the Doctor has been attempting to remove his presence from history, something he started doing as a result of the events of 2011's "The Wedding of River Song." We see flashes of the previous ten incarnations of the Doctor. Mr. Clever puts on a northern accent to imitate the ninth Doctor and says, "Fantastic!" He also says, "Allons-y" and "He's had some cowboys in here" (from "The Girl in the Fireplace") to imitate the tenth.

**The Impossible Girl Effect** Mr. Clever knows that Clara is the impossible girl and knows that this is why the Doctor's so interested in her. Since her memories were erased in "Journey to the Centre of the TARDIS," this is the first time she's aware that the Doctor has a special interest in her. However, she has no idea why he thinks she's impossible.

**Who Is the Doctor?** He threatens to regenerate in order to stop Mr. Clever, although he doesn't want to, because he's afraid of who he'll become next. (And, as we'll later learn, for another reason.) Even when it looks like he will lose the chess match, he insists that Mr. Clever release Artie and Angie, continuing to prove Amy's observation in 2010's "The Beast Below" that he can't help but stop the suffering of a child.

**The Doctor and Clara** The Doctor trusts Clara enough to put her in charge of the military platoon. She knows him well enough to know that even if he had feelings for her, he'd rather die than say so. When asked if he thinks she's pretty, he says she's short and bossy, with a funny nose. The Doctor comically insulting Clara is a theme that will continue.

**Monster of the Week** The Cybermen have upgraded, in both design and abilities. They can now move much faster than before, have tiny Cybermites that can convert people and non-humans. They have access to the Cyberiad, a collective consciousness of all Cybermen. Every time someone finds a weakness, they upgrade themselves. They need children to build a Cyberplanner, because a child's brain has infinite potential.

**Stand Up and Cheer** The reveal that Porridge — all three feet and six inches of him — is actually the emperor of a thousand galaxies, defender of humanity and imperator of known space is quite magnificent. The fact that it's Angie who figures it out is just sublime.

**Roll Your Eyes** What kind of nanny is Clara? Not only does she allow her charges to blackmail her, she wilfully exposes them to a lifestyle she knows to be highly dangerous. And then — surprise, surprise — said adventure turns out to be not only highly dangerous but incredibly traumatic for the children. Somebody call Child Protective Services.

**You're Not Making Any Sense** Okay, so we get that the Doctor's companions usually receive special treatment and bring a world of experience and compassion that you can't find elsewhere. But . . . putting a nanny in charge of a military operation? Really?

**Interesting Trivia** Originally, the companion for the second half of Series Seven was going to be someone from the Victorian era. The first concept was someone named Beryl, who was an actual stern, moralistic Victorian nanny to contrast with the irrepressible eleventh Doctor. This eventually changed to Clara, who wasn't stern but was still a nanny, with Francesca and Digby Latimer as her two charges. Fairly late in the day, the character was reworked to a modern-day Clara, which necessitated several changes. One of these was the impossible girl arc. However, Neil Gaiman's script had already been written with the Victorian version of Clara. This required the introduction of Angie and Artie, as well as the fairly sudden tag scene at the end of the previous episode to get them into the TARDIS here.

Actress Eva de Leon Allen accidentally left a copy of her script (then titled "The Last Cyberman") in a taxi, and it was subsequently found by two *Doctor Who* fans, who posted sneak previews to Facebook and Reddit. The BBC arranged with the fans to have the script returned.

**The TARDIS Chronometer** Hedgewick's World of Wonders, 3526.

**Cool? (RS?)** Oh, this is brilliant. I'm so clever already, and now I'm a million times more clever. And what a brain. I mean, I'm going to have to completely rework the parameters of evaluating an episode, but this is going to be the most efficient review. And for such a pathetic story too.

*Get out of my head! And you're wrong. "Nightmare in Silver" is a great story! What's not to love?*

Stalemate then? We each control 49.881% of the opinion of this story — 0.238% of the assessment is still in the balance. Whoever gets this gets the whole thing. Which should be easy in my case, because the episode is totally boring.

*Winner takes all. Fine. But it's not boring at all. What about Matt Smith's tour de force performance as the Doctor and Mr. Clever, subtly supported by some perfect camera angles that never leave you in doubt about who's who? It's a complex set-up, but Smith delivers the goods to perfection.*

Pah. Matt Smith spends all his time waggling his arms and talking loudly and flapping about in a series of children's presenter acting tics that substitute for —

*Are you my cybernetically enhanced brain, or are you Graeme Burk off on the same old rant again?*

Sorry. But the story still manages to make a Cybermen invasion dull.

*What are you talking about? The Cybermen are the perfect slow burn in this story. They start with a simple echo of a long-gone threat, with the Cybershell as the perfect fake-out. The stakes are raised with the ominous Cybermites. And then there's a full-on invading army.*

Yes, but there's no sense of realism here. One Cyberman is scary, but a thousand is ludicrous. The army is a perfect illustration of that. They're far too efficient to ever be stopped by a motley crew of ragtag soldiers in a comedy castle, so they have to be artificially eunuched or else they'd have killed Clara and discarded her headless body at the halfway mark.

*True, but that's the conventions of television for you. And it ties into the A-plot of the Doctor's chess battle. Besides, they can upgrade in a flash, so every time they lose, they win. Now that's terrifying.*

Don't even get me started on the Borgification of the Cybermen!

*Hey, it's a logical extension of their premise. And the Borg were Cyber rip-offs, anyway. Fair's fair. What about the setting? The amusement park gives us some great gothic imagery, while defending the planet in a comical castle gives us some levity.*

Oh sure, it sounds good on paper. But there's no menace to the setting, just some low lights and a bunch of burnt-out rides. And the comical castle blows its entire comedy in the name. There's no other game here.

*Well, at least we don't get the shock revelation that the TARDIS has been choosing the Doctor's destinations for him all this time like we did in "The Doctor's*

*Wife." Oh my, how I would never have guessed that in a million years if it hadn't been up onscreen for everyone to —*

Are you my human brain, or are you Robert Smith? off on the same old rant again?

*Sorry. But "Nightmare in Silver" does use all its main cast to good effect.*

Oh, now I know you're messing with me! Sure, the Doctor gets a meaty role. But Clara the nanny leading a battalion of soldiers? And don't even get me started on those kids.

*It makes perfect sense that the Doctor would put Clara in charge! Besides, she's really there to stop them blowing up the planet. He needs someone he can trust to make sure this doesn't happen.*

You're not disagreeing with me about the kids? They're awful! And their appearance here is incredibly contrived.

*Well . . . sure. But who cares? They're kids. Nobody expects child actors to be any good. You just tune out the acting and move on.*

Eh. The Latimer children in "The Snowmen" were pretty good. Why couldn't we have had them instead?

*I won't argue that they were much better actors. But there's utility in having present-day companions. The fact that the producers realized that it wasn't working with the original direction speaks volumes. And the change does mean that we have characters of colour as pseudo-companions, for the first time in close to a decade. That's no bad thing.*

Meh. [censored] [censored] [censored]

*Are you my cybernetically enhanced brain, or the ECW Press editors off on the same old rant again?*

Sorry. But what about the ending? Blowing up whole planets to stop a single outbreak of Cybermen is ridiculous.

*It's drastic, sure. But it's an appropriate response to what's become a huge threat. And it means the story isn't a game-changer, because each new infestation has to start at a baseline and do the upgrading again.*

So your argument is that "Nightmare in Silver" is good because it's only mediocre? Checkmate in four, I think.

*No, mate in three. Move one: it's scary as hell. Move two: it's a wonderful Cyber romp. Move three: it has the perfect raison d'être — it gives us quintessential Matt Smith at his finest, playing a dual role and sustaining the entire adventure with a combination of brilliant acting, dead-on voice impressions and a perfect route through the complexities of the script thanks to acting so amazing that it proves how lucky we were to have him in the role in the first place. Checkmate.*

That's cheating!

**Second Opinion (GB)** Well, I don't see much point in being here since my co-author and Mr. Astute have covered off most of what I love and hate about this story.

So let me focus on a couple of things. First of all, the kids. I disagree with Robert and Mr. A. above; I think it's a terrible idea to bring kids into *Doctor Who*. Every time, it lets things down. Every. Time. It's not about their ability to act; I actually do find Artie and Angie irritating, though I don't know if that's down to the acting or the fact that making kids work in an adventure series never quite sounds right. Neil Gaiman is a genius writer ("Journey to the Centre of the TARDIS" made me appreciate again how incredible "The Doctor's Wife" is), and he's written some amazing fiction using children, but even he can't quite get them to work. It doesn't help that, great as the moment is, Angie pointing out Porridge is the emperor is undermined by Porridge and Ferrin already saying as much 20 minutes earlier.

Also, I think children in *Doctor Who* create a phenomenon I call "jeopardy-bending" whereby you can't have horrible things happen to kids onscreen, so you inexplicably change the rules of engagement. If adults were standing in for Artie and Angie, they'd be cyberized in a second. Instead, they talk in a terrible monotone because, well, they're kids.

I think the pre-emptive strike is quite cute, but I'm not as wild about Mr. Clever as my split personality co-author is . . . are. I think Mr. Clever is just a shoutier, snider version of the children's presenter persona Matt Smith adopts when he's bored with a script. (It's a fascinating tell that should make you realize what scripts Smith didn't actually have much time for — including, possibly, this one.)

But . . . that final scene when the Doctor beats Mr. Clever in three moves, that's a really great scene. It hinges on the absurd premise that the Doctor can bluff even himself — and then makes that somehow work.

The other thing I love about this story is Warwick Davis as Porridge. That man has gravitas and charm to burn. I would have been quite happy to have half a dozen characters eliminated across the entire season just to give him more screen time.

The thing here that's been unremarked upon is that originally this was supposed to be called "The Last Cyberman." It was meant to be a story set in the far future with the most advanced version of the Cybermen ever. Of course, the sad part is — without spoiling anything — this is going to be undermined, repeatedly.

So that's all I had to say. Sorry Robert and Mr. Astute, I just made the best of local resources.

# 7.14 The Name of the Doctor

**Written by** Steven Moffat **Directed by** Saul Metzstein

**Original airdate** May 18, 2013

**The Big Idea** The Doctor has a secret, one that he will take to his grave. And it is discovered.

**Roots and References** The 1917 Sherlock Holmes short story "His Last Bow" (the Doctor imagines his retirement will involve beekeeping, which is what Holmes did). Vastra and Jenny play "Spring" from *The Four Seasons*.

**Adventures in Time and Space** We see all the Classic Series Doctors, some from clips and some with stand-ins. The scene with the first Doctor and Susan is a colourized version of a scene from 1964's "The Aztecs," with dialogue from 1965's "The Web Planet." The third Doctor driving is from 1983's "The Five Doctors," as is the clip of the second Doctor running. The fourth Doctor is shown on Gallifrey in a clip from 1978's "The Invasion of Time." The fifth Doctor is seen trapped in the Time Lord Matrix in 1983's "Arc of Infinity." The seventh Doctor hangs from his umbrella in 1987's "Dragonfire." There are also a number of audio quotes, such as "Have you ever thought what it's like to be wanderers in the fourth dimension?" from 1963's "An Unearthly Child"; "Do I have the right?" from 1975's "Genesis of the Daleks"; "Daleks, Cybermen; they're still in the nursery compared to us," from 1986's "The Trial of a Time Lord"; "There are some corners of the universe that have bred the most dangerous things," from 1966's "The Moonbase"; and "It was the daisiest daisy I'd ever seen," from 1972's "The Time Monster." The domed Capitol of Gallifrey was first seen in 2007's "The Sound of Drums." River as seen here is the version saved in the library after her death in 2008's "Silence in the Library"/"Forest of the Dead," chronologically her last appearance.

As the Great Intelligence destroys the Doctor's timeline, he's killed in the Dalek asylum ("Asylum of the Daleks") and Androzani (1984's "The Caves of Androzani"). The Doctor's murder of the Sycorax leader in 2005's "The Christmas Invasion" is questioned, along with leaving Solomon to die in "Dinosaurs on a Spaceship." The Great Intelligence mentions the Doctor's evil self, the Valeyard (from 1986's "The Trial of a Time Lord").

The most important leaf that led to Clara's birth from "The Rings of Akhaten" is summoned by the Doctor to help her out of his timestream. Trenzalore and its importance to the Doctor was first mentioned in 2011's "The Wedding of River Song." There are flashbacks to "Journey to the Centre of the TARDIS" (Clara remembers climbing through a wrecked TARDIS with the Doctor),

"Asylum of the Daleks" and "The Snowmen." We see Oswin and Victorian Clara among Clara's many doppelgängers.

**The Impossible Girl Effect** This is where the entire arc about the impossible girl essentially begins and ends. Because Clara leapt into the Doctor's DNA, she was thus present throughout his lives, likely displacing the Great Intelligence. As a result, the Doctor ran into two of her, who had Clara's last words ("Run, you clever boy, and remember [me]") imprinted on them. This is how she was able to die twice. It also explains why Emma saw nothing out of the ordinary in Clara in "Hide" — because, at the time, there wasn't.

**Who Is the Doctor?** We start this episode seeing something we've never seen before: the Doctor's "origin story," as we see him steal the TARDIS and leave Gallifrey with his granddaughter, Susan. (He's even directed to what will become his TARDIS by one of Clara's doubles.) The Doctor discovers that his final resting place is at Trenzalore, where he will die in battle. He's buried underneath his TARDIS, which swells to great size once the dimensionally transcendental effect wears off. He's now saved the universe so many times over that almost all of it exists solely because of him.

The episode ends with the revelation that he has a secret previous incarnation he doesn't talk about (so well hidden that Clara never even sees him), one who apparently committed great crimes and who isn't worthy of the name "Doctor."

**The Doctor and Clara** When the moment comes, Clara jumps into the Doctor's timestream without hesitation to save him, and it turns out that Clara has been saving the Doctor all his lives, albeit without him noticing (likely because she's simply undoing what the Great Intelligence was doing to change his history).

**Monster of the Week** The Whispermen are blank-faced, except for their mouths, which are red and full of teeth. They dress in Victorian suits, complete with hats, and speak in rhyme. They're embodiments of the Great Intelligence, but aren't properly corporeal, as Simeon's aspect can be downloaded into any one of them.

**Stand Up and Cheer** If you're a Classic Series fan, the flashbacks to all the past Doctors are utterly glorious. The mix of existing clips with stand-ins and even colourized black-and-white footage can really get the continuity juices flowing. We watched it about 50 times in a row when we first saw it. And that was just on the first day.

**Roll Your Eyes** Surely there was a better way to tell us who John Hurt was that didn't involve *actually writing it in text on the screen*? That's just the height of laziness.

**You're Not Making Any Sense** The letter that gets delivered to Clara is dated "Twenty thousand & thirteen." So why is the Clara of two thousand and thirteen getting it, rather than the one who flies with a jetpack and lives on an asteroid?

**Interesting Trivia** In our book *Who's 50: The 50 Doctor Who Stories to Watch Before You Die*, we postulated that when Clara jumps into the Doctor's time-line, she defeats the Great Intelligence by simple displacement: two objects can't coexist in the same space, so she overwrites him and, in so doing, deletes the Great Intelligence's corruption to the Doctor's timeline. To do that, she must have manifested herself in beings born throughout time and space to fulfill their destiny of encountering the Doctor at whatever convergence point the Great Intelligence broke through, which is why — for the most part — she doesn't actually meet multiple Doctors. Somehow, there's a timey-wimey, spacey-wacey way that Clara's DNA (with echoes of her personality and her memories) imprinted on these people. (How they all have the same family name — even names like "Oswin," which was a login Clara used — are questions we can't answer.)

And yet, that's just an explanation. The most important thing to note is that, outside of this episode, the entire "impossible girl" effect is basically in the Doctor's head. Clara was never hiding anything from him, making all those scenes of him looking ominously at the scanner redundant. Yes, she retroactively affects the Doctor's past and intersects with it, in the form of multiple women with similar names who exist just slightly to the right of the Doctor's reality. But Clara herself was never a mystery and hence never the impossible girl. It retroactively makes the Doctor stalking her somewhat creepy and also places undue expectations on the companion, thanks to all the buildup for something that fundamentally wasn't what it was made out to be.

Multiple mini-episodes were released to accompany this episode. There was a prequel called "Clarence and the Whispermen," where Clarence DeMarco (the prisoner) learns the space-time coordinates of the Doctor's grave. Another prequel, "He Said, She Said," features monologues from the Doctor and Clara about how little they know about the other and the upcoming trip to Trenzalore. There were also three "Strax field reports" with Strax informing Sontaran High Command about an upcoming battle in the first two and the newly discovered incarnation of the Warrior in the third.

Not only does this story feature the Doctor stealing the TARDIS for the first time, it's also the first time we see the TARDIS in its default shape, although we saw other such TARDISes in that shape in 1969's "The War Games." It's also the first to use colourized footage from the black-and-white era.

**The TARDIS Chronometer** London and Glasgow, 1893. Trenzalore, the future. Plus a variety of locations from the Doctor's past.

**Cool? (RS?)** In a flashback, we see exciting moments from all the Doctors, like the time the seventh Doctor climbed off a railing and hung over a cliff for no reason whatsoever or when the second Doctor jogged too close to the camera. Classic! And then a prisoner imparts information so incredibly vital that he doesn't bother to correct the simple misunderstanding that arises from his not-at-all-strange phrasing about the Doctor's grave. The Doctor kisses in mid-air, because that's what happens at seances, and it just proves you shouldn't meddle with forces from the beyond, like your dead wife. Meanwhile, some mime artists totally and absolutely kill Jenny to death, with only minutes left to bring her back . . . so everyone makes their way to an alien planet in the future, though we're a bit fuzzy on exactly how, but presumably it was done quite quickly.

The Doctor says that there's one place he must never, ever go, no matter what. Except for that one time, about five minutes later, when he decides to. Because this is the Doctor's grave, he has a tombstone in the shape of a giant TARDIS. Which is a bit like me being laid to rest beneath a huge Toyota Prius, which would actually be pretty cool, come to think of it. Only it turns out to be the real TARDIS, and apparently the TARDIS has been expending all this energy keeping the inside part on the inside, rather than in a separate universe as you might have been expecting (based on things like dialogue and so forth). This means the TARDIS interior is only about as big as the thing we see, which is actually not all that impressive when you think about it.

Inside the TARDIS is scar tissue, formed from the Doctor having travelled in time and everything that resulted from it. It's like how whenever I go jet-setting, I get dry rot at home for some reason. The Great Intelligence plans to commit suicide by rewriting the Doctor's history, which is one of the less-impressive plans by a disembodied villain in *Doctor Who*'s long history. As a result, Clara jumps inside the Doctor's timeline and appears absolutely everywhere throughout the Doctor's life, such as all those times he walked by at chest height or away from her in a park, making it a bit strange he didn't recognize her in "The Snowmen" as that weird stalker he always sees everywhere. Or all those times he searched the universe for her and creepily painted her picture in a cave, when she was supposedly living in the next cave over all along and always kept variations of her own name, so was presumably Claraoswindelunder on Gallifrey.

Clara gives the Doctor her secret code, only she must have mumbled the last word, because none of the Claras we meet ever included that, which might have been a bit helpful. She spends all her lives being the Doctor's acquaintance, next-door neighbour, random woman on a bus, et cetera, which is an even odder thing for the Great Intelligence to have wanted, now that I come to write it down.

Inside the Doctor's mind, Clara and the Doctor are totally trapped with no idea how to get out. So naturally the episode reveals some other guy we've never seen before and then just ends, because we don't need to know how our heroes survived when we've had text onscreen telling us that John Hurt is the Doctor!!! Which must be completely true, even though Matt Smith said he wasn't. But the BBC are in on this too, because they've called him the War Doctor ever since, even though the point of this episode, including the title, is that he's the one who *isn't* the Doctor.

So, let me get this straight. If the Doctor doesn't like something about himself, he can just live in denial and pretend an entire incarnation doesn't exist? What I want to know is: what else is this guy hiding? Was there a bearded incarnation of him that liked to hang out with Daleks, had a Cyberman girlfriend and sold secrets to the Voord? Did one of his previous lives spend all his time swearing, sleeping in a cardboard box and stealing candy from children, only to be entirely forgotten about later? Was there an incarnation who had a buzzcut, wore a leather jacket and talked in a northern dialect? We need to be told!

But that's all okay, because there's a follow-up webisode that has Paul McGann in it, so it really is all kinds of worth it.

**Second Opinion (GB)** As a season finale, "The Name of the Doctor" is a bit wonky. Actually, it's totally wonky. A lot has been placed on Clara's mystery throughout the season — except there is no mystery. While the Doctor has been going on about Clara as an impossible girl, Clara has just continued being a pretty ordinary *Doctor Who* companion learning about travelling with the Doctor and having adventures.

Add to that the problematic resolution of that arc: it turns out that Clara was, um, something, something, Doctor's timestream, something, something? Robert and I have offered you a reasonably decent (and I think reasonably watertight) explanation of what happened elsewhere in this entry, but it would have been nice if it had actually been explained properly in the episode itself. As it is, it's a non-explanation to paper over an otherwise inert story arc.

I don't even understand what need there was for a mystery around Clara. It certainly made "Asylum of the Daleks" mind-blowing, but honestly Oswin turning out to be Clara was icing on a pretty great cake. (You could have made Oswin a free-standing character and the reveal of her as a Dalek would still have been really cool.) Yes, they changed their minds on her being Victorian (which I still think was a bad idea, though future seasons have warmed me to 21st-century Clara), but they could have done "The Snowmen" with another character. All these multiple Claras did was ultimately build expectations while making people think that Clara was nothing but the mystery surrounding her — which did a disservice to both viewers and Clara as a character.

The things that work in "The Name of the Doctor" are Matt Smith's reactions to his impending death, the use of River (I love watching the Doctor reveal his feelings about her), showing the Doctor's origin in flashback and revealing John Hurt. I wish we had more of that.

How sad so much of it had to be devoted to the nonexistent impossible girl.

# THE 2013 SPECIALS (2013)

**Starring**
Matt Smith as the Doctor
David Tennant as the Doctor (2013.01)
John Hurt as the Warrior (2013.01)
Jenna Coleman as Clara Oswald

**Executive Producers**
Steven Moffat
Faith Penhale (2013.01)
Brian Minchin (2013.02)

**Producer**
Marcus Wilson

# 2013.01 The Day of the Doctor

**Written by** Steven Moffat **Directed by** Nick Hurran

**Original airdate** November 23, 2013

**The Big Idea** The Doctor has to revisit the worst day of his life — the day he ended the Time War — three times over.

**Roots and References** The 1983 film *WarGames* (the Moment as a machine you have to reason with to prevent or cause destruction); the 1982 film *Raiders of the Lost Ark* (the Black Archive and the warehouse at the end of that film). UNIT uses real-life mentalist Derren Brown as a cover story for bringing the TARDIS to Trafalgar Square. The eleventh Doctor calls the tenth "Dick Van Dyke," a reference to Van Dyke's cod English accent in the 1964 film *Mary Poppins* but also a sly remark on David Tennant's faux-English accent as the Doctor. Cup-a-Soup is a popular brand of instant soup. The show opens with Clara offering a Marcus Aurelius quote (from Book X of his *Meditations*, written 121–180 CE): "Waste no time arguing what a good man should be. Be one." A number of phrases from *Doctor Who* script editor, writer and author Terrance Dicks are used, including describing the TARDIS having a "wheezing, groaning" sound (Dicks's usual way of describing the TARDIS sound effect in his novelizations of Classic Series stories). The idea that the Doctor is "never cruel or cowardly" is taken from Dicks's 1976 book *The Making of Doctor Who*.

**Adventures in Time and Space** The episode starts with the original titles from 1963–67 and has several callbacks to the very first serial "An Unearthly Child" by having a police officer walking by a sign pointing to the scrapyard at 76 Totter's Lane before passing by the Coal Hill School (where original companion Ian Chesterton is a school governor). The time on the clock that Clara rides past shows 5:16 p.m., the time the original episode aired. Clara snaps her fingers to shut the TARDIS door, a trick first learned by the Doctor in 2008's "Silence in the Library"/"Forest of the Dead." UNIT still has its base in the Tower of London (2005's "The Christmas Invasion") and is still run by Kate Lethbridge-Stewart ("The Power of Three"). Kate mentions UNIT's scientific advisor, Malcolm Taylor (from 2009's "Planet of the Dead"). Kate's associate Osgood is a Doctor fangirl and sports the fourth Doctor's scarf. The Doctor tries (unsuccessfully) to convince Clara he used to work for UNIT, which he did back in the third Doctor's era.

The Doctor reminds Clara that he had a previous incarnation that has been disavowed by his other selves ("The Name of the Doctor"). We get to see that incarnation, the Warrior, during the last day of the Time War, a part of the mythology of the Modern Series since 2005. The High Council's plans have failed. (This was presumably Rassilon's plan to escape Gallifrey's time lock and destroy all sentient life in 2009's "The End of Time." The Doctor's theft of the Moment was mentioned in passing there as well.) The Fall of Arcadia had already been described as something the Doctor might one day come to terms with back in 2006's "Army of Ghosts"/"Doomsday." The Omega Arsenal on Gallifrey, from where the Moment is stolen, is named after the Time Lord engineer Omega from 1972's "The Three Doctors." The Moment takes the form of Rose Tyler — more specifically, Rose as Bad Wolf from 2005's "Bad Wolf"/"The Parting of the Ways."

The tenth Doctor's adventure in 1652 has several elements of other tenth Doctor adventures. He is carrying a lashed-up machine that goes "ding," rather like a similar device he had in 2008's "Blink," and the Doctor makes a speech ("I'm the Doctor, I'm 904 years old . . .") that's quite like one he gave in 2007's "Voyage of the Damned." This story goes some way to explaining the complicated history the tenth Doctor had with Queen Elizabeth I, in particular why she wants to kill him when she's much older in 2007's "The Shakespeare Code." In "The End of Time," the Doctor mentions getting married to Elizabeth (and a bit more) as a means of delaying the Ood's summons — which suggests that "The Day of the Doctor" may be set quite close to the tenth Doctor's final adventure.

The Zygons last appeared on television in 1975's "Terror of the Zygons" (which also happened to be their only appearance). An offscreen adventure mentioned in "The Power of Three" suggests the Zygons have been in the Tudor court since the time of Elizabeth's father, Henry VIII. The Doctor's interest in fezzes (which dates back to 2010's "The Pandorica Opens"/"The Big Bang") is once again questioned, and both the tenth and eleventh note, with approval, each other's affectation for wearing glasses (mentioned in 2007's "Time Crash"). The Warrior mocks his future selves' use of "timey-wimey" as a term (which dates back to "Blink"). Both the tenth and eleventh Doctors have trouble reversing the polarity — a piece of technobabble made popular by the third Doctor.

Kate Lethbridge-Stewart is looking for a file on Cromer to do with multiple incarnations of the Doctor, which is a reference to "The Three Doctors." As usual, she's vague on the dates, saying "Seventies or eighties depending on the protocol" (a nod to the fan debate of dating UNIT stories of the Pertwee era). It would take us a dozen paragraphs to document everything in the Black Archive (particularly the photographs on the bulletin boards, which showed companions from different eras together, like Sara Kingdom with Captain Mike Yates, for example), so we'll refrain (though we'll point out that River Song's shoes from 2010's "The Time of Angels"/"Flesh and Stone" are there).

While in the Black Archive, Clara uses a time-vortex manipulator that belonged to Captain Jack Harkness, and the Doctor uses the space-time telegraph the Brigadier used to contact the Doctor in 1975's "Revenge of the Cybermen." The Doctor's phone number is the same one he had back in 2008's "The Stolen Earth"/"Journey's End."

The tenth Doctor's TARDIS returns, until it starts glitching its desktop theme ("Time Crash") into the Warrior's TARDIS (which has the ninth and tenth Doctor console but with the Classic Series' TARDIS walls with "round things"). The friction contrafibulator on the TARDIS console was first mentioned in 2010's "Vincent and the Doctor." The tenth Doctor not liking his future self's console room is a gag that dates back to the second Doctor not liking the third Doctor's TARDIS in "The Three Doctors." (This time, the eleventh Doctor calls the tenth on it, saying "You never do!")

The Warrior says, "Bad Wolf girl, I could kiss you." To which the Moment says, "Yeah, that's going to happen." (It does for the tenth Doctor and Rose . . . a few times.) The scenes with past Doctors are clips (visuals only) from a number of stories, including 1963's "The Daleks" (first Doctor), 1967's "The Tomb of the Cybermen" and 1968's "The Mind Robber" (second Doctor), 1971's "Colony in Space" (third Doctor), 1976's "Planet of Evil" (fourth Doctor), 1984's "Frontios" (fifth Doctor), 1985's "Attack of the Cybermen" (sixth Doctor), 1989's "Battlefield" (seventh Doctor), the 1996 TV Movie (eighth Doctor) and "Bad Wolf"/"The Parting of the Ways" (ninth Doctor).

We see the Warrior regenerate into the ninth Doctor, mentioning that his old body is wearing a bit thin, which echoes something said by the first Doctor in his final story, 1966's "The Tenth Planet." The eleventh Doctor admits he found his grave on Trenzalore ("The Name of the Doctor"), and the tenth Doctor uses his last words from "The End of Time": "I don't want to go."

**Who Is the Doctor?** The Moment sends the Warrior to see his future after his decision to destroy the Time Lords and Daleks and finds the tenth Doctor is the one who regrets those events, while the eleventh is the one who forgets them. Seeing his future incarnations come to terms with what the Warrior did and be the Doctor again strengthens the Warrior's resolve to end the Time War. However, the tenth and eleventh Doctors decide to join him, telling the Warrior he was the Doctor "when no one else could" and are prepared to press the button with him . . . when the eleventh Doctor decides to change history instead and save Gallifrey.

**The Doctor and Clara** Realizing the paintings in the Under Gallery are about the end of Gallifrey, the Doctor reflexively holds Clara's hand. Clara can see in the Warrior's eyes that he's a younger version of her Doctor. She's also able to get through to the Doctors, particularly the eleventh, that they are much better than they think and can't let Gallifrey burn.

**Monster of the Week** The Zygons are shapeshifters who can assume various animal shapes and can duplicate humans, provided they retain the original body (which they keep in a form of stasis). They're refugees, having lost their homeworld during the Time War.

**Stand Up and Cheer** It's beautiful when the twelfth Doctor and then the others suddenly realize that they don't have to press the button and burn Gallifrey after all. The maturity Matt Smith brings to that moment is incredible: his Doctor seems like the oldest man there, despite the fact that Matt Smith is the youngest.

**Stand Up and Cheer (again!)** "No sir . . . ALL THIRTEEN!" and we see a tight close-up of the eyes of the twelfth Doctor as played by the just-cast Peter Capaldi. It's the punch-the-air moment that defines a story filled with them already.

**Stand Up and Cheer (one more time!)** Just when you think things can't get any more wonderful, TOM BAKER shows up. And he's as barmy and amazing as he ever was. We're sorry. We need a second to compose ourselves . . .

**Roll Your Eyes** The eleventh Doctor throwing shade on the tenth Doctor's last words borders on being a bit meta and a bit snide on the part of the writer.

**You're Not Making Any Sense** Forget the technobabble about timelines synching up . . . the Doctor changes history all the time. Why wouldn't he remember what he did and change history so the ninth Doctor has less survivor's guilt, the tenth Doctor is less emo and the eleventh Doctor can stop being so damn awkward about the past?

**Interesting Trivia** It may be years before we get the real story of what happened with the fiftieth anniversary of *Doctor Who*. At one point, it was hoped to have a story featuring all the Modern Series Doctors: Christopher Eccleston, David Tennant and Matt Smith. There was not only a script with this iteration, there were storyboards as well (by Andrew Wildman, *Doctor Who*'s storyboard artist at the time) that featured the ninth Doctor in the barn with the Moment, originally intended to be played by a little girl. At some point, for whatever reason, Eccleston refused to participate in the project, and this necessitated a rethink. Moffat felt that Paul McGann's Doctor was too romantic a figure to start the Time War, so the decision was made to have a hitherto unseen incarnation of the Doctor, and John Hurt was cast to play him. In order to include an element from Eccleston's era, Billie Piper was cast as the Moment. It may have been even more complicated than that. Steven Moffat has commented that it was down to the wire to get David Tennant; early on, there was a period when the only person under contract was Jenna Coleman. (Moffat thought Clara could encounter various aspects of the Doctor, played by famous actors, though he admitted this idea was only explored for a day or so). Fortunately, Smith's and Tennant's services were acquired, otherwise we might have had a fiftieth anniversary special with just Clara!

As the anniversary neared, there was a great deal of content produced for both television and the web. The special webisode "The Night of the Doctor" (which we cover in an appendix) gave us the eighth Doctor's final adventure and showed us how, and why, he became the Warrior. Another webisode, "The Last Day," was from the point of view of a soldier in Arcadia the moment Gallifrey's sky trenches failed and the Daleks began to invade. For television, Mark Gatiss wrote and produced *An Adventure in Space and Time*, which told the story of the early days of *Doctor Who*, with David Bradley playing William Hartnell. And after "The Day of the Doctor" aired, the BBC website showed *The Five(ish) Doctors Reboot*, a comedy written and directed by former Doctor Peter Davison, which saw Davison, Colin Baker and Sylvester McCoy playing (versions of) themselves as they attempt to convince the powers that be to let them appear in "The Day of the Doctor." (Ultimately leading to them being in the episode as the "statues" underneath the tarps!) It also featured appearances by Steven Moffat, Russell T Davies, Paul McGann, David Tennant and John Barrowman, along with Peter Jackson, Sir Ian McKellan and a host of others.

"The Day of the Doctor" was simulcast around the world, both on broadcast TV and in 1,500 cinemas worldwide. On November 23, 2013, at 7:50 p.m. U.K. time, viewers in 94 countries all watched at the same time — a record for simulcasting drama that went into *The Guinness Book of World Records*. It's been hard to find an actual number of viewers (77 million was initially reported, but that apparently is the number of people who watch *Doctor Who* worldwide generally), but 10 million watched overnight on BBC1; BBC America broke its ratings records with 2.5 million watching; and the Canadian channel Space broke records as well, with 1.5 million viewers (not bad considering it was Saturday afternoon there).

A 3-D version of the episode was broadcast on the BBC's red-button service and simultaneously screened in cinemas, which required extra work on the part of Steven Moffat and director Nick Hurran. This episode was the first (and to date only) time *Doctor Who* was shot using stereoscopic cameras. This led to the idea of Gallifreyan paintings being a slice of time in 3-D as a way of making the most of the process. There were also extras made for the cinema screening, including an introduction featuring Strax and the tenth and eleventh Doctors.

In 2018, "The Day of the Doctor" was one of the first *Doctor Who* stories to be novelized in the revived Target Novels range. The adaptation was by Steven Moffat, and it breaks the story into several narratives. Among the more interesting details found in it: River Song was the one to send the tenth Doctor on the hunt for Zygons; Osgood and her Zygon duplicate formed a sisterly bond, which is why they didn't alert anyone when they realized only one of them had the inhaler; and the Curator is indeed a future Doctor with the same face as his fourth incarnation.

The surprise appearance of a 79-year-old Tom Baker was kept totally secret. In fact, the actor was driven into Wales in the middle of the night to ensure no one knew he was involved in filming. Baker would later claim he was irritated at the time that no one welcomed him on the set . . . except Matt Smith, whose enthusiasm delighted Baker. Ever the improviser, Baker did the "Who knows" thing while tapping his nose — delighting every fan over the age of 35 who watched him do this sort of thing when he was the Doctor.

By 1562, Queen Elizabeth I would have been queen of England for four years and only 29. The following year, she caught smallpox and barely survived the experience (the friend who nursed her through her illness also survived but was badly scarred). She never married, despite considerable pressure to do so — perhaps because of her feelings for the Doctor?

It never made it into the final product, but Osgood was intended to be the daughter of Sgt. Osgood, the UNIT engineer who helped the Doctor break the heat barrier in 1971's "The Daemons" — which would explain the younger Osgood's fangirling of the Doctor. Moffat decided to leave this out in order to let fans make their own determination, but we rather like it, even if Sgt. Osgood didn't seem to get along with the third Doctor very well. (Then again, who did?) Another cut element was that the Black Archive was supposed to have movie posters from the Peter Cushing Dalek movies of the 1960s. (Moffat included this aspect in the novelization.)

This story also has what we might call a Fez Paradox: the eleventh Doctor takes a fez from Queen Elizabeth's collection in the Under Gallery in the present day. Only if it's in Queen Elizabeth's personal collection from 1562, it was therefore probably the fez left behind by the eleventh Doctor, who then picks it up in the Under Gallery in the present day and . . .

**The TARDIS Chronometer** London, the present day; England, 1562; and Gallifrey (particularly Arcadia and its Capitol) during the last day of the Time War.

**Cool? (GB)** Being the Doctor is a *promise*.

This may be my favourite lesson of "The Day of the Doctor." The idea that being the Doctor means something: it means being the person who always finds a better way; the person who finds a solution — a brilliant solution — when there is no hope.

But this promise comes with a problem: the Doctor's backstory since 2005 is that he destroyed his own people and their enemies to end a terrible war. And that backstory helped give an edge to the Doctors of the Modern Series and even helped to define the Eccleston and Tennant eras of *Doctor Who*. However, it means the Doctor — a hero who is never cruel or cowardly — has committed genocide.

Which brings us to the subtle, and overt, retcon that Steven Moffat performs in "The Day of the Doctor." The last time we explicitly touched on the Time War in "The End of Time," the Doctor was clear that the war had made the Time Lords as bad as the Daleks. Which was a nice way of having one's cake and eating it too, because the Doctor did a bad thing for the right reasons. But "The Day of the Doctor" retcons this, showing us children on Gallifrey, even turning the Doctor into a warrior who renounces his name, which puts the lie to the previously stated justification. Which brings us to the story's biggest retcon: the Doctor saving Gallifrey.

There are reasons this central change to the series' recent mythos does not sit well with me. But, equally, there are reasons why I love it. Pressing a giant reset button feels disrespectful to the Russell T Davies era of *Doctor Who*. I love the ninth Doctor because of the way he struggles with his guilt and complicity in killing his people and how he moves on from that. Sometimes people, sometimes heroes even, do horrible things, and it's how they live with these things that makes them still worthy of love and respect. Changing that so he simply *thought* he was guilty diminishes that. And I feel cheated and a little disappointed that a complex, nuanced life lesson is lost to a timey-wimey do-over not afforded to ordinary mortals.

And yet . . .

I also equally love the eleventh Doctor's assertion to his predecessors, "Gentlemen, I have had four hundred years to think about this. I've changed my mind." Being the Doctor also means what Craig Ferguson sang on his late-night show: the triumph of intellect and romance over brute force and cynicism. And if that means taking 400 years to figure out how to right this wrong, I feel this is fair too. Because even ordinary mortals must face up to difficult circumstances to correct their bad decisions in some way.

The great thing about "The Day of the Doctor" is that this meditation on the Doctor as a hero and ending the Time War are essentially bookends to some of the best fun *Doctor Who* has had in 50 years. The Zygon story in Elizabethan England and the present day is, in its own way, a jauntier restatement of the Time War story as the Doctors — through wit, dumb luck, lateral thinking and sheer brilliance — achieve the impossible and stop a war. In many ways, just as it shows the Warrior how much his successors have moved on, it shows how *Doctor Who* has moved on from needing the Time War as character motivation.

But it's also quite, quite wonderful.

It's so damn funny. Doctors bickering with each other is always delightful in multi-Doctor stories, but Steven Moffat practically weaponizes this, as each Doctor takes shots at each other's clothes, manner and accent (the eleventh Doctor mocking the tenth for potentially snogging a Zygon is a sight to behold). Giving us a retroactively created older incarnation in John Hurt's Warrior also gives the opportunity to skewer the traditions of the Modern Series, by mocking the proliferation of younger actors playing the lead, the propensity for cute catchphrases and the abundance of kissing that came after 2005. While the Doctors are bickering elsewhere, we even get a lovely bit of suspense as Osgood and Clara discover the Zygon infiltration, while the tenth Doctor's mini-adventure with Elizabeth (Joanna Page is a hoot!) is charming and funny.

Matt Smith has some amazing moments: I love the way he stops an argument with the other Doctors by saying, knowingly, "This is what I'm like when I'm alone." The maturity of Smith's Doctor throughout is a thing of beauty here — and that's no mean feat with John Hurt and David Tennant in the room. And John Hurt's performance is incredible. For a character with the weight of an implied backstory like the Warrior (not to mention standing in for all the pre-2005 Doctors in some way), it's astounding how Hurt makes us feel he's simply reprising a part that he played in some alternate universe from 1997 to 2005, rather than being a character created out of desperation. It's a shame David Tennant gets short shrift, being limited to a lot of balloon-puncturing comedy, but he and Matt Smith have glorious onscreen chemistry.

The real unsung hero of this story is director Nick Hurran. Hurran was already the standout director of the Matt Smith era, but his use of short inserts here to emphasize the mood or internal thoughts of the characters is a beautiful flourish. And there are so many incredible moments: The Warrior taking out the Daleks and blasting "NO MORE" into the wall! The tenth and eleventh Doctors effortlessly bringing about a Zygon/human ceasefire! Peter Capaldi's eyes! Tom *Bloody* Baker! You could have done only those things and made "The Day of the Doctor" wonderful on just those merits. But it went the extra mile and asked, "Why is the Doctor a hero?"

Because, in the end, being the Doctor is a promise: a promise never to be cruel or cowardly. To fight monsters when no one else will. And to always find a solution that will save lives and bring hope — no matter how long that might take.

Thanks for the Day, Doctor.

**Second Opinion (RS?)** Pretty much everything my co-author says I agree with. But I'd like to add one more thing, because I've had 400 years — erm, weeks — to think about this, and I've finally figured out what makes "The Day of the Doctor" so good. It's the simple fact that it's about learning to be a grown-up.

Not just an adult, despite getting married and talking about having a desk job. The Warrior is a grim, serious figure in his initial appearances, but he's fundamentally at a crossroads, about to make a decision he knows will define the rest of his days. That's basically what it's like being a teenager entering adulthood. Everything seems deep and dark and bombastic, with the paths before you holding what seems to be infinite promise, except that so few people actually take more than the most common of those options.

The tenth Doctor is the man defined by his past. He's done the terrible thing, and he's full of angst because of it. He's someone who's just a little bit past his prime, facing the onset of middle age and knowing that some doors have closed forever. As much as he sometimes acts youthful, it's a performance, recalling older days, when the world lay less heavily on his shoulders. And when he drops the act, he's full of fury and disappointment. But this isn't really what being an adult is about. You can spend all your days in regret, but that's not living.

The eleventh Doctor is initially the one having the mid-life crisis. He pretends away the past and lives in the moment, attempting to move on from what happened by ignoring it and hoping it'll go away. But that's not how these things work. Instead, he's caught in a hamster wheel of mania, endlessly distracting himself for fear that he'll stop and have to face himself.

Until he does. "The Day of the Doctor" breaks all the rules in order to bring three Doctors to a barn, where they have to press the button. The Warrior is resigned to doing it, the tenth Doctor is resigned to having done it, but the eleventh has doubts. And doubts are good.

What he realizes, thanks to Clara's prodding, is that being a grown-up isn't about holding on to resentment or trying to forget; it's about making amends. Doing what you can to put it right, even if it's hard. Where his two predecessors are trying (and failing) to be a warrior and a hero, the eleventh Doctor realizes that he's a Doctor. And the point about being a Doctor — the promise, in fact — is that a Doctor is someone who fixes things. Who puts it right, every day. Even on this Day.

## The Psychic Papers: Multi-Doctor Stories

For years, the *Doctor Who* production office had received letters from particularly geeky children asking, "Could you please have an adventure with all the Doctor Whos?" In 1972, with *Doctor Who*'s tenth season looming, producer Barry Letts decided to take them up on the idea. Bob Baker and Dave Martin wrote a script called "The Black Hole," and William Hartnell and Patrick Troughton were contracted to reprise the roles of the first and second Doctors, respectively, to play opposite the incumbent Doctor, Jon Pertwee. However, these plans for a full-fledged team-up of all three Doctors had to be rewritten when one of those Doctors turned out not to be as available as they'd hoped. Letts received a phone call from William Hartnell's wife, informing them Hartnell's health was not great (and, indeed, his appearance here would be his final acting role before his death, three years later). Consequently, the script for what eventually became known as "The Three Doctors" was rewritten by script editor Terrance Dicks so that Hartnell's scenes were pre-filmed inserts of the first Doctor giving advice from the TARDIS monitor, while Patrick Troughton and Jon Pertwee carried the story, comically bickering like siblings throughout.

This started a tradition of multi-Doctor reunions on anniversaries, though Jon Pertwee was the one to suggest to producer John Nathan-Turner that it might be nice to have a reunion for the series' twentieth anniversary. And so, in 1983, "The Five Doctors" featured the return of Patrick Troughton and Jon Pertwee, alongside incumbent Peter Davison. You'll notice that this only accounts for three of said Doctors. Plans for a full-fledged team-up of all four living Doctors (and one replacement) had to be rewritten when one of those Doctors turned out not to be as available as they'd hoped. Tom Baker had discussed appearing but ultimately refused to take part in the special on the grounds that it was too soon after he'd left; he thus appeared only in clips from an unmade story. (A waxwork of Baker from Madame Tussauds appeared in publicity photos.) Hartnell had died by this time and was replaced by a look-alike (starting a tradition of its own), although it's interesting that Richard Hurndall's first Doctor gets treated with just as much respect as the established Doctors.

What these stories do best is give us a chance to revisit old friends, as well as contrast the various eras and styles. The only time the Doctor encounters a Yeti outside of the 1960s is when the second Doctor finds one in "The Five Doctors." The fifth Doctor's consensus-based rapport with his companions is sharply contrasted with the first Doctor ordering them to make food. And the well-ordered style of the UNIT family is given a chaotic kick in the pants when the second Doctor drops in for "The Three Doctors."

The next multi-Doctor story occurred only a few years later and wasn't initially tied to any anniversary. Patrick Troughton had had such a good time on "The Five Doctors" that he came back two years later for "The Two Doctors" alongside Colin Baker. Unlike the previous stories — where the various Doctors were pulled out of time in a moment of crisis — "The Two Doctors" had the sixth Doctor rescuing his second incarnation after he had been kidnapped as part of an experiment to isolate the genetic code Time Lords possess for time travel. The story wasn't quite in continuity; the second Doctor, still travelling incognito during the TV stories of the 1960s, was now on a mission from the Time Lords. Then again, continuity to the source material is a perennial problem bedevilling most multi-Doctor stories. At the time, almost every story was being turned into a book, and the adaptation of "The Two Doctors" was a perfect fit for the one-hundredth novelization, making it an anniversary story (of sorts) anyway.

Classic Doctor Who ended a few years later, but, incredibly, this wasn't the end of the multi-Doctor story. For the thirtieth anniversary, a 13-minute special, "Dimensions in Time," was made as part of 1993's Children in Need broadcast. It was a crossover with the British soap opera EastEnders, starring Jon Pertwee, Tom Baker, Peter Davison, Colin Baker and Sylvester McCoy, along with many of the companions, and was even filmed in 3-D. (Sadly, it's not very good, but it's easy to find on YouTube.)

When the show returned in 2005, the abrupt departure of Christopher Eccleston meant that multi-Doctor stories were initially in short supply. However, in 2007, Children in Need again needed a special. Steven Moffat — who agreed to write what was stipulated to be a scene on the TARDIS set — thought it would be fun to team David Tennant with Peter Davison, who was a friend of Moffat. "Time Crash" affectionately sends up the Davison era and the fifth Doctor's quirks, ending with the tenth Doctor telling the fifth "You were *my* Doctor!" in a clear homage to Tennant's own feelings about watching Davison's Doctor on television. Interestingly, just a few years after this, Davison would end up being Tennant's father-in-law!

However, it was the fiftieth anniversary that saw the true return of the multi-Doctor story in its purest form. Plans for a full-fledged team-up of all three Modern Series Doctors had to be rewritten when one of those Doctors turned out not to be as available as they'd hoped. When Christopher Eccleston bowed out of appearing, the bold decision was made to retroactively insert a brand new "mayfly" Doctor into the mix. John Hurt's Warrior only appears in two stories (one of them a cameo), but "The Day of the Doctor" functions just as the Classic multi-Doctor stories did, with comedic bickering among the Doctors and the replacement being treated with just as much respect as the established Doctors. It also features clips from all the Doctors and a surprise cameo at the end from Tom Baker.

That wasn't quite the end of the multi-Doctor team-ups, however. Peter Capaldi's final story, "Twice Upon a Time," unlinked to any anniversary, saw the twelfth Doctor and the first together. Once again, a replacement was needed, this time with David Bradley stepping into the role, as he'd played William Hartnell in a docudrama for the fiftieth anniversary.

The more Doctors there are, the more chances we get for TARDIS team-ups. They're a sweet-tasting dessert, best doled out sparingly so as not to feel sick, but when done right, they can be magnificent. We look forward to Doctor Who's one-hundredth anniversary starring the current hologram Doctor, a digital replacement for the first Doctor and a surprise cameo from an 81-year-old Jodie Whittaker. We'd watch that!

# 2013.02 The Time of the Doctor

**Written by** Steven Moffat **Directed by** Jamie Payne
**Original airdate** December 25, 2013

**The Big Idea** The Doctor spends the last years of his final incarnation on Trenzalore, keeping the peace in the town of Christmas.

**Roots and References** The holiday-themed lithographic prints by Currier and Ives (the Victoriana look of Christmas Town); the 1939 movie *Destry Rides Again* (a peaceful man becomes the new sheriff in town); J.M. Barrie's 1904 play *Peter Pan* (Clara begging the Time Lords to save the Doctor is reminiscent of Peter getting the audience to wish Tinker Bell back to life). The Oswald family is watching a Christmas episode of *Strictly Come Dancing*.

**Adventures in Time and Space** Among the races surrounding the planet are Daleks, Sontarans, Cybermen (the Cyberiad version from "Nightmare in Silver"), Weeping Angels, Slitheen (2005's "Aliens of London"/"World War Three") and Terileptils (1982's "The Visitation"). The Church of the Papal Mainframe is the updated version of the Catholic Church first seen in 2010's "The Time of Angels"/"Flesh and Stone." The Silents (first seen in 2011's "The Impossible Astronaut"/"Day of the Moon") are priests in this church, used mostly for confessions (since people forget they told them anything). The Doctor uses the seal of the High Council of Gallifrey that he purloined off the Master way back in 1983's "The Five Doctors" (kudos to the prop department; they duplicated it perfectly). The celebration after defeating the wooden Cyberman features a puppet play with a Monoid (from 1966's "The Ark") and the Doctor doing his "cool" dancing from 2010's "The Pandorica Opens"/"The Big Bang."

Much of this episode concludes various story arcs from throughout the eleventh Doctor's tenure, particularly from Series Five and Six, so buckle up. The planet the town of Christmas is on is Trenzalore, the apparent site of the Doctor's death after a great battle according to "The Name of the Doctor." The Doctor and Clara discuss Gallifrey's fate from "The Day of the Doctor" and conclude it's in another dimension. But Gallifrey is using the crack in the universe found way back in 2010's "The Eleventh Hour" (there's even a flashback to it) as a bridge into our universe. Thus Dorium's prophesy about the Doctor in 2011's "The Wedding of River Song" —

> On the fields of Trenzalore, at the fall of the Eleventh, when no living creature can speak falsely, or fail to answer, a question will be asked.
> A question that must never, ever be answered . . . The first question.
> The question that must never be answered, hidden in plain sight. The

question you've been running from all your life. Doctor who? Doctor who? Doctor Who.

— turns out to be more or less literally true: if the Doctor utters his real name in the truth field, then the Time Lords will manifest themselves and create catastrophe. This prompts the Church of the Papal Mainframe to become the Church of the Silence, which bedevilled the Doctor throughout Series Six. Their mission is to protect Trenzalore so that the Doctor never utters his name.

It's revealed that a splinter group of the Church of the Silence, led by Madame Kovarian (first fully encountered in 2011's "A Good Man Goes to War"), travelled back in time to prevent the Doctor from even getting to Trenzalore and were the ones behind the "destiny trap" of the TARDIS blowing up in "The Pandorica Opens"/"The Big Bang" and then attempted to brainwash River to murder the Doctor ("The Impossible Astronaut"/"Day of the Moon," though it was foiled in "The Wedding of River Song").

The Doctor reveals he's actually regenerated 12 times (the limit for regenerations established in 1976's "The Deadly Assassin"). One of those regenerations was the Doctor dispelling the regeneration into his severed hand back in 2008's "The Stolen Earth"/"Journey's End." The human Dalek sleeper agents (last seen in "Asylum of the Daleks") are back. And it turns out that the greatest fear the Doctor saw in his room in 2011's "The God Complex" (which wasn't revealed in that episode) . . . was the crack in the universe. The new Doctor doesn't like the colour of his kidneys, which follows on from the recently regenerated tenth Doctor being able to visualize his dorsal tubercle in the 2005 Children in Need special.

**Who Is the Doctor?** In a past incarnation, the Doctor had some kind of an intimate relationship with Tasha Lem, the head of the Church of the Papal Mainframe. Finally made to stay in one place for centuries, the Doctor becomes the go-to person for toy repairs (and repelling alien invasions) in Christmas. At first, he stays because the TARDIS's return is delayed, but even when he goes back to Earth with Clara, the sight of Barnable waiting for his return brings him back. (As ever, the sight of a child in need is enough to bring him back to Trenzalore.) It is revealed that the Doctor is at the end of his life, having used up his regenerations, and he seems ready to face his fate until the Time Lords (and Clara) intervene. Clara explains to the Time Lords that their demand for the Doctor to answer "Doctor who?" misses the point: "His name is the Doctor. All the name he needs. Everything you need to know about him." Also . . . the Doctor is not bothered in the slightest with being naked. As we might have guessed.

**The Doctor and Clara** Under the effects of the truth field, Clara admits that she fancies the Doctor. The Doctor for his part is awkward when talking about his relationship with Clara in front of Tasha Lem, settling on calling Clara his "associate." Time and again, Clara's affection for the Doctor motivates her: she holds onto the TARDIS as it dematerializes when he tries to send her back to Earth, she's despondent when she thinks the Doctor has abandoned her, and she advocates for the Time Lords not to let him die.

**Monster of the Week** Pretty much every major monster from the eleventh Doctor's tenure makes an appearance (including Dan Starkey's comedy Sontarans!). However, as usual, the Daleks become the dominant adversary by attrition.

**Stand Up and Cheer** The eleventh Doctor's final scene is beautiful, as he tries to sum up the briefness of life before coming to a beautiful summation of not only being the Doctor but being human as well: "We all change, when you think about it. We're all different people all through our lives. And that's okay, that's good, you've got to keep moving, so long as you remember all the people that you used to be."

**Roll Your Eyes** The really on-the-nose poem in the Christmas cracker is a bit much. We're amazed Clara didn't read a limerick that began "One time would a Doctor soon regenerate . . ."

**You're Not Making Any Sense** We get that the Doctor had just been given a new life cycle worth of regenerative energy but even so . . . being able to use regeneration energy to blast a Dalek saucer to smithereens (along with all the Daleks circling Christmas) seems a wee bit excessive.

**Interesting Trivia** A lot of fans felt that Tasha Lem was simply a stand-in for River Song (or even a hitherto unseen incarnation of River). The similarities to River are pronounced given their flirting and how much she knows about the Doctor (even knowing how to fly the TARDIS). But Tasha Lem — who explicitly states she hasn't met or even seen this incarnation of the Doctor — opens another possibility for the Doctor . . . that he's had intimate relationships like the one he has with River in his past. Perhaps the fifth Doctor or seventh Doctor had been close with Tasha back when she was a novice?

The events of "The Name of the Doctor" indicate that Trenzalore is the site of the Doctor's death, with the TARDIS there as a tomb and the Doctor's "corpse" within it (albeit it's now a space-time "scar"). The Great Intelligence described the circumstances of the Doctor's death as "a minor skirmish" by the Doctor's standards, and the Daleks attacking a superannuated elderly Doctor presumably might qualify as that. But history has clearly changed by the end of the story — and quite possibly what changed it was the Doctor saving Gallifrey in "The Day of the Doctor." Because Gallifrey is saved, the Time Lords can give the Doctor a new life cycle, which enables him to defeat the Daleks. And Trenzalore is no longer the site of the Doctor's grave. That said, Dorium is still correct: the (original) Doctor died here, at the end of his thirteenth life. It just so happens that he unexpectedly got a new cycle of regenerations, but the prophecy is essentially fulfilled.

Shortly before broadcast, Steven Moffat teased fans by saying "count the regenerations." Which was thought by some (including the less-than-clever co-author without a question mark) to be about John Hurt's retroactive renumbering of the Doctors (the question-marked co-author was in a bunker, remaining spoiler-free). In actual fact, Moffat was pointing out that the tenth Doctor's abortive regeneration in "The Stolen Earth"/"Journey's End" was a legitimate regeneration. At the time, it was presumed that, because the transformation didn't occur, the regeneration didn't happen. But in actual fact, it was one of times the Doctor regenerated, regardless of whether he "counted" it or not.

Steven Moffat used the extra regenerations to force a question that had bedevilled fans for decades. (The authors of this volume can attest to this: at many of our convention panels before 2013, we were asked, "What happens when the Doctor reaches 13 lives?") The answer of course was pretty simple: the Doctor gets a new life cycle. And it wasn't without precedent: the Master was offered a new life cycle of regenerations by the Time Lord as a reward for rescuing the Doctor in "The Five Doctors" (not surprisingly a story called back to in this episode). The Master also clearly had a new life cycle by the events of 2005's "Utopia." It was heavily implied that Rassilon was also resurrecting Time Lords all over the place in "The End of Time." Clearly it's not hard to grant the Doctor a new set of regenerations; the only people who seemed to have a hard time believing this were the fans who were convinced *Doctor Who* would go off the air once number 13 snuffed it.

One element this story reiterated from its preceding Doctor finale, "The End of Time," was that there's a reset period that takes place before the regeneration happens, whereby the damaged cells are restored before the transformation occurs. Here it completely de-ages the Doctor. Which of course was more for production convenience so Matt Smith could do his final scene without old-age makeup, but it's also now an established part of the regenerative process that, no spoilers, we will return to in future.

Matt Smith was indeed wearing a wig when he made "The Time of the Doctor." Smith had just come off making the film *Lost River*, which required him to sport a buzzcut. Steven Moffat doubled down on this and made it a gag in the episode that the Doctor was actually bald and wearing a wig! The funny thing is . . . Smith wasn't the only cast member to wear a wig. Karen Gillan was filming *Guardians of the Galaxy* at the time her cameo was shot and had to wear a wig over her own shaved head.

**The TARDIS Chronometer** Earth, the present day, and the town of Christmas on the planet Trenzalore over an 800-year period some time in the future.

**Cool? (GB)** I love this story. It's probably my favourite story to star Matt Smith as the Doctor. It's ranked high among my favourite Steven Moffat stories as well. In many ways, what I love about it is that it's the culmination of so many aspects of this era of *Doctor Who*.

Let's first talk about Matt Smith's performance. I have occasionally given Matt Smith a rough ride — mostly because my co-author is so unconditional in his love of him that I feel he can be blind to when Smith isn't particularly engaged in playing the role. But I love Matt Smith as an actor. I think he's incredible, particularly when he has a script that's worthy of him. And we have that here.

Matt Smith has always played his Doctor as an old soul in a young man's body. It was an astonishing trick back in "The Eleventh Hour," and he built that over three seasons into one of the great performances in *Doctor Who* history. The wonderful thing about "The Time of the Doctor" is we get to see the Doctor become the elderly man Smith has been playing all this time. And he's amazing doing it. Playing old is not easy; makeup can help, but not nearly as much as you'd think. Smith makes it look effortless; he makes us love him as an old man as well. Which, when you think about it, shouldn't be that surprising because the Doctor's personality hasn't changed — his body has just caught up with his soul.

We see the Doctor's ageing in a lovely series of vignettes. And I think here is the other aspect of the eleventh Doctor's era finally coming to a close: the super-compressed storytelling. This was an era that told so much in so little time, whether that be the Doctor and Rory tracking down Amy at the start of "A Good Man Goes to War" or the life in the changed Earth without stars in "The Big Bang" or even the mini-adventure at the start of "The Doctor, the Widow and the Wardrobe." So much of the Matt Smith era was made up of vignettes: short little sequences, packed with action and designed to deliver the maximum amount of backstory. (Unsurprisingly, this is an era that thrived on making a lot of additional vignettes for YouTube and DVD release.) "The Time of the Doctor" celebrates this super-compression, zooming through 800 years of adventures in an hour or so by offering just a few key set pieces full of action (the standoff with the wooden Cyberman is smashing), emotion (Clara's gran has a lovely moment) and some lovely montages (the Doctor partying with the town is so charming). Sometimes all you need is a single image, like the Weeping Angels surrounded by mirrors, and sometimes there's more elaboration, like the wonderful sunrise and sunset.

These two things add up to give us something we've never seen happen in a Doctor's final adventure: the Doctor simply lives to death. I found this beautiful and deeply moving. I loved watching this Doctor get older, as his stand to save an ordinary town is to just live with them and fix their toys.

What it also gives us is the resolution to a three-year-long story about the eleventh Doctor, where the unknown forces that haunted him from his first story turn out to have been created in his last. I think the execution is a bit rushed — Matt Smith announced his resignation just as the fiftieth-anniversary stories were being made; in a perfect world, we might have had a half season leading up to his departure to build all this up a bit more — so maybe the origins of Madame Kovarian's machinations could been dealt with in more than a couple of lines of dialogue. And maybe Tasha Lem could have been developed as a character as opposed to being given a couple of bullet points we have to take as understood.

While we're talking about things that don't quite work, I'm not wild about Clara admitting she fancies the Doctor, because it seems awfully sudden. There's a complexity to Clara and the Doctor's relationship that I think gets boiled down a little too much with that, though making the Doctor her boyfriend for the purposes of Christmas dinner makes it not exactly subtextual, either. (I wasn't thrilled with her confession of being a control freak.) And yet, maybe we needed it, because my favourite scene is Clara with the now very old Doctor tenderly helping him with his Christmas cracker.

And that last scene is among the very best of the Doctor's end-of-life valedictions. It's a smidge meta ("I will always remember when the Doctor was me" feels like Matt Smith, Steven Moffat and the Doctor speaking all at once) but not unpleasantly so. And yes, the eleventh Doctor really can't let go, so of course he fantasizes about saying goodbye to Amy (which might explain the next incarnation's Scottish accent!). But his speech about how everyone is different people at different times of their life is powerful because it's true.

Coming back to the Matt Smith era for this book reminded me how much I loved this Doctor and this era. And this story is a fitting end to the eleventh's hour. We'll always remember when the Doctor was him.

**Second Opinion (RS?)** The sun rises over a valley, then sets over the same valley about ten minutes later. So . . . does that valley face east or west? What shape is the planet Trenzalore for this to be possible? Does it orbit on a strange axial rotation? Forget about the appalling misfired jokes about the Doctor and Clara being naked for half the episode or the fact that this all centres on Tasha Lem, who is clearly a replacement for River Song, who was unavailable for filming that week — this sunrise/sunset mystery is clearly the real problem here.

Never mind that the idea of the Matt Smith incarnation being the Doctor's last regeneration is thrust upon us with no warning and no buildup. Instead of making this a season-long or Doctor-long arc full of thrills and suspense about how this Doctor only has one life to live and hence actual stakes . . . nah, better to have a massive infodump to create artificial tension. And then handwave it away. Artificially.

Because "artificial" is this story's watchword. Along with the massive infodump about the regenerations, we get a massive infodump about what the Silence were up to all along . . . that still makes absolutely no sense. The Silents' plan for silencing the Doctor apparently goes like this — Step 1. Destroy the universe. Step 2. ??? Step 3. Profit! Okay, yes, technically that would actually silence him, but . . . WTF?

That and the fact that letting the Doctor age to death is just about the most boring reason for a regeneration since having him hit his head on the console after falling off an exercise bike due to a deranged Time Lady shooting his spaceborne TARDIS from a planet using a handgun. At least that had a so-bad-it's-good vibe going for it. This doesn't even do that. It's just dull. Oh, and Clara apparently has never seen the moon landing, which is the only explanation for why she doesn't try to brutally murder the Silents on sight. More's the pity, because that would at least have been funny. Trenzalore has a truth field, which should be a licence to print jokes. Instead, it's barely used and only seems to exist so that Clara can confess her feelingszzzz . . .

Sorry, I nodded off there. Man, those sunsets come around quickly.

# SERIES EIGHT (2014)

**Starring**
Peter Capaldi as the Doctor
Jenna Coleman as Clara Oswald

**Executive Producers**
Steven Moffat
Brian Minchin

**Producers**
Nikki Wilson (8.01–8.03, 8.06, 8.09)
Peter Bennett (8.04–8.05, 8.07–8.08,
8.11–8.12)
Paul Frift (8.10)

# 8.01 Deep Breath

**Written by** Steven Moffat **Directed by** Ben Wheatley

**Original airdate** April 27, 2013

**The Big Idea** The regenerated Doctor and Clara crash-land in Victorian London and stumble upon a plot by robots to harvest human body parts.

**Roots and References** Philip K. Dick's 1968 novel *Do Androids Dream of Electric Sheep?* and its 1982 film adaptation *Blade Runner* (the Half-Face Man's desire to become human); the 1993 film *Jurassic Park* (the dinosaur); the 2000 film *Crouching Tiger, Hidden Dragon* (Vastra and Jenny's rescue of Clara, the fight scene); *Titanic* (Vastra "painting" Jenny); Lt. Data from *Star Trek: The Next Generation* (the Doctor makes fun of the Droids' refusal to contract "do not," saying, "I don't think of it . . . Droids and apostrophes"). (That said, the Half-Face Man says at one point, "He'll know better than to follow me." However in the script, it's "he will," so that's an unfortunate error on Peter Ferdinando's part.) The Doctor goes through several of the seven dwarfs' names trying to figure out who Strax is. The sound effect for crashing to the ground in Hanna–Barbera cartoons is used when Vastra knocks the Doctor out. The Doctor quotes from Walt Whitman's poem "O Captain, My Captain" (popularized in the 1989 movie *Dead Poets Society*).

**Adventures in Time and Space** The Doctor knows his face looks familiar (a reference to Peter Capaldi having played Caecilius in 2008's "The Fires of Pompeii"). Vastra echoes the Brigadier at the end of 1974's "Planet of the Spiders" when she says, "Here we go again." The Doctor can understand what the dinosaur and the horse are communicating, continuing the conceit that he speaks the language of any animal (humanoid or otherwise) established in 2005's "The Parting of the Ways" and 2010's "A Good Man Goes to War." The Doctor's regeneration has made him initially erratic and a little bit amnesiac, a tradition that began in 1966's "The Power of the Daleks." He talks of having a big long scarf like his fourth incarnation had. Once he and Clara reconcile, he asks if she wants chips (and then admits he has no money), echoing the ending of 2005's "The End of the World." The code word for Vastra, Jenny and Strax to intervene is the eleventh Doctor's catchphrase "Geronimo!" While they're struggling to get the sonic screwdriver while restrained, the Doctor wishes Amy was still around (presumably because she had long legs . . . and not because he wanted to be even ruder to Clara!).

Though the Doctor can't remember them, the robots are evolved from the Clockwork Droids from 2006's "The Girl in the Fireplace": in fact, according to one of the fuses, the crashed ship is the SS *Marie Antoinette* (the fuse also states, helpfully, "Sister ship of the *Madame de Pompadour*"). The ad in the paper says "Impossible Girl," the term for Clara throughout Series Seven.

Continuing on from "The Time of the Doctor," the Doctor confuses Clara for Handles, and the eleventh Doctor calls Clara in the future from Trenzalore just before his regeneration (explaining why the phone panel was open and the phone was off the hook at the end of that story).

**The Heaven Effect** The robots, led by the Half-Face Man, are desperate to reach a place they call the "Promised Land." After his death, the Half-Face Man awakens to find himself in garden with a woman called Missy welcoming him to Heaven. What this place is, and who Missy is, will comprise parts of this season's arc.

**Who Is the Doctor?** The new Doctor has a Scottish accent (and, apparently, attitude as well, proclaiming, "I'm Scottish! I can complain about things!") and is puzzled as to why his new face looks familiar to him. After being somewhat abstemious, even naive, about alcohol in his previous incarnation, he's quite happy to have a drink. He seems very anti-heroic, though he's ultimately doing the right thing: he appears to abandon Clara but is actually disguising himself as a robot. And even if he didn't kill the Half-Face Man, he certainly encouraged him to consider suicide — all of which is not out of character for the Doctor . . . but it is unusual for him to own it so readily. He is also terribly insecure, despairing that Clara can't see who he really is anymore and doesn't understand how scared he is. He also is now not a hugger, and seems incapable of comprehending the emotional stimulus of a hug.

The Doctor claims to be over 2,000 years old — which tallies with his lengthy stay on Trenzalore in "The Time of the Doctor." Vastra postulates that, with this regeneration, the Doctor has simply decided to let Clara see how old he really is and that he previously wore a young face "to be accepted."

**The Doctor and Clara** Following from her last words to the eleventh Doctor ("Please don't change!"), Clara does not initially accept this new, older Doctor, even telling Vastra, "How do we fix him?" The result of that, and the difficult relationship they seem to have at the restaurant (the Doctor calls her a needy, egomaniacal control freak and game-player, while Clara refuses to let him smile first), means that both Clara and the Doctor are forced to re-evaluate their relationship. Both are confronted with the fact that, whether the relationship was platonic or not, they liked the idea of the Doctor as a dashing, young hero, with the Doctor telling her, "I'm not your boyfriend" and then admitting he said that for his own benefit. With the help of the eleventh Doctor, Clara is able to see that this new Doctor is still her friend and finally accepts him.

**Monster of the Week** In "The Girl in the Fireplace," the Clockwork Droids were robots that had been damaged with their ship and began using the human crew for spare parts to repair their ship. The robots here were similarly damaged, but since they crash-landed so long ago, they decided to turn themselves into humans to get to the Promised Land. They cannot breathe and can only detect humans from their breath.

**Stand Up and Cheer** The phone call from the eleventh Doctor is an amazing surprise (and was a cunning bit of advanced planning on Steven Moffat's part, since they filmed it the previous year), but it's more than just a clever flourish. What really makes it transcendent is the vulnerability in the new Doctor's face when he realizes that, even with the phone call, Clara doesn't get he's actually the same man as the one who called her. It's that momentary vulnerability that lets Clara — and the viewer — finally love him.

**Roll Your Eyes** We'd be willing to give Clara a pass for mourning the loss of her Doctor given how different he's become, but the obsession with him being old is, frankly, ridiculous. The previous story has Clara seeing the Doctor not only older but elderly. The story before that saw her comforting and connecting with the Warrior (even saying she can tell he's the Doctor from his eyes). The one before that saw her living entire lives with the Doctor, notably in his first and third incarnations. This is nonsensical.

**You're Not Making Any Sense** Even in an age before there was technology, it stretches credibility that Mancini's restaurant could operate in full view with no one noticing that it's actually an abattoir for any hapless customer who would step inside. Yet the implication is that it's been doing this for centuries.

**Interesting Trivia** With the "Impossible Girl" ad, we once again return to a mystery started in "The Bells of Saint John": who keeps bringing Clara and the Doctor together? And why? Some of these mysteries might be answered soon, while others might be answered later . . .

On the one hand, the Doctor's remarks about Clara's face and how she looks seems intent on portraying the Doctor as a bit of a jerk. But he just doesn't seem to recognize her or understand how old she is or, as we'll see, if she has her makeup on or not. It's plausible that the Doctor is simply face-blind when it comes to Clara. Or maybe he's just a jerk.

As the Doctor suddenly despairs why everyone has an English accent when he has a Scottish one, Vastra speaks to the Doctor with a Scottish accent, which is Neve McIntosh's actual accent.

The tramp from whom the Doctor gets a coat was played by Brian Miller, the widower of Elisabeth Sladen, who played Sarah Jane Smith. This is not the only connection to Sladen: Clara Oswald was apparently named after Elisabeth Clara Heath Sladen.

In July 2014, the scripts for the first five episodes of Series Eight were leaked. Like all *Doctor Who* scripts, they were watermarked, so they were traced to an employee of BBC Worldwide's Latin American division, which was preparing a Spanish-language version of the upcoming season. The scripts didn't come from the employee but rather an easily hackable vulnerability on the BBC Worldwide Latin America's website, where items were stored at a root directory and could be found by a few keystrokes in the navigation bar! But things got worse: it turned out that viewing copies of the first five episodes were also so hacked. These viewing copies were in black and white, used a rough-cut edit and lacked special effects but were nonetheless complete and, in some cases, contained scenes not in the broadcast versions. One of your co-authors gleefully watched the rough-cut versions, while the other remained just as gleefully spoiler-free. We're counting that as a win for all parties.

**The TARDIS Chronometer** An unspecified date in Victorian London. Judging from the Paternoster Gang's ease with the modern Clara, it's clearly after the events of "The Crimson Horror" and "The Name of the Doctor," both set in 1893.

**Don't Be Stupid? (GB)** As a *Doctor Who* fan, I'm all about the first story of a new Doctor. I love watching those early moments: when we get to hear the new Doctor speak, the moment when they take on Doctorish authority, the first really good gag, watching them pick out the new costume, all of that. Sign me up for "Spearhead from Space," "The Eleventh Hour," "Robot," "The Christmas Invasion," even "The Twin Dilemma." I love all that stuff.

And yet, even with all that, "Deep Breath" is a really disappointing debut. The thing about "Deep Breath" is that for every positive thing about it there is an equally negative thing that cancels it out. For example, you have Ben Wheatley's direction, which is astonishing and demonstrates the eye of someone used to making films . . . but it's let down by how terrible all the green screen CG sequences are, particularly in the first half of the story.

Then there's Clara's obsession about the Doctor being old, which is, let's face it, designed to stand in for the audience. (But, just to ask . . . did we really need someone to stand in for the audience here?) It makes Clara look superficial and heartless. However, we also have the beautiful closing scene where Matt Smith calls her and Peter Capaldi's brilliant moment of exasperated vulnerability to set things right.

Actually, that moment also compensates for another big problem with the story, which is that the Doctor has become kind of unpleasant and anti-heroical. On the one hand, I don't mind it because it's Peter Capaldi, who is an established heavyweight actor finally getting his dream job; on the other hand, he has no allies in this story. He's actively hostile to Vastra and Jenny; he's rude to Clara; and the drama hinges on a solo confrontation that leads to a climax — elided by editorial fiat — where either the Doctor has pushed Half-Face Man out of the ship or has convinced him to kill himself. Even the Doctor's rescue of Clara is tainted by the fact that he looks like he's turning his back on her.

We're not given a way to understand this Doctor. We just know he's Doctorish because he's brilliant, rude and daft enough not to realize it's his own coat that smells. Which is why the closing phone call is such welcome relief.

Even the supporting cast has a similar cancelling effect. There was a time in *Doctor Who* when the Sontarans were credible villains. There was even a time in *Doctor Who*, when he first appeared, that Strax was a tragic figure — a creature bred for war forced to be a nurse — but now he's an annoying comedy figure who lets the air out of every single scene he's in. Which is a real shame, because Vastra and Jenny are never better than they are here; it's their finest story. For one thing, the pretence of Jenny being a maid is done away with, and Jenny and Vastra flirt and banter as a married couple still in love and lust with each other gloriously throughout. (I adore how even after Jenny realizes Vastra wasn't painting her she goes back to posing anyway.) If only Strax wasn't there to ruin things.

The main plot with the robots, such as it is, is kind of a letdown. Partially because the whole "don't breathe or you'll be detected" feels like a pale shadow of "Blink," though Ben Wheatley does an amazing job at making it work. The robots are unpleasantly generic, but Clara running circles around Half-Face Man's interrogation makes it worth the ennui, as does the delightful promise of whatever Missy is up to.

The result of all these advances and defeats, these unpleasantries and delights, is that "Deep Breath" as a whole is kind of inert. If you're looking for something where the new Doctor is summed up with a single scene, come back for the pre-credits sequence of the next story. This is the first time I've been disappointed by a new Doctor's debut.

**Second Opinion (RS?)** This is the first time I've been disappointed by a new Doctor, period.

Everything my co-author says above is true: this is a shambles of a story. But I have a bigger problem than the appalling dinosaur (why was it even there?) and that's Peter Capaldi's acting.

He's not very good.

Graeme makes the point that we were promised a heavyweight actor for the Doctor, but Capaldi fumbles the ball here, time and time again. The opening scene was billed by the production team as the first time a new Doctor filmed his opening scene as his first scene. And it's rubbish. I don't mind an unlikeable

Doctor (I have an unholy love of the sixth Doctor, companion strangulation and all), but Capaldi acts like someone who hasn't even finished drama school. It's appalling and unwatchable.

This was the first *Doctor Who* episode I saw on the big screen, having missed "The Day of the Doctor" in that format. I actually cringed on behalf of my fellow cinema-going patrons that they were forced to sit through this embarrassing nonsense. Worse, Capaldi doesn't even get a chance to make good; I can intellectually see why they didn't show us the resolution of the Doctor's debate with the Half-Face Man before his fall, but it removes the possibility of a meaty confrontation scene, which this new Doctor could have desperately used.

But then the phone call from Matt Smith arrives, and it's amazing. I couldn't care less about the Doctor being old, but as someone who hadn't warmed to this new incarnation at all, I desperately needed that. So that phone call does exactly the job it was supposed to do: it passes the torch. And, even better, all my problems with Capaldi's acting will vanish with the next story, never to return. So "Deep Breath" is a blip, where the best thing about the new Doctor is in fact the old Doctor. Goodbye, Matt Smith. Miss ya.

. . . . . . . . . . . . . . . . . . . . . . . . . . . . . . . . . . . . . . . . . . . . . . . . . . .

## Peter Capaldi

On June 20, 1972, Sarah Newman, the production secretary for *Doctor Who*, wrote to P. Capaldi in Bishopbriggs, Glasgow, Scotland: "Dear Peter — Thank you for your letter. Firstly, the pictures aren't ready yet, and secondly, I'm afraid we have an official Dr. Who Fan Club secretary." While there have been people cast as the Doctor who watched the program as kids (like Peter Davison) or were big fans of the series (like David Tennant), Peter Capaldi was already a superfan: as a 14-year-old living in Glasgow in the early 1970s, he was well known to the *Doctor Who* production office, looking for photos from the series and trying to muscle in on the presidency of the then nascent *Doctor Who* fan club (whose president was another Glaswegian teenager).

Born in 1958, Capaldi grew up with *Doctor Who*. As a teenager, he wrote articles and drew pictures for *Doctor Who* fanzines, and he was treated by the people making *Doctor Who* with equal measures of disdain and affection. *Doctor Who* producer Barry Letts was charmed by his questions on how the show was made, which led to him being sent the scripts and set drawings for the 1972 Jon Pertwee story "The Mutants"!

Capaldi had put his fan career behind by the time he went to art school in Glasgow (during that period, he played in a punk group called the Dreamboys with Craig Ferguson). Alongside visual art and music, Capaldi was interested in acting, and his breakout role was in the 1983 film *Local Hero*. In a 30-year career that has spanned stage, screen and TV, he was probably best known for playing profanity-laden spin doctor Malcolm Tucker in the political comedy *The Thick of It* (2005–12) and its film version, *In The Loop* (2009).

Curiously, for a vast film and TV career, Capaldi has committed to very few TV shows that lasted more than a year. That changed with *Doctor Who*. Producer Steven Moffat wanted an older actor, and Peter Capaldi was at the top of his list. His audition, such as it was, was a video shot at Steven Moffat's home by Moffat's son on his phone.

After leaving the role of the Doctor, Capaldi went on to play Mr. Micawber in the 2019 film *The Personal History of David Copperfield*. Capaldi has also written and directed for film and TV, and his 1993 short film *Franz Kafka's It's a Wonderful Life* won an Academy Award — making him the only actor to play the Doctor who's won an Oscar.

## 8.02 Into the Dalek

**Written by** Phil Ford and Steven Moffat **Directed by** Ben Wheatley
**Original airdate** August 30, 2014

**The Big Idea** Honey, I shrunk the Doctor. And put him inside a Dalek. Fantastic idea for a *Doctor Who* story. Terrible idea for a proctologist.

**Roots and References** The 1966 movie *Fantastic Voyage* and 1987's *Innerspace* (shrinking the main characters to explore the inside of a body on a macro scale); 1989's *Honey I Shrunk the Kids*; Steven Moffat's 2000–04 TV series *Coupling* (romantic comedy featuring nonlinear scenes to highlight the awkwardness). The school secretary seems to be doing a variant on the "Nudge nudge, wink wink" sketch from *Monty Python's Flying Circus*.

**Adventures in Time and Space** Back in 2005's "Dalek," the lone Dalek known as Metaltron stated that the ninth Doctor would make a good Dalek. Here the lone Dalek known as Rusty outright says that the Doctor is a good Dalek. The Doctor's claim that he doesn't like soldiers is an outgrowth of his earlier claim not to like guns (2008's "The Sontaran Stratagem"). Scenes from "Dalek" and 2008's "The Stolen Earth"/"Journey's End" play on the screen as the Doctor and Rusty merge. The Doctor mentions his first trip to Skaro, which took place in 1963's "The Daleks."

**The Heaven Effect** Gretchen is killed by Dalek antibodies, screaming as she does . . . only for the scream to continue in an Edwardian room, where she meets Missy, who offers her tea and welcomes her to Heaven.

**Who Is the Doctor?** The Doctor asks Clara to tell him whether he's a good man or not. (Clara concludes that she doesn't know, but he tries, and that's what is important.) Rusty the Dalek looks into his soul and sees pure hatred of the Daleks. The Doctor has defined himself in opposition to the Daleks ever since he first met them, even stating that his title was just a name until he met them, after which it became a manifesto. Even though his hatred is the key to saving everyone, the Doctor realizes that hatred isn't a victory. He's taken his dislike of soldiers to new extremes as he refuses to take Journey Blue with him as a companion.

**The Doctor and Clara** When Clara remarks that she's his carer, the Doctor quips, "She cares so I don't have to." And yet, faced with the Doctor's seeming satisfaction that Daleks are irreversibly evil, she pushes him to look further, saying that this is not the lesson that they've learned. Using her educational skills, she helps the Doctor come to a different conclusion on his own: namely, that making a Dalek good is actually possible and can thus be replicated.

**Monster of the Week** Rusty the Dalek is a "good" Dalek, one who rejected his programming because he saw the beauty of a star being born. Despite all the death and destruction its fellows have rained on the universe, the fact that new stars were still being born showed Rusty that life prevails and that resistance was futile. This came about because of leaking trionic radiation, but he ends the story as a fifth columnist inside the Dalek hierarchy, thanks to relearning the lesson of hatred of the Daleks from the Doctor.

**Stand Up and Cheer** At the story's conclusion, having reached an unsteady moral equilibrium, Rusty leaves the station but gives the Doctor a look that's incredible in its badassery. It's hard to believe so much could be conveyed with a lingering eyestalk staring out of a metal dome, but the message is incredibly clear. It's a powerful smackdown from the Doctor's worst enemy, who just got the upper hand. And did it with one look.

**Roll Your Eyes** Having the new Doctor be abrasive and quirky is cool. Having him insult his companion is less cool. Having him make cracks about a woman's looks, age and body is very far from cool indeed. When are we getting female writers again?

**You're Not Making Any Sense** Let's see if we can get the timing right here. The military capture someone on a base so secret they almost murder him, just because. When it turns out he can help them, do they a) shrink him immediately and put him to work, b) place the only doctor they have under 24-hour armed surveillance, or c) let him leave in his spaceship, unaccompanied by guards or anything, hoping he'll return out of the goodness of his heart?

**Interesting Trivia** Steven Moffat originally thought up the idea for this episode as a premise for a *Doctor Who* computer game but then decided to use it for an episode. The idea floated around for a while until Phil Ford fleshed it out, pitching it as "*Die Hard* in a Dalek!" Ford had to write the script before the twelfth Doctor had even been cast, so he wrote the first draft imagining Tom Baker's Doctor. Moffat later described the new character as "a raging Billy Connolly," which gave Ford some better focus. Moffat contributed a lot of the domestic scenes, as they were set-ups for the season arc.

In the *Who Is The Doctor* entry for 2005's "Dalek," we referred to the lone Dalek as "it." Here, the Doctor refers to Rusty as "him." So . . . do Daleks have gender? This episode aside, they never have. But they've never had names either. So we're going with the convention that Daleks with a name have gender; otherwise, they're an "it."

Being a *Doctor Who* fan from way back, Peter Capaldi spent a lot of time on set even when he wasn't working. He was particularly interested to watch the special effects in relation to the Daleks, hanging around for entire days when he didn't have a single line. Bless.

The rough cut for "Into the Dalek" contains a very different ending as Rusty transmats aboard the Dalek mothership (the "beam up" sound effect from *Star Trek* is used as a "temp track," presumably to be replaced by a more on-brand effect), and Rusty blows up the ship and himself.

**The TARDIS Chronometer** Med Sec 07, a hospital in an asteroid belt in the middle of a Dalek battle; Coal Hill School, 2014.

**Don't Be Stupid? (RS?)** Everyone always forgets about "Into the Dalek."

This might just be one of the greatest forgotten episodes of all time. It has it all! It sets up all the character arcs of the season, from the Doctor questioning whether he's a good man to his dislike of the military; it introduces Danny Pink and Clara's complex attempt to live in two worlds. It introduces Courtney and Principal Armitage, who will go on to have significant roles in the series (or its spinoffs). It has Clara not just working as a teacher but actually being one, thus stabilizing her character in a way that had previously been lacking. It even introduces the TARDIS blackboard, which will be a staple of the twelfth Doctor's era.

But it's more than the continuity. The central idea is sublime. Shrinking the Doctor and putting him inside a Dalek is such a laugh-out-loud moment that you wonder why they didn't try this in 1972 with plywood sets, string and a lot of hope. Intercutting the asteroid-belt story with the domestic scenes of Clara's first meeting with Danny works really well. The situation comedy is both romantic and genuinely funny, and it provides a great contrast to the sci-fi action going on elsewhere. Danny is immediately likeable, but their relationship is likewise flawed from the beginning.

Samuel Anderson is easily the most attractive male pseudo-companion the show has ever had. However, what could easily be just a pretty-boy role is so much more, thanks to Anderson's charming awkwardness and edgier side. He and Jenna Coleman have immediate chemistry, so their connection feels genuine, even if it's only painted in broad brushstrokes in the script.

Journey Blue is my favourite one-off character since Rita in "The God Complex." She's smart, adaptable and learns to think outside her military training. I can see why the script demands that the Doctor doesn't take her along with him, but oh how I wish that he had! She's great.

After a rocky start in "Deep Breath," Capaldi nails the role perfectly in this episode. From the very moment he talks down a gun-wielding soldier by waiting until she asks nicely — while holding a tray of coffees, no less! — he's immediately both gruff and likeable. The Clara insults do him no favours, but the rest is very well done. Perhaps the most shocking moment is Ross's death, which is a brilliant bait-and-switch moment that shows how different this Doctor is from his predecessors.

I also really love the unexpected direction the script takes. Rusty having a moment of seeing beauty is a neat idea, so the obvious path is for the Doctor to recreate that (brilliantly espoused in a scene that shows Clara teaching the Doctor in a way that isn't didactic but communicates the lesson nonetheless). And then the rug is pulled out from under us, because what recreates the "good" Dalek isn't the beauty of a star being born, it's the sheer amount of hatred the Dalek sees . . . in the Doctor.

I'm reminded of the eleventh Doctor realizing who the Dream Lord was in "Amy's Choice" by virtue of the fact that only one person hated him that much: himself. With Matt Smith's lovable Doctor, that was a hard sell. But with Peter Capaldi, you're never in doubt that there's a dark fire of hatred burning at his core. Hatred for evil, sure. But it's hatred nonetheless. It makes the final look that Rusty gives him entirely earned.

And the motif of learning is so well executed here. The Doctor thinks he's learned that the Daleks are irreversibly evil, but Clara calls him on that. She does what all the best teachers do: she challenges him with questions, getting him to really think it through. The first conclusion isn't always the right one, which is something Clara knows all too well. It's not just the Doctor's realization either; Journey undergoes significant growth, as does Rusty (who revises his first conclusion about the star with a deeper one about the Doctor), while Danny is constantly challenging the conclusion that all soldiers do is shoot people.

So we have an episode that has high-octane battles, with Dalek fleets fighting a beleaguered and morally dubious military. Meanwhile, you have a domestic romantic comedy with a new love interest for Clara and an examination of what her life must be like. You've got the wondrous exploration of somewhere both beautiful and terrifying inside the Dalek itself. And you've got a moral dilemma about the nature of good versus evil, with both the Doctor and the Dalek taking different turns on either side. Surround that with a learning motif that ties into the central characters and leads all the way back to the second-ever adventure, and you have a recipe for one of the best episodes of *Doctor Who* you're likely to experience.

I really don't know why more people don't love this. I think it's one of the best things ever and an excellent true start to the season. Give it another shot; you can thank me later. If you remember.

**Second Opinion (GB)** My favourite scene in "Into the Dalek" — indeed my favourite scene from the first half of this season — is the opening sequence, where the Doctor forces Journey Blue to drop her weapon and to *ask nicely* to be taken back to her base. And he does it with nothing more than a sternly Scottish "Not like that. Get it right!" It's an amazingly commanding performance by Peter Capaldi as the Doctor that instantly defines him in a way that 60 minutes of "Deep Breath" failed to do. But . . . watching "Into the Dalek" again, I do wonder if they laid on the anti-heroical nature of this new Doctor a bit too thick.

For the most part, I enjoy it, mostly because of Capaldi's performance. A lot of actors would have added a note of self-pity to a line like "Tell me, am I a good man?" but Capaldi takes the Doctor's instruction to Clara to be brutally honest and runs with it. He's seeking a data point, not necessarily wanting to self-improve. It's a wonderful study in understated but compelling acting.

But where I break company with what's going on isn't with Ross's death (I'm fascinated that the Doctor has lost his sense of affect in turning Ross's last moments into collecting another data point), it's the Doctor's gleeful smugness and defeatism when Rusty goes back to becoming a Dalek, saying, "I gave it a shot. It didn't work out." If Clara hadn't slapped him, I would have gone into the TV and done it myself. There's portraying the Doctor as cold and harsh, but *this* . . . the Doctor is just an asshole here. There's no other word for it. He's cruel and cowardly. But . . . he's the Doctor; Clara shouldn't have to make him come up with a better solution. With any other Doctor, Rusty's judgment of him as a good Dalek would be about the glimmerings of darkness under the surface of the character. Here it's right up front. And I'm not sure if that's a good idea.

Everything my co-author says about "Into the Dalek" is true otherwise. It is a forgotten classic. Ben Wheatley's direction is astonishing. Wheatley is a director of some brilliantly idiosyncratic films, and it shows here: every shot in this is framed beautifully, and it has a gloss and sense of auteurship to it that so much *Doctor Who* doesn't.

But the bold experiment they're doing with the Doctor — take a very popular character at the summit of its fiftieth-anniversary success, make the risky decision to cast an older actor, and then take away the character's heroism and make him brittle and selfish — might be going a little too far.

Without spoiling things, Capaldi's Doctor will get rejigged, and the character goes on a journey (either intentionally or by fiat to make him more accessible) that brings him to the realization of the importance of kindness. And it can be argued that "Into the Dalek" is an example of the twelfth Doctor at the start of this journey, incapable of offering kindness. Or it might be they've gone too far by redefining the Doctor in terms of what he's not anymore. In short, not like that. Get it right!

## 8.03 Robot of Sherwood

**Written by** Mark Gatiss **Directed by** Paul Murphy

**Original airdate** September 6, 2014

**The Big Idea** The Doctor takes Clara to 1190 to see Robin Hood, even though Robin Hood is a myth . . . except he's not. And there are robots in Sherwood Forest. Coincidence?

**Roots and References** Just about every iteration of the Robin Hood story, though particularly the 1938 film *The Adventures of Robin Hood* (Robin here closely matches the laughing, swashbuckling version played by Errol Flynn, and the Sheriff is very much a pastiche of Basil Rathbone's version) and the 1989–94 British comedy series *Maid Marian and Her Merry Men* (Clara's co-opting of the Merry Men); *Lethal Weapon* and a host of 1980s buddy comedies (the Doctor and Robin's "opposites attract" relationship). The title is a parody of the 1984–86 British TV series *Robin of Sherwood*; Clara references the 1993 film *Robin Hood: Prince of Thieves*; the Robots' computer shows various images of Robin Hood in popular culture, including an image of Patrick Troughton as Robin in the 1953 BBC production of *Robin Hood* (before he played the second Doctor). The Sheriff says, "Who will rid me of this turbulent Doctor?" which is a spoof of a quote attributed to King Henry II regarding Thomas Becket.

**Adventures in Time and Space** The Doctor makes references to the Ice Warrior hives (seen most recently in "Cold War"). One of his theories for Robin Hood's existence is that they're in a miniscope, an electronic zoo seen in 1973's "Carnival of Monsters." The Doctor once again is using a variant on "pudding brains" (in this case, "pudding heads") as his go-to insult, following on from "Deep Breath." He also uses his third incarnation's cry of "Hai!" The Doctor learned sword fighting from King Richard (whom we met in 1965's "The Crusade"), as well as the fictional Cyrano de Bergerac, seen in 1968's "The Mind Robber."

**The Heaven Effect** The Robot ship is headed to the Promised Land, which the Half-Faced Man mentioned in "Deep Breath."

**Who Is the Doctor?** Robin tells the Doctor that their legends are vastly similar, both having been born into wealth and privilege and both finding the plight of the underdog too much to bear. In spite of this reasonably accurate summary, the Doctor denies — as he does throughout — that he is a hero.

**The Doctor and Clara** The Doctor seems irked at the presence of Robin Hood more because he's taken Clara's fancy than that he's a real historical figure. The two spend the episode jostling for her attention.

**Monster of the Week** The Knights are robots who have crash-landed on Earth and are using the Sheriff of Nottingham to get the necessary quantity of gold to repair the circuitry in their ship and escape the planet. They fire cross-shaped beams of light from their helmets.

**Stand Up and Cheer** The Doctor and Robin chained up and arguing with each other is freaking hilarious as they debate who would die slower (the Doctor: "I think you'll find I have a certain genetic advantage"), reveal that neither of them have any semblance of a plan (Clara: "Can you explain your plan without using the words sonic screwdriver?") and argue as though it's a competitive sport. ("Execute me now!" "You heard him. Execute the old fool." "No hang on. Execute *him*!") It's capped by the guard coming in and determining that Clara is the ringleader of the group. Which is a fair assumption.

**Roll Your Eyes** No way! You mean the only woman in the production who's not Clara is actually Maid Marian!? What are the chances?!? And this was seriously worth holding out as a secret until the very end . . . *why* exactly?

**You're Not Making Any Sense** The climax is so ludicrous it pains us to even break it down. The ship needs enough gold to prevent a reactor leak in order to take off. Apparently, a golden arrow fired from the ground can do the trick even though 1) it is relatively small, 2) an arrow of gold is going to be too heavy to shoot and would probably plummet to the ground after a few feet in the air, 3) there's no way it could reach a spaceship far in the sky, 4) it's unlikely to seal a reactor by puncturing a hole in it . . . we're pretty sure if we kept going, we could get to 100 on this.

**Interesting Trivia** The original climax — which can be seen in the leaked rough cut — featured Robin cutting off the Sheriff's head in the swordfight, only to reveal that the Sheriff was a robot, who then forced Robin to put his head back on his body. The week before broadcast, two American journalists were beheaded by ISIS, so the producers chose to cut that sequence. However, the continuity following that scene remained unedited, including Robin's remark that the Sheriff is now "half man, half engine" and the Sheriff attempting to emerge from the molten metal (which makes more sense if he's a robot).

Whether or not Robin Hood was an actual historical figure has been a debate that has lasted centuries. (It doesn't help that both "Robert" and "Hood" were relatively common names in the 12th century, as Robin is a diminutive of Robert.) The earliest accounts of Robin Hood date back to the 15th century. The character grew popular in medieval times, mostly through ballads and plays (the earliest of which dates back to the 1470s.) All these were compiled by antiquarian Joseph Ritson in 1795 into the work *Robin Hood: A Collection of All the Ancient Poems Songs and Ballads Now Extant, Relative to That Celebrated Outlaw*. Ritson's work provided the backbone of the narrative that Walter Scott would use in his 1818 historical novel *Ivanhoe*, which is probably the best-known version of the Robin Hood myth.

**The TARDIS Chronometer** 1190 CE (ish), sometime in autumn.

**Don't Be Stupid? (GB)** Always wanted to write your own review of a *Doctor Who* story but never had the time, inclination or interest in using the word "astonishing"? We're here for you! Simply take whatever thoughts reflect your interests, put it in an order you like and presto! An instant review! Ready?

### The *Who Is The Doctor 2* Write-Your-Own-Review Kit:
### "Robot of Sherwood" Edition

A. It's astonishing that no one has thought of doing a *Doctor Who* story about the Robin Hood mythos. How strange that they should pick "Robot of Sherwood" to finally do that, as it veers drunkenly from *The Adventures of Robin Hood* to the *Muppet Show* rendition of the legend of Sherwood Forest.

B. The Doctor sword fighting with a spoon (and, not only that, wearing a gauntlet to hold it) may be the most absurdly *Doctor Who*–ish thing done this season. And Peter Capaldi is all in.

C. You have to love a villain like Ben Miller's Sheriff of Nottingham. His ambitions are so mundane they're sublime: first he takes Sherwood, then Derby, then Lincoln. The fact that he's so completely bamboozled by Clara's patently obvious attempt to obtain information is actually charming as well. It's a shame the Sheriff's cyborg nature was cut from the final broadcast, but the character makes so much more sense as a narrow-minded parochial martinet.

D. On the one hand, the Doctor is still just as much a miserable sod as he's ever been. On the other, putting this miserableness to the service of comedy is a genius move. I still laugh at "Do people ever punch you in the face when you do that?" "Not as yet." "Lucky I'm here then, isn't it?"

E. It's a shame the plot was written on the back of a packet of Walker's Crisps and most of the writing was subsequently obliterated because a packet of crisps doesn't offer an ink-absorbing surface.

F. What's up with the whole subplot where the Doctor is working his way towards the discovery that Robin Hood is actually a robot and suddenly it's "Nah, he's really Robin Hood"?

G. Peter Capaldi is clearly enjoying the comedy, and you have to love the very sweet reaction he has to Marian's kiss. This is a story that indicates a more layered version of this Doctor than we've seen thus far.

H. Here's the thing about "Robot of Sherwood": it's the best buddy comedy *Doctor Who* has ever done. All the scenes where Robin and the Doctor are imprisoned are gloriously winning.

I. Every five minutes, it comes remarkably close to self-parody but, somehow, manages to course-correct narrowly in time. For the most part.

J. The ending is absolutely, totally, completely and irrefutably rubbish.

K. Does anyone in *Doctor Who* understand the actual properties of gold?

L. It's really funny, and at this point we desperately needed a comedy.

M. My co-author will very likely say something about Mark Gatiss in his review. It will likely not be flattering. With this story, there's good reason to both agree and disagree with that sentiment.

**Second Opinion (RS?)** Always wanted a bog-standard disagreement with an alphabetical list? Do you not have enough bitching about Mark Gatiss's lack of writing abilities in your life? Well, fear not! We've got you covered.

### The *Who Is The Doctor 2* Write-Your-Own-Second-Opinion Kit: The Robert-Still-Isn't-Happy-about-Mark-Gatiss Edition (Part XXVIII)

N. Ooh look, it's another really clever set-up (Robin Hood can't be that perfect; no wait, yes he is) that only exists as a one-line joke that can't possibly be sustained for a whole episode.

O. I mean, I'm happy for my co-author that he finds this stuff funny. I don't.

P. Man, but those photos Mark Gatiss has of Steven Moffat with a Weeping Angel must be REALLY compromising. No wonder they cover their eyes.

Q. If *Doctor Who* were the kind of show that could jump the shark, this is the shark.

R. Peter Capaldi was incredible in "Into the Dalek." I've seen "Into the Dalek." "Into the Dalek" was a classic of mine. "Robot of Sherwood," sir, is no "Into the Dalek."

S. "The Crimson Horror" proved that Gatiss could break his own curse if he worked hard enough. So I'm adding the charge of "lazy" to this script.

T. My girlfriend saw this as her first-ever episode of *Doctor Who* while watching it with her best friend who was a twenty-plus-year *Doctor Who* fan. (I wasn't present at this viewing.) The friend has since refused to watch *Doctor Who* and will decry Peter Capaldi to anyone who'll listen.

U. You would not believe the amount of damage control I had to do in order to (eventually) convince said girlfriend to watch another episode of *Doctor Who.*

V. Thank god for Matt Smith, that's all I'm saying.

W. The Doctor cheating in the arrow competition is pretty funny, though.

X. That Patrick Troughton photo is the most awesome one-second cameo imaginable.

Y. And the links between Robin and the Doctor are good. Okay, I'll admit I liked that bit.

Z. I liked that bit a lot, actually.

## 8.04 Listen

**Written by** Steven Moffat **Directed by** Douglas MacKinnon
**Original airdate** September 13, 2014

**The Big Idea** What if a creature evolved the perfect hiding mechanism? How would we know?

**Roots and References** Stanley Kubrick's 1980 film adaptation of *The Shining* (the madness of isolation at the end of the universe, the ambivalence of whether there is something actually haunting people). The Doctor ponders why he can't find Wally in every book, a reference to Martin Handford's *Where's Wally?* series of books (known in North America as *Where's Waldo?*).

**Adventures in Time and Space** Clara and Danny gossip about their student Courtney (last seen terrorizing Clara in "Into the Dalek"). When the Doctor wakes up from being knocked out, he says, "Sontarans perverting the course of human history," just as the fourth Doctor did after regenerating (1974's "Robot"), both of which are referencing 1973's "The Time Warrior." The Doctor saying "not a click or a tick" paraphrases a similar line from 1974's "Death to the Daleks." We see a flashback to the Warrior walking to the barn from "The

Day of the Doctor." The Doctor is described in opposition to cruel or cowardly, a mantra for him invented by 1970s script editor Terrance Dicks. The boy sleeping alone in the barn echoes the ninth Doctor telling Nancy that he knows what it's like to sleep in the cold (2005's "The Empty Child") and Madame de Pompadour identifying the tenth Doctor as a lonely little boy (2006's "The Girl in the Fireplace"). Finally, the hope that Clara gives him in the line "Fear makes companions of us all" is from the third episode of the very first *Doctor Who* story (1963's "An Unearthly Child").

**Who Is the Doctor?** It's revealed here that the Doctor has been driven by a primal fear since he was a child, thanks to a waking dream of a hand under the bed. But being scared became his superpower, something that makes him run faster and fight harder. He puts Rupert to sleep with a finger to the forehead, claiming it's "Dad skills." Clara's description of Dan the Soldier Man, an action figure missing its weapon, is clearly about the Doctor himself, saying that he's a soldier so brave he doesn't need a gun.

**The Doctor and Clara** She had a profound influence on him as a child, giving him the ability to both accept and hide his fear, turning it into a strength. They each give the other orders at different points, both arguing against them but ultimately obeying them. Once again, the Doctor appears to be face-blind when it comes to Clara, saying he can't tell whether Clara has makeup on and attempts to lie to her about her figure, even though she wasn't looking for comfort. She hugs him, despite his insistence that he's against hugging. In a telling piece of foreshadowing, when he insists on staying to confront the creature, Clara tells him he's an idiot. His response: "I know."

**Monster of the Week** Is there one? The Doctor posits a creature so perfectly evolved at hiding that you'd never know it existed. And every strange occurrence has a perfectly plausible explanation that's also offered. So if there was such a creature, we'd never have seen it anyway . . .

**Stand Up and Cheer** The moment when Clara realizes just whose bed she's hiding under, thanks to the mention of "a Time Lord," is priceless. Jenna Coleman sells it perfectly with her facial expression — and it's also the moment you know you're watching something really special.

**Roll Your Eyes** Okay, we accept that Clara's dressed up for a date. But is climbing a ladder in high heels really that sensible? Why doesn't she take them off, especially when she did so earlier?

**You're Not Making Any Sense** The orange spacesuit Orson wears is emblazoned with the SB6 logo of Sanctuary Base 6 from 2006's "The Impossible Planet"/"The Satan Pit." Although why Orson Pink, who hails from 100 years hence, should have the spacesuit from a far-future Sanctuary Base is anyone's guess. There are nearly 3,000 years separating the two! (Complicating matters, 2009's "The Waters of Mars" has a crew 75 years in the future who are unfamiliar with the orange spacesuit.) It can't be the Doctor's suit, because Orson is seen wearing it in the archival footage (albeit without the logo being visible) before he launches in his time machine.

**Interesting Trivia** Steven Moffat decided to write a chamber piece — a three-act play with a minimal cast and few sets — in the middle of the season to "prove I could write," as he says. His inspiration was wondering what the Doctor does when he's got nothing to do.

In the *Doctor Who Storybook 2007*, Moffat published a short story called "Corner of the Eye," featuring a race of beings called the Floofs. They hide out of sight but have effects on people's lives, such as moving their keys around and stealing important letters, much like the description of the perfectly evolved hiding creature here. Interestingly, the Floofs were short humanoids with bald heads, not unlike what might be glimpsed out of focus when the bedspread is removed. The actor who was under the bedspread, Kiran Shah, is also short with a bald head!

The fact that the TARDIS brought Clara back to the Doctor's past on Gallifrey returns us to the question asked by the tenth Doctor in "The Day of the Doctor": Gallifrey's past is time locked (as established in 2009's "The End of Time"). The TARDIS shouldn't be able to travel there. What we are seeing — though no one, especially the Doctor, has realized it — is that the TARDIS *can* travel to Gallifrey and Gallifrey's past, given the right circumstances.

**The TARDIS Chronometer** Present-day London, a planet at the very end of time, and a barn on Gallifrey.

**Don't Be Stupid? (RS?)** At last, after four long weeks of waiting, we reach the Series 8.5 season finale! This finale has it all: scares, thrills, tie-ins to the previous season and a stunning revelation about the Doctor's past.

Some may complain that this was the shortest season yet, but I don't think it matters. Not when the quality of the story we get here is so good. Series 8.5 has dealt with the Doctor and Clara's much more antagonistic relationship, which here comes to a head when he orders her into the TARDIS, later followed up by her ordering him to never look back at where they'd landed. These are stunning moments and the perfect payoffs to a season full of conflict and mistrust in this new Doctor–companion relationship.

After episodes of buildup, Danny and Clara finally get their long-awaited date — and it's a disaster. "Listen" echoes the flashback structure and headbanging from as far back as "Into the Dalek" in order to show Clara and Danny's poor attempts at communication. The listening motif plays out beautifully, with both of them simultaneously listening far too much and not at all. Meanwhile, in a perfect payoff to a long-running thread, the Doctor inadvertently creates Danny the soldier, with the ultimate season-long punchline being that he and Danny Pink never actually met!

Past seasons have had a recurring monster appear in the season finale, but that's not quite what happens here. Instead, we have a riddle: could all of the depicted events have been caused by a perfectly evolved creature or did the more prosaic explanations carry the day? One would think that a creature perfectly evolved to hide might not bang on doors, turn off televisions, write on chalkboards or steal bedspreads, so it's likely that the true explanations are the air pressure, a faulty set, the Doctor forgetting and a friend playing a trick. That said, such a creature could well have been present all along, just hiding in a better way. It's fitting that, without a recurring monster from the preceding season, the "monster" of this very special episode may not exist at all.

The last person on the last planet at the end of the universe isn't the Doctor. Nor is it the immortal Captain Jack Harkness or Lady Me. It's not even the Toclafane or the Futurekind. No, it's Orson Pink. Well . . . I just lost several bets.

The entire season comes together in the final scene, told in a disjointed way for maximum effect. Having taken the TARDIS safeties offline, Clara inadvertently gets distracted once again, sending the TARDIS into the childhood of her other friend. This is a brilliant piece of writing, taking us full circle from the "Is he too old?" dilemma of the season opener to precisely the opposite. We even have an emotionally resonant flashback of the Warrior to remind us that Clara had once met a much older Doctor, despite her protestations in "Deep Breath."

And what a scene it is, with the terrifying hand under the bed belonging to Clara herself and the implication that this same nightmare was seeded throughout the universe by the Doctor, just as he earlier tried to persuade Clara to admit she'd had the dream, who in turn peer pressures Orson into saying he had too, in a classic example of Stockholm syndrome. One can't help but wonder if, since the episode is telling us that fear is a superpower, then perhaps the Doctor was trying to seed superpowers throughout the universe.

The season ends on the perfect note by resolving a 51-year-old mystery. Way back in 1963, we all sat on the edges of our chaise longues when the first Doctor said, "Fear makes companions of us all" in the third-ever episode. Where did he get that line from, we all wondered. Whose words was he speaking? Well, I'm happy to report that the long national nightmare is over: it was Clara Oswald, having time travelled by TARDIS telepathic interface to the Doctor's childhood and whispered it to him as a talking dream that only clever people can hear. Whew. And I so nearly guessed it too.

"Listen" has so much going on that you really have to pay attention. It wraps up several longstanding issues, gives us the first-ever look at the Doctor's childhood (and parents, maybe?), creates the ultimate terrifying non-monster and makes Clara the most pivotal person in the Doctor's long life. Again! And all in a story so pivotal and so profound that it could only exist as a season finale.

**Second Opinion (GB)** Okay, I need to give readers ample warning. You're about to hear a high-pitched squeal coming from somewhere, possibly everywhere, in just a few moments. That squeal is the sound of my co-author wailing after what I'm now about to say.

I don't really care for "Listen."

I'm going to prolong question-mark boy's agony by quoting from *Family Guy*. There's a really funny scene where, while the Griffin family is facing certain death by drowning in a rapidly flooding room, Peter admits that he never liked *The Godfather*. When asked by the other family members to explain himself, Peter simply says, "It insists upon itself."

That's kind of how I feel about "Listen." *It insists upon itself.* Now, my co-author would argue, as Chris Griffin does, "It's insistent because it has a valid point to make!" Or he would argue all this balderdash he does above about it being the perfect curvature of the Doctor's character arc or something. Whatever.

Now there's a lot in this story I admire: I like having a monster for which we have no explanation; I like the quiet, moody atmosphere throughout. I adore the introduction, which is groundbreaking, and the scene by Rupert's bed, which is tense without anything actually happening other than someone sitting up with a blanket on their head.

But the rest of it . . . it insists upon itself. It starts with insisting that we should care that this is an interesting situation and continues with insisting that the Doctor would be so monomaniacally obsessed with this idea, and yet never previously given it a thought onscreen, well, ever. All the Clara and Danny bits feel forced and awkward. Then there's the ending, where everything good and bad about the Doctor boils down to being a scared little boy comforted on the edge of his dreams . . .

Actually, that bit was rather good.

But it does feel like we're supposed to appreciate this because it's great and significant, rather than because it's interesting, coherent or emotionally engaging.

And yet . . . that's the thing about something like "Listen." It doesn't have to tick the boxes of everyone watching. That's the thing about experiments in storytelling like this, or, in a bygone age, "Love & Monsters" or "Ghost Light" or "Kinda" (and the fact that I had to jump back to 2006 for a previous example and then to the 1980s tells you how rare experimental stories are in this "make something everybody loves every time" era we live in): it will connect with some people; others will run a mile. I'm genuinely glad Robert got so much out of it and that it's there to be that litmus test for other viewers in future.

I still think it insists upon itself.

## 8.05 Time Heist

**Written by** Steve Thompson and Steven Moffat **Directed by** Douglas Mackinnon
**Original airdate** September 20, 2014

**The Big Idea** The Doctor and Clara have to rob the biggest bank in the galaxy. The only thing is . . . they don't remember why or how they came to be in this dilemma in the first place.

**Roots and References** The 2004–12 British TV series *Hustle* (the heist with lots of misdirection given to the audience; even the slow-motion walk into the bank lobby is a pastiche of a similar flourish used in that series); *The X-Men* (Saibra is a mutant and has to wear gloves to prevent physical contact, like Rogue from that series, though Saibra's abilities are closer to that of Mystique); the DC Comics character Cyborg (Psi); *Mission: Impossible* (the briefing on the mission); *Pulp Fiction* (the glowing briefcase).

**Adventures in Time and Space** The Doctor reminds Clara once again of the mysterious woman in the shop who brought them together in "The Bells of Saint John." The memory worms, seen in "The Snowmen," return, although we've forgotten what they were used for. The Doctor recalls having a big scarf (the fourth Doctor) and a bowtie (the eleventh Doctor). Get ready to freeze-frame: among the mugshots of the worst criminals ever are a Sensorite (1964's "The Sensorites"); the Gunfighter ("A Town Called Mercy"); *Torchwood* adversary Captain John Hart; the Doctor's Terileptil nemesis from 1982's "The Visitation" (and it's that specific Terileptil, as he is disfigured the exact same way); *Doctor Who Magazine* comic strip character Abslom Daak, Dalek Killer; a criminal from Raxicoricofallapatorius (though it could be a Slitheen); and *The Sarah Jane Adventures* monsters Androvax and the Trickster. Whew.

**Who Is the Doctor?** Once he figures out he's actually the Architect (though before he spells this out to his companions), the Doctor describes the Architect as "Overbearing, arrogant and likes to think he's clever. I hate him." In spite of being initially abrasive with Psi and Saibra, he becomes quite chummy with them by the end, even taking them out for a meal and joking with them. Compared to how he treated Journey Blue and Robin Hood, this is huge.

**The Doctor and Clara** Psi calls out Clara on her tendency to make excuses for the Doctor's behaviour. The Doctor's remark to himself at the end — "robbing a bank, beat that for a date" — and his attempts to get Clara to do something other than go out at the start indicates he might be jealous of Clara's affections for someone else. It could explain — poorly — why the Doctor is persisting with his alleged face-blindness towards Clara even when it clearly bothers her.

**Monster of the Week** The Teller is a large, telepathic alien with a hide like a rhinoceros and eyes on the end of thick antennae. It can sense guilt and has the ability to violently absorb thoughts, liquefying the brain and skull cavity.

**Stand Up and Cheer** The payoff to the episode is quite lovely, as the Doctor takes Madame Karabraxos's call and we see how all the pieces of the puzzle fit together, but there's still a genuine surprise as it's revealed that it's not a heist but a rescue mission of the Teller's mate.

**Roll Your Eyes** "It's a time-travel heist!" exclaims the Doctor. Everyone throws their remotes at the screen in disgust. Fromage, fromage, fromage . . .

**You're Not Making Any Sense** It's never explained to any satisfaction how the Doctor managed to time travel back to supply all the suitcases with supplies at key junctures and open up a few safety deposit boxes throughout the bank without tipping off the Teller.

**Interesting Trivia** Of the criminals that Psi tries to fool the Teller into thinking are in the bank, one that pleased a certain older generation of fans was Abslom Daak, the self-styled Dalek Killer who was popular in comic strips beginning with *Doctor Who Weekly* 17 (February 1980). Daak was a hardened criminal sent on a suicide mission to kill Daleks in lieu of execution and then took on Dalek killing as his life's mission when his lover was murdered. The character proved popular, as he managed to capture the zeitgeist of grim, offbeat anti-heroes in British comics of that era. Daak reappeared intermittently throughout the next 30 or so years in comics (and occasionally cameoed in books), but this is the first appearance of the character in the TV series. Naturally, only a drawing of Daak appears, as it reprints art from the comic by original artist Steve Dillon. Good times.

And . . . of the criminals that Psi tries to fool the Teller into thinking are in the bank, one that pleased a certain *younger* generation of fans was Captain John Hart, who made three appearances in the second season of *Torchwood*. The character, played by James Marsters, was a homicidal ex-lover/nemesis to John Barrowman's Captain Jack Harkness. There was a great deal of . . . heat exchanged between the two captains. Good times.

**The TARDIS Chronometer** The Bank of Karabraxos, sometime in the future.

**Don't Be Stupid? (GB)** If you've never watched an episode of *Hustle*, you honestly should. It was the best program the BBC was making in 2005 not called *Doctor Who*. It's *Ocean's Eleven* on a TV budget but with Marc Warren from "Love & Monsters" and should-one-day-be-cast-as-the-Doctor Adrian Lester. It's about a bunch of grifters performing cons and occasionally heists, and it's done with real style and panache. And when the Doctor, Clara, Rogue from *The X-Men* and Cyborg from *The New Teen Titans* came into the Bank of Karabraxos in slow-mo, that was totally a *Hustle* move.

Now, with *Hustle*, if you're moderately observant, after a while you can see how you're being misdirected and predict what the end result will be. When I first watched "Time Heist," it wasn't until the first conversation between the Doctor and Saibra about the Architect that my wife realized the Architect was really the Doctor. I'm going to make the humble and yet unbelievably sad brag that I figured it out in the first two minutes (but I did *not* figure out the point of the mission, which was a great reveal).

But here's the thing about *Hustle*: it doesn't matter if you figure it out. It's just so damn entertaining. The same is true of "Time Heist."

I mean, this is a show that has the following exchange between the Doctor and Clara when the former wants to blow a hole in the floor of the room they're standing in.

> *Clara:* What if the plan is we're blowing up the floor for someone else?
>   What if we're not supposed to make it out alive?
> *The Doctor:* Don't be so pessimistic, it'll affect team morale.
> *Clara:* What, and getting us blown up won't?
> *The Doctor:* Only very, very briefly.

This is the thing that bugs me about TV in the social-media age. Everyone wants television to be superawesomeincredibleamazing. And when it's not superawesome-incredibleamazing, they get upset, and then the echo chamber of the internet starts adding some beats to it, and then all across Twitter you start hearing *DOCTOR WHO* IS NO LONGER SUPERAWESOMEINCREDIBLEAMAZING LIKE IT WAS TWO WEEKS AGO. EVERYTHING IS AWFUL. MOFFAT MUST GO.

Here's the thing. Television isn't designed to be superawesomeincredibleamazing. Superawesomeincredibleamazing television is meant to happen once in a while . . . because it's superawesomeincredibleamazing. Most of the time, television is meant to be entertaining.

Which brings back me to "Time Heist."

This veneration of superawesomeincredibleamazing has led us to forget that highly entertaining television is actually *really* good television. If an episode has left you entertained, it's not something to be disappointed about. It's done the job it set out to do. Which is why I like *Hustle*, even the later years where its superawesomeincredibleamazing hit rate was astonishingly low. Because it was still always entertaining.

I harbour no illusions that "Time Heist" is the best story of the season. It's a heist story with time travel twists and the Doctor being too devious for his own good. But, by the Architect, it was entertaining! Every time I watch it, I come away with a smile on my face.

It's such a delightful story. There's something for everyone. There's a great-looking monster with the scary ability to melt people's brain into soup. (And, ew, when the counterfeiter lowers his arm . . . ) There's Keeley Hawes — I still have a crush on her from *Ashes to Ashes* — who is so-so as Ms. Delphox but rocks for the entire three minutes she gets to play Madame Karabraxos. (Hawes is so wonderful when her character realizes there's no reason to have her hands up.) And while their character arcs are pretty simple, Psi gets some great moments with Clara, just as Saibra shows us the Doctor's tortured conscience.

What I love most about this story is that the Doctor is so damn funny — and Peter Capaldi does comedy like a boss. I love it when he tells Karabraxos, "Frankly, you're a career break for the right therapist." And "Come on, then, Team Not-Dead." My favourite Capaldi moment in all five episodes thus far is the Doctor hanging out with his crew after it's over, having a meal, making a joke about the Borgias and the Leaning Tower of Pisa and laughing. After four episodes where he hardly made more than a sardonic smile, the grumpy Doctor tries to connect with humans, just a little. It's a moment where one could get the feels, as the kids say.

"Listen" and "Into the Dalek" are superawesomeincredibleamazing. But "Time Heist" . . . it's entertaining. And that's wonderful.

**Second Opinion (RS?)** I like the idea of a story being in one genre and then switching to a love story in the last few minutes. I like that a lot. I liked it slightly more when it was called "Hide" last season, but that's by the by.

As my co-author says, entertaining television is perfectly wonderful. And this is. But I think there's a case to be made that "Time Heist" is actually much closer to superawesomeincredibleamazing than Graeme gives it credit for. If it were just a heist, that would be perfectly fine weekly entertainment. But the story has a lot more going on.

The opening is fantastic. It's one of the sharpest, most engaging openings since, well, Steven Moffat last wrote one of these. I have no insider knowledge, but my guess is that Steve Thompson submitted a straightforward story about a heist and Moffat added the timey-wimey elements and jazzed up the intro. That opening is sheer perfection.

But it's more than whizzes and bangs. The series has been very careful to keep Clara's romantic interest focused on Danny, ever since the phone call from the eleventh Doctor made it clear that her romantic feelings were only for that incarnation. And yet the twelfth Doctor's final line here ("robbing a whole bank; beat that for a date") is loaded with potential. Clara's gone off to have dinner with Danny, but in his private moments, the Doctor is showing the nearest thing he can to jealousy and one-upmanship. She may have lost interest in him after his regeneration, but he's still carrying a torch for her and competing with a romantic rival he hasn't even met yet.

A story with an engaging hook, a brilliant opening, thrills, spills and the hint that there's a lot more going on than we realized? I don't know about you, but that sounds superawesomeincredibleamazing to me.

## 8.06 The Caretaker

**Written by** Gareth Roberts and Steven Moffat **Directed by** Paul Murphy
**Original airdate** September 27, 2014

**The Big Idea** To smoke out an alien killing machine, the Doctor goes undercover at Clara's school as the janitor.

**Roots and References** The 1976 film adaptation *Logan's Run* (the Skovox Blitzer is reminiscent of the design for Box). The Doctor whistles the "We don't need no education" opening of Pink Floyd's "Another Brick in the Wall, Part 2," their most famous hit from the 1979 concept album *The Wall*.

**Adventures in Time and Space** Coal Hill School was in *Doctor Who*'s first episode, "An Unearthly Child," in 1963. This is the first story to be fully set at the school since 1988's "Remembrance of the Daleks." The Doctor, perhaps predictably, thinks Clara's boyfriend is the one who looks like his eleventh incarnation. The Doctor's antipathy to a former soldier who's now a maths teacher, however, causes one to raise an eyebrow, as the Doctor's best friend from the Classic Series, Brigadier Lethbridge-Stewart, who led UNIT throughout the '70s (or was it the '80s?) eventually became a maths teacher in 1983's "Mawdryn Undead." The Skovox Blitzer is attracted to "artron emissions," a reference to artron energy, a key element of time travel first mentioned in 1977's "The Deadly Assassin." Both 2010's "The Lodger" and 2011's "Closing Time" saw the eleventh Doctor trying to fit into his (temporary) companion's ordinary life, with hilarious consequences. This is repeated here, with all three episodes written by Gareth Roberts. Clara mentions Orson Pink ("Listen") when introducing the Doctor to Danny, but he fails to notice the resemblance, despite both being played by the same actor. The Doctor reminds Clara of when she had to eat two meals in a row, which happened in "Time Heist." The Doctor mentions sulking after a fight with River Song.

**The Heaven Effect** The police officer killed by the Skovox Blitzer turns up in a processing area, where we met Seb, an associate of Missy. He names where they are as the Afterlife, the Promised Land or — his preference — the Nethersphere. He implies that Missy is God.

**Who Is the Doctor?** The twelfth Doctor's next-level antipathy to soldiers, which first surfaced in "Into the Dalek," once again returns with a vengeance, as the Doctor outright rejects Danny because of his background. He grudgingly accepts Danny in the end but not before Danny calls the Doctor on his aristocratic airs. Once again, the Doctor thinks he can pass for a normal human, but it doesn't quite work out. He's read Jane Austen's *Pride and Prejudice*.

**The Doctor and Clara** They've been taking daily trips for some time now, forcing Clara into a double life. The Doctor is sometimes nice to her "because it works." This week's teasing about Clara's appearance is about how she hasn't washed. The Doctor is happy enough for Clara to be in a relationship when the new boyfriend is the spitting image of his eleventh self, but he acts like a stern, disapproving Victorian parent when he learns that Clara's dating a soldier.

**Monster of the Week** The Skovox Blitzer is an armoured alien that walks on four spider-like legs and has a built-in machine gun for a hand. It's one of the deadliest killing machines ever created.

**Stand Up and Cheer** "Is this part of the surprise play?" After Clara's flimsy excuse for what's been going on falls entirely flat with Danny, the Doctor swallowing the story whole is delightful.

**Roll Your Eyes** The Doctor being invisible and running from the Skovox Blitzer should be dramatic and exciting, but it's directed with all of the flair of your dad filming a distant niece's birthday party.

**You're Not Making Any Sense** Can Danny Pink really somersault faster than a deadly killing machine with a built-in automatic weapon can shoot? Really? He can do that?

**Interesting Trivia** Writer Steven Moffat pitched the idea to Gareth Roberts about the Doctor becoming a caretaker at Clara's school and her two worlds colliding. However, Moffat failed to tell Roberts who the new Doctor would be, so Roberts was just finishing the first draft when he saw the announcement on TV, like everyone else. It was producer Nikki Wilson who had the idea to give the Doctor a bonding moment with one of the pupils, and Roberts initially wrote her as an Amelia Pond–type before deciding it would be funnier to have her as a "Yeah, what?" character. Peter Harness, who was writing the next script, liked the idea so much he asked if he could incorporate the character into *his* story, so it was decided to retroactively add her to the previous school-based stories this season. Indeed, the script for "Into the Dalek" simply referred to her as "the girl from episode six," illustrating her roots in this story.

Courtney's mother mentions having talked to Danny Pink a year ago about her daughter. Since Danny was new to the school in "Into the Dalek," this suggests that Clara and Danny have been dating for months by now. Given the TARDIS is said to be taking Clara on daily outings, it's no wonder she's exhausted from her double life. She's been doing this for the better part of a year!

**The TARDIS Chronometer** An alien planet with sand piranhas and two suns; Coal Hill School, London, and surrounding areas in the present day; in space to dispose of the Skovox Blitzer.

**Don't Be Stupid? (RS?)** "The Caretaker" is a monumental failure, but at least it's an interesting one.

First of all, what's with the Skovox Blitzer? It's the most underdeveloped alien menace in the history of *Doctor Who*. It's a deadly killing machine, fighting in a war and . . . no, that's it. We're never told anything about the machine, the war or its planet. It's a reasonably effective visual, but it has absolutely nothing else going for it. No backstory. No character. Just a generic monster of Generia.

My theory is that the mysterious war it's fighting is the epic battle against drama and entertainment — that thing sucks the life out of every scene it's in. The invisible chase is rubbish. The other invisible chase is not only rubbish, it's hard to even notice that Danny was actually invisibly chasing! And I don't know what training they give these things in the war on fun, but try sitting in a chair and getting one of your friends to jump over you and see if you can't hit them with a nerf gun. Let alone a multi-firing automatic weapon built into your hand. (Your choice.)

Speaking of idiotic things Danny does, let's follow his chain of logic here: 1) Suspect girlfriend is lying to you. 2) Discover aliens are real. 3) Go into near-catatonic shock as a result. 4) Ask said girlfriend why she lied about that. Um, okay, but maybe you have all the clues already, buddy? But . . . sure, let's go with the idea that the most pressing concern on Danny's mind after discovering that aliens exist and one of them almost destroyed the world because of his blundering is to immediately start controlling his girlfriend. It's good to keep your priorities straight in these situations.

And then he levels a devastating charge at the Doctor, one that visibly upsets Clara: namely, that the Doctor is an officer. You know, the kind of person who does the planning and sends others to do the actual fighting while he defeats the higher menace. I'm sorry, but how is this a revelation? Why does the Doctor react in any way other than to nod and say, "Yep, pretty much my job description"? Has the Skovox Blitzer's war on drama been more successful than we realized?!

But wait, it gets better. Clara's immediate response to Danny calling her out on lying is . . . to immediately lie to the Doctor via making Danny invisible and secreting him aboard the TARDIS. So this brilliant plan will make Danny discover you're a trustworthy, non-lying type of a person, will it?

It's not rocket science to point out that this is a poor man's version of "The Lodger" and "Closing Time." But why were those considered two hugely successful episodes whereas this is a miserable failure? First, the setting of a school just doesn't have the intrinsic comic potential of a wacky houseguest or two inept guys babysitting. Second, those episodes featured the comic delights of Matt Smith, who was put upon this Earth to be the charmingly awkward friend whom you love anyway despite his klutziness. Peter Capaldi . . . was not.

Don't get me wrong, I love some of Capaldi's stuff. He's amusing when he's insulting people. And the look he gives Clara when she says that Adrian (the bowtie-wearing guy with the big chin) isn't her type is utterly priceless. But Capaldi isn't madcap zany the way Matt Smith is, and that's what this script really needs.

Capaldi's other problem is that he's a much stronger personality than anyone around him, so his insults are harsher than they would be in the hands of a lesser actor. His supposedly comic insults of Clara's appearance seem sexist rather than naive, which has been a running problem all season. And the optics of him cheering along the white teacher and insulting the Black guy are not good, particularly since he's reclassifying the Black guy as too mentally feeble for maths, assuming he must be into physical activity instead. Yes, we know it's supposed to be a commentary on his dislike of soldiers, but that's not how it's going to read to anyone born after 1980.

Peter Capaldi, Jenna Coleman and Samuel Anderson are all good actors — at times brilliant. And yet none are able to make their characters likeable in a story that's supposed to be a bit of a laugh. Meanwhile, the direction is absent, the script is generic, and the only people still in the game are the design team, who've poured their entire energy into a guy in a chair. With "Time Heist," you can see the Steven Moffat bits poking through. With this one, he added his name as a co-writer apparently because he'd never yet had an out-and-out failure of a *Doctor Who* story and wanted to see what that was like. Well, it's good to have goals.

So "The Caretaker" has a decent premise, but everything after that actively derails it. Damn, I think the war against drama just claimed another victim.

**Second Opinion (GB)** My co-author has been sniffing Skovox Blitzer smoke — how else could he call "The Caretaker" an *interesting* failure?

It's a clever defence to say the problem is that the heavyweight actor is too overpowering . . . except the problem doesn't even begin with the actor. The problem is this choice of a character for the Doctor. "Arsey Tom Baker" (as writer Phil Ford described to me how he wrote the character in "Into the Dalek") is one thing; *the Doctor actually tells Clara she needs to justify who she's seeing to him.*

What. The. Actual. Ever-living. (Come-on-now.) Fuck.

Yes, Danny is equally off-the-charts controlling (his "good guy" persona has not aged well, if it even played decently in 2014), but the Doctor should have been sent packing the second he felt he could dictate who his friend could or could not date. This isn't making the Doctor slightly unlikeable; this is making the hero of the program actively unpleasant.

Are the people in charge actually reading the scripts or watching the rushes? Clara going out with a bowtie-wearing white guy is okay, but a Black soldier is not?! This is so many levels of not cool, you could build a skyscraper on top of another skyscraper. The backstory — that the Doctor is denying that he *did* know a soldier who was a maths teacher — is a detail that only diehard fans (and/or readers of this book) will intuit, because nowhere is it explicitly stated in dialogue.

There's one thing I like about "The Caretaker." I flat-out disagree with question-mark boy about Danny's criticism of the Doctor. He's not taking issue with the Doctor being an officer; he's taking issue that he's an aristocrat in spite of the Doctor's self-delusion that he's a man of the people. In that moment, Danny is speaking truth on behalf of the audience: he's pointing out that, actually, the Doctor has become a bitter, nasty snob. And I can't begin to tell you how terrible it is that this has to be pointed out.

## 8.07 Kill the Moon

**Written by** Peter Harness **Directed by** Paul Wilmshurst
**Original airdate** October 4, 2014

**The Big Idea** The moon turns out to be an egg, containing a newly gestated creature that might threaten all of Earth. Clara faces a terrible choice: save the creature or kill the moon.

**Roots and References** *The Twilight Zone* (the moral dilemma facing the humans when they discover the moon is an egg); Jules Verne's *First Men on the Moon* (visiting the moon). Courtney mentions Neil Armstrong's speech on the moon landing. While it's in the background, the whiteboard in Clara's classroom has a quote from Charles Dickens's *David Copperfield* that seems deliberately chosen for its appropriateness to the story: "Whether I shall turn out to be the hero of my own life, or whether that station will be held by anybody else, these pages must show."

**Adventures in Time and Space** The orange spacesuits that have been seen since 2006's "The Impossible Planet"/"The Satan Pit" appear again. The Doctor mentions Blinovitch, who is responsible for the Blinovitch Limitation Effect, first mentioned in 1972's "The Day of the Daleks."

The Doctor uses a yellow yo-yo to do a gravity test, just as he did in 1975's "The Ark in Space." In that same story, he determined the year the ark was constructed by judging a Bennett oscillator; here he does the same thing to the spaceship, only with a prototype Bennett oscillator. Clara's comment about the moon existing in the future has strong echoes of Sarah Jane Smith's line in 1975's "Pyramids of Mars" about the past not being able to affect the present.

The setting on the moon means there are also a number of implicit references to the second Doctor stories that take place in the 21st century. "Kill the Moon" is set in 2049, just before "The Moonbase" (1967), which was set in 2070 and obviously features the moon. There's also a callback to 1969's "The Seeds of Death," which was set at the end of the 21st century and similarly had no spaceships except for one in a museum that had to be repurposed for a trip to the moon. In yet another echo of the second Doctor, the twelfth Doctor says, "When I say run, *run*," a catchphrase dating back to Patrick Troughton's first story, 1966's "The Power of the Daleks."

**Who Is the Doctor?** We return to a facet of the Doctor we've seen throughout the Modern Series but which was finally articulated in "The Fires of Pompeii" (2008) and "The Waters of Mars" (2009): the Doctor has the ability to perceive how moments of time can change, as he immediately understands what happens with Earth's history when the creature emerges. Indeed, the Doctor is motivated in this story by the fact that there are some "little eyeblinks" in time that he can't see, meaning the outcome could be vastly changed by decisions made in the present. He therefore refuses to participate in the decision of whether to kill the moon or not, leaving it up to the humans, since Earth isn't his home. (He says it's the same logic that prevents him from killing Hitler in the past.) The Doctor talks about his new regenerative cycle and admits that he doesn't know if it has a limit: if he's shot, he's not sure if he'll keep regenerating forever.

**The Doctor and Clara** This story ends with the Doctor and Clara breaking up. In many ways, it was headed to this point at the start of the story when Clara makes him tell Courtney to her face that she isn't special, which he can't do.

But it comes to a head after he abandons her to make her choice. While the Doctor tells Clara he had faith that she would always make the right choice, she is angry about being abandoned and about the Doctor abdicating his responsibility to help them. She tells him to leave and not come back. Danny later points out that she was angry when she said this, so she can't be sure she meant it.

**Monster of the Week** The "spiders" infesting the surface of the moon are actually enormous germs, said to be a prokaryotic unicellular lifeform with non-chromosomal DNA — otherwise known as bacteria. They're large by our standards but tiny compared to the creature in the egg.

**Stand Up and Cheer** Clara's retort to the Doctor's actions after Courtney leaves the TARDIS is just stunning. She shuts down his attempts at grandstanding and calls him on his patronizing. She makes the excellent point that he walks the Earth and breathes the air, so he therefore has some responsibility to the planet . . . and then makes the even more important point that he was supposed to be her friend and yet made her scared and feel like an idiot. It's a bravura performance from Jenna Coleman, who doesn't let up the intensity.

**Roll Your Eyes** The Moon.

Is.

An Egg.

**You're Not Making Any Sense** If the issues with the moon have caused "high tide everywhere" — so high that tides drown whole cities — why is the tide out when the Doctor lands on the beach at the end of the story? Also . . .

The Moon.

Is.

An Egg.

**Interesting Trivia** The fact that this story makes a lot of references to stories produced in the 1970s by Philip Hinchcliffe is no coincidence. Hinchcliffe's era was known for its high horror content, so Steven Moffat's note to Peter Harness about writing the first half of the episode was that he should frighten the audience and "Hinchcliffe the shit out of it."

Courtney Woods becomes president of the United States by 2049. The Doctor mentions that this is rather bizarre. We can't help but agree. There are three eligibility requirements that the U.S. president must satisfy: they must be a natural-born citizen of the United States; they must be at least 35 years old; and they must be a resident of the United States for at least 14 years. The middle requirement is fine, as Courtney would be 50 in 2049. And the last option is certainly possible during the intervening 35 years. But is she a natural-born citizen? We can't conclusively rule it out, but both Courtney and her parents (seen in "The Caretaker") have strong British accents, which makes it unlikely. Possibly the rules change within the next few decades. Or there's another out: the man Courtney meets in the future is called Blinovitch, whom we've never met but we know is responsible for the Blinovitch Limitation Effect, which deals with time paradoxes. So perhaps there's something timey-wimey and paradoxical that causes Courtney to be retroactively born in the U.S. Nonetheless, it's still bizarre. (Or perhaps the Doctor is just being flippant in order to avoid his impending conflict with Clara.)

We have some scientific questions:

1.  If the moon has gained mass, then why is it high tide everywhere? More mass would mean that the high tide was higher, but the low tide would also be lower. More moon would mean larger tidal oscillations; it wouldn't just suck the oceans outwards in all directions.

2.  The moon has put on weight: 1.3 billion tonnes, to be precise. How? Eggs don't get heavier the closer they are to hatching; unlike a pregnant woman (whose weight gain is mostly from external sources of energy), the moon is a closed system with no food cravings.

3.  The gravity changes because the mass is unstable. So the creature is not only gaining weight somehow, it also loses so much of it that the gravity becomes a fraction of what it normally is. And it does this within a matter of seconds. How, exactly?

4.  Can a creature that hatched from an egg then lay an egg of precisely the same size, moments later? I guess we're not experts on space chickens, but . . . really?

5.  If a giant space chicken is going to lay an egg the same size as the previous one that was pockmarked from a hundred million years of asteroid impacts, why would it have exactly the same crater markings as the old one?

6.  Why do germs exist in proportion to the thing they're infesting? Rather than, say, being the size that germs always are? Do elephants have bigger germs than mice?

7.  What did science ever do to Peter Harness?

8.  Why is the moon an egg? No, really, *why*?!

**The TARDIS Chronometer** The Moon and Earth in 2049, plus Earth in the present day.

**Don't Be Stupid? (RS?)** I'm going to dive right in to the big question: Is this entire story a metaphor for the abortion debate?

Let's examine the evidence. First, there's a choice between killing an embryo versus not. Second, the Doctor — the only man still in the story — decides he has no place in this debate and hightails it out of there, leaving the women to decide. Third, external votes are taken but ignored, turning the ultimate decision back to personal choice. Fourth, said ultimate decision is to let the fetus come to term, and all's well that ends well.

One of these things is not like the others.

As a metaphor, it's a thinly veiled one. The idea that *Doctor Who* would ever even vaguely approach the abortion debate is wild; the fact that it comes right up into its face, as here, is shocking. Courtney's position is clear, right from the beginning — "It's a little baby," she says, seeing the creature as alive even though, by definition, it isn't. Lundvik represents the point of view of those who favour aborting a fetus if it poses a danger. And Clara's caught in the middle, sympathetic to both sides, and entirely out of her depth at having to make the ultimate call.

The first half of the story is a mix of thrills, scares and terrible science. Or, in other words, a pretty typical *Doctor Who* story. I'm a scientist myself, and I don't need *Doctor Who* to have accurate science to enjoy it; my problem here is that the bad science alienates people from the story for entirely superfluous reasons. For a story deliberately painting an enormous target on its back, it's unfortunate that it inadvertently paints a second one.

However, that first target is an incredibly brave one. As soon as there's a choice to be made, the story does a complete 180-degree turn. The fact that the Doctor is so eager to leave is vastly out of character. The idea that the three people left wouldn't simply take a vote among themselves is bizarre. (The story could have played out almost exactly as is if they had, with Clara being the swing vote who shifts at the last minute.) The possibility that not one single person down on Earth would leave their lights on beggars belief. I really must visit this entirely homogeneous planet Earth someday, where everyone has the same opinion on any issue, let alone a contentious one. Must be a very quiet and calm place.

And yet, none of this really matters, because the central dilemma is so strong. "Kill the Moon" isn't being subtle about its metaphor. The reason every single person on Earth turns off their lights in unison is because they represent the policymakers and voters who think they should have a say over someone else's choice. The Doctor leaves because that's an easy cop-out answer for any man faced with this decision. Even if it ultimately does affect him, it's not really his decision in the moment, so he can throw his hands up and avoid making a choice. He even says, "It's your moon, womankind, it's your choice," in case the metaphor wasn't clear.

But where this goes is more complicated. The episode appears to pick a side by having Clara save the moon and let it hatch, something that's narratively endorsed as correct. As a dyed-in-the-wool, third-wave feminist from way back, I find this deeply uncomfortable. Yes, it's about choice, not a unilateral position. Yes, it was a fetus almost at term, which is the kind of rare situation where abortion only occurs to save the mother's life — which is far more the direction the story is leaning in, except that it cheats by making the resolution entirely without cost and laughably ridiculous with a space-dragon egg exactly the same size and layout as the previous egg. And true, *Doctor Who* is not — and probably should not be — a show only for lefty intellectuals like me. But it's still picking a side, and that's going to alienate a lot of people.

Like the Doctor, I believe that a man has no role in what a woman does with her own body. That's abhorrent. But I'd like to address his position anyway, because I think he's wrong. Not in staying out of the argument, but in the way that he does. And Clara's entirely right in what she says to him afterwards.

The Doctor leaving the scene was meant to be a gesture of respect, but that simply isn't good enough. Too many progressive men are scared to say anything one way or the other for fear they'll be yelled at for joining in at all. But that's actually not being supportive. And every time this debate rages, the policymakers tend to be a bunch of white blokes who are not physically or directly affected by the outcome. Yes, Clara should be the one making the ultimate choice, but it's not as though she couldn't have used some support and friendship along the way, rather than being — and feeling — abandoned. The problem here isn't that he lets the women make the choice; it's that he jumps into the TARDIS and runs away as soon as things gets tricky. For her part, Clara could have simply abided by the majority vote via Earth's lights and washed her own hands of the situation, but she's not taking the easy way out and hence refuses to let the Doctor do the same.

So is this entire story a metaphor for the abortion debate? It's probably intended only to be one for late-term abortions in the case of risk to the mother, but it's very easy to read it as something encompassing the whole spectrum. And it's about as polarizing too. Some people hate it for attempting the metaphor in the first place. Some people love how brave it is, doing things no other *Doctor Who* story has ever dared try. Others can't get past the resolution, seeing yet another assault on abortion within popular entertainment. Whichever camp you fall into will depend on your point of view and your upbringing. But it's your choice . . .

. . . okay, that was pretty heavy. I'm going to let my co-author talk about something else entirely now.

**Second Opinion (GB)** Here's a confession: I love "Kill the Moon."

Everything my co-author says above is absolutely true. The bad science, the awkward metaphor that the writer and showrunner have publicly stated was unintentional and yet clearly is there . . . not to mention the inexpert handling of the implications of said metaphor. (Once again, I repeat: only one woman had written for the Modern Series of *Doctor Who* at this point, and that was back in Series Three and Four.)

And yet . . . I love "Kill the Moon."

There is a school of thought in producing television that drama needs to be safe. You want as big an audience as possible, so you make the scenarios as anodyne as possible, or you take the side of an issue the majority of your audience will take.

What "Kill the Moon" does is neither of these things. It's decidedly unsafe. And it's deliberately uncomfortable viewing. "Kill the Moon" confronts an awful moral and ethical dilemma and takes the magic man who makes everything all right out of the picture to settle that dilemma. And it doesn't settle the matter to the satisfaction of many of the audience — myself included.

It's meant to anger you, frustrate you, bewilder you. Even alienate you.

Case in point: the final scene with the Doctor and Clara. When the Doctor says, "I had faith that you would always make the right choice," Clara replies, "Honestly, do you have music playing in your head when you say rubbish like that?" The actual answer is no he doesn't — but the viewer heard music when Matt Smith or David Tennant made similar heroic speeches. Within the context of the drama, the Doctor is motivated by letting humanity determine their own fate. The Doctor genuinely believes he's respecting Clara and humanity. (And had the Doctor been the emo boyfriend and not the grumpy jerk, maybe things would have played out differently.)

And yet Clara is also right. The Doctor has faced other moments in history where humans have to decide their fate, and he has intervened willy-nilly. He spends enough time with humans, he could help. She rightfully calls him on his arrogance, saying, "Don't lump me in with the rest of all the little humans that you think are so tiny and silly and predictable." Which is actually pretty arrogant on her part.

The truth of the matter is both the Doctor and Clara are right and wrong to varying degrees here, and that's uncomfortable. But at the same time . . . you know when drama is great? When you connect with what motivates disparate characters and you have sympathy for many sides of an argument.

It's not satisfying. It's messy as hell. But so is life. And that's why I love "Kill the Moon."

# 8.08 Mummy on the Orient Express

**Written by** Jamie Mathieson **Directed by** Paul Wilmshurst

**Original airdate** October 11, 2014

**The Big Idea** There's murder most foul on the Orient Express . . . only the Orient Express is in space and the murderer is a mummy who kills its victim 66 seconds after it is seen.

**Roots and References** Agatha Christie's 1934 novel *Murder on the Orient Express* (the title, the setting and the passengers; the Doctor also plays the Poirot role, a little); the films based on *The Mummy* since its 1932 debut (the Foretold); the 1968 film version of *2001: A Space Odyssey* (Gus the murderous computer is the literary progeny of the HAL 9000); *Red Dwarf* (the extra passengers are "hard-light holograms"). The mystery shopper is a consumer-protection practice that dates back to the 1940s. The Queen song "Don't Stop Me Now" is sung on the train by the singer Foxes.

**Adventures in Time and Space** The Doctor mentions that Gus had been tempting him to ride the Orient Express for a while — something seen onscreen back in 2010's "The Big Bang" (then it was an "Egyptian God" on board, which sort of tracks with this story). The Doctor offers Hargreaves a jelly baby, a sweet favoured by the fourth Doctor in particular, in an elegant cigarette case. The Doctor asks the Foretold, "Are you my mummy?" riffing off the catchphrase in 2005's "The Empty Child"/"The Doctor Dances." It's been more than a month since the events of "Kill the Moon."

**Who Is the Doctor?** This story marks a notable shift in the Doctor's attitude. He seems callous about the Foretold's victims, even harsh about putting Maisie in jeopardy. However, by the end he is vulnerable enough to tell Clara the horrible position he always finds himself in and that, if he had to, he would have sacrificed everything to stop the Foretold. He also candidly admits to Clara he does find his jeopardy-prone lifestyle addictive. Perhaps it's no surprise Perkins turns down the opportunity to travel with the Doctor because he notes, "That job could change a man." The Doctor sadly agrees.

**The Doctor and Clara** Clara is at first still dealing with her unresolved anger towards the Doctor, but, by the end, the Doctor's admission that he had no idea if saving Maisie would work forces Clara to recognize that her life adventuring with the Doctor is an addiction and she enjoys it — so much so that she lies to Danny about calling it quits with the Doctor and chooses to continue travelling.

**Monster of the Week** The Foretold is an ancient creature, wrapped in bandages, that looks like an Egyptian mummy. Only it's a weapon used on a long-forgotten battlefield that can't be seen by its victim until exactly 66 seconds before it kills them.

**Stand Up and Cheer** Clara says to the Doctor, "So you were pretending to be heartless." And there's a slight pause before the Doctor replies, "Would you like to think that about me? Would that make it easier?" and he says it like he wishes Clara *could* think that about him, before letting Clara in and telling her about the awful series of choices he has had to make. It's a scene where Clara finally forgives the Doctor. Perhaps the same is true for many viewers as well.

**Roll Your Eyes** British pop sensation Foxes' appearance was a much-hyped event leading up to broadcast, but it was just a glorified cameo singing a subpar remake of "Don't Stop Me Now."

**You're Not Making Any Sense** The Doctor had nearly passed out from asphyxiation before the scene cuts away to the ship exploding. How did he manage to get to the TARDIS — around which Gus had placed security — and use it to rescue the other passengers? Perhaps he wasn't joking with Clara and actually let them suffocate.

**Interesting Trivia** Jamie Mathieson was commissioned to write this story on the strength of his work on "Flatline," which he wrote first but was transmitted after this. Steven Moffat was so impressed by Mathieson's work that he gave him "Mummy on the Orient Express," which was originally to have been written (with the basic premise) by someone else but fell through due to scheduling conflicts. The writer has never been identified, but, given the fact he had been involved in every season except this one, Toby Whithouse remains the prime suspect.

In Britain since 2005, *Doctor Who* has tended to air in a "teatime" slot that ranges between 5:30 p.m. and 7:30 p.m. on Saturday nights (television in the U.K., unlike in North America, has great success with family viewing on weekends and starts prime programming far earlier). As family viewing, the teatime slot has been a key part of *Doctor Who*'s DNA since it began. "Mummy on the Orient Express," however, had the latest start time of any *Doctor Who* story ever, at 8:30 p.m. — which meant the show ended for the first time after the 9 p.m. "watershed" for more adult programming. Part of the problem was that the series was now going out in the autumn after seven seasons of airing primarily during spring. Scheduling obstacles with sports and the BBC ratings behemoth *Strictly Come Dancing* meant *Doctor Who* was shown much later. This was to the detriment of the series' overnight ratings, which, while still popular, were declining somewhat. All this would have a hand in the series' move to Sunday nights in 2018.

**The TARDIS Chronometer** On the space-faring replica of the Orient Express, somewhere in space (near the Magellan Black Hole), sometime in the future.

The Doctor and Clara's conversation at the end takes place on the nearby civilized planet, while we also briefly see Danny in the present.

**Don't Be Stupid? (GB)** Up until now, the twelfth Doctor has been a paradox: an unpleasant anti-hero who is hard to like or understand but played by an actor so good he's impossible to ignore. This story finally, beautifully, shows us the Doctor's actual vulnerability.

Thank the universe.

And the actual revelation is earned. At first, the Doctor is showing this incarnation's inability to process emotional cues as he tries to talk about the stars while Clara pours out her heart about how hard it is to forgive him. Then the monster and the terror happens, and it turns out the Doctor knew this was coming. And then the Doctor asks Clara to betray Maisie by giving her false hope, and we're back with the asshole Doctor again.

But I would argue that something shifts subtly within the Doctor with every death caused by the Foretold that the Doctor witnesses first-hand. The Doctor is openly bewildered that Professor Moorhouse would abandon giving the Doctor his precious information about the Foretold to beg for his life; he is rebuked by Moorhouse, who says, "This is my life, my death. I'm going to fight for it how I want."

But it's Captain Quell's death that really seems to change the Doctor. Because Quell dies as the Doctor wants — giving the Doctor his vital data — and then actually thanks him for the experience. (And he's an ex-soldier, no less.) There's a brief glance Peter Capaldi gives at the moment when Quell thanks the Doctor that's utterly haunting.

After Quell's death, something changes in the Doctor not only in this story, I would argue, but in the twelfth Doctor's personal story as well. The Doctor stops using people for emotionless data collection and finds a way to put himself in the line of fire. (You'll note that he starts talking about the possibility of doing so only after Quell dies.) As he later admits, he might have had to keep sacrificing people if his gambit with Maisie failed, but one thing is for certain: he was going to face down the monster himself and not analyze it either.

All this is why the Doctor's moment of vulnerability is so precious and so earned. It's because he's seen what results from being callous — and it turns out he's not a person who wants to be thanked by someone for giving them their death. To top it off, he expresses his most basic fear: that Clara will reject him if he admits the truth. And then he tells her the horrible burden that being the Doctor can be.

And if that's all "Mummy on the Orient Express" was, I would be overjoyed. But it's not.

Because "Mummy on the Orient Express" isn't solely about the burden of being the Doctor; it's about the burden of being Clara, as the Doctor's confession forces Clara to recognize that she's addicted to the thrill of travelling. It's about the burden of being Quell, who has become a cowardly shell of himself because of PTSD; he only becomes truly alive again in the moments before his death. It's about the burden of being Maisie — abused by an overbearing mother figure — and it's about the burden of being the Foretold, forced to kill again and again, waiting for someone to say, "We surrender." Almost everyone in this story has demons of their own that drive them towards or away from things. (The one exception is Perkins, who seems to have been burdened with working with the Doctor; no wonder he turns down the opportunity to travel with him.) In creating an hour this thematically rich, Jamie Mathieson has established himself as a writer to watch.

There's so much more I could say about "Mummy on the Orient Express." It's a brilliantly constructed thriller: the pre-credits sequence establishes the premise of the monster perfectly, and, yes, the sequences with the Foretold are scary AF, as the kids say. The countdown clock is a brilliant touch. The reveal that the whole train ride was a sham to get people on board to investigate the Foretold was a twist worthy of Agatha Christie.

But I'm always going to remember it for the Doctor standing on the beach saying, "Would you like to think that about me?" Because that's the scene where the Doctor became the Doctor again.

**Second Opinion (RS?)** Unlike my co-author, I'm a massive spoilerphobe. My view is that you get only one chance to view the episode for the first time, so I'd like that to be as pure an experience as possible. I don't even watch the "next time" preview; I don't need to watch a preview to know I'll be tuning in the following week.

But how far does this extend? My co-author and I have had many friendly arguments over the years about whether story titles count as spoilers. Mostly these involve Graeme spluttering in apoplexy at the very idea, but I remain resolute. So much so, that I have a sneaking suspicion that the (brilliant!) comedy sequence "Spoiler Cops!" that he created for his *Reality Bomb* podcast was pretty much based entirely on my recalcitrance on this issue.

It's no picnic avoiding the titles of episodes, let me tell you. I have to dance very carefully around social media. I've successfully trained my co-author to discuss upcoming tidbits in only the broadest of terms, and even then using code words. (This can make planning these books challenging.) But sometimes it's all entirely worth it.

With this episode, I was proved gloriously, incandescently right! (In my own mind, at any rate.) Watching the opening, I had no idea that there was a mummy, no idea that the train was the Orient Express and no idea that it was in space. You simply can't imagine the effect of the teaser on a viewer like me, who was whooping in delight in the first few minutes — and pretty much never stopped all episode long.

There's much to admire about this episode, as Graeme aptly illustrates. Watching the "next time" preview retroactively, I was pretty appalled at how much it gave away. Happily, there's so much more than just the hook to this story. But, as much as I love it, the version of the episode I watch now is not — and cannot be — the same version I watched for the first time, completely unaware of how smacked upside the head I was going to be. That's an amazing feeling — and one I can't wait to experience next episode, with a story that Graeme has assured me will be a tour de force for Jodie Whittaker when she stars in "The Noun of Noun."

## 8.09 Flatline

**Written by** Jamie Mathieson **Directed by** Douglas Mackinnon
**Original airdate** October 18, 2014

**The Big Idea** The Doctor is trapped in a TARDIS that has shrunk to a foot tall, leaving Clara to solve the problem when a community service crew is terrorized by two-dimensional beings that can literally flatten anything.

**Roots and References** The works of Banksy (the tunnel "mural," Rigsy's name and interest in graffiti art); the 1884 Edward Newton Abbot novel *Flatland* and the *Star Trek: The Next Generation* episode "The Loss" (communicating with two-dimensional beings); the Scissormen from Grant Morrison and Richard Case's 1989 DC Comic *The Doom Patrol* (making people two-dimensional). Clara mentions *The Addams Family* (specifically the 1991 film), and the Doctor obliges by using his hand to move the TARDIS like Thing in that movie. The Doctor's final line, "Goodness had nothing to do with it," is a quote from Mae West's character in the 1932 film *Night After Night*.

**Adventures in Time and Space** The Doctor returns to using "pudding brains" as his favourite insult ("Deep Breath" and elsewhere this season). The TARDIS door-opening sound effect from the 1980s is used when the Doctor opens the doors from the console.

**The Heaven Effect** At the episode's conclusion, Missy watches the Doctor and Clara on a tablet and says, of Clara, "I *have* chosen well."

**Who Is the Doctor?** Trapped inside the TARDIS, the Doctor is forced to cede his role to Clara, who acts as a substitute Doctor. This offers him an opportunity to understand how he seems to others, as Clara reflects back his cynicism, his lateral thinking and his lies. When the TARDIS is restored, the Doctor assumes his role as the defender against monsters and banishes the Boneless from this dimension.

**The Doctor and Clara** While playing substitute Doctor, Clara takes the opportunity to mock the Doctor, saying of his academic credentials, "Well, I'm usually quite vague about that. I think I just picked the title because it makes me sound important." The Doctor, for his part, is appalled when he discovers that Clara has been lying to Danny about her travels with him. When the Doctor thinks he's dying, he admits that Clara made a "mighty fine" Doctor, though he's more reluctant to concede this once he survives.

**Monster of the Week** The Boneless are two-dimensional creatures from outside this universe, who have the ability to flatten objects or people into two dimensions and then take their form. In spite of the Doctor and Clara's attempts to communicate, their intentions appear to be hostile.

**Stand Up and Cheer** The scene with Clara and Rigsy trapped in the rapidly flattening apartment is thrilling, visually striking — the outline of PC Forrest's nervous system on the wall is visceral and yet entirely gore-free, while the door handle and couch flattening are great images — and, best of all, funny, as Clara has to maintain a casual conversation with Danny throughout it all.

**Roll Your Eyes** The Doctor is on his way to a real corker of a speech after defeating his enemies . . . and then he names them "the Boneless" before banishing them. Um, really? You can't just save the day? You now need to dramatically name your enemies? Apparently, this was meant to be the culmination of a running gag where the Doctor tries to come up with the name for the creatures. Even so, "And I name you 'the Boneless'" is a bit much from the man who thought a deflattener should be called a "2Dis." Doctor, stick with speeches from now on.

**You're Not Making Any Sense** Rigsy must be a phenomenally good artist if he can come up with a realistic-looking painting of a door in a matter of minutes.

**Interesting Trivia** While the double-banked, Doctor-lite stories of old like "Blink" were mostly gone by 2014, production needs still placed limits on Peter Capaldi's availability, leaving the Doctor stranded in the TARDIS and only appearing in two short scenes on location. Thus Jenna Coleman carried the bulk of the episode, complete with her own temporary companion in Rigsy.

The Doctor claims that the TARDIS is always lighter because if it landed with its true weight, it would crack the surface of the Earth. Leaving aside the fact that the Doctor is conflating "weight" (the amount of gravity exerted on an object) and "mass" (the amount of matter an object has), this is something the series mythology has not been entirely consistent about. In 1981's "Full

Circle," Romana says the TARDIS would be "5×10⁶ kilos" (5,000,000 kilograms, or 5,000 metric tons) in the local gravity. (Then again, a band of Marshmen were able to pick it up ten minutes later.) In 1982's "Castrovalva," the Doctor says a quarter of the TARDIS's architecture would create about 17,000 tonnes of thrust, so presumably the TARDIS is 68,000 tonnes. Again, mass and weight are not the same, but, either way, while the TARDIS shouldn't crack the planet with its true weight (or mass), it's clearly heavier inside than out.

Writer Jamie Mathieson had pitched to Steven Moffat before, but Moffat balked at his previous idea because it was too conceptual and there was no monster. When Mathieson returned to pitch, he came armed with four ideas, complete with illustrations of a monster. "Flatline" and the Boneless landed with Moffat, who enthused about how kids would be afraid of the drawings on walls coming to life.

**The TARDIS Chronometer** Bristol, the present day.

**Don't Be Stupid? (GB)** This book is being written as the BBC is broadcasting the adventures of a female Doctor. During Series Eight and succeeding seasons, we will see a number of steps taken to establish that as a possibility in *Doctor Who*.

However, in many respects, "Flatline" was the first move to a woman as the Doctor. Because, for one night only, Jenna Coleman played the Doctor. And boy does she do it well.

Okay, the Doctor in this story wasn't the Doctor; it was Clara *emulating* the Doctor. And she really played the part to the hilt: she's funny, quirky, whip-smart and very good at running from danger. She inspires others, shuts up her critics and stops a horrific threat by turning their power against them through a clever trap and witty quips. Kind of like the hero we used to have fronting the program before production fiat made him miserable and unlikeable.

In fairness, the actual Doctor does get some great moments to shine, and I love watching Peter Capaldi parading around the TARDIS set. The little triumphant shuffle he does after he moves the TARDIS off the train tracks is frankly adorable. And his insistence on naming everything is the ultimate in dad humour. It's a shame he also talks about how giving hope can help them run faster and all that. But he does compliment Rigsy at the end, briefly. He's learning.

"Flatline" is a great pilot to test out a female Doctor. The Boneless make a brilliant monster, and part of the fun is watching the Doctor and Clara first figure out that the paintings aren't paintings and then, later, that the people aren't people. Mostly though, "Flatline" is a giant chase sequence, with Clara trying to save everyone from the looming threat as the stakes get higher and higher, and, ultimately, it's her playing the Doctor without support from the real thing. The cast of characters alongside Clara are a lot of fun, from her pseudo-companion Rigsy to Fenton (a man so unimaginative the psychic paper doesn't work on him!) to the train driver who is too nice for words.

But "Flatline" doesn't skimp on thrilling set pieces for our Doctor-for-a-day. The scene where Clara tries to get her and Rigsy out of Roscoe's rapidly flattening apartment is genuinely exciting (adding a phone call with Danny — who is nerdily excited at the prospect of sitting at a particular park bench — is a brilliant touch), as is the moment the Boneless graduate to 3-D and a giant hand grabs Al, carrying him bodily down the tunnel. Clara is pretty amazing throughout, especially her speech lamenting Rigsy's attempted sacrifice and how it could have been prevented by her favourite hairband, which is pretty funny, charming and a little inspiring.

In the end, Clara tosses the sonic screwdriver back to the Doctor, who assumes the part with a rousing speech. But, for just one episode, you got to see a woman play the Doctor with charm, humour, intelligence and a good deal of twinkle.

How about Jenna Coleman as the Doctor for real in 2023? I think she'd be brilliant doing it as a full-time job.

**Second Opinion (RS?)** Jenna Coleman as the next Doctor? That's genius! Wow.

Clara as the Doctor really works, not just for Jenna Coleman's stunning performance but also for a fundamental examination of what the Doctor's role actually is. She's equipped with a superior tool, a sharp mind and access to more knowledge than anyone else around her. That's it. That's all it takes to be the Doctor. She almost scares off Rigsy by talking in non-sequiturs but then gains his trust by showing him something spectacular (the tiny Doctor in the tiny TARDIS) and saves the day by turning her enemies' power against them (the painting of the door is brilliant, even if we really should question why the Boneless can't turn a work of art into a 3-D object). When interrogated about who she is, Clara's response is pure Doctor: "I'm the one chance you've got of staying alive, that's who I am."

All that's well and good. But while Clara's attempt to emulate the Doctor is fantastic, unfortunately the script fares less well in its attempt to emulate *Doctor Who*. For me, this falls apart entirely because of the insistence of making the Boneless yet another evil invading race of alienzzzz . . . Oh, sorry, I nodded off there.

It's a shame, because the set-up is so good. The very first thing that happens after the credits is the Doctor marvelling at not knowing something (in this case, about the shrunken TARDIS). Everything that proceeds from this point is about Clara and the Doctor learning, as they piece together disparate clues in order to deduce what's happening. That's excellent.

Having an alien race inadvertently dissecting people to understand or communicate with them is a great idea, and the moral dilemma is given some decent weight for the first two-thirds. But, by the end, it's all so pat. How much better would it have been to have the Boneless not actually be evil, as the Doctor postulates? Instead, the episode is forced to come down on the side of the unlikeable Fenton, who dismisses every attempt to understand or learn — and turns out to be right, sadly.

It's deeply unfortunate that an episode so interested in examining what fundamentally makes the Doctor tick has to fall back on a tired *Who* cliché. And it's frustrating as all get-out, because it could so easily have been so much better. Had they simply reversed the outcome at the end, we would have had a bona fide classic on our hands, one that showed us the value of learning and thoughtfulness over simply assuming the worst. Sadly, the end result turns out to be something we could have guessed all along. Aliens are bad, and the Doctor (or Clara) has to stop them while restoring the TARDIZZZ . . . Sorry, did I doze off again?

## 8.10 In the Forest of the Night

**Written by** Frank Cottrell-Boyce **Directed by** Sheree Folkson
**Original airdate** October 25, 2014

**The Big Idea** Overnight, Earth has been covered in a forest, and solar flares are about to destroy everything.

**Roots and References** Ursula K. Le Guin's *The Word for World Is Forest* (a planet covered in trees); *12 Monkeys* (zoo animals being released in the midst of a global catastrophe). Danny and the class sing the hiking song "Everywhere We Go" by Dave Benson Phillips. The title of the story derives from William Blake's 1794 poem "The Tyger."

**Adventures in Time and Space** The Doctor uses Clara's description of him ("I walk your Earth; I breathe your air") from "Kill the Moon." He references the solar flare that destroyed the bank of Karabraxos ("Time Heist").

**The Heaven Effect** Missy watches the solar fire on a monitor from an office in the Nethersphere and comments on how surprising the outcome is — presumably because she was expecting a great many people in Heaven who have now failed to appear.

**Who Is the Doctor?** He describes himself as masculine, although he trips over the word slightly. He claims that Earth is his world, as well as humans', a reversal not only from "Kill the Moon" but from most of the series' history. When he has his breakthrough about the trees, he calls himself "Doctor Idiot" (stay tuned for more on that). He's never seen *Les Misérables*.

**The Doctor and Clara** She manipulates the Doctor into returning to the TARDIS under the pretext of saving the children, but she's doing so only to save him. She refuses to join him, preferring to die with the rest of the planet, because she doesn't want to be the last of her kind, like he is.

**Monster of the Week** Intelligent trees cover the Earth and can withhold oxygen to avoid fire or inflate the atmosphere with excess amounts that can burn off solar flares. Despite initial assumptions, they're not actually monsters (nor are they aliens).

**Stand Up and Cheer** The pull-back in the teaser showing Trafalgar Square and then all of London covered in trees is just gorgeous. It's a stunning visual image, saying so much without uttering a word.

**Roll Your Eyes** Our eyes rolled back pretty far when the Doctor decided to call everyone on Earth. They rolled back even further when he decided that a 12-year-old girl should be the one to make the call. They were facing the inside of our skulls when he delayed saving the trees for some considerable time so that a bunch of children could plan a message. By the time the Earth was saved, on account of governments of the world listening to a Year Eight schoolgirl telling them not to do something, our eyes had completed their rotation and were facing forward again.

**You're Not Making Any Sense** Mental illness is serious. It can rob people of their lives, their family, their dignity. It's been stigmatized for centuries or ignored or underappreciated. That Maebh's mental illness turns out to be some form of psychic sensitivity and she shouldn't be medicating herself is not only lazy but an irresponsible choice, particularly in a program watched by children who may face mental health difficulties themselves. Clara isn't the only person who is responsible for children who isn't bothering; *Doctor Who*'s makers aren't either.

**Interesting Trivia** The Doctor mentions Tunguska and Curuçá as examples of previous times the trees have saved us from fireballs. The former was a meteor impact in the Tunguska province of Russia on June 30, 1908, which exploded in the air, rather than hitting the ground; despite the lack of a crater, it remains the largest impact event in recorded history. The latter refers to the Curuçá River event of August 13, 1930, in Brazil, when a Franciscan monk catalogued a meteoric air burst in the region after talking to witnesses, although the event wasn't widely known until the mid-1990s. Subsequent investigation discovered a potential meteorite impact crater in the area.

It's visible only for a brief second, but one of the red London buses has an ad on the side that might look familiar: it's for the TV show *Doctor Who*, featuring

Peter Capaldi, Jenna Coleman and the TARDIS! Capaldi's face is hidden behind a tree, but Jenna Coleman is quite visible. Some of the children are looking right at it, although oddly don't comment on their teacher being in a bus ad . . . This isn't a production error, because real buses weren't used; due to difficulties manoeuvring them through the forest, all the buses seen in the background were cardboard cut-outs. The crew clearly decided to hide an easter egg for the fans. What's interesting is that it had slightly more exposure than was intended, since it also appeared in the "Next Time" trailer shown at the end of the previous episode.

The Doctor tells Clara that humanity will forget about the day the trees came and went. You mean the trees that toppled over Nelson's Column in Trafalgar Square . . . a global landmark?

**The TARDIS Chronometer** London, 2016. Despite being made in 2014, the "present" of *Doctor Who* has been running a couple of years ahead, so this is consistent with other "present day" stories of recent years.

**Don't Be Stupid? (RS?)**

1. Wow, this is gorgeous! The visuals are stunning, the mystery is sublime, and the reveal of Trafalgar Square is done with incredible style. The Doctor effectively taking on a small child as a companion is masterful: her no-nonsense style contrasts magnificently with his, and the joke about her needing an "appointment" to see the Doctor — which is beautifully juxtaposed by her mentioning that something is chasing her — pays off beautifully with a subtle nod from Peter Capaldi. Best. Episode. Ever!

2. Neat. The museum is a cool visual with some great props, and the kids are realistic but not overly annoying. The screens showing the TV reports from around the world are fun, harkening back to the Russell T Davies era without feeling derivative.

3. The Doctor and Clara's banter is passable, but segueing into Danny's suspicion about Clara's behaviour works really well. Their relationship is a bit spiky though, as apparently the only way to deal with accusations ("You were with *him*!") is with counter-accusations ("You lost a *child*!").

4. Clara's right: Danny being fiercely protective of the kids is very attractive. The navigator joke is so-so.

5. Maebh countering the Doctor's comments about communication only being through technology is a nice reversal of expectations. But Maebh's mum probably wasn't put on this Earth to do comedy.

6. It's very important to get in some good nut-allergy jokes. That'll have them rolling in the aisles at the gluten-free society, you mark my words.

7. The flashbacks to problem children in the classroom are okay. The fact that Clara and Danny are both inadvertently shown to be terrible teachers is less okay. Clara pays no particular attention to bullying in her classroom, while Danny fails to change nouns when a student doesn't understand his question, merely repeating the same thing in exactly the way that no decent teacher would.

8. The discussion about the forces of time affecting the trees would probably be better if anyone followed this up in any way whatsoever. But the single ring in the new trees is a neat touch.

9. The Doctor not being able to tell the children apart is a cool idea, ruined by the fact that one of the children would likely just answer him, rather than wordlessly waiting for him to stare weirdly into every face, one at a time.

10. Nelson's Column looks pretty fake when it falls.

11. The Doctor describing himself as masculine is just odd.

12. Most of this episode is just a holding pattern, isn't it?

13. Maebh waving her hands in the air is dumb. But the menace of escaped wolves is a nice escalation.

14. Can a little girl really outrun a pack of wolves? A pack that was about a metre away from her when she started running? A pack that chases her for several minutes? Rather than, you know, devouring her in the first second? And don't even get me started about the method of dealing with a tiger . . .

15. Once the wolves run off in one direction and the tiger in another, nobody is particularly worried for any residents of London who might be eaten? Okay.

16. The talking tree tries its best to explain the plot. It fails.

17. For no clearly explained reason, Clara decides it would be best if everyone she knows and loves, including small children, burns to death. Rather than take the safe option that's right in front of them, it's far better for her to dictate that small children should die in screaming pain because otherwise they might miss their parents. When are the teacher-of-the-year awards given out, again?

18. So the world is going to be saved by 12-year-old children who ring everyone on Earth and tell them what to do, and they will then do it? Uh-huh.

19. Danny tells Clara he only wants to know the truth and doesn't care what it is, but his past actions have clearly demonstrated that this is not the case. So he's basically boxed her into an impossible choice: tell

the truth and be punished, or lie and be punished. This is a desirable boyfriend *how* exactly?

20. Annabel returns home because Maebh asked her to on the world-wide phone call — and apparently climbed inside a thicket of trees once she got there, presumably because it was comfy or something. Nobody else was suddenly trapped inside trees, so why is Annabel? And, more importantly, why are we ending on a subplot that had no dramatic pizzazz whatsoever and was barely even acknowledged? Worst. Episode. Ever!

**Second Opinion (GB)** It starts out so well. The pre-credits sequence is brilliant, and not just for the reveal of seeing London covered in forest. Maebh finding the Doctor in the TARDIS and the subsequent tour of the TARDIS is funny, charming and delightful (Capaldi is wonderful, channelling Peter Cushing from the 1960s *Doctor Who* films), and it's one of the best directed scenes in a season full of great direction.

At first, I found it hard to find fault in quite so much. Even though there are all the gaps of logic my co-author correctly lists above, I still love the beauty of it; it's a story that's full of gorgeous, lyrical imagery: the scene of the kids marching to "Everywhere We Go" while the Doctor contemplates Earth's imminent destruction is disturbingly haunting.

But I think this favouring imagery over logic points to the problem with "In the Forest of the Night."

There was a behind-the-scenes clip where writer Frank Cottrell-Boyce talked about his process for writing this episode: he showed the scrapbooks he assembled in preparation, which had collages of things about Tunguska and trees and global disasters, and it was intensely fascinating and detailed. I think he was so fascinated with the process of researching the story that he forgot to actually write the story.

Because gorgeous, lyrical imagery and a stunning cold open can take you only so far. And this episode has not a lot once the goodwill from that is expended. Clara is a *terrible* teacher: inept, selfish and more interested in adventuring and one-upping the Doctor than showing the duty of care she lectures the Doctor about. Danny isn't much better, but he's constrained by playing, alternately, Buzz Killington to the Doctor or Controlling Boyfriend to Clara. The kids are stock annoying children except Maebh, who is Too Precious for Words. No, here we have the Doctor basically stigmatizing mental health treatment. Way to go, people.

And the climax is even stupider than Robert describes it. It's an embarrassment to drama.

I remain quite mystified by "In the Forest of the Night." Frank Cottrell-Boyce is an amazing writer of children's fiction, and his film *24 Hour Party People* is a triumph of British cinema. But this is what happens when you admire your research a little too much.

## 8.11–8.12 Dark Water / Death in Heaven

**Written by** Steven Moffat **Directed by** Rachel Talalay

**Original airdates** November 1 and 8, 2014

**The Big Idea** A tragic accident leads Clara and the Doctor on a quest to the afterlife, where they discover Missy's ultimate plan to harvest the dead as Cybermen.

**Roots and References** The 1964 film version of *Mary Poppins* (Missy descending to the ground, holding an umbrella); 1984's *Return of the Living Dead* (a storm raining on a cemetery causing the dead to rise from their graves); *The Thick of It* (the Doctor's sweary psychic paper is a nod to Peter Capaldi's character Malcolm Tucker from that show); the 1968 *Doctor Who* story "The Invasion" (the Cybermen descending the steps near St. Paul's Cathedral is a direct visual reference to that story, hence why we're including it here); the 1991 film adaptation of *The Silence of the Lambs* (Missy in restraints); Marvel Comics' *Iron Man* (the Cybermen's new jet boots); recent war films such as 2008's *The Hurt Locker* (the scenes from Danny's past as a soldier); the Nethersphere is a Dyson Sphere, a concept which began with Olaf Stapledon's 1937 science-fiction novel, *Star Maker*. Steve Jobs's death three years previous is mentioned by Seb, while the Doctor, Osgood and Colonel Ahmed debate whether Cloud Base is in *Thunderbirds* or *Captain Scarlet and the Mysterons* (the latter actually; the Doctor namedrops Sylvia Anderson for good measure). Clara's birthday is the same as *Doctor Who*'s: November 23. Missy sings "Happy Birthday, Mr. President," like Marilyn Monroe did to John F. Kennedy in 1962 and sings a parody of Toni Basil's 1981 single "Hey Mickey." A TARDIS key is hidden in a copy of Audrey Niffenegger's 2003 novel *The Time Traveler's Wife*. (Niffenegger and Steven Moffat have been making references to the other in their work since 2006's "The Girl in the Fireplace"; Moffat is now working on a television adaptation of her novel.)

**Adventures in Time and Space** Clara's bookshelf is littered with Post-it notes with references to elements of every story this season. Clara's gran returns after last being seen in "The Time of the Doctor." The sleep and dream patches were first seen in 2007's "Gridlock." Clara is once again hooked up to the telepathic circuits like she was in "Listen." The Cloister Bell (first heard in 1981's

"Logopolis") is tolling the doom of the TARDIS as Clara destroys the TARDIS keys in her trance. The Nethersphere is actually a Matrix data slice, referring to the Matrix (or Amplified Panatropic Computer Network, as it's more properly known) on Gallifrey, which collected the minds of dead Time Lords in 1976's "The Deadly Assassin." Missy refers back to the Doctor's last tangle with her when she was the Master in 2010's "Last of the Time Lords."

UNIT shows up, with Kate Stewart and Osgood. Kate is carrying the head of a Cyberman from (judging by the design) 1968's "The Invasion." Osgood now sports a bowtie, emulating the eleventh Doctor in "The Day of the Doctor." Osgood points out that UNIT has files on all former British prime ministers, referring to the Master's stint as PM in 2007's "The Sound of Drums"/"Last of the Time Lords," and the Doctor mentions the UNIT skybase *The Valiant* from that same story. A painting of Brigadier Lethbridge-Stewart (using a photo from 1989's "Battlefield" as a reference) is on the UNIT plane, and it's heavily implied, though never said, that Kate is saved and Missy is dispatched by a cyberized version of the Brigadier. (The Doctor even salutes him!)

The emotional inhibitor in the Cybermen's chest plate was first established in 2006's "Rise of the Cybermen"/"The Age of Steel." Missy gives the coordinates for Gallifrey first used in 1975's "Pyramids of Mars." There are flashbacks to "Into the Dalek," "The Caretaker" and "Robot of Sherwood."

While pretending to be the Doctor, Clara claims many things about him. The ones that can be verified are that Gallifrey is in the constellation of Kasterborous ("Pyramids of Mars"), the Doctor is in the Prydonian chapter of the Time Lords and the TARDIS is a type 40 ("The Deadly Assassin"), his medical doctorate is from Glasgow (1967's "The Moonbase") and the Doctor has a non-Gallifreyan daughter (2008's "The Doctor's Daughter").

Oh, and the woman in the shop who gave Clara the Doctor's phone number in "The Bells of Saint John" and who helped Clara and the Doctor find each other in "Deep Breath"? Turns out it was Missy.

**The Heaven Effect** Missy, the latest incarnation of the Master, has been absorbing the minds of the recently dead (and travelling across time and space to do it) and putting them on a Gallifreyan Matrix data slice. The hosts remain connected to their bodies, but they are enticed to edit out their emotions so they can be beamed back into their bodies and remade as Cybermen. Missy is doing this to give the Doctor an army.

**Who Is the Doctor?** The Doctor rejects Clara's claim that he interferes with history all the time, saying, "I know when I can; I know when I can't." Which must prove awkward for him, because it turns out that the people of Earth have decided that, when the planet is under global extraterrestrial threat, the Doctor becomes emergency president of Earth. The Doctor is insistent that Cyberized Danny keep his emotions — even though Danny is in agony — saying, "Pain is a gift." Danny, however, calls out the Doctor on his hypocrisy in having Clara turn off Danny's emotional inhibitor. Missy tempts the Doctor with an army to aid the Doctor in wiping out injustice around the universe; however, this only causes the Doctor to reflect on events of the past season and conclude that he is an idiot with a box and a screwdriver. At the end, we learn why this incarnation is not a hugger, when he says, "Never trust a hug. It's just a way to hide your face."

**The Doctor and Clara** Clara's grief over the loss of Danny drives her to force the Doctor to reverse Danny's death, threatening to destroy all the TARDIS keys if he doesn't help. Turns out she's actually in a suggestible trance, but it lays bare her betrayal of the Doctor. And yet the Doctor forgives her and is even willing to see if he can find Danny after death. By this point, the Doctor and Clara have clearly forged some considerable degree of closeness: she knows exactly where the Doctor hides all of the TARDIS keys and knows enough about his past to pass herself off as him. Their relationship is put to the test when she wants to kill Missy; the Doctor knows how it will change her and agrees to do it himself instead (a Cyberman intervenes and shoots Missy before that happens). The Doctor and Clara lie to each other about their circumstances: Clara says Danny came back when he didn't, and the Doctor says Gallifrey was found when it wasn't. Clara insists on hugging the Doctor one last time before they part company.

**Monster of the Week** The Cyberiad Cybermen return, this time created by a nanite swarm that builds the Cyber-exoskeleton on the dead, with their emotionless consciousness beamed back into the host body from the Nethersphere. Oh, and the Master is back, only she's a woman now, and she calls herself Missy.

**Stand Up and Cheer** The whole "go to Hell" moment has no reason to work: it's a line purely based on the confusion between "go to Hell" as a statement and as a plan — and, as most plans don't involve going to Hell, it's a little too contrived. But . . . it works, mostly because Peter Capaldi says it as both admonition *and* destination and because his subsequent speech — "Do you think I care so little for you that betraying me would make a difference?" — is so perfect. And the awkward smile he gives when the Doctor says he'll try to get Danny back is utterly beautiful.

**Roll Your Eyes** So what was the point of 3W being in St. Paul's Cathedral, other than the fan service of recreating the sequence of Cybermen marching down the steps near it from 46 years earlier — something that only the hardcore cognoscenti of *Doctor Who* fans would notice anyway?

**You're Not Making Any Sense** Actually, what was the point of 3W at all? There's some handwaving about 3W funding Missy's work, but she's a Time Lord using

Gallifreyan technology, a TARDIS and the means to weaponize the dead and create Cybermen within human graves. Why the ridiculous cover, other than to stall the Cybermen's reveal and give us the cool walk down St. Paul's steps?

**Interesting Trivia** When the Cyberiad Cybermen were introduced in "Nightmare in Silver," it was implied they had a long history. One of the interesting ideas proposed by this story is . . . what if Missy invented them? By the future of "Nightmare in Silver," these Cybermen have become incredibly adaptable, they can build themselves around a host body and upload their consciousness as they did with the Doctor and his party in that story. What if this story is their origin, with a Time Lord poking around and figuring out how to make better Cybermen? This might also account for one of the unexplained elements of this year's story arc: all the varieties of robotic creatures searching for the "Promised Land." Perhaps Missy was using them (she clearly was able to transfer the consciousness of Half-Faced Man in "Deep Breath") to assist her in her upgrades to the Cybermen.

Missy as the female incarnation of the Master is an important step leading towards casting a woman as the Doctor (as is showing Clara's face in the title sequence). Naturally, at the time, it was done with tremendous secrecy, which was hard as Missy's reveal was recorded in a busy tourist location in London! Michelle Gomez only mouthed the words, and sound was added in an ADR session later. Phony dialogue was prepared to use on location with Missy revealing herself instead as the 1980s' Time Lady villain, the Rani.

At the time this episode was made, it was unknown if Jenna Coleman would continue with the series. It was thought at one point that Clara would depart in this story, though Coleman decided to stay on until the Christmas special, which was filmed as part of this season.

The Post-it notes on Clara's bookshelf mostly list plot elements of the past season ("Dinosaur in London," "Courtney on the Moon," "Miniature Clara"). But there are several Post-it notes that might be important. There's one that says "lying," another that says "truth" and one, which she picks up as she calls Danny, that says, "Just *say* it." However, the fact that this had the potential to be Jenna Coleman's exit casts an interesting light on the *two separate Post-it notes* that say "three months." Could it be just how long she's been travelling with the Doctor again — or is she pregnant with Danny Pink's child? Granted, she doesn't look very pregnant at the story's end a few weeks later (and there are double Post-its for "Impossible Girl" and "Robin Hood"), but it would explain how Orson Pink in "Listen" looked like Danny and had Danny's childhood toy. Of course, Jenna Coleman didn't depart the series with this episode, so even if that was a possibility, it couldn't have happened. Or did it . . . ?

**The TARDIS Chronometer** Locations around London, 2016.

**Don't Be Stupid? (GB)** Cleverness + emotions = *wow!*

This for me is the simplest distillation of the formula for this season of *Doctor Who*. It's not enough to have a brilliant puzzle. (Copies of Clara are scattered through the ages! The Doctor dies on Lake Silencio!) You must undergird that puzzle with emotions and character motivation.

I would argue that Moffat started trying this more vigorously in *Doctor Who* with "The Day of the Doctor." But Series Eight is the first time he really does it in the context of an ongoing season. He gives Clara a boyfriend (and an emotional life beyond the Doctor that harkens back to Russell T Davies's families for Rose and Donna more than it does to Amy and Rory). He gives the Doctor an inability to connect emotionally and an abundant insecurity about who he is and his place in the world. Both these characters' emotional arcs collide throughout the season.

This is a long preamble to explain why "Dark Water"/"Death in Heaven" is such an amazing *Doctor Who* story.

Cleverness + emotions = *wow!*

Up until now, the model of a Steven Moffat season finale was finally shoving the puzzle pieces together and having the Doctor overturn the table the puzzle was on. (The Pandorica is a trap . . . but the Doctor can beat it and fix the crack! And so on.) It's not devoid of emotions — indeed, the relationships are often central — but the thrill is bound in discovering, for example, that the Doctor is inside a Teselecta and isn't actually dead, rather than other concerns.

Here the story arc for the season is very different. The solution to the puzzle — how and why people are getting picked up after they die — is kind of mundane by Steven Moffat's standards. But what's important here is *how* the puzzle is being employed. Missy is motivated to defeat the Doctor, not by destroying him but by corrupting him. It's an approach that adds a new palette of colours to everything.

All this perfectly collides with Clara's part in the story. Pretty much everything in the first 20 minutes of "Dark Water" is heartbreaking but wonderful, as we see Clara go to terrible lengths to get Danny back (watch the frightening way Clara, after listlessly talking about how boring Danny's death was, suddenly fakes enthusiasm when the Doctor answers her call). Jenna Coleman and Peter Capaldi are electrifying as Clara tries to force the Doctor to save Danny, and the Doctor tells Clara what she means to him.

But let me talk about a few other things I love about "Dark Water"/"Death in Heaven." Because it's not just an angst fest. There are other emotions being explored, like being excited and thrilled. (Rachel Talalay is probably the best directorial hire the modern show has made.) Clara keeping herself alive by pretending to be the Doctor; the Doctor jumping out of a freaking plane and free-falling after the TARDIS; Missy breaking free and killing Osgood. Missy doing just about *anything*, really.

Michelle Gomez is incredible. I didn't think anyone could outdo John Simm for his sheer bonkers approach to the Master, but Gomez does it in her first scene — while Missy is pretending to be an android and secretly having a laugh at the Doctor and Clara's expense. She's hilarious, charming, weird and completely dangerous in every scene. I will confess I was always a smidge conservative when it came to a female Doctor, but it took a single scene with Missy to realize how wrong I was. I only mention the gender of the character to briefly make that point. By every accounting, for me, Michelle Gomez is as good a Master as the original, played by Roger Delgado. That's the highest praise an old-school fan can offer.

There are some elements that grate a little: 3W is a ridiculous waste of time. The St. Paul's setting is pointless. The Doctor berating Colonel Ahmed is just cruel. It spends maybe a tad too long in the cemetery.

But what it does right is spectacular. Especially that moment where the Doctor realizes who he is and what's important. I had mixed feelings rewatching this season about how sternly the Doctor was portrayed: I felt they made a terrible miscalculation. And it's more than a little dodgy to have the hero of a program watched by kids say, "Never trust a hug." But then Missy's plan comes together, and it cuts to the heart of the Doctor's insecurity this season — am I a good man? — which makes the final confrontation, and the Doctor's decision and declaration, so remarkable.

Danny's sacrifice is wonderful (sacrifices, actually: he gets Clara off the phone, he saves the Earth, and he gives up his route out of the Nethersphere to the boy). Danny has been a frustrating character — really decent, but a little too controlling, and his conflict with the Doctor made the viewer side against him, even when Danny was right — and it's a shame his fate was ultimately to be the character that makes Clara sad. (It's also frustrating given his is the first significant role for a person of colour since Martha Jones.) And yet Samuel Anderson makes us believe that love can conquer even a Cyberman.

"Dark Water"/"Death in Heaven" is one of the most satisfying season finales *Doctor Who* has ever had. The eighth season of *Doctor Who* was one of the biggest experiments of the Modern Series since it came back in 2005. Not all aspects of the experiment worked. But this one did, and it will be built upon in the coming seasons.

Cleverness + emotions = *wow!*

**Second Opinion (RS?)** Pretty much what he said. The only thing I want to add to this analysis is the ending, which gets a bit lost in light of what comes afterwards.

The changed plans that resulted in Clara returning mean the bite got taken out of what could have been the most daring final companion scene ever. Had this been the last Clara story, we'd have gone out not with some tragic death or heartbreaking separation but two characters lying to each other's faces.

This has been a fundamental part of Clara's arc this season. She's lied to Danny. She's lied to the Doctor. And here, finally, she lies to herself. She does it for the best of reasons — she cares deeply about the Doctor and wants him to be happy in what she thinks is a perfect ending for him, and she also wants to live the lie of being happy with a still-alive Danny — but nevertheless she lies.

Worse, it appears she's taught the Doctor a thing or two. Yes, Rule 1 is that the Doctor lies, but it was never like this. The Doctor usually lies to trick villains or withhold crucial plot information until the right time. We've never seen him do it for emotional reasons before. The sheer unbridled anger he expresses when he discovers Gallifrey is not where Missy said it would be (the result of another lie) is shocking. Almost as shocking as the calm he shows when talking about it with Clara in the café afterwards.

In an alternate universe, Clara's arc would have ended here, in about as perfect a way as possible for these two complicated characters. Two people who care deeply about each other lying to protect both their friend and themselves from emotional harm. And the final hug — where neither can see the other's face, but we can — is just perfect, rounding off a similar long arc for this Doctor.

I'm not sad that Clara ended up coming back. But if I said I thought that detracted from an otherwise perfect ending . . . I'd be lying.

## The Psychic Papers: Regeneration

It's a fundamental rule of the series: a Time Lord has 13 lives.

Of course, that rule was broken in the very story that introduced it, 1976's "The Deadly Assassin." There, the Master had burned through his regenerative cycle and was harnessing powers of the Time Lords to get himself a new one. But it's something the media always glommed onto when describing the character to a general audience, along with the idea that the Daleks couldn't climb stairs (something else debunked decades ago).

As the Doctor's regenerations hit the double digits, many *Doctor Who* fans lived in dread of the day of the thirteenth regeneration. It almost seemed as though, regardless of the show's popularity when it happened, *Doctor Who* would simply pack up and go home when the Time Lord hit the 13 lives limit — presumably fans would just move on to *Supernatural* or something else. (No other TV show has a fandom so resigned to ending their favourite series like this one!) It was therefore something of a shock when the number fast-forwarded not once but twice in 2013.

First, we learned of a regeneration we never knew about, in the form of the Warrior. Despite not calling himself the Doctor, the John Hurt incarnation nevertheless used up one of those precious 13 lives, cleverly sneaking into a gap that we'd all assumed didn't exist. We even got to see the regenerations onscreen, first in "Night of the Doctor" and then in "The Day of the Doctor," the Warrior forming part of an unbroken regenerative chain from William Hartnell through to Matt Smith.

Second, just as the eleventh Doctor's era was ending, we learned that he'd double-counted his tenth body. There's an onscreen regeneration in "The Stolen Earth"/"Journey's End" that everyone dismissed because it doesn't seem to happen, but in "Time of the Doctor," we learn that it had indeed happened and we'd miscounted. (Let's gloss over the same thing happening in "Let's Kill Hitler" when River gives him her regeneration energy.) Suddenly and shockingly, the Doctor's time was up.

There are two responses to this. One is to mourn the loss of what could have been a thrilling story arc, as a final Doctor spends their entire incarnation knowing that this was it. That ups the stakes, because this time if the Doctor dies, it's all over. Of course, we'd all know that there would be a fix by the end, but getting there would be fun. The other response is to breathe a sigh of relief that the writers chose *not* to dwell on it. By fast-forwarding the schedule and giving the Doctor a whole new set of regenerations, it negates any sense of the show coming to an end, even if that would ultimately be undone. One of the unique things about *Doctor Who* is that it has no beginning and no end, and it's best to keep it that way.

This does open up some confusion with regard to the numbering of the Doctors. It's fair enough that the Warrior didn't call himself by that name, so he doesn't count. But with the second David Tennant regeneration, does this mean Peter Capaldi is actually the thirteenth Doctor, in his fourteenth body? Actually, it may be even more complicated than that: if we consider "regeneration" to be the process that transforms one body into another and "incarnation" to be the form the Doctor has, then that pesky Tennant fake-out was a regeneration that didn't result in a new incarnation, so perhaps Capaldi is the thirteenth Doctor in his thirteenth body . . .

. . . but it's a lot easier if we try not to overthink this and just go with the situation we're given or else everything is going to get very confusing very quickly. So Peter Capaldi is the twelfth Doctor. He just is, okay?

However, the new regeneration cycle opens up a number of questions that even the Doctor doesn't seem to be able to answer. How many new bodies can he have? Nobody is sure. The Doctor in "Kill the Moon" doesn't know. That's probably for the best, because otherwise everyone would be stressing about the 502nd Doctor regenerating into hir final holographic body in the year 5177, and who needs that?

Playing with the ultimate number wasn't the only trick Steven Moffat had up his sleeve when it came to pushing the regeneration envelope. Until the reveal of Missy in the cliffhanger to "Dark Water," we'd never seen a gender-swapping regeneration before. (The Corsair is said to have done so in "The Doctor's Wife," but that takes place offscreen.) With the benefit of hindsight, there seems little doubt that having the Master regenerate into a woman was paving the way for the Doctor to do the same.

The Capaldi era didn't stop there, however. In "Hell Bent," we actually see a gender (and race) switch in front of our eyes when the General — someone we've seen in multiple stories by this point — regenerates. Amusingly, she notes that the old bald guy was the anomaly and that she's usually female. This was great for normalizing the idea for the viewer.

And so, by the time the Doctor regenerates into a woman, it's a well-established part of Time Lord lore. Because why wouldn't shapeshifting aliens who take on different accents, personalities, mannerisms and hairstyles not add gender and race into the mix? To which we can only say: aww, brilliant!

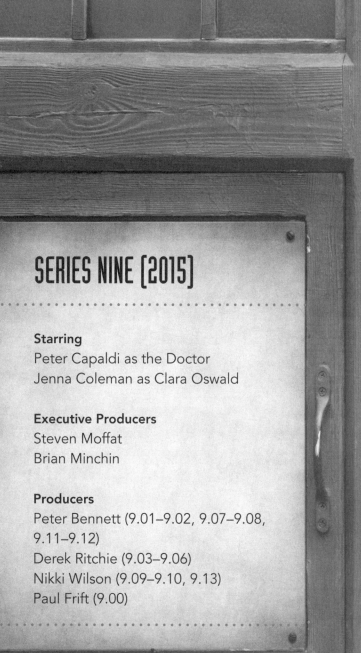

# SERIES NINE (2015)

**Starring**
Peter Capaldi as the Doctor
Jenna Coleman as Clara Oswald

**Executive Producers**
Steven Moffat
Brian Minchin

**Producers**
Peter Bennett (9.01–9.02, 9.07–9.08, 9.11–9.12)
Derek Ritchie (9.03–9.06)
Nikki Wilson (9.09–9.10, 9.13)
Paul Frift (9.00)

# 9.00 Last Christmas

**Written by** Steven Moffat **Directed by** Douglas Mackinnon

**Original airdate** December 25, 2014

**The Big Idea** When Clara, the Doctor and the crew of an Arctic base are trapped in their dreams by terrible creatures, the only one who can save them is . . . Santa Claus?

**Roots and References** The pop-cultural version of Saint Nicholas a.k.a. Santa Claus as devised by Clement C. Moore in his 1837 poem "A Visit with St. Nicholas" and designed by Haddon Sundblom for 1930s Coca-Cola ads (Santa Claus); Robert L. May's 1939 creation Rudolph the Red-Nosed Reindeer (Rudolph's cameos throughout); the 2010 film *Inception* (the dreams, the dreams within dreams and the is-it-a-dream? ending); the 1983 film *Videodrome* (the head coming out of the TV); the 1947 film *Miracle on 34th Street* (Santa is real); the 1951 film *Thing from Another World* (the Arctic base setting); the 1979 film *Alien* (the Dream Crabs' resemblance to the face-huggers from that movie is mentioned, and the Doctor's response to a horror film called *Alien* is "That's offensive! No wonder everyone is invading you!"). Actually, *Alien*, *Thing from Another World* and *Miracle on 34th Street* are listed on Shona's Christmas Day itinerary, along with a *Game of Thrones* marathon. Shona dances to "Merry Christmas Everybody" by Slade. "Who ya gonna call?" from the 1984 film *Ghostbusters* is used as a catchphrase throughout, as is "God bless us, every one!" from Charles Dickens's *A Christmas Carol*.

The title of the story is derived from Wham!'s 1984 song, "Last Christmas," which peaked at number two on the charts, behind "Do They Know It's Christmas?" . . . which, amazingly, has never been used as the title of a *Doctor Who* Christmas special.

**Adventures in Time and Space** The episode picks up on developments at the end of "Dark Water"/"Death in Heaven" as the Doctor's and Clara's lies to each other are exposed and Danny Pink's death is revisited. Santa does a parody of "timey-wimey" from 2007's "Blink" with "It's a bit dreamy-weamy." (For good measure, Nick Frost's impression of Peter Capaldi is impeccable.)

**Who Is the Doctor?** The Doctor is hostile to Santa at first but eventually softens to the point where he goes with the dream and, while steering Santa's sleigh, thoroughly enjoys himself. He claims to have deleted all the crew's names after he briefly left the base, opting for basic nicknames (though he calls the older Bellows "sexy one"). He still seems to have some kind of face-blindness, as he genuinely doesn't know if Clara is old or not.

**The Doctor and Clara** Still grieving the loss of Danny Pink, Clara is angry when the Doctor jokes about Danny (the Doctor still thinks Danny has come back from the Nethersphere). But once Clara says goodbye to the dream version of Danny, her affection towards the Doctor blossoms. At the end, when the Doctor asks her if she believes in Santa, Clara says, "I've always believed in Santa Claus. But he looks a little different to me." And then hugs the Doctor, who doesn't protest. If anything, the Doctor's affection for Clara has become more apparent. When visiting Clara as an old woman in the final dream, the Doctor helps Clara open a Christmas cracker — the same way Clara did for the superannuated eleventh Doctor in "The Time of the Doctor." Once everything is restored, the Doctor and Clara find themselves with a second chance of travelling together.

**Monster of the Week** The Kantrofarri, otherwise known as the Dream Crabs, are creatures that attach themselves to humanoids and put their hosts into a dream state to effectively anaesthetize them while the Dream Crabs dissolve the hosts' brains. They become active if you think about them, including in a dream, which can lead to dreams being nested in dreams.

**Stand Up and Cheer** Santa saving the day for the first time — complete with tangerines, a toy parade, witty quips, an explanation of how Christmas actually works and then Santa taking the Doctor's technobabble away from him — is funny and delightful. Nick Frost is charming enough to upstage Peter Capaldi, which is no mean feat.

**Roll Your Eyes** Most of the Santa jokes really land, but the whole "calling someone an elf is racist" thing feels like Dad trying to write topical jokes.

**You're Not Making Any Sense** Okay, let's get this straight . . . the Dream Crabs only wake up when they're being thought about, including when they're in dreams. So why are they dormant on the base even though everyone is talking about them in the next room? Why are they dormant when Santa Claus brings one inside in a container?

**Interesting Trivia** This story was really, truly supposed to be Jenna Coleman's departure from the series, with the final twist being that Clara is now old and the story ending with the Doctor having one last Christmas with a presumably dying Clara before saying goodbye. Jenna Coleman's decision to stay happened just before the first readthrough, so the ending we see — where the Doctor discovers that to be a dream and then finds a younger Clara and they decide to resume travelling together — was hastily added.

Many people watching thought Shona was being groomed to be the next companion. Certainly her introductory scene is designed that way. But Faye Marsay was only cast for the Christmas special (given the next season wouldn't begin production for several months after "Last Christmas" was filmed, there wasn't any rush). Steven Moffat has admitted that he was moving in the direction of someone earthier and less posh than Clara, like Shona. Certainly, those qualities are present in the next companion.

Two of the players in this episode had connections to the broader world of *Doctor Who*. Michael Troughton, who played Smithe, is the son of Patrick Troughton, the second Doctor (and he wrote a biography of his father). His older brother, David, appeared in 2008's "Midnight," where he also played a professor. Meanwhile, Dan Starkey, who played Ian, is better known as a variety of Sontarans, particularly Strax from the Paternoster Gang. Moffat wrote the part for Starkey so he could finally play a role without heavy prosthetics.

Clara being written off as an old woman presumably would have supported the idea that she had Danny Pink's child, which would explain how a hundred years or so later Orson Pink in "Listen" looks just like Danny. Only that ending didn't happen, so presumably the whole question of how Orson can look like Danny and have Danny's soldier toy will forever remain a mystery. Or . . . here's a fan theory you can keep for yourself: Clara did have Danny's baby and gave it up for adoption some time before the events of "Last Christmas" (because it was too painful a reminder of everything, perhaps?). Not only would this enable Orson Pink to exist, it might explain several details of "Last Christmas," like why she's dreaming of Santa Claus. And maybe it might explain Clara's motivation for why she throws her lot in with the Doctor so recklessly. It would also explain why Orson is in possession of the toy but doesn't recognize Clara. Or . . . maybe Orson Pink is not descended from Clara and Danny.

**The TARDIS Chronometer** Clara's grandmother's house, in the present day, plus a variety of undated locations and a number of places (such as the Arctic base) within dreams. The Doctor wakes up on a volcano planet.

**Don't Be Stupid? (GB)** Let me make something clear at the outset: I think Steven Moffat is a gifted writer, a talented showrunner and — in the interests of full disclosure — a pretty funny man with whom to hang around a hotel lobby discussing James Bond. What Steven Moffat doesn't do well is a very small number of things, and one of them is the *Doctor Who* Christmas special. I have called Mr. Moffat's many contributions to this subgenre things like "lightweight," "soulless confection" (which admittedly is about "A Christmas Carol," which everybody else likes), "silly" and "forgettable." Caveat: I tend to think of "The Time of the Doctor" as a regeneration story, not a Christmas special.

All this is to provide valuable and important context for when I say that I think "Last Christmas" is the best *Doctor Who* Christmas special of all time.

First of all, it does *Doctor Who* incredibly well. The Dream Crabs are a brilliant menace that are genuinely scary (which is something Christmas specials have shied away from generally, but here it works amazingly well). Moreover, it demonstrates best how *Doctor Who* filches from stories and genres: it takes something people recognize and then riffs off it and deconstructs it. It isn't that it borrows from *Inception* or *Alien*; it's that it puts *Alien* inside *Inception*, which is glorious.

But it also follows the "cleverness + emotions = *wow!*" paradigm beautifully. The dream sequence that finally writes out Danny Pink is scary and dramatic — the blackboards saying "Dying!" are really creepy — but it's also lovely too, as Danny goes back to being charming. (I adore the way Samuel Anderson tells the Doctor, "Compliments of the season!") Dream Danny gives Clara advice on grief that feels both right and a little wrong-headed, and — just like he did in life — he sacrifices himself, again. The result is bittersweet and beautiful.

Which brings me to the other thing "Last Christmas" does exceptionally well: Christmas. For once it isn't shoehorned into a planet's name or a coincidental time of year the story is set. Santa Claus is integral to the success of the story. I suppose it could be another mythical figure, but Santa is perfect for it, as this lighthearted children's whimsy suddenly strolls onto the set of *The Thing*. Nick Frost plays the role utterly straight, and Steven Moffat has a ball giving him dialogue where he deflects all criticism. But it does something more with the concept of Christmas, as it takes the pop-song title and makes it into a sublime message: every Christmas is last Christmas; we have to love what we have when we can.

Perhaps unusually, this is the rare Christmas special not focused on the Doctor regenerating that has both the Doctor and the current companion in it, so "Last Christmas" benefits from a centre of gravity these stories don't usually have. The result is that it does the character stuff powerfully. I've talked about Danny and Clara's final scene together, but you could argue (and I would) that this is the story where Clara accepts that she loves the Doctor, and the Doctor accepts that he truly loves Clara. The ending on Santa's sleigh is delightful, and the potential that Clara has become old feels like a gut punch, as I worried the Doctor was, for once, too late to see everything.

If you're lucky, most Christmas specials get one element right — the *Doctor Who*, the Christmas or the emotions. If you're very lucky, two of them will be right. But every so often, you have something miraculous like "Last Christmas" where everything aligns, and it's perfect. But you need to treat it like a last Christmas — with reverence for the moment — because these things are rare and special indeed.

**Second Opinion (RS?)** It's an utterly sublime idea: Santa Claus meets *Doctor Who*.

In fact, as my co-author outlines above, that makes it perhaps the most Christmassy of all possible Christmas specials, assuming the TARDIS will never materialize in Bethlehem. And they do it by going full-bore Santa, with the toys, the reindeer, the sleigh, the housebreaking-in-a-red-suit-with-bells, you name it. This is vastly preferable to having Santa be a misunderstood alien or something.

The problem is how you get those two to mesh. The answer is basically "It was all a dream," which is usually the laziest of all plot contrivances. But where "Last Christmas" works is that it drills down into the dream idea. By nesting dreams within dreams and seeding clues from the very beginning — such as the four sleepers wearing the same four jackets that the base personnel are wearing — the story weaponizes the dream as a solution.

I have no particular problem with the fact that *Inception* did this already. *Doctor Who* has a long history of paying homage to other sources, with particular success when it makes the source material scary. And I found "Last Christmas" more effective than its big-budget cousin on that score.

Where it gets a bit hairier is the story's central premise that you know you're dreaming if ridiculous things are happening. Coming from a time traveller in a police box who's dressed as a magician, that's a dangerous line to skirt. Yes, they play it for humour, which is well done, but the risk is that you undermine the whole of *Doctor Who* for a plot point in a single episode. Surely Clara should spend every day of the next season rubbing her temple to see if it's cold, given that she lives in a world that's clearly not real? It puts the story in a terrible bind: you can have the Doctor meet Santa so long as it's a dream, but the price you pay will be accidentally undermining the entire premise of your show.

The only way to get away with this is if the resultant story is good enough to warrant such a narrative-destroying concept. Fortunately, "Last Christmas" is sublime in just about every way. Not only as a Christmas special, as Graeme points out, but as one of the best Modern Series episodes, bar none. Our brains may be slowly dissolving, but at least the dream that is *Doctor Who* is a great one. Totes worth it.

## 9.01–9.02 The Magician's Apprentice / The Witch's Familiar

**Written by** Steven Moffat **Directed by** Hettie MacDonald
**Original airdate** September 19, 2015

**The Big Idea** If someone who knew the future pointed out a child to you and told you that that child would grow up totally evil, to be a ruthless dictator who would destroy millions of lives, could you then kill that child?

**Roots and References** The 1981 film *My Dinner with Andre* (the Doctor's lengthy conversation with Davros about their lives); the 1967 film adaptation of *The Jungle Book* (Colony Sarf resembles Nag, a little); the 1993 film *Dazed and Confused* (the Doctor makes "dude" all the rage in the Middle Ages). The Doctor plays Roy Orbison's "Pretty Woman" on the guitar and references Mott the Hoople's "All the Young Dudes." Missy is back to parodying Tony Basil's song "Mickey" by typing "You So Fine" when she hacks UNIT's computers.

**Adventures in Time and Space** The opening battle, with weaponry from different eras, is a logical extrapolation of the war between the Kaleds and the Thals in 1975's "Genesis of the Daleks." The amplifier for the Doctor's guitar is from Magpie Electricals (2006's "The Idiot's Lantern"). We visit the Shadow Proclamation, complete with the Shadow Architect (2008's "The Stolen Earth"/"Journey's End") and a Judoon (2008's "Smith and Jones"). We also see the Sisterhood of Karn (1976's "The Brain of Morbius"), led by Ohila ("Night of the Doctor").

The planet Skaro, destroyed in 1988's "Remembrance of the Daleks" has been built again and brought back by the Daleks, as briefly seen in "Asylum of the Daleks." Skaro looks similar to how it looked originally in 1963's "The Daleks." Virtually every type of Dalek is here, from the original model in that story to the special weapons Dalek (1988's "Revelation of the Daleks") to the Supreme Dalek ("The Stolen Earth"/"Journey's End").

The Maldovarium was first seen in 2010's "The Pandorica Opens"/"The Big Bang." There we find an Ood in the bar (2006's "The Impossible Planet"/"The Satan Pit") as well as a Skullion (from the 2011 *Sarah Jane Adventures* story "The Man Who Never Was"), a Kahler ("A Town Called Mercy"), a Hath (2008's "The Doctor's Daughter"), a Blowfish (from the 2007 *Torchwood* story "Kiss Kiss Bang Bang") and a Sycorax (2006's "The Christmas Invasion"). You have to be really fast with the pause button to catch some of these. Some we found only because the end credits listed their creators! Clara being inside a Dalek echoes "Asylum of the Daleks." Davros asks, "Am I a good man?" just as the Doctor asked Clara in "Into the Dalek." There are references to three possible versions of Atlantis, from the Classic Series episodes "The Underwater Menace" (1967), "The Dæmons" (1971) and "The Time Monster" (1972). Clara mentions the helicopter used to collect the TARDIS in "The Day of the Doctor," while the Doctor tells Davros that Gallifrey is back, which he discovered in that same story.

Missy has a vortex manipulator, just like Captain Jack and River Song. (Its catchphrase, "cheap and nasty time travel," which dates back to 2005's "The Empty Child"/"The Doctor Dances," is mentioned.) We learn that she survived in "Death in Heaven" because of it (and there's a *very* brief flashback to that episode showing this). Her brooch is made of Dark Star Alloy, which may be related to Dwarf Star Alloy from 1981's "Warriors' Gate." Likewise, the Doctor's mention of the TARDIS's Hostile Action Dispersal System is probably a reworking of the Hostile Action Displacement System from 1968's "The Krotons."

Davros plays a clip of the famous scene of the Doctor holding two wires together from 1975's "Genesis of the Daleks." We see images of the first and fourth Doctors in the background of Missy's narrated story. We also hear the Doctor talking to Davros about unleashing a hypothetical virus in the same story; potentially executing him in 1984's "Resurrection of the Daleks"; Davros's scheme to feed people their dead relatives in 1985's "Revelation of the Daleks"; unlimited rice pudding in "Remembrance of the Daleks"; and everything they've lost in 2008's "The Stolen Earth."

**The Hybrid Effect** There's a prophecy on Gallifrey that talks of a hybrid. It says that two warrior races will be forced together to create a warrior greater than either. Davros posits a Time Lord/Dalek hybrid, but Missy (separately) suggests that the Doctor and Clara make up a hybrid. The Doctor's confession dial — a last will and testament for the Doctor — is introduced, while Davros tells the Doctor to take the darkest path into the deepest hell in order to protect his own. We'll be seeing more of this in due course . . .

**Who Is the Doctor?** He has a profound sense of shame about abandoning the young Davros and assumes he's going to die when he goes to meet the elder version. This sense of shame is so strong he even abandons using the sonic screwdriver, given its association with the boy he left on the battlefield; instead, he switches to the sonic sunglasses, as wearable technology. Thinking he's going to die, he throws a party, which goes against the solemn expectations of Time Lords. His idea of a fun time is playing the guitar on top of a tank in the Middle Ages while wearing a hoodie and a T-shirt and introducing anachronistic words. Missy plays Two Truths and a Lie in reference to the Doctor, claiming that she has cared about him since the Cloister Wars, since he was a little girl and since the night he stole the moon and the president's wife. We're not told which is the lie. In response to the accusation "This isn't you," he says, "I spent all yesterday in a bowtie, the day before in a long scarf." Either he's speaking metaphorically or the Doctor just cosplayed as himself. We're hoping for the latter.

**The Doctor and Clara** After the Doctor's recent opposition to hugging ("Death in Heaven"), he immediately hugs Clara, indicating something is very wrong. If he lies to her, she doesn't want him to apologize; she wants him to make it up to her. Missy describes their dynamic as a friend inside an enemy and an enemy inside a friend and says that this is why she put Clara and the Doctor together in the first place. Clara's shocked to realize the Doctor has given the confession dial to Missy.

**Monster of the Week** We learn a few new things about the Daleks: since they're hard-wired to keep on living, the contents of their sewers are actually millions of decaying Daleks. Once inside the casing, kind or understanding words like "I love you" or "You're different from me" are translated into "Exterminate." A Dalek experiencing emotion is what fires the gun, while the word "Exterminate" reloads it. We also discover that Davros can open his eyes.

**Stand Up and Cheer** It's the most perfect lead-in to the credits ever devised: an ugly war. Terrifying hand creatures with built-in eyes that can suck a man into the earth in seconds. A boy stranded in the middle. Whereupon the TARDIS arrives and the Doctor throws him the sonic screwdriver, giving hope to the hopeless. And then we hear the boy's name . . . only for the Doctor to display a look of sheer horror on his face. The genius of this is that the credits leave time for new viewers to quickly google "Davros" on their phones and come up to speed — and time for more experienced viewers to wipe the tears away.

**Roll Your Eyes** Why does Kate Stewart, a UNIT operative who works in the field of security — and has presumably heard about 9/11 — need to be told by a schoolteacher that planes might be a dangerous weapon?

**You're Not Making Any Sense** The sewer Daleks overwhelm the Dalek Missy has poked holes in because they want its casing . . . and yet they promptly leave the casing alone and, despite said holes, never try to overwhelm it again once Clara is inside. Did they get distracted by Dalek Twitter or something?

**Interesting Trivia** There was both a prologue and a mini-story ("The Doctor's Meditation") preceding this season opener. The prologue comprised a single scene between the Doctor and Ohila on the planet Karn, where the Doctor gives Ohila his confession dial and decides to meditate. We've added "The Doctor's Meditation" to the appendix, although it's not crucial. The major impact on this story is the apparent importance of Bors and a mention of digging some wells. Both are available as extras on the Series 9 DVD boxset.

Back in Halloween 2014, actor Sean Pertwee dressed as the third Doctor as played by his dad, Jon Pertwee, and posted a photo to Instagram where most people, including your co-authors, marvelled at the resemblance. We weren't the only people to have noticed. Sean Pertwee stated in an interview with the *Radio Times* in 2016 that the he was asked to cameo as the third Doctor during Series Eight. While the nature of the cameo was never mentioned, it's easy to picture it being the opening sequence of "The Witch's Familiar" where there's a vignette told by Missy using the fourth and twelfth Doctors, though she posits it could have been any incarnation. Unfortunately, Sean's schedule on *Gotham* wouldn't permit the cameo.

If you're a long-term fan who's paying attention, the opening scene has a few clues. Soldiers wearing gas masks and attempting to shoot down a laser-firing biplane with a bow and arrow is familiar to anyone who's seen "Genesis of the Daleks." There's also the need to stand very still in the middle of a minefield and a reference to "clam drones" that's an in-joke to a poor special effect in the original. These probably weren't meant to be noticed by the unwary first-time viewer, but if you're familiar with the original story — and it's the Classic Series story most people would know — then everything slots beautifully and tragically into place once you hear the boy's name.

As with "Asylum of the Daleks," we see a plethora of different types of Daleks coexisting. (Missy's partial to the Supreme Dalek and tickles a Dalek's, erm, ball.) But if you look carefully, you'll notice that the New Paradigm Daleks are completely absent. They aren't even immobile in the background, the way they were in "Asylum of the Daleks." (And there was much rejoicing.) Apparently, the Daleks decided to recreate their home planet, which they happened to make invisible for some reason and pointedly didn't invite one group to the party. Even for Daleks, that's cruel.

Wait, so Davros's eyes work (albeit with considerable effort)? They've worked all this time? That third eye is not, as we all thought, a cybernetic replacement for burnt-out cinders stemming from his tragic accident that does all the seeing for him, but rather some sort of fashion accessory? Huh.

**The TARDIS Chronometer** The original Skaro, in the distant past; Earth in the Middle Ages and the present; and a rebuilt, semi-invisible Skaro. Colony Sarff also travels around the universe searching for the Doctor.

**Don't Be Stupid? (RS?)** Peter Capaldi's second season opens in considerable style with what could have been a very fannish and introspective story about a debate that started in 1975, starring two old men who sit around and have a bit of a chat. For an hour. Instead, it's nothing short of sensational.

It helps that the sensation is right at the beginning. The post-credit scenes have it all: the Doctor is missing from the universe. Planes everywhere are frozen. UNIT calls in Clara. Missy is alive! The Doctor's delayed entry — on a tank while playing guitar in the Middle Ages — is astonishing. You think it can't get any better . . . and then you realize that all this is a cover for something we've never seen the Doctor experience before: shame.

*The Doctor leaves a child to die.*

The stylish writing and editing of these scenes bring us perfectly to the disguised melancholy of Peter Capaldi's Doctor. He's done something truly terrible and is genuinely prepared to die as penance. The ageing rocker act is good (and plays to Capaldi's strengths brilliantly), but it's the effect of the pre-credits sequence hanging over the story that makes it great.

That opening scene with the young Davros is jaw-dropping. It's seeded brilliantly, with the mix of technological styles and a terrifying new monster in the hand mines (the soldier asking the boy when he's seen one before, only for the boy to glance down at the soldier's foot, is extremely well done). The reveal of the boy's name is one of those "Oh crap!" moments that forces you to rethink everything you've just seen, driving the Doctor's natural warmth and compassion into a brick wall. And then we find out what happened next: the Doctor simply leaves. *He leaves a child in a minefield to die.*

The genius of this is that it ups everybody's game. The writing has to be totally on point for this to work — and by goodness it is. Peter Capaldi sells it like nobody's business, as he takes the Doctor on a deeply uncomfortable journey. And it ups the game for *Doctor Who* itself as well, taking a time-travel hypothetical from "Genesis of the Daleks" — about killing a dictator as a child — and putting it onscreen. And when you think it can't be any more powerful, you discover that the very dictator you're seeing is exactly the same one we first met in "Genesis," only now he's the child. This is the ultimate example of show, don't tell.

*And then the Doctor leaves a child to die.*

Fundamentally, this is a morality play about compassion. One involving two old men having a philosophical debate in a room. Yet it's working overtime to make sure that we aren't bored, with every trick in the Moffat playbook being used — but they're done in service of the story, not as gimmicks. Missy's story of the Doctor surviving the attack is illustrated with snatches of past Doctors, shown in black and white, teased in snippets and capped with a funny joke about the Doctor falling into a nest of vampire monkeys. It's utterly sublime. It's also there entirely to keep us distracted from the two-hander at the heart of the story.

This debate is the culmination of a millennia-long disagreement between two incredibly strong characters. One of the appeals of Davros is that he isn't a ranting villain; he's an intellectual equal to the Doctor, as interested in philosophical debate as he is in creating a genocidal murder machine. Almost every Davros story has stopped the action for an argument between the two characters — with such scenes usually being the episode's highlight. "The Magician's Apprentice"/"The Witch's Familiar" takes that tradition and makes it the whole story.

Knowing how hard a sell that is for a modern audience, we're also treated to delights such as the Doctor in Davros's chair (the Daleks backing away in fear is hilarious), Missy owning every scene she's in, the only other chair on Skaro and an invisible planet. We have a number of firsts, such as Missy and Davros meeting or the horrific sight of Davros out of his life-support system.

But it's the talk of mercy and compassion that takes this story to a deeper place. Davros is still trying to prove his point that empathy is a weakness: faced with the option to wipe out the Daleks entirely, the Doctor chooses compassion. Davros's comeback is devastating: he likens it to a cancer, saying that it will kill the Doctor.

And it's the Doctor's compassion that leads him to give Davros his regeneration energy. Here lies the story's only flaw, because the immediate result of this is that multiple rugs are pulled out from beneath everybody's feet — Davros planned it all along!; but wait!!; the Doctor knew this and counter-planned!!! — but it's too much, too quickly and fundamentally unearned.

Everything else, however, is sublime. The Doctor and Davros laughing over a shared joke is the kind of thing you'd never have imagined ever seeing (and it's a pretty funny joke too!). The Doctor's solution, to awaken the sewer Daleks, is excellent in exactly the way the regeneration energy one-two wasn't: because it's been seeded throughout, so even though it comes from left field, it's surprising, not arbitrary.

Putting Clara back inside a Dalek was a winning move. Especially because we learn that some words simply don't translate, making the tension skyrocket when Missy suggests that the Doctor kill her. Everything comes together beautifully here, with genuine tension . . . and then a stunning realization that the word "mercy" does in fact exist in the Dalek vocabulary, and the Doctor's comprehension of precisely why that would be.

The Doctor going back to save young Davros is, for me, what *Doctor Who* is all about. He can't kill a child, not even by his absence, and even though saving said child doesn't stop the horrors to come, it's still the right thing to do. The fake-out cliffhanger involving the Doctor shooting at what we think is Davros is perfectly fine for what it is, but only because the resolution is so clever. The final image of the Doctor leading the boy Davros by the hand is just amazing.

*And then the Doctor doesn't leave a child to die.*

There are some *Doctor Who* stories where everything fires on all cylinders. Where the show becomes more than a quirky, lighthearted action-adventure series, something much more important — while still being a quirky, lighthearted action-adventure series. "The Magician's Apprentice"/"The Witch's Familiar" hits all the grace notes beautifully. It's the most fun morality tale involving two old men debating philosophy that you'll ever see. It's also the deepest character examination of an eccentric time-travelling rocker and his crippled, ranting arch-nemesis on an invisible planet that you could hope for. I love this show.

And there's not a single time I watch that opening scene of the battlefield where, when the boy says his name and the Doctor looks aghast, I don't tear up and start crying uncontrollably. Dammit, it's happening again . . .

**Second Opinion (GB)** Yeah, so I don't like this story quite so much as my co-author does.

For one thing, it's the first in a trend you're going to see all season where stories that really shouldn't be two-parters are joined up so they can save some cash on sets and cast. Case in point, this story, which has 60 minutes of story and 90 minutes of running time. Oh, and they spent most of the money on the first episode so they could give us UNIT and a cool scene with Missy. Most of the story is a lot of lengthy scenes in Davros's laboratory, and they're pulled off only because Peter Capaldi and Julian Bleach are so good at what they do. With any other actors, the paucity of the script would be immediately apparent.

I could almost forgive that because Capaldi and Bleach are such a brilliant double-act — the scene where Davros and the Doctor laugh at a joke is heart-achingly tender and sad — and because Jenna Coleman and Michelle Gomez are just as good, though playing a much more broadly comedic duo. But . . . I can't.

You see, my other problem is my co-author is just flat-out wrong about the morality of this story.

The "moral dilemma" of this story is as bullshit as the "moral dilemma" put forward back in 1975 in "Genesis of the Daleks." There the Doctor kept on hemming and hawing about whether he has the right, and everyone uses that as a brilliant clip, except the Doctor does end up deciding to blow up the Daleks' incubator room . . . before a Dalek, conveniently, does it for him.

Here, the Doctor gets confronted with the scenario he discusses back in "Genesis of the Daleks" when he said to Harry and Sarah, "If someone who knew the future pointed out a child to you and told you that that child would grow up totally evil . . . could you then kill that child?" (And to make sure we don't miss this, Davros helpfully plays a clip of this; good thing he has the DVD lying around.) Only . . . no matter how many times question-mark boy writes, *"And then the Doctor leaves a child to die,"* in italics, it doesn't escape the fact that the Doctor, once again, skates around the moral dilemma while pretending he's not.

Because the Doctor isn't doing this to save Davros. (What's more, he knows Davros must have survived, because he's still there to point the sonic screwdriver of guilt at him.) He goes back so he can save Clara. So he can introduce the word "mercy" as a meme to Little Davros, so he'll remember it and maybe keep it in the Dalek's memory banks, even though living battle machines have no use for it whatsoever.

That isn't the resolution of a moral dilemma. It's bullshit. Timey-wimey bullshit, no less.

I enjoyed "The Magician's Apprentice"/"The Witch's Familiar," even though it's 30 minutes too long. But it's not all that deep. Some day, they'll probably use clips of it to claim that it is — just like "Genesis of the Daleks," when it comes down to it.

**Third opinion (RS?)** Wait, so your argument is basically "This is a story of the same quality as 'Genesis of the Daleks'"? Well, then. That'll have them all aghast down at the next monthly *Doctor Who* tavern, I'm sure.

Oh, and the idea of a season of two-parters where each part functions like a different story is utterly brilliant. Almost as brilliant as a morality tale involving Daleks and their creator, in fact . . .

**Fourth opinion (GB)** Um, no. I'm saying this story and "Genesis of the Daleks" claim to have weighty moral arguments but are actually cowardly in how they handle them. But that's okay, Robert?. You're the one who enjoyed "The Doctor, the Widow and the Wardrobe." I'll just be over here being smug.

# 9.03—9.04 Under the Lake / Before the Flood

**Written by** Toby Whithouse **Directed by** Daniel O'Hara
**Original airdates** October 3 and 10, 2015

**The Big Idea** Ghosts are haunting an underwater mining base. The Doctor goes back in time to investigate, and then Clara discovers that one of the ghosts is his.

**Roots and References** *The Abyss* (aliens in an underwater base); the U.S. Fort Irwin National Training Center (building a fake town for military exercises); the moon landing ("one small step"); the 2002 film adaptation of the Marvel Comic *Daredevil* (Cass "seeing" the vibration of the axe being dragged is a lot like how Daredevil's radar sense is depicted); the legend of the Fisher King, probably best known from the 1991 film *The Fisher King*, although T.S. Eliot's *The Waste Land* is thought to be based on this legend. Funeral director Prentis's business card makes a *Star Wars* pun ("May the remorse be with you"). The Doctor mentions "Mysterious Girl" by Peter Andre as an earworm and plays Beethoven's Symphony No. 5 in C minor (Op. 67) on his guitar at the end of the cold open to "Before the Flood."

**Adventures in Time and Space** The Cloister Bell (1981's "Logopolis") rings several times, including — in a first — loudly enough to be heard outside the TARDIS. The Doctor references the Nethersphere ("Dark Water"/"Death in Heaven"), gangers (2011's "The Rebel Flesh"/"The Almost People") and his previous meeting with the people from the planet Tivoli in 2011's "The God Complex." Their current oppressors are the Arcateenians, previously seen in spinoffs *Torchwood* and *The Sarah Jane Adventures*. As a fan of the Doctor's exploits, O'Donnell references Rose, Martha, Amy, Harold Saxon (2007's "The Sound of Drums"/"Last of the Time Lords") and the moon exploding and a big bat coming out ("Kill the Moon"). The TARDIS's holographic security protocol (which dates all the way back to 2005's "Bad Wolf"/"The Parting of the Ways") has the Doctor wearing his costume from last season.

Sharp-eyed (and long-time) viewers looking at the Doctor's flashcards will note that the second one is a reference to him having dropped Sarah Jane Smith off in the wrong place at the end of 1976's "The Hand of Fear," as we discovered in 2006's "School Reunion."

**Who Is the Doctor?** The Doctor is clearly trying to move on from his more awkward days last season, as he has flashcards for delivering bad news or for socially awkward situations. He acknowledges that Cass is very smart and is excited by the ghosts to an unseemly degree. He's also quite the Shirley Bassey fanboy. He forces himself to act in order to save Clara but not O'Donnell. He not only has a UNIT code, he remembers it!

**The Doctor and Clara** The two have become quite close. Clara refuses to face the idea that he could die, telling him, "I don't care about your rules or your bloody survivor's guilt. If you love me in any way, you'll come back." (Clara clearly knows him too well.) The Doctor, for his part, is very anxious about how much Clara has become enamoured of their travels, telling her that he has a "duty of care" and he's worried that she doesn't understand there's only room for one Doctor.

**Monster of the Week** The Fisher King is immensely tall, with a skull-like face and a hood made of bone. He and his armies enslaved Tivoli for a decade until it was liberated by the Arcateenians, who decreed that the body of the Fisher King be interred on a savage outpost. However, the Fisher King wasn't dead after all and embedded a message in the afterlife of anyone who saw his code that would direct his armies to rescue him. He dies in the flood, but the code lives on.

**Stand Up and Cheer** Clara's flashcards for the Doctor are hilarious. The statements are:

1. I completely understand why it was difficult not to get captured.
2. It was my fault. I should have known you didn't live in Aberdeen.
3. I didn't mean to imply that I don't care.
4. No-one is going to get eaten/captured/vapourised/exterminated/upgraded/possessed/mortally wounded turned to jelly. We'll all get out of this unharmed.
5. I'm very sorry for your loss. I'll do all I can to solve the death of your friend/family member/pet.

In a moment of great comedy, the Doctor simply reads the last one out verbatim, complete with slashes.

**Roll Your Eyes** You're Cass, a deaf woman searching a dark base that you know is haunted by ghosts of your fellow crewmates. You've split up from the person you were with and are walking down a corridor when you suspect something might be behind you. Which of these options is most plausible to you? a) Turn your head to look. b) Kneel down, placing your hand on the floor and closing your eyes to feel the vibrations before diving out of the way of an axe-wielding ghost at the last moment. Or c) did you really not think of turning your head to look?

**You're Not Making Any Sense** The coordinates that the Fisher King gives the ghosts are "the dark, the sword, the forsaken, the temple," which correspond to "space, Orion's sword, the empty town, the church." Three of these are fine, assuming the Fisher King doesn't mind his friends checking out Chernobyl, or any number of other abandoned towns, first. But Orion's Sword is so named because of the way the constellation looks from the vantage point of Earth, so it wouldn't look similar from elsewhere. It also doesn't point to Earth. We can see the sword horizontally, which means it lies laterally. If the three stars were in alignment with Earth, then we'd be able to see only a single star.

**Interesting Trivia** If you search Google Trends for the term "bootstrap paradox" in 2015 (hey, you never know, you might be bored!), you'll see a huge spike in searches. On October 9, there are hardly any searches. On October 10, this increases by a factor of 41. On October 11, the increase is more than a hundred fold compared to two days earlier. The reason? The twelfth Doctor says, "Google it!" in the cold open to "Before the Flood" when explaining what the bootstrap paradox was. Basically, it's a paradox that creates itself, explained here by a man picking himself up by his bootlaces (which would of course be impossible) or a time traveller using Beethoven's sheet music to write Beethoven's music. Where did this music come from in the first place, then? Actually, the answer is simple: in a bootstrap paradox, there is no "first place"; the music exists because it always existed, and there's no need for it to have ever had an origin. It's just one of the many unexpected consequences of time travel.

So what exactly are the ghosts? They appear whenever a person dies, can pass through walls, touch metal objects and only appear at night (even if "night" is artificial on the base). They're even shown walking upside down and sideways at one point. The Doctor pooh-poohs the idea that ghosts could exist, then later says that the Fisher King hijacked other people's souls and turned them into electromagnetic projections that were out of phase with the base's day mode. But what does that actually mean? Well, it means they're ghosts.

At one point, the Doctor sticks his finger into what looks like coffee and is able to calculate the passage of time. This isn't some Time Lord gift; it's physics. Newton's law of cooling says that the rate at which temperature decreases is proportional to the difference between the temperature of the object and the ambient temperature. Since coffee is mostly water, which was probably heated to 100° Celsius in a 20° room, all the Doctor would need to know is a) the cooling rate of water, b) the surface area of the liquid, and c) the temperature that the liquid is now. The latter is the only part that's not easily accessible to the rest of us, as our fingers aren't that sensitive.

Actress Sophie Stone, who plays Cass, was the first deaf actor to be admitted to the Royal Academy of Dramatic Arts (RADA). (She's not the first deaf actor to appear in *Doctor Who*; that was Tim Barlow, in 1979's "Destiny of the Daleks.") Zaqi Ismal, who plays Dunn, Cass's interpreter, knows sign language, as his sister is deaf.

Peter Capaldi is six feet tall. And yet the Fisher King towers over him. That's not a special effect; it's because the actor inside was professional basketball player Neil Fingleton, who stands at seven-foot-seven and, at the time, was the tallest man in Britain. That isn't the Fisher King's only claim to fame: he's partially voiced by Corey Taylor, known for his screaming vocals in the band Slipknot. Whereas Peter Serafinowicz is responsible for the speaking voice, Taylor is credited as "Roar of the Fisher King." This may be the most bizarre onscreen credit in *Doctor Who* since Rosyln de Winter was credited for "Insect Movement" in 1966's "The Web Planet."

Yes, that is Peter Capaldi playing the *Doctor Who* theme on his guitar.

**The TARDIS Chronometer** The Drum, an underwater mining facility in Caithness, Scotland, in 2119; the same location in 1980 when it was a military training camp, before it was flooded.

**Don't Be Stupid? (RS?)** Back in the 1960s, there was a house style of *Doctor Who* called "base under siege": a single, remote location, where the TARDIS crew and a small group of unfortunates could be stalked by creeping horror. It arose largely from budgetary restrictions, because this kept the cast small and the sets limited. *Doctor Who*'s 2015 budget is a lot healthier than it was in the 1960s — but there's also a lot to be said for the claustrophobia that arises from the base-under-siege format.

Which brings us to "Under the Lake." The first episode of this two-parter is a triumph of thrills and scares, using darkness to let the viewer's imagination fill in the gaps and some very effective makeup on the ghosts to add the right amount of creepiness. The base is sprawling, but that doesn't lessen the tension, given the ghosts' abilities to pass through walls.

Indeed, a great deal of plot logic gets sacrificed in service of the atmosphere. What were the ghosts if there's no such thing? Meh, basically just ghosts. Why can they pick up only metal objects? Let's not bother to explain that. What are the philosophical implications for the afterlife if ghosts really do exist? Never mind.

The cast is pleasantly diverse, which is also in keeping with the 1960s stories, though happily less stereotypical. My one complaint is that Cass, who's easily the strongest character here, appears to be deaf solely because of the ensuing plot function. How terribly convenient to have someone on board who can read lips, rather than (say) in a story just because. (What's worse is that this is the second time Toby Whithouse has offered us diversity for plot convenience: he pulled the same trick with Rita in "The God Complex," which had a strongly written, exceptionally cast Muslim almost-companion, purely because they needed a Muslim for the story.) In the 1990s New Adventures line of *Doctor Who* novels, Kate Orman's *SLEEPY* also had a deaf character, except she wasn't there for plot purposes, which made her a lot more credible.

Interestingly, *SLEEPY* also had the (seventh) Doctor take the TARDIS back in time to investigate how it all started. Which is where "Before the Flood" comes in. Unlike many Steven Moffat stories, the genius of this one is to keep its eye on the prize: there's a single time jump, and we go from there. Okay, there is a brief 30-minute jump back at one stage, but that only serves to clutter the plot. One of the cleverest things here is how different the second part looks compared to its predecessor, yet the two are intricately linked. That's exactly what you want from a two-parter. Compare this to "The Rebel Flesh"/"The Almost People" and weep.

Switching moods is where 2015 storytelling comes to the fore. We can enjoy an entire fake town, a towering (and terrifying) alien and a spectacular set piece of the dam bursting in precisely the ways that 1960s TV could never have managed. These are all excellent additions, but it's the atmospheric scares in the claustrophobic base that will stay with you long after the other elements have been forgotten. Spectacle is great, but it's the ability to tap into the imagination that really hits home.

One of the nicely understated moments is when Bennett is struggling with his grief over O'Donnell's loss and Clara steps forward, because she can truly understand where he's coming from. We haven't seen much explicit fallout this season from Danny's death, which makes sense from the viewpoint of an adventure series, but there's a continuing undercurrent that suggests that Clara is barely holding on and that everything she's doing this season is a performance for the Doctor — and herself. Grief over the loss of a loved one doesn't just dissipate, but the demands of a weekly TV show also don't lend themselves to dealing with this sort of thing head-on. So it's nice to see that it hasn't totally been forgotten.

Having Cass and Lunn get together at the end is a little too twee, mainly because it reduces all the female base staff to objects of male desire. You can see why they want an uplifting moment at the end, but it's a shame that they went for the lazy option. Bennett calling the Doctor on his crap should be a standout moment, but it's undercooked. Yes, the Doctor cares more about his friend than a stranger, but so what? That might not have been the way things were in the Classic Series, but it's been blatantly true for the past 13 years. What especially harms this moment is the fact that so much of the story's ethos is ripped from the past. In a modern-looking and -paced Moffat story, this charge might hold water. Here, it's just flooded.

A few complaints aside, "Under the Lake"/"Before the Flood" is a definite winner. It's a triumph of the season's two-parter approach, mixing old-fashioned scares with modern time-travel wackiness. There's an effective monster, scary ghosts, a base under siege and some impressive set pieces. Works for me.

**Second Opinion (GB)** I agree this story is brilliant; I disagree with my co-author about why and why not.

Let's talk about why not: the budgetary problems continue from the previous story, and here the action is padded out with extraneous talky scenes. It also looks cheap and nasty once the story moves to the empty base in the 1980s. That's disappointing, but thankfully not fatal.

I agree with Dr. Smith? about Bennett and O'Donnell, but I think the biggest problem with it is that it completely misses a trick: Bennett should have been killed, not O'Donnell. Had Bennett died, the Doctor fangirl would have had to face the fact that her hero knew that the guy she was interested in was going to be killed, which would have expanded the range of dramatic possibilities considerably.

But I think what works in this story far outweighs what doesn't. First of all, I can't believe we haven't talked about the opening monologue for "Before the Flood," which is stunning. Not only does it explain the paradox at the episode's end, but it does it in a funny and really engaging way. It's one of my very favourite sequences of the whole Capaldi era. It's a little meta (who is the Doctor talking to?) in a way that only *Doctor Who* can be (probably himself!) and the fact that it decides to lean into the skid by having Peter Capaldi jam on the theme song is sublime.

The story really shines when Toby Whithouse shows us how he would do a timey-wimey story. You know, the ones Steven Moffat does that are almost considered ten a penny now? I think Whithouse's genius is that the story is, in many ways, almost relentlessly linear. Plot elements come into being in the present only when they're close to happening or have immediately happened in the past. The result is less mystery than the usual puzzle boxes we get when things like this happen, but it's also brisk and hugely exciting.

And the story continues this season's move to rehabilitate the Doctor: the ageing rock star persona is a delightful refinement, as are the flashcards, which show that the Doctor sees he needs to make a better effort with people. This is a guy no longer treating others like data points (he really does try to stop O'Donnell, and his concern for Clara is unbelievably touching), and he's a more complex and more engaging character for it. And I can't agree more with Robert's assessment about how unstuck Clara probably is.

"Under the Lake"/"Before the Flood" is not just a winner, it's one of this season's best stories. It's entertaining, thoughtful, brilliantly cast and creepy. It more than works for me.

## 9.05 The Girl Who Died

**Written by** Jamie Mathieson and Steven Moffat **Directed by** Ed Bazalgette
**Original airdate** October 17, 2015

**The Big Idea** When a Viking village declares war upon a technologically advanced race of warriors, the Doctor has 24 hours to save the entire town. But can he save everybody?

**Roots and References** The 1967–77 BBC sitcom *Dad's Army* (the Doctor's disastrous attempt at creating an army from farmers and peasants echoes the classic World War II–set comedy about civilian members of the Home Guard); the Norse legends of Odin and Valhalla; Terry Jones's 1989 film *Erik the Viking* (comedy antics with Vikings); the 1975 film *Monty Python and the Holy Grail* (the projection of Odin's head in the clouds is very similar to Terry Gilliam's animated God in that film). The Doctor references the band ZZ Top and the children's TV character Noggin the Nog when nicknaming the Vikings. Clara adds the *Benny Hill* theme to the video of Odin cowering from the puppet, referencing the popular 1969–89 British comedy show. The Doctor, when translating what the baby is crying, cites it in the metre and style of Norse poetry.

**Adventures in Time and Space** The Cloister Bell (first heard in 1981's "Logopolis") rings, for the third episode in a row. The Doctor again uses a yo-yo (1975's "The Ark in Space"), this time to try to intimidate the villagers. He says that Ashildr is now immortal, barring accidents, which is how the second Doctor described the Time Lords in 1969's "The War Games," and he leafs through a 2,000 year diary, which is a update of the five hundred year diary he had in 1966's "The Power of the Daleks" and the nine hundred year diary in the 1996 TV Movie. He says, "Time will tell, it always does," a direct quote from 1988's "Remembrance of the Daleks," in which he also mused about the effects of ripples on history. He reverses the polarity of the neutron flow, a phrase commonly associated with the third Doctor, and he can speak baby, as first shown in 2011's "A Good Man Goes to War." The Doctor also shouted at the sky to address the Time Lords in 1985's "Attack of the Cybermen." Ashildr coming back to life is staged in exactly the same way as with the also-immortal Captain Jack Harkness (2005's "The Parting of the Ways").

The episode finally answers the question first uttered in "Deep Breath": why does the twelfth Doctor's face look so familiar to him? We have a flashback of Donna convincing the tenth Doctor to save Caecilus (as played by Peter Capaldi) and his family from 2008's "The Fires of Pompeii."

**The Hybrid Effect** The Doctor here turns Ashildr immortal and notes that, with alien tech inside her, she isn't human anymore; she's a hybrid. This links back to Davros's prophecy of two great warrior races merging (then thought to be the Time Lords and the Daleks, but here suggested to be the Vikings and the Mire).

**Who Is the Doctor?** The Doctor realizes that he has chosen the face of Caecilus from "The Fires of Pompeii" and surmises that he chose it because he needs to remind himself that sometimes he needs to save people no matter the consequences. He's also motivated because the death of Ashildr leaves him tired of saving the day but losing people (this could be informed by the previous story, where something similar happened to O'Donnell). And yet, after he saves Ashildr, the Doctor worries he has made an emotional decision because of his anger over Ashildr's loss, and he fears he may have made a terrible mistake.

**The Doctor and Clara** Clara accuses the Doctor of always talking about what he can and can't do but not telling her the rules, so the Doctor decides to try to explain how the rules work. He outright abandons his "no hugging" rule and runs to Clara and throws his arms around her when she comes back from the Mire spaceship. Just as the Doctor uses the baby translation to motivate the villagers, Clara uses it to motivate the Doctor to act. He says that immortality is the curse of watching everyone die and that he can't bear to lose her; someday the pain of losing Clara will hurt so much that he won't be able to breathe, but he will do what he always does: get in his box and run. It's hinted that they both have a bit of a crush on Ashildr.

**Monster of the Week** The Mire are a warrior race who feed on adrenaline and testosterone, which they harvest from warriors on other planets and drink as nectar.

They wear clunky metal armour and use holograms to take on the appearance of local gods. Underneath their helmets, they have huge mouths full of teeth.

**Stand Up and Cheer** The scene where the Doctor realizes why he chose this incarnation's face is stupendously good. His reflection reminds him, by way of flashbacks to "Deep Breath" and "The Fires of Pompeii," that he can break the laws of time, just as the tenth Doctor did, drawing on the compassion that Donna showed him to save someone. He now wears the face of the nobody he once saved in order to hold him to the mark: that he's the Doctor, and he saves people. Excuse us, we appear to have something in our eye . . .

**Roll Your Eyes** While the idea of using electric eels to magnetize the Mire helmets is fun, the actual shock produced by an eel amounts to 860 volts and one ampere of current for a duration of two milliseconds, which is vastly lower than that needed for the electromagnetic current we see here. And what are South American fish doing in a Viking village in the first place? It's enough to make a baby cry.

**You're Not Making Any Sense** The Doctor says that the battlefield medical kit will never stop repairing Ashildr. But would the battlefield medical kit itself last forever? Do the Mire helmets also outlive eternity?

**Interesting Trivia** This was the hundredth *Doctor Who* story since its revival in 2005. It's the hundred-and-twentieth actual episode, but there have been 20 two-parters during that time. Interestingly, the hundredth episode was "The Day of the Doctor," but everyone forgot that, as they were too busy celebrating other things. Only 61 more, and the New Series will have told more stories than the Classic Series. (Some of us may find that fact a little mind-boggling.)

In one of the great "if only" scenarios in *Doctor Who*, Odin was originally supposed to have been played by Brian Blessed, who has made a career playing larger-than-life roles, particularly Vultan in the 1980 cult classic *Flash Gordon*. Which would have been kind of perfect. Alas, Blessed fell ill, and the part had to be recast.

**The TARDIS Chronometer** Deep space, a Viking village and on board the Mire spaceship. The next story is set in the year 1651, where Ashildr mentions having had 800 years of adventure, putting this adventure circa 851 CE.

**Don't Be Stupid? (RS?)** For 38 minutes, this is the quintessential *Doctor Who* story.

The mini-adventure that kicks off the episode even does this in fast-forward. Clara's adrift in space with a spider in her spacesuit, while the Doctor is under attack from four battle fleets, having lured a race of aggressors across the universe and drained their weapons. When Clara asks if the aggressors will re-arm and try again, the Doctor admits that this is perfectly possible, but it was the best he could do. All of this takes precisely two minutes and 20 seconds. That's a *Doctor Who* story in a very tiny nutshell.

The slightly larger nutshell is the next 35 and a half minutes. The Doctor has no TARDIS, no sonic and has to save a village that's lost all its fighting men. He does this by way of baby speak, a party, electric eels and a bad special effect. That's just glorious — and everything that's wonderful about *Doctor Who*.

But it's not solely the resolution that's great; it's how he gets there. The Doctor starts off by telling the villagers to flee the invading army. When they refuse, claiming that they prefer to die with honour, he pauses to let the sound of an infant crying seep through and then asks, "Do babies die with honour?" That's a magnificent line . . . but it doesn't work.

When *Doctor Who* started, it was about a man on the run. So it makes perfect sense that this is the Doctor's first instinct. However, the second-ever story saw the Doctor convincing pacifists to fight, by way of his companion at the time. Later, the second Doctor's ethos became defined by some evils in the universe needing to be fought. So the Doctor's next move is training the villagers to fight. Clara criticizes this as not being what the Doctor does, but he counters that he learned it from his companion.

They've clearly been learning from each other, because Clara's impersonation of the Doctor on board the Mire spaceship is note-perfect. She's almost successful in convincing Odin to leave the village in peace, thanks to a combination of bluster, trickery and superior technology. It's only Ashildr who gets in the way, foreshadowing not only the rest of this story but the season as well.

Clara makes the point that the Doctor will win; he just doesn't know how he's going to do it until the last minute. This is the Doctor's "third way": not running, not fighting, but the unexpected. "The Girl Who Died" is a graceful sprint through the history of *Doctor Who* in order to set up something from totally out of left field. And, sure enough, it's the Doctor's ability to speak baby that leads him to "fire in the water," which he discovers are electric eels, which he tethers to something even more powerful: stories.

Ashildr's great ability is to tell stories. The Doctor points out that she's not the first to try to reshape reality through stories. The genius of his plan is to illustrate that stories aren't just for fun, they're also used for intimidation. So disrupting the Mire's story of themselves is the goal.

The execution of that goal is perfect. The Doctor wins by using Classic Series techniques with a New Series sheen. The attack on the Mire looks stupendous: the CGI serpent is convincing, terrifying and effective. But it's not real. As the Doctor points out, viewing reality through technology makes it easy to feed in a new reality. So while Odin thinks he's seeing a modern special effect, he's really being duped by theatrics: string, magnets, pulleys and wire. The puppet dragon is, as Clara points out, rubbish. But that's the point. Rather than try to create the best effect imaginable, the Doctor instead uses a bad special effect and a superior story, a trick he learned from the Classic Series.

This is utterly sublime.

And then, 38 minutes in, the battle has been won, the village saved and the monster defeated (while threatening to return someday). The only loss has been the guest star of the week, who died while saving everyone else. The Doctor and Clara briefly mourn her death and then depart the story in the TARDIS, another successful *Doctor Who* adventure under their belt.

Except that they don't do this last part.

Had the story finished there, it would have been a fun adventure of the week, with laughs and spills and tragedy. Instead, it becomes something much greater — and much more complicated.

The twelfth Doctor is the only Doctor who wasn't just left to his own devices from his predecessor. It's the first time a Doctor has had to point his next incarnation in the right direction, and he does it twice. Back in "Deep Breath," the eleventh Doctor phoned Clara to guide her in the transition, knowing how unsettled his successor would be. We again call back to that story here, as — in one of the most magnificent scenes ever filmed in *Doctor Who* — the Doctor discovers why he chose the face he did.

By returning to "The Fires of Pompeii," complete with a vision of a much more confident and determined tenth Doctor, we're reminded of the Doctor's relationship with fixed time and of the compassion he's capable of, if nudged by the right companion. Clara is not that companion . . . but Donna was.

And so, having been pointed in the right direction, what's the first thing the twelfth Doctor does with this newfound certainty? He makes a terrible mistake. One that will go on to cost him dearly. In response to having broken the rules and brought Ashildr back to life, he does the only thing he was ever going to do: he runs. He knows that her immortality isn't good, and he knows from experience that she won't like it. He throws her a bone, in the form of a second repair kit, but it's not enough. Because he's already aware that he's seen her before, in the future. From the first moment the Doctor laid eyes on Ashildr, he had a premonition in the form of future memory. And now he knows what he's done. Except that he won't fully know until the season's end, and it will cause nothing but heartache.

Indeed, the final shot of this episode, with the camera swirling around Ashildr as the days rush by, shows her initially happy to be alive, then horrified and then determined. The rest of the season is mapped out in those few moments, in yet another superb touch to what might be the greatest and most terrible *Doctor Who* story we've ever seen. I love it to pieces.

**Second Opinion (GB)** I really want to say that my co-author has covered everything I love about this story. And he has . . . for the first 38 minutes he speaks of above, which are just as delightful as he describes; if anything, the *Dad's-Army*-with-Vikings scenario is even funnier. (The Doctor introducing swords, with the jump-cut to the entire village in disarray as a result, is the funniest thing this season.)

It's the final six or so minutes I completely disagree about.

I really don't think we needed an explanation for why the Doctor has the face of a random guy he saved hundreds of years earlier in his own timestream. Colin Baker never got a scene noting how similar he looked to that Time Lord guard he'd once met. (Plus, we have Peter Capaldi playing a completely different character in *Torchwood*.) But that's not the reason it bothers me.

I feel with the fiftieth anniversary and a superfan of the series playing the Doctor, the fan service quotient is becoming dangerously high. This season, we've had a Skaro that used every imaginable version of Daleks (and a city design straight off the drawing board of Raymond Cusick in 1963), and that was just the first episode of the season. Now we're in episode five, and we're explaining why the Doctor looks like Caecilus? Really?

It bothers me because I feel like the Doctor should be motivated by what's in front of him — not by cute attempts to square the circle and explain why he looks the same as another character who hasn't been seen on television in seven years. Why can't the Doctor just be, you know, sad about a teenager dying? I'd even live with a flashback to Bennett telling the Doctor off about O'Donnell's death, as it aired only a week prior. At least it's to do with something in the Doctor's recent memory.

I understand my co-author's case for why it's cool that the Doctor is being directly influenced by his past. I just don't get the point of it. Sure, it adds an interesting element of predestination, I suppose — but I think it could have gotten there more effectively without answering a question that no one needed an answer to in the first place.

## 9.06 The Woman Who Lived

**Written by** Catherine Tregenna **Directed by** Ed Bazalgette
**Original airdate** October 24, 2014

**The Big Idea** What do you do when you're immortal and have survived the Dark

Ages? If you're Me — formerly Ashildr — you become a highwayman and steal an amulet in a bid to get off-world with a cat alien.

**Roots and References** The legend of real-life highwayman Dick Turpin (Me's alter-ego as the Knightmare); Daniel Defoe's 1722 novel *Moll Flanders* (Me's trials and tribulations, all journaled); Henry Fielding's 1749 novel *The History of Tom Jones, a Foundling*, particularly the 1963 film adaptation (comical adventures in the Middle Ages; Sam Swift has echoes of the ineffectual highwayman Partridge); Andrew Lloyd Webber's musical *Cats* (the look of Leandro); *The Muppet Show* (the riffing between the Doctor and Sam Swift is a saltier version of "Veterinarian's Hospital"). The Doctor calls the masked Knightmare "Zorro."

**Adventures in Time and Space** The Doctor warns Me that the Terileptils will bring plague and also fire to London (which they do to 1666 England in 1982's "The Visitation"). The Doctor mentions Captain Jack Harkness, who became immortal as a result of the events of 2005's "The Parting of the Ways." The story continues several themes from "The Girl Who Died," as the Doctor reconsiders the difference between ripples and tidal waves in history that he pondered in that story. The second dose of the Mire cure is used to save Sam Swift.

**Who Is the Doctor?** The Doctor has been following Ashildr/Me in her travels but refuses to take her off-world, asserting that, as an immortal, Me needs to connect to humans, telling her that humans are "mayflies. They know more than we do." He continues his declared mission in "Robot of Sherwood" of being anti-banter, adding that he's anti-puns as well. That said, when he needs to, he banters with Sam Swift like a pro.

**The Doctor and Clara** Clara is off this week, seen briefly at the end, but she hugs the Doctor, and the Doctor readily admits that he missed her.

**Monster of the Week** The Leonines are race of lion-like humanoids from Delta Leonis who travel great distances using a portal opened by the life energy of a dying person. They can breathe fire and have eyes that gleam in the dark.

**Stand Up and Cheer** The Doctor is forced to stall Sam Swift's (and his own) death by making a series of groaners not seen on British TV since the days of Tommy Cooper. "Doctor! Doctor! I'm a robber!"/"Have you taken anything for it?" and "He's so old, he farts dust." It's terrible. And it's hilarious — both at the same time.

**Roll Your Eyes** How did they get a Wanted poster for the Doctor that quickly? Though don't get us wrong, it's a great silhouette . . .

**You're Not Making Any Sense** Me remembers the Doctor and Clara but not her own name. Yes, it makes the point that she's not the same person anymore . . . but who forgets their own name?!

**Interesting Trivia** One of the stylistic experiments of this season was that almost every story was a two-parter or linked, carrying characters, ideas or themes from one standalone episode into another. Thus we have this episode, which continues the narrative of Ashildr/Me but is in every other respect its own story, so — despite the "To Be Continued . . . " at the end of the previous episode — we've decided to split the entries for this book.

The DVD/Blu-ray release includes in its deleted scenes a small but important moment for "The Woman Who Lived": After Me mourns the death of her children who died of the plague, she talks to a plague doctor — a physician who treated people with plague while wearing a bird-like protective mask with a long beak. (Its protective qualities were nil; there were some scented herbs in it that prevented "bad air.") Me tells the plague doctor that she's leaving and that the plague is actually created by poor sanitation (which it was). After she's gone, the plague doctor takes off his mask to reveal he's the Doctor. The implication of the scene is that the Doctor was keeping closer tabs on Me than was stated previously.

Comedian Rufus Hound, who plays Sam Swift, is a huge *Doctor Who* fan. He was one of the guests on the TV special where Peter Capaldi was announced to be the new Doctor. Hound infamously misfired during that appearance — making a joke about "he will knock four times" from David Tennant's final episodes, Hound accidentally said, "three times." ("Of all the places to get this wrong!" Hound immediately said.) The producers clearly forgave him, as he appears here. Hound later became the voice of a new incarnation of the William Hartnell–era villain the Monk in the Big Finish *Doctor Who* audio range.

When the initial trailer for Series Nine was released, in time for San Diego Comic Con, the very last shot was of Maisie Williams as Me, dressed as the Knightmare and saying to the Doctor, "What kept you, old man?" This caused fandom to collectively lose their shit, as the oldsters say, as speculations ran high that this character was anyone from the Doctor's granddaughter Susan to a new incarnation of River or any number of established characters. Of course, it turned out it was just someone the Doctor had met in the previous episode, and the scene was put at the very end of the trailer because of Maisie Williams's fame from *Game of Thrones*.

**The TARDIS Chronometer** England, 1651.

**Don't Be Stupid? (GB)** I love the idea of "The Woman Who Lived," just as I love the idea of Catherine Tregenna writing for *Doctor Who*. Tregenna was the one superstar on the writing staff at *Torchwood*. While everyone else was doing potboiler genre TV, she was writing thoughtful stories with a real emotional kick and an almost lyrical quality. And the idea for this story — a simple meditation on the nature of immortality — should be amazing.

Instead, "The Woman Who Lived" is a thoroughly damp squib. What happened?

I don't watch *Game of Thrones*, so all I have to go on with regard to Maisie Williams's talent is "The Girl Who Died," and I was very impressed with her there. Here, less so. Part of the problem is that Ashildr in "The Girl Who Died" was bold, imaginative and passionate. Ageing several hundred years has made her sullen and disengaged — which, I get, is the point, but I have no sympathy for the character. This is awkward when the Doctor and Me are talking about how fabulous Me has become in the intervening years. The journal entries show us everything she's lived *through* but not what she's lived *for*. It shows vignettes of miseries and tragedies but never of profound loves or moments of joy. Again, yes, I get that's the point, but it's an uninteresting one.

It's made all the more uninteresting because the plotlines to do with Leandro and Sam Swift and stealing the jewel aren't very interesting either. The viewer knows within seconds of meeting Leandro that he isn't being honest and his plan is going to lead to something nasty . . . so why doesn't the allegedly stupendously awesome Me get it? Also, Leandro is so flat and boring that I don't find him credible even as a *Doctor Who* monster. Sam Smith is a one-joke character. The climax is funny, but it feels like it could have been saved for a worthier story.

It's all a lame compromise. What it ought to be is a two-hander with the Doctor and Me. It should embrace the scenes with a recent immortal learning from an immortal who has lived for thousands of years and make that the heart of it. But it runs far from this idea to commit the most uninteresting heist scene in the history of filmed media (and I've seen *Ocean's 8!*).

Probably the most damnable thing about it is that the Doctor is so badly used in the story. If you're going to do a two-hander, don't reduce the Doctor's role to being the guy who reads the book that describes how awesome the secondary character is.

The only thing Me wants out of the Doctor is a ticket to the stars . . . not any insight into the pains and joys he's suffered being immortal. Worse, the Doctor doesn't offer any insight beyond suggesting she might take on some human companionship. (Me decides instead she'd rather take up the hobby of saving the world. B-o-r-i-n-g.) It's a waste of a character like the Doctor, and it's a waste of Peter Capaldi's talent.

This story could have featured two highly regarded actors examining what it's like to be someone who never dies, where both share their hopes, fears and pains with the other. You could have done it and still made it sufficiently *Doctor Who*-y (just put the house under siege, for example). You just need to trust the material you have in front of you.

I do hope Catherine Tregenna comes back to *Doctor Who* and tries again someday. Me (the character) . . . not so much.

**Second Opinion (RS?)** I'd like to apologize for my co-author's surly mood this week. Me, I kind of liked her.

I'm not convinced that a two-hander with Peter Capaldi and an immortal frenemy would be a good idea, given that this is exactly what the season opener was. And we've had a lot of darkness recently, not least in the preceding story. Here we get a lighthearted romp that's fun and funny, with some depth to it. I'm fine with that.

It's not that I don't agree with much of what Graeme says (the heist scene is pretty dull), but I think it misses the point. Yes, the Doctor lacks agency in this story . . . but that's because it's about showing him in contrast. Me is an excellent foil to the Doctor: also an immortal who (ultimately) wants to help people, but her choices are a reaction to the Doctor's lifestyle. By taking the long route, she gets a perspective on his life that he misses: namely, the detritus that's left behind. The fallout from this is going to be massive, so I like that it's effectively seeded here.

But it's more than that. The Doctor spends all his time trying to distract himself from his own immortality; Me does exactly the same thing, using different methods. Her journals are like the long history of *Doctor Who*: there if you want to access them (with a few gaps), but not terribly relevant in the present (though there are some excellent set pieces). Like the Doctor, she's not above theft or impersonation. And she yearns for her freedom when trapped. The difference is: he can escape, but she can't. The image of her in the selfie at the story's end is incredibly ominous.

Me is a dark mirror to the Doctor's soul. That this gets wrapped around a cheerful romp with gallows humour and a hilarious fight scene is pretty impressive. No complaints here. Not from Me.

# 9.07—9.08 The Zygon Invasion / The Zygon Inversion

**Written by** Peter Harness and Steven Moffat **Directed by** Daniel Nettheim
**Original airdates** October 31 and November 7, 2015

**The Big Idea** The ceasefire between humans and factions within the Zygon population has broken down. It's the nightmare scenario. The only thing left is the Osgood box.

**Roots and References** The 1956 film *Invasion of the Body Snatchers* and its 1978 remake (shapeshifting alien invaders bringing paranoia in their wake); the 1988 film and 1988–89 TV series *Alien Nation* (aliens immigrating to Earth and living among us); *24* (the mixture of ripped-from-the-headlines terrorism and larger-than-life action); the 2012 film *Zero Dark Thirty* (the Turmezistan sequences); *The Spy Who Loved Me* (the Doctor's parachute has the Union Jack on it). The Zygon representatives Jemima and Claudette have *Cinderella* and *Monster High* backpacks. The Doctor is playing "Amazing Grace" when Osgood texts him.

**Adventures in Time and Space** The story begins with a flashback to the Doctors forging the Zygon/human truce in "The Day of the Doctor," with a brief allusion to Osgood's death in "Dark Water"/"Death in Heaven." There's a picture of the first Doctor (who never met UNIT except briefly in 1972's "The Three Doctors") in front of the safe in the UNIT safe house. Much of the Zygon hardware (and its fronds, which need titillating) were in 1975's "Terror of the Zygons"; when talking about the events of that story, Kate Stewart adopts the usual vagueness about whether it was set in the '70s or '80s.

The Doctor flies on a presidential plane similar to the one in "Dark Water"/"Death in Heaven." (Once again, it's destroyed while in flight — the Doctor should stick to trains!) When the Doctor tells Walsh he's president of the world, Walsh says, "We know who you are," a nod to the running gag with Harriet Jones that began with 2005's "The Christmas Invasion." The Zygon-destroying gas was developed by the fourth Doctor's companion, Harry Sullivan (whose final regular story was "Terror of the Zygons"). Harry — who was called an "imbecile" by the fourth Doctor in 1975's "Revenge of the Cybermen," something the twelfth echoes here — developed this gas in Porton Down, which tallies with where the Brigadier said Harry was stationed in 1983's "Mawdryn Undead."

The Black Archive is as we saw it in "The Day of the Doctor," complete with the memory-wiping devices (though it now has the helmet of a Mire from "The Girl Who Died"). Kate kills the Zygon using "five rounds rapid," a catchphrase her father, the Brigadier, used when dispatching a "chap with wings" (in that case, an animated gargoyle) in 1971's "The Dæmons."

For those keeping track of Osgood's Doctor-inspired fashion choices, here she sports the eleventh Doctor's bowtie (while still wearing the fourth Doctor's scarf), the seventh Doctor's pullover and tie and the fifth Doctor's shirt with a question-marked collar. The Doctor and Osgood also reminisce about the Doctor's predilection in 1980s stories for question marks; he claims they're on his underwear now!

**The Hybrid Effect** The Doctor's response to Osgood's philosophy that she's now both Zygon and human — and it doesn't matter which — is "Like a *hybrid*?" Stay tuned for the Doctor to be offered a ride in a Prius, only for him to say, "Travel in . . . a *hybrid*?"

**Who Is the Doctor?** He's more facetious than usual, calling himself "Doctor Disco" and "Doctor Funkenstein" and even telling Osgood his real name is

"Basil." But this may just be the Doctor deflecting from the experience of getting Zygons and humans to renegotiate the ceasefire, which leads him to talk about his trauma in the Time War for the first time in quite a while. It's clear that the anguish of it is still very much with him.

**The Doctor and Clara** Even though Bonnie has taken Clara's form, leaving Clara without much to do, her impact on the Doctor is evident, as he credits Clara with helping him change the course of the Time War in "The Day of the Doctor." When Clara asks what the Doctor felt when he thought she was dead, he says it was "the longest month of my life." When she points out it was only five minutes, his response is "I'll be the judge of time."

**Monster of the Week** The Zygons return, having agreed to live on Earth in human form after the events of "The Day of the Doctor." Most are happy to live this way, though a faction opposes it. The Zygons can now take human form using memories and only need to store bodies in stasis as a live link if they need more information from them. They emit electrical stings that can disintegrate beings into a small hairy mass.

**Stand Up and Cheer** Okay . . . take "The Zygon Inversion." Watch it from 30:39 to 39:51. Watch nine minutes and 12 seconds of Peter Capaldi delivering the best performance in *Doctor Who* you'll ever see, while giving the best speech that anyone has ever made in *Doctor Who*. Or possibly anywhere. Watch it again. And again. It's that good.

**Roll Your Eyes** What the hell is up with the crowd of people who are completely unresponsive as Etoine runs around, freaking out before transforming into a bloody great monster? Are they Zygons? Completely stoned? Played by extras who were on break?!

**You're Not Making Any Sense** How is Clara able to become aware, much less able to have this symbiotic connection to Bonnie? Even the other characters marvel about it, yet no one explains how Clara, out of the hundreds of people who are held in stasis by the Zygons, is able to do it. Just . . . plot convenience?

**Interesting Trivia** The premise for this story was given to Peter Harness to develop. Unusually, Harness wrote the first episode on his own but co-wrote the second episode with Steven Moffat.

*Truth or Consequences*, which began in 1940 on the radio before moving to television, was a game show that involved contestants performing stunts if they failed to answer general knowledge questions. For its tenth anniversary in 1950, the show's host and creator, Ralph Edwards, stated that the show would broadcast its anniversary episode from a town that would rename itself "Truth or Consequences." The town — formerly known as Hot Springs, New Mexico — accepted the challenge. Truth! (And also some consequences.)

Just how is the Doctor still emergency president of the world? He's certainly acting as though he has the role, though based on what we're told in "Dark Water"/"Death in Heaven," the powers are only given to him when there's a global crisis agreed to by all the world leaders. However, Operation Double, the covert operation to rehouse the Zygons, is done without the knowledge of global authorities. Perhaps they never rescinded it after Missy's Cybermen invasion? Or Kate simply gave the Doctor the plane to ponce around in to keep him happy?

Operation Double, being done "off the books" by UNIT U.K., brings up some thorny problems. UNIT rehoused 20 million Zygons around the world without telling the leaders of those countries. And, more critically, they did it without any infrastructure to support them. If Norlander's account of what happened in Truth or Consequences is to be believed, the Zygons had no money, no skills training and, more importantly, no emergency support when a Zygon accidentally reveals themself. No wonder there was an anti-British sentiment in New Mexico or that the Doctor has had to come back 15 times to renegotiate the peace. It might have gone a lot smoother had they thought the details through.

There are a few missing credits on this story. Nicholas Briggs, who tends to get called in every time they need a Classic Series monster voice, voiced the Zygons but was accidentally left off the credits when the story was broadcast. (He was put in when it was released on DVD.) Missing altogether is creator credit for Robert Banks Stewart, who wrote "Terror of the Zygons." It has been suggested that perhaps Stewart's estate subsequently sold the rights to the Zygons to the BBC. Or, as with Briggs, the BBC overlooked it. Either way, it's a conspicuous absence in the Zygons' first full story in 40 years.

**The TARDIS Chronometer** London, Turmezistan and New Mexico, the present day.

**Don't Be Stupid? (GB)** This is one of those stories that initially seems to work, then you realize it doesn't . . . and then it suddenly does anyway. And it owes it all to The Speech.

It starts with *Doctor Who* doing a rather impressive assaying of the modern thriller, as we watch the Doctor and UNIT arrive too late: the Zygons are rebelling and infiltrating everyone, including Clara. (The Zygons' elevator and Sandeep's parents weren't coincidental!) They've run circles around Colonel Walsh's crew and wiped out UNIT troops in London.

It's the first *Doctor Who* story to use the language of the war on terror as the Doctor talks about "radicalized" Zygons and the Zygons are treated as a race that wants to live peaceably (like the twins and Etoine and Osgood) but for a fanatical few. And the makers know they're ripping from the headlines as the Doctor makes the uncomfortably true quip, "Well, you can't have the United Kingdom. There's already people living there. They'll think you're going to pinch their benefits."

And, like in "Kill the Moon," Peter Harness brilliantly gives us the whole picture, as we understand what's motivating both humans and Zygons. The visit to New Mexico is sobering, as we see that Zygons faced xenophobia and discrimination in their human forms before things became dire. No wonder they want to live as themselves.

The problem is it's a sort of dream logic where everything holds together until you take a step back from it. At that point, the logic of "The Zygon Invasion"/"The Zygon Inversion" falls apart. How would a planet that regularly does a pretty terrible job of administrating health care oversee the rehousing of 20 million shapeshifting aliens *in secret*? How did no one in London notice Zygons building extensions on their apartment elevators? What the hell is up with the non-threatening-but-threatening police officers? Why are the Doctor and Osgood the only souls on the airplane with parachutes? How the hell is Clara the only person in 40 years of Zygon stories able to wake up, much less influence Bonnie? Even the centrepiece of the episode is hinged on the idea that every time the peace breaks down, the Doctor has to give an emotional speech that puts everything right.

But just as the story is about to have the cruel daylight of plot and logic burn everything away, suddenly we have The Speech.

You know how I've been complaining about this season and how it's so budget-strapped that it's doing lots of two-part stories with long talky scenes? With this story, they weaponize the talky scene. The weapon is Peter Capaldi, one of the great British actors of this or any other generation, with *nine minutes* to monologue about the limitations of tyranny and war, the need for people to talk and reason together (all the more prescient now) and the terrible burden the Doctor carries as a former warrior. Cataloguing what happens during The Speech doesn't do it justice, because it's performed with a supernova of intensity by Capaldi (aided by Jenna Coleman as Bonnie, who is a revelation). It's funny and electrifying and smart and devastating. And when the Doctor suddenly rasps that he's going to do the unthinkable and forgive Bonnie, it's unforgettable. When the Doctor wearily thanks Kate for standing down, I burst into tears. When he gives Bonnie that sad, sad look, and she does too, I do so again.

The Speech transcends the good and bad of this story. It makes you forget the dream logic and bad plotting and remember the creepiness and the great villainy. It makes you realize how precious Peter Capaldi is as the Doctor. But it does more than that. It makes you ask: what other show could have a heavyweight actor spend nine minutes making an impassioned speech about forgiveness?

The answer is: only *Doctor Who* would do this. The Speech is one of the things that makes this show so goddamn great.

**Second Opinion (RS?)** My problem with this story is almost exactly the same as my problem with "Kill the Moon": the utterly brilliant central debate gets lost because of the stupid. Previously, it was the science. Here, it's the televisual clichés. My co-author identifies a great many of them, but for me it's those damn soldiers in Turmezistan.

I'm usually pretty forgiving of televisual language shortcutting stuff that isn't central to the story. People sometimes walk into obvious traps (like Clara does in her building or Jac does underground) that the audience knows they shouldn't, and which any rational person would probably avoid, but hey, that's TV. But where this falls down is when the plot has smart people acting like utter morons.

How are the UNIT troops in Turmezistan so badly fooled by Zygons — who they know shapeshift — pretending to be their families? It's their job to face down aliens. Fair enough with the woman who can't launch a missile at what might be her child. But the rest are laughable. They've been highly trained and specifically warned about this very possibility — so if they're really unsure about who's who, why don't they take all their "relatives" into custody and sort things out later, instead of following them into an obvious trap? You know, the relatives who won't even answer simple questions about birthdays, despite having been plucked from someone's memories?

Meanwhile, the Doctor stands idly by as a UNIT commander orders her men to murder all those people. Whether they're humans or Zygons, would he really do this? He even says, "Try to kill as few of them as possible." Rather than — oh, I don't know — "Don't kill any of them," as the Doctor we know actually would.

The result is a story that should be gripping and intense falls apart because the central character isn't consistent and skilled soldiers can't do their job. Not only does this undermine the central premise, it turns a deathly serious story into a laughing stock.

But let's fast-forward to The Speech. My co-author is absolutely right about how intensely marvellous it is and how it single-handedly redeems the entire story. It's a shame that the story even needs to be redeemed in the first place, as it's clear that Peter Harness is one of the most interesting voices that *Doctor Who* has ever had on the writing staff. But if he could stop distracting us from his amazing ideas with the stupid, that would be nice. (And probably very, very good for his career, to boot.)

I actually deeply love this story, and I've watched The Speech on its own more times than I can count, but it's a bit like dating a fiery redhead who argues with you when you tell them how great they are. Why are you making it so hard for me to like you?! I guess maybe that's the Inversion.

## The Psychic Papers: The Zygons

For a very long time, the Zygons had the distinction of being the most famous monsters who never were.

They first appeared in 1975's "Terror of the Zygons," in a story where six of them were disguised as people in a Scottish village, using the Loch Ness Monster to attempt to take over the world. Yes, *that* Loch Ness Monster. The same one Sarah Jane Smith plays as her trump card when comparing notes with Rose in 2006's "School Reunion."

One of the things that makes the Zygons so rich is their backstory. Having crashed on Earth millennia ago, their planet destroyed and relying on the milk of the Skarasen, an enormous cyborg creature (a.k.a. the Loch Ness Monster), to survive, they're immediately sympathetic. And their leader, Broton, is played utterly straight, spending much of the story in the guise of a stiff-upper-lip member of the Scottish aristocracy, talking about the power of organic crystallography as though it were his prized membership at a gentlemen's club.

It's a brilliant story in an era full of brilliant stories. But perhaps the highlight was the design of the monsters themselves. Costume designer James Acheson — who went on to become a three-time Oscar winner — fashioned them as walking, bulbous embryos, with John Friedlander, who sculpted the actual suits, creating the details of the face. Designer Nigel Curzon also added to mix, providing the organic controls that had to be manipulated with smooth, almost sexual movements. In an early glimpse of what was to come, Tom Baker even sends this up by being far too graphic with the Zygon controls for children's TV, while making adults realize that the man they were watching on TV was an acting deity.

Certainly, their raspy voices added to the effect. Their nature as shapeshifters who could look like anyone (including the Doctor's then-companion Harry Sullivan) added to the allure. But what set the Zygons apart was that, even in the mid-'70s, at a time when *Doctor Who* looked lush and rich, the Zygons stood out as particularly visually arresting. As a result, they were the go-to visual for the media, who used images of them in newspaper and magazine articles about *Doctor Who*. As a result, they punched above their weight as *Doctor Who* adversaries: people knew them much better than, say, the Kraals, even though both only turned up once in the Classic Series, a few months apart. Little wonder they were David Tennant's favourite monster.

So why didn't they appear for another 40 years?

The Hinchcliffe era, as the first half of Tom Baker's tenure is known, was famous for ditching regular monsters for memorable one-offs. Sutekh, Morbius and Magnus Greel (from, respectively, 1975's "Pyramids of Mars," 1976's "The Brain of Morbius" and 1977's "The Talons of Weng-Chiang") are fantastic creations that never return, but they're all villainous individuals, rather than races of monsters. However, monsters such as the Mandragora Helix, the Voc Robots and the Krynoids (1976's "The Masque of Mandragora," 1977's "The Robots of Death" and 1976's "The Seeds of Doom") are equally memorable and equally absent from any future TV stories.

It's a testament to the Zygons' staying power that they did show up again, for the fiftieth anniversary in "The Day of the Doctor." They were used as shorthand for an alien invasion in a story that needed to move its plot beats along efficiently. With the advent of CGI, demonstrating the Zygons' shapeshifting abilities had become a lot easier. The only downside was that the costumes never looked quite as real as they did in the '70s. With "The Zygon Invasion"/"The Zygon Inversion," we see the Zygons' fate linked inexorably with humanity's, which offers even more story potential.

Let's just hope we don't need to wait another 40 years for their return . . .

## 9.09 Sleep No More

**Written by** Mark Gatiss **Directed by** Justin Molotnikov

**Original airdate** November 14, 2015

**The Big Idea** Gagan Rassmussen has edited together a video of the ill-fated rescue mission on LeVerrier Station, which has been overrun by monsters made of the stuff created in your eye when you sleep.

**Roots and References** Found-footage movies popularized by the 1997 film *The Blair Witch Project* and 2008's *Cloverfield*; the Marvel Comics villain the Sandman; *Babylon 5* (the space station, Rassmussen's uniform). The Doctor sings a line of "Consider Yourself" from *Oliver!* People who reject the Morpheus machine are called "Rips" after Rip Van Winkle from the 1819 short story of the same name by Washington Irving. Actor Reece Shearsmith asked for Rassmussen to have big glasses as a tribute to the spectacles Lawrence Payne wore when he played Dastari in the 1985 *Doctor Who* story "The Two Doctors." The title takes its inspiration from a line in *Macbeth* (which the Doctor quotes). Throughout, we hear the 1954 song "Mr. Sandman," popularized by the Chordettes (but sung here by sound-alikes).

**Adventures in Time and Space** The story is set in the 38th century, sometime after the great disaster referred to in stories like 1975's "The Ark in Space."

When Clara names the Sandmen, the Doctor says, "It's like the Silurians all over again," referring to the titular creatures from 1970's "Doctor Who and the Silurians," even though they're from the wrong geological age. The reference to Space Pirates not only disproves the Doctor's notion that you can't put "space" in front of any old word, but it could also allude to the 1969 story "The Space Pirates."

**Who Is the Doctor?** The Doctor is initially keen to save Deep-Ando, though he becomes less keen to save others once he's cornered. Following on from "Flatline," he seems to take being able to name the monsters very seriously; he's irritated that Clara comes up with "Sandmen" first.

**The Doctor and Clara** In a rather sweet moment, the Doctor asks Clara to hold his hand, and when Clara says she's okay, he tells her, "I'm not." She holds his hand.

**Monster of the Week** Okay, give us a second here. This is going to be hard to do. The Sandmen are creatures made of the hardened mucus that accretes in the eye during sleep, who have become weaponized and carnivorous because of the Morpheus process.

Gigantic, walking eye-boogers. God, this is a strange job . . .

**Stand Up and Cheer** Deep-Ando desperately trying to get into a locked room with a password that's a song he's too scared to sing is a really great moment. It's enhanced by an uncredited performance by producer Nikki Wilson as the flirtiest computer voice interface ever.

**Roll Your Eyes** Rassmussen was the villain all along! We'd never have known that except . . . who else could it be?

**You're Not Making Any Sense** The Doctor doesn't actually explain how Morpheus turns human mucus into sentient, carnivorous beings. He just restates that's what it does in the hopes we'll accept it. Sorry, but . . . no.

**Interesting Trivia** This is the first *Doctor Who* story to not have a title sequence. Unlike subsequent occasions where this has occurred, it hedged somewhat by highlighting the letters for "Doctor Who" in the datastream of names after the introduction.

Bethany Black, who plays 474, is the first transgender actress on *Doctor Who*. Black is a stand-up comedian, and *Doctor Who* was her second dramatic role. Black is a *Doctor Who* fan who even asked writer Mark Gatiss if the 38th-century setting was because it was set in the same era as the 1977 story "The Sun Makers." (It wasn't.)

How do dust specks act as a camera? And if there's no CCTV footage, just how is some of the footage not from a human point of view in black and white, while other footage (like from Chopra's gun) is in colour? Perhaps Rassmussen was doing colour grading along with editing and narrating — though we're not entirely sure when he was able to do all that in the first place.

**The TARDIS Chronometer** LeVerrier Station, orbiting Neptune, sometime in the 38th century. On a Tuesday.

**Don't Be Stupid? (GB)** No. Just . . . no.

I love experiments in storytelling in *Doctor Who*. I only ask for three things: don't bore me; don't cheat; and be as bold as possible.

"Sleep No More" is an epic fail on every single count.

The worst thing is the cheating. Using found footage in *Doctor Who* should be the most exciting thing ever. In theory, it should be everything we love: the thrills, the jeopardy, the race against time with a Time Lord with all artifice stripped out of it. It should be *Doctor Who* but with tremendous immediacy, as everything is from a limited number of perspectives.

Unfortunately, "Sleep No More" pretends to uphold the idea of using found footage while only using it in the most superficial way. With the revelation that cameras are in the dust, they're not limiting the number of points of view on the characters — which is, frankly, *the whole point* of found footage — they're doing a middling episode of *Doctor Who* with some hand-held camerawork that's as omniscient as any other episode. It's just given the illusion of found footage.

Part of the problem is the setting is too large and too artificial. Found footage works better the more limitations you have. *The Blair Witch Project* is a perfect example: it works because you don't see the threat — or when you do, it's in partial glimpses — and so it relies on the reactions of the characters. In fact, if I were to take a story from the Modern Series and give it a found-footage treatment, the likely candidate would be "Midnight": a story with an enclosed setting and a menace you can't quite see or that defies being filmed. Instead, "Sleep No More" wants to tempt fate by putting it in a *Doctor Who* story made up of the usual sets in Roath Lock and a couple of supplementary locations and throwing in a bunch of men-in-suit monsters to make matters worse.

The result is absolutely no immediacy. (It doesn't help that the characters are largely ciphers; the only exception is 474 and her crush on Chopra, which merely meets expectations rather than exceeds them.) Every scene in a found-footage version of *Doctor Who* should be like the scene with Deep-Ando trying to get into the room: it's heavily from a character's point of view, living with their terror and, when they turn their backs . . . BOO! Most scenes in "Sleep No More" are the Doctor and company just running around. It's less *Blair Witch* and more *Scooby-Doo*.

It's even more terrible than that, because it doubles down by having Rassmussen present the whole thing as an unreliable narrator. Rassmussen's narration is boring and clichéd. (Outside of a 1940s B-movie, no one has *ever* said something like, "Deep-Ando. Conscript. Likes to think of himself as the joker of this little group. Well, he *did*.") It adds nothing to the story beyond compressing things that probably should be kept in . . . like the Doctor explaining what the Sandmen are. Worse, it telegraphs that Rassmussen isn't reliable since he's still narrating after allegedly being killed. It's all in service of the slam-dunk of the closing scene where he's inexplicably revealed to be the monster . . . only it's not even remotely earned.

And then there are the Sandmen. My problem isn't that they're a gross idea for a monster; it's that they're the prime example of "because I said so" as explanation in *Doctor Who* history. They're not even particularly scary — which is a really egregious sin in a found-footage story; in a story where body horror might have been welcome, they only show the end result of the creatures rather than showing people becoming them.

I would still really like to see *Doctor Who* tackle a found-footage story. "Sleep No More" is not so much a pretender as an outright imposter. And an insult to my intelligence on top of it all.

**Second Opinion (RS?)** What he said. Though I thought it was perfectly serviceable as an opening episode. I'm sure it'll all be explained in part two . . .

# 9.10 Face the Raven

**Written by** Sarah Dollard **Directed by** Justin Molotnikov

**Original airdate** November 21, 2015

**The Big Idea** Clara's friend Rigsy calls her and the Doctor in when he wakes up with a tattoo counting down on his neck. The answer lies in a hidden street where aliens are taking refuge, but the laws of the street are absolute — and deadly.

**Roots and References** The 1949 film *D.O.A.* (Rigsy only having 24 hours to live); the 2009 film *District 9* (the alien refugee camp); the 1996 *Doctor Who* novel *Return of the Living Dad* (a hidden settlement on Earth made up of former *Doctor Who* monsters); the 1994 film version of *The Crow* (there, a mythical black bird gives back a soul; here, it takes it away). Clara once again mentions Jane Austen, this time in the context of someone whom she pranks and who is a friend (or possibly more).

**Adventures in Time and Space** Rigsy previously featured in "Flatline," while Me was last seen in "The Woman Who Lived." There's a flashback to the Doctor's sighting of Me in the present day at the end of that story, while Me has followed through on her promise to pick up the pieces in the Doctor's wake. Some of the aliens on Trap Street include Sontarans, Ood, Cybermen, Judoon (appropriately disguised as policemen!) and the Lugal-Irra-Kush, the crested aliens previously seen in "The Rings of Akhaten." There are also very brief flashes of a Silurian (in a mask) and an Ice Warrior (out of its armour).

Rigsy's memory loss is achieved with the drug Retcon, which featured in the spinoff show *Torchwood*. The cue cards from "Under the Lake" make a brief appearance. Clara references Danny Pink dying well in "Death in Heaven" (specifically his final death, when he sends the boy back), Me references Zygons out in the world ("The Zygon Invasion"/"The Zygon Inversion"), and the Doctor threatens to bring UNIT and the Daleks to Trap Street.

**The Hybrid Effect** The Doctor is trapped by unknown enemies and forced to surrender the confession dial he's been carrying around all season.

**Who Is the Doctor?** With Clara facing death, the Doctor threatens Me, saying, "The Doctor is no longer here." Which sounds like he's dangerously close to forsaking his name and becoming the Warrior again. (Clara even says, "Don't be a warrior.") We see a very ugly side of the Doctor here, as he promises to end not only Me but everyone she loves, threatening to bring in every force that would expose and destroy them. Clara stops him, reminding him once again that his reign of terror would end with the first cry of a child. Even so, he notes that it's a very small universe when he's angry with someone. He has a whole room in the TARDIS devoted to surveilling Me throughout the ages.

**The Doctor and Clara** Clara's desire to be more Doctor-like results in her making a terrible mistake that the Doctor would totally make, except that he's less breakable. Even so, the Doctor's fury is palpable, even threatening to forsake what he stands for to save her. But Clara refuses to let the Doctor destroy Trap Street, going so far as to order him not to insult her memory and wreak revenge. At the end, she prevents him from telling her how he feels, saying, "Everything you are about to say, I already know. Don't do it now. We've already had enough bad timing."

**Monster of the Week** A Quantum Shade is a kind of spirit that binds itself to a victim using a chronolock (a tattoo on the neck that counts down to zero). You could run across all of time and space, and it would find you. Here, it appears in the form of a raven that kills people by flying into someone's back and then emerging from the body as black smoke.

**Stand Up and Cheer** Although it ultimately fails, Clara's plan is absolutely ingenious. Taking in the snippets of information she's heard, she realizes that Rigsy can give the tattoo to her, knowing that she's protected by Me's promise. It's a very Doctorish solution.

**Roll Your Eyes** We get to meet Rigsy's baby why . . . exactly? Oh, that's right: because giving him a cute offspring will make him worth saving. Rather than, say, because he's a human being in his own right who did nothing wrong.

**You're Not Making Any Sense** Why can't Clara just give the tattoo back to Rigsy? Me says that she can't but doesn't explain why not. Me also says that her taking it changes the terms of the contract, but why is that, exactly? When Me promised that Clara would be under her personal protection, she said that this was absolute. Absolute doesn't mean "unless you do something to change the terms of a contract you knew nothing about." It means that it's absolute. Clara's plan really should have worked!

**Interesting Trivia** Clara's right that a trap street is a nonexistent street on a map that cartographers use to determine if other mapmakers are stealing their work. The phenomenon isn't limited to streets, however; it can include fictitious towns or mountains at the wrong elevation. In order to avoid confusing people navigating with the map, the traps may be subtler, like a bend in a street that has none. Although these are usually kept quiet, for obvious reasons, there's a popular driving atlas for Athens, Greece, that has a warning at the front about trap streets.

The original script (with the title "Trap Street") had more Rigsy, including a moving scene where the Doctor told Rigsy to remember what Clara did for him. He also ordered Ashildr to not Retcon Rigsy a second time in order to allow him to remember. Rigsy's partner Jen (unseen in the broadcast episode) appeared throughout the original script and in the epilogue, talking to baby Lucy about what Clara did, while Rigsy painted Clara's portrait on the TARDIS. The final lines were Jen saying, "He won't be mad you painted his TARDIS?" and Rigsy replying, "I hope he is mad. I hope he comes back and properly goes off at me." It included the stage direction, "But Rigsy frowns. He isn't holding his breath." All these scenes were shot, with Naomi Ackie cast as Jen, but in the end, they were cut, presumably for timing reasons.

This is the first time in the Modern Series that a companion has been killed off in order to write them out. However, it's not the first companion death in *Doctor Who*: the Classic Series killed off two short-term companions in the first Doctor's era, as well as Adric, a long-running companion of the fourth and fifth Doctors. That story broke with tradition and ran the end credits silently, superimposed over the remains of Adric's badge for mathematical excellence.

"Face the Raven" also breaks with tradition after a long-running companion death, by being the first episode of *Doctor Who* to have a scene after the end credits. It's fairly brief — Rigsy painting a mural on the TARDIS — but the idea is so unusual that one of us entirely missed it the first several times he watched the episode. In case that's you, stick around until the end; it's a lovely coda.

**The TARDIS Chronometer** London, present day.

**Don't Be Stupid? (RS?)** There's no other *Doctor Who* story this bleak.

For the past three years, Clara has been slowly turning into the Doctor. Back in "Death in Heaven," she even told some Cybermen that she was the Doctor and that Clara Oswald didn't exist, complete with her headlining the opening credits. Again and again, we've seen Clara attempt to emulate the Doctor, with greater and greater success: she almost perfectly talks down the Mire on board their spaceship in "The Girl Who Died," for example, and effectively becomes him for the majority of "Flatline."

Here, it all comes to a head. She does exactly what the Doctor would do to save Rigsy (who was essentially her companion in "Flatline") by taking all the information about the world she's found herself in and using the tools at hand to create an innovative solution. She even describes it as "Doctor 101," hoisting the opposition with their own petard. The genius of this plan is that it twists the pre-established rules of the trap street into a shape we weren't expecting, simultaneously upping the threat by having Clara take the tattoo. You can imagine the Doctor doing the same thing at the triumphant climax of an episode.

But then it all goes horribly wrong.

The real problem here isn't that she keeps it from the Doctor (she even uses the Doctor's presumed disapproval as part of her plan). And it's not at all a bad strategy; the only weak spot in the episode is that they gloss over the reasons that Clara's plan doesn't work. Had we been privy to information that Clara wasn't, that would have been fine. Instead, Me simply tells us flat-out that she can't keep her earlier promise and that Clara can't give the tattoo back to Rigsy, but these aren't explained. The result is authorial fiat: Clara dies because the story cheats, which is unfortunate.

The tragedy of Clara's death is that she's overlooked one vital thing about the Doctor: he can regenerate. This is the ultimate get-out-of-jail-free card for the Time Lord; he can be far more reckless than his human companions, because if things go wrong, he can die and be reborn. Clara can't.

Even the trap street itself is a response to the Doctor's lifestyle, full of his enemies. Following the promise in "The Woman Who Lived," that Me would protect Earth from the Doctor, here we see the result of that, and it's dirty, uncomfortable and full of traumatized people. It's a refugee camp, although it's left unclear from what the aliens are seeking refuge. Rump mentions a war zone, but there are also suggestions that the residents are the collateral damage of the Doctor's lifestyle, so Rump's war may well be one of the Doctor's.

By the story's end, that collateral damage has come home. The chain of events stretches back to the tenth Doctor saving a family in Pompeii, by way of the twelfth Doctor breaking the rules and bringing a teenager back to life, and concludes with the death of the Doctor's companion. The result is a story where the Doctor loses, and loses badly. His companion is killed, and he's captured by enemies unknown and teleported elsewhere, separated from his TARDIS.

There have been a few other stories where the Doctor loses, such as "The Aztecs" from the show's very first season. And there have been stories where the Doctor's companions have died, but at least there an overall victory was achieved. Here we get neither of those things, which is an incredibly brave choice. It may be bleak, but it does at least take that bleakness and run with it.

It's probably not possible to love this story, but you do have to respect it.

**Second Opinion (GB)** She used to have a book that she brought everywhere. It was called *101 Places to See*. She had a leaf that was the start of her mum and dad. And was the start of her.

She once asked her friend why they were running from a girl in danger, and she learned then that they never, ever ran away from trouble.

Her friend thought she was an impossible girl. Which is ridiculous, really, because she was *herself*. She had responsibilities. She had a life. She had somebody occasionally stop by with a blue box to take her anywhere. And he was cute. Not that she would ever tell him that.

She was willing to do anything to save his life. To become impossible if she had to. But even then, she was herself.

One time — one extraordinary time — she got a rare glimpse into her friend's past. She looked into his sad, old, young eyes and saw a terrible heartbreak. And she told him the truth: that he was smarter and better than the ghosts that haunted him.

Then came the day when her friend changed. And then followed the days where she mourned what was. But then she realized . . . her friend was scared, like her. Her friend had lost his way. So she reminded him what was important: that there were things to learn from every experience.

She didn't look at her friend the same way, though she still loved him. And she learned to love someone else. Her friend hated her boyfriend, but she loved him because . . . love doesn't make sense. Love never makes sense. But it's something humans do.

Her friend hurt her, and she cut him off. He came back, and she forgave him. But she did more than forgive; she understood something about herself, about who she wanted to be. And it scared her and thrilled her.

One day, she discovered that people just . . . end. Her boyfriend died. She went to hell and back and found herself alone.

But her friend came back. This time, she remembered all the things she really loved about him. True, he was grouchy and socially awkward. But he would do anything to help a crying child. And he would do anything for her.

She became less scared being with him. She stood up to bullies and faced down monsters. It was as though, perhaps, she wanted to forget the pain of loss: the loss of her mum, the loss of her boyfriend. Perhaps she overcame that sense of loss by becoming more like her friend.

And her friend was, well, *incredible*.

She wanted to be like him. But she couldn't be like him. Because it was her friend who was impossible, not her.

One day, she did something she thought was clever, and she was wrong. She faced her death the only way she could: as herself. Begging the universe to let her be brave. Whatever happens next, this will be her final end.

She used to have a book that she brought with her everywhere. In that book, she wrote down her age every year and crossed it out to write a new one every birthday. That book was called *101 Places to See*.

Her name was Clara Oswald, and she's one of my very favourite companions. She was called the impossible girl, but, really, she was just herself. And that's why I loved her.

## 9.11 Heaven Sent

**Written by** Steven Moffat **Directed by** Rachel Talalay
**Original airdate** November 28, 2015

**The Big Idea** The Doctor is trapped in a prison, while being stalked by a monster that will never, ever stop.

**Roots and References** James Joyce's *Finnegans Wake* (a dream state that runs in a loop); the 1998 films *Dark City* and *Cube* (the self-contained environment that changes its configurations); the *Babylon 5* episode "Intersections in Real Time" (an unending series of torture sessions that continues in a loop); Steven Moffat's other TV show *Sherlock* (the storeroom in the Doctor's mind is uncomfortably similar to Sherlock's mind palace); the 1967–69 cult TV series *The Prisoner* (the Doctor in a banal setting he cannot escape from unless he confesses something); *Star Trek*'s transporter, in particular its pattern buffer (the teleporter maintaining a perfect copy). Much of the music seems to be based on (or an outright pastiche of) Beethoven's 7th Symphony. The story of the bird is from "The Shepherd Boy" by the Brothers Grimm.

**Adventures in Time and Space** We see a flashback to Clara's death in "Face the Raven." Gallifrey returns, last seen in "The Day of the Doctor," with the dome first seen onscreen in 2007's "Last of the Time Lords." In 1969's "The War Games," the Doctor claimed he left Gallifrey because he was bored, although we find out here that this was a lie.

**The Hybrid Effect** Long before the Time War, the Time Lords predicted that a hybrid creature would arise to destroy Gallifrey and stand in its ashes. The Doctor knows that the Hybrid is not half Time Lord and half Dalek, as previously assumed, but rather that "the Hybrid . . . is Me." (It sounds like he's referring to himself, but the script and the closed-captioning for the episode both capitalize "Me.") The Doctor's confession dial, seen throughout the season, here turns out to be the place of his imprisonment.

**Who Is the Doctor?** Being scared of dying is a new feeling for him. He's nothing without an audience. When he finally runs out of corridor, he decides that this sums up his life. His three confessions to the Veil are:

1. He's scared of dying.
2. He lied when he said he left Gallifrey because he was bored; he left because he was scared.
3. He knows what the Hybrid is and is afraid.

**The Doctor and Clara** The Doctor smiles fondly at the painting of Clara in his room in prison. She appears in his dreamscape in the TARDIS but with her back turned, asking questions. When he asks her what she would do, she replies, "Same as you," which largely sums up her life and death.

**Monster of the Week** The Veil is a creature based on a nightmare the Doctor had as a boy after seeing an old lady who died; she wore a veil and was surrounded by flies. The creature will keep coming and only stops when you make a confession. It's made of cogwheels and teleports away each time it finally gets the Doctor.

**Stand Up and Cheer** In a story with so many scenes that make you stand up and cheer, the reveal that the Doctor has finally emerged on Gallifrey — after 4.5 billion years of repeated torture — is astounding.

**Roll Your Eyes** The note to the Doctor says, "I am in 12." Of course it does, because it's Steven Moffat's *Doctor Who*, and every time a number is mentioned, it *always* ties in with what number of Doctor it is.

**You're Not Making Any Sense** Everything in the castle resets every time . . . except for the abzantium wall, for some reason. Why doesn't this revert as well? Who took the paving stone in the centre of the kitchen and drew arrows to the missing stone? And who wrote "I am in 12" on the paving stone and buried it? Presumably it was part of the confession dial's mechanism . . . but why?

**Interesting Trivia** Steven Moffat was inspired by the idea that a teleport could keep a person alive indefinitely and keep creating a person living again and again in the same causal loop. It was an idea he had had for decades (he even thought of pitching it to Big Finish back when the audio maker was the only game in town producing *Doctor Who*), but he liked the idea of combining it with writing a "one-hander" where the Doctor was the only character. While many fans and critics laud this story, Moffat has noted that the BBC's audience appreciation index score was one of the lowest it's had — though "Sleep No More" scored lower.

The Doctor is shown for about five or six days in the tower, and then he says it'll take a day and a half to climb up the tower, so let's say for the sake of argument it takes seven days for a full loop. Assuming a relatively Earth-standard year, that's 52 new versions of the Doctor a year. In the next episode, we learn the Doctor has been in the confession dial for 4.5 billion years . . . that means the Doctor has gone through the full loop 234 billion times.

The dry clothes are hanging by the fire because the previous iteration left his wet ones there. This means that, 234 billion teleports ago, the first version of the Doctor teleporting in spent half his time running around naked.

The story of the bird that once a year uses its beak to whittle away at a mountain is meant to illustrate the sheer length of time that eternity represents, but the analogy is a poor one. The Doctor says that the whittled-away mountain represents merely the first second of eternity, but infinity doesn't work like that. What this does is expand the scale for our human minds, so that something that takes a geological age would seem like a mere eyeblink as far as eternity is concerned. This analogy suggests that infinite time is basically the same as finite time, only longer — but it isn't. Infinity isn't a very large number, as this analogy suggests; instead it's best understood as the limit of a process that never ends. Interestingly, there are multiple forms of infinity. If you count 1, 2, 3, . . . then the "last" number (even though it doesn't exist) is a countable infinity. On the other hand, how many decimals are there between 0 and 1? The answer is infinite, yet it's uncountable — and, mind-bogglingly, it's a much "bigger" infinity than the countable one. Even more extreme: there are an infinite number of types of infinities, and that infinity isn't countable. As the Doctor says, that's one hell of a bird.

It's just a quick flash, so you might have missed it the first time (as we did), but the word "HOME" appears superimposed over the abzantium wall when the Doctor first sees it. He concludes that this is where the TARDIS is, which is a reasonable mistake to make under the circumstances . . . except that those circumstances would presumably include knowing that the word "HOME" has appeared. Was this superimposed for our benefit — or for the Doctor's?

This is the first episode of televised *Doctor Who* to use the word "arse." We thought you might want to know that.

**The TARDIS Chronometer** Inside the confession dial, about a light year from Earth, over a 4.5 billion year period, as well as Gallifrey.

**Don't Be Stupid? (RS?)** . . . *ACCEPTANCE.*

DENIAL: When rumours circulated that this season of *Doctor Who* was going to feature a story where Peter Capaldi was the only actor, I sighed. There was no way they were going to pull that off. I thought they could do it for half an hour, tops. But there was no way they could sustain 55 minutes of television with one guy.

ANGER: How the hell do you pull off a story with one actor, a couple of similar sets and a shambling monster that never speaks? It can't be done.

BARGAINING: This is Peter Capaldi's star turn. Please don't let it suck.

DEPRESSION: The Doctor realizing the implications when he sees the abzantium wall is just stunning. He's simultaneously facing the horror of what's been happening to him, as well as grieving Clara. And it's written all over his face, with nary a word.

ACCEPTANCE: What I didn't reckon on was the fact that the production team had a superweapon at their disposal: actor Peter Capaldi. Actually, make that two superweapons. The other being Steven Moffat as a writer.

*DENIAL: The last time the Doctor grieved a companion, he went up into a cloud, refused to get involved in worldly affairs and was lured down only by the promise of a mystery he couldn't solve, known as the impossible girl. This time around, he spent the closing moments of "Face the Raven" in denial, desperate to spare Clara the fate she couldn't escape.*

*ANGER: The opening of "Heaven Sent" sees him with barely controlled rage, threatening to rain down fire and fury on whoever was responsible for Clara's death, refusing to honour her orders not to.*

*BARGAINING: The confessions to the Veil are only a temporary solution. In each case, the confession is the same: he's scared. If he confesses enough or runs far enough or slows down his thinking effectively enough, he can buy himself time. Just not all that much of it.*

*DEPRESSION: Yet even as he uses the TARDIS mindscape to solve the problems at hand, it's here that the Doctor reaches his lowest ebb. We're used to seeing the Doctor pull out a miracle solution at the last minute, making an amazing leap or using an enemy's strength against itself. Here he collapses in a heap, wishing that for once he could just lose.*

*ACCEPTANCE: Despite all the ways in which the Doctor cleverly outthinks his pursuer, none of them leads to freedom. Instead, the answer is something that goes against everything the Doctor is about: he punches a wall and sacrifices himself. Neither is clever or innovative, transcending the unwritten rules of* Doctor Who, *a show that eschews violence and has an immortal lead character.*

DENIAL: The Doctor survives the story. Of course he does.

ANGER: The first iteration of the Doctor in this story, the skull at the very bottom of the pile, is the man we've been following for over 50 years. That's the Patrick Troughton and Tom Baker and Matt Smith Doctor down there.

BARGAINING: It's not really death, since his pattern got stored in the teleporter. The last iteration would remember Clara dying, then a while spent in a castle and then emerging on Gallifrey. Right?

DEPRESSION: He's dead. They killed the Doctor. Offscreen.

ACCEPTANCE: It's okay, because the Doctor willingly sacrificed himself — something that the Patrick Troughton or Tom Baker or Matt Smith Doctors would have done too — knowing that his death would achieve the miraculous: at long last, he'd return home.

*DENIAL: The Doctor doesn't really live through 4.5 billion years.*

*ANGER: Nobody can do that without going mad. You can't do that to our favourite character.*

*BARGAINING: Since each iteration died off, he wouldn't remember. Would he?*

*DEPRESSION: He lived through 4.5* billion *years.*

*ACCEPTANCE: He took the slow way, but he triumphed. And not only returned home, he did so with his secrets intact. He won in a no-win situation. That's what the Doctor does.*

DENIAL: This story structure can't possibly work with this set-up.

ANGER: Having a single actor is challenge enough. Looping around is going too far.

BARGAINING: Maybe this is a cul-de-sac that doesn't actually feature the real Doctor, just a transporter copy trapped in a loop?

DEPRESSION: For an episode that spends much of its time running in a loop, there sure are a lot of flashbacks — to the very episode we've been watching.

ACCEPTANCE: Do what the Doctor always does and turn your weaknesses into strength. In this case, you make the repetition a feature. In fact, you go all the way and speed up the repetitions, while at the same time showing — not telling — the sheer magnitude of what the Doctor has gone through.

*DENIAL: This can't actually be the showcase episode of all of* Doctor Who.

*ANGER: It has a generic monster and only two speaking parts, one of whom is onscreen for about a minute.*

*BARGAINING: Can we at least agree that* Doctor Who *can have a lot of "best" stories? It depends on the era, the writer, the actors, my mood . . .*

*DEPRESSION: All the other* Doctor Who *stories I love — they pale in comparison to this, don't they?*

*ACCEPTANCE: Yes.*

DENIAL: No.

ANGER: Why?

BARGAINING: Please?

DEPRESSION: Sigh.

ACCEPTANCE: Okay.

*DENIAL, ANGER, BARGAINING, DEPRESSION, ACCEPTANCE*

DABDA.

*DABD . . .*

**Second Opinion (GB)** What he said. Can't top that.

## 9.12 Hell Bent

**Written by** Steven Moffat **Directed by** Rachel Talalay

**Original airdate** December 5, 2015

**The Big Idea** The Doctor returns to Gallifrey and will go to any length to get Clara back. Has he finally gone too far?

**Roots and References** Sergio Leone's 1960s spaghetti westerns, specifically 1966's *The Good, the Bad and the Ugly* (the outside sequences on Gallifrey are shot in a similar fashion to Leone's work; composer Murray Gold does a pastiche on *The Good, the Bad and the Ugly*'s whistled main title, using 2005's "The Doctor's Theme," and the Doctor acts like Clint Eastwood's taciturn Man with No Name); Richard Stark's 1962 crime novel *The Hunter* and its 1967 film adaptation *Point Blank* (the Doctor's return to Gallifrey to exact revenge and get back what was taken from him); the 2004 film *Eternal Sunshine of the Spotless Mind* (the Doctor needing to forget Clara). The Doctor quotes from the 1931 film version of *Frankenstein* when he quips, "You're aliiiive!" The sign for Jackson, Nevada, has the slogan "No matter where you go, there you are," which is the catchphrase from the 1984 cult classic film *The Adventures of Buckaroo Banzai Across the 8th Dimension*. In what must be one of the most metafictional things *Doctor Who* has ever done (and that's saying something), the Doctor plays a song he calls "Clara," which is in fact Murray Gold's theme for Clara (called "Clara"!), which we've been hearing since Series Seven.

**Adventures in Time and Space** The version of "Don't Stop Me Now" (sung by

Foxes) back in "Mummy on the Orient Express" is playing on the radio (which is probably the first sign that the diner is a TARDIS, since that version of the song is from the future!). The Doctor returns to the barn where the Doctor ended the Time War in "The Day of the Doctor" and where he lived as a child (as revealed in "Listen"). The General from "The Day of the Doctor" returns, as does a newly regenerated version of Time Lord president Rassilon from 2009's "The End of Time," complete with a variant on the resurrection gauntlet seen in his last appearance (and first used in the 2006 *Torchwood* episode "Everything Changes"). Rassilon asks the Doctor, "How many regenerations did we grant you?" ("The Time of the Doctor"; he doesn't quantify it, though Rassilon does say he could spend all day repeatedly killing the Doctor).

We hear the Cloister Bells, though for once it's actually emanating from Gallifrey's cloisters and not the Doctor's TARDIS. Ohila and the Sisterhood of Karn are back (after "The Magician's Apprentice"/"The Witch's Familiar") and are even chummy with the Time Lords (something they never were, even back in 1975's "The Brain of Morbius"). The Matrix is a database that uses the minds of deceased Time Lords to predict the future, as established in 1976's "The Deadly Assassin." The Doctor goes back to retrieve Clara from the events of "Face the Raven," while Missy's role in bringing Clara and the Doctor together in "The Bells of Saint John" is briefly discussed, as was Missy's discussion of the Doctor's antics as a youngster in "The Magician's Apprentice." Prisoners of the Cloister Wraiths include the Weeping Angels, Cybermen and an actual Dalek that weeps.

The stolen TARDIS has a console room quite similar to the one used in the first and second Doctors' eras. When Me knocks on the door, she does so four times ("It's always four knocks") as per the prophecy that featured in the tenth Doctor's final stories. Me asks, indirectly, if the Doctor is actually half human, which the Doctor claimed to be in the 1996 TV Movie, and here he says, "Does it matter?"

Clara reversing the polarity on the neural blocker is referring to the great piece of technobabble from the third Doctor's era: "Reverse the polarity of the neutron flow." The Doctor says he has wiped the memories of others before, alluding to what he did to Donna in 2008's "The Stolen Earth"/"Journey's End." He fondly remembers some of his adventures with Clara, including "Cold War" and "Mummy on the Orient Express." As the Doctor collapses, he talks about his dislike of pears, which was mentioned in a deleted scene from 2007's "Human Nature"/"The Family of Blood." The Doctor notes that the diner is the same one from 2011's "The Impossible Astronaut"/"The Day of the Moon" and makes mention of meeting Amy and Rory there. The Doctor gets to admire Rigsy's handiwork with the graffitied TARDIS from the very end of "Face the

Raven." Clara's final note to the Doctor, on the TARDIS blackboard, is, in part, "Run you clever boy," which echoes Oswin Oswald's final words to the Doctor way back in "Asylum of the Daleks."

**The Hybrid Effect** Gallifrey has developed an interest in the Hybrid because all Matrix prophesies now state that the Hybrid will stand in the ruins of Gallifrey and destroy the web of time. They believe the Doctor knows who the Hybrid is because he learned about it when he was younger and encountered a Cloister Wraith.

Except that the Doctor *doesn't* know who the Hybrid is. The Doctor thinks the Hybrid is Ashildr/Me because of the Mire technology that makes her immortal. But Me makes the Doctor realize that the Hybrid is actually the Doctor and Clara, or rather the Doctor's desire for Clara to live, which has made him abandon his personal code. The Doctor thinks the only way to stop this from happening is for Clara to forget the Doctor and never be found by the Time Lords . . . but Clara realizes that it could be achieved by the Doctor forgetting Clara.

**Who Is the Doctor?** The Doctor tells Clara, "Well, I can't be the Doctor all the time," which echoes the Doctor's fury-filled phrase, "The Doctor isn't here" from "Face the Raven." He's profoundly broken, both from grief about Clara and by 4.5 billion years inside the confession dial. The Doctor is becoming more and more like the Warrior during the Time War: he dismisses the murder of the General's tenth incarnation and the psychic pain of regeneration (the one that *the Doctor* described as a form of death in his tenth incarnation in "The End of Time") as Gallifreyan "man flu." He is willing to steal, to forcibly mindwipe Clara to save her and even to destroy time itself, as her death is a fixed event in space and time.

**The Doctor and Clara** When Clara asks why he suffered torture for so long, the Doctor falls back on the explanation he gave back in "Under the Lake"/"Before the Flood," saying, "I had a duty of care." But it's perhaps more than that. Clara finally insists (after avoiding the subject in "Face the Raven") that she and the Doctor tell each other how they feel (although, since it happens offscreen, how much of it was "I love you" and how much of it was "stall Ohila and the General while I sneak below and steal a TARDIS" is unclear; we suspect there was more of the former than the latter). Clara's insistence that she die on her own terms — even going so far as to sabotage the memory-wiping neural blocker — stops the Doctor in his tracks and makes him realize he had gone too far to bring her back. So much so that he's willing to submit to losing his memories of Clara. Even so, Clara makes sure he's okay before leaving him to travel alone once more.

**Monster of the Week** The Cloister Wraiths are manifestations of dead Time Lords that are uploaded to the Matrix. They glide around the cloisters that surround the Matrix as guards, trapping anyone who tries to break into the Matrix. They look like Time Lords with the familiar collars, but their faces look like computer projections of a face at the moment of death.

**Stand Up and Cheer** When Clara realizes the Doctor has repeated his torture in the confession dial for over four billion years, it leads to the heartbreaking scene where she tells him, "My time is up. Doctor, between one heartbeat and the last is all the time I have. People like me and you, we should say things to one another. And I'm going to say them now." We don't get to see the rest . . . but the damage is already done.

**Roll Your Eyes** You have to pity President Rassilon just a little. Not only did he lose his (literal) James Bond good looks after "The End of Time," he seems to have lost his near omnipotence. His gauntlet could previously do crazy stuff to beings in space-time, but now he's forced to surrender to a gun?

**You're Not Making Any Sense** It feels churlish to say this of "Heaven Sent" but . . . what was the point of the Doctor's torture in the confession dial? Given everything they've seen the Doctor say and do over various millennia — including saving them from the Time War itself — did the Time Lords really think they could torture a lousy secret out of him? Their idea stinks all the more, since the Doctor's theory on the identity of the Hybrid is actually wrong.

**Interesting Trivia** Steven Moffat's original script for "Hell Bent" describes the scene when the Doctor is first inside the 1960s-inspired retro TARDIS console room thusly: "The Doctor is flying around the classic console like a distinguished Scottish actor who's slightly too excited for his own good." Which is abundantly evident onscreen. The console prop is the replica of the version Hartnell and Troughton used in the 1960s that was created for the 2013 docudrama, *An Adventure in Space and Time*, about the creation of the series.

The timeline for this story seems to be off; if the Doctor has travelled "the long way around" 4.5 billion years into the future, how is Gallifrey even remotely close to the end of the universe? Five billion was the setting of a reasonably stable universe in "The End of the World," "New Earth" and "Gridlock." Presumably it's much further in the future than the Doctor thinks.

For those of you who think the ending is a little too cheery, here's a depressing thought: ever wonder why Me is in the Gallifreyan Cloisters in the far future? And why she goes along with Clara in the stolen TARDIS afterwards? Perhaps she's an immortal happy to joyride after being too close to the end of the universe . . . or maybe she was planted there by the Time Lords to take Clara back to

Gallifrey. So perhaps there aren't happy adventures in a diner in time and space after all. Sorry to have bummed you out . . .

As the Doctor points out, the diner looks exactly like the one the Doctor went to with Amy, Rory and River in "The Impossible Astronaut"/"Day of the Moon," though that one was in Utah and this one is in Nevada. So either the TARDIS being piloted by Me and Clara pulled the diner somehow from the Doctor's memories when it used the chameleon circuit, or the Doctor, Amy, Rory and River were in Clara and Me's TARDIS and didn't know it. (We never actually see any of the diner's staff.) Or it's an excuse for returning to the American-themed Eddie's Diner in Cardiff Bay, about ten minutes away from *Doctor Who*'s studios.

Missy says in "The Magician's Apprentice" that she's cared about the Doctor, "Since always. Since the Cloister Wars. Since the night he stole the moon and the president's wife. Since he was a little girl. One of those was a lie. Can you guess which one?" The Doctor says here of the president's wife, "Ah, well, that was a lie put about by the Shabogans. It was the president's daughter. I didn't steal the moon, I lost it." Hmmm.

**The TARDIS Chronometer** Gallifrey, in the very far future and in the even further far future near the end of the universe. Also Nevada, in the present day.

**Don't Be Stupid? (GB)** The ending to this season is so frustrating, for many reasons.

First of all, we wait nine seasons to finally have a story set on Gallifrey and . . . it's kind of boring. There's a reason why Russell T Davies blew up Gallifrey in the first place and why, even when he brought Gallifrey back, Steven Moffat kept it off the board for as long as possible. The mystery of the Time Lords is so much better than the reality. Because to have this species that created ships that can travel in space and time and can change their near-immortal form turn out to be, well, *Star Trek* aliens, is a wee bit lacking.

But . . . if we're stuck on Gallifrey, doing a Sergio Leone pastiche is so much better than trying to repeat the John Frankenheimer pastiche they did when they made "The Deadly Assassin." The first 20 or so minutes — the Doctor barely says anything and does little more than eat a bowl of soup and yet deposes the ruling class of Gallifrey — is pretty amazing. What's more, he does it by letting Rassilon become a raving loony while the Doctor relies on the loyalty of the people he saved. That's really cool. These sequences are directed and filmed brilliantly.

The problem is if they're going to bring Gallifrey back, the story has to merit it. And I'm not sure it's worth it here. Part of the problem is that the Hybrid story arc is probably the worst one *Doctor Who* has ever done. (What's particularly galling is that it follows from the Death in Heaven arc, one of the best they've ever done.) As a repeated meme, it's frankly rubbish. Any time there's a mention of two species interacting, the Doctor quietly intones, "You mean . . . like a *hybrid*." If there had been some evidence that the Hybrid is a threat — if the Doctor had some kind of foretaste of the devastation it might cause — it might have made the Hybrid, and the fact that the Doctor turns out to be part of it, more meaningful. As it is, it's not so much a damp squib as a completely waterlogged one.

Then we have the revelation that it's the Doctor and Clara who are the Hybrid all along. Except not really; it's more the Doctor's feelings for Clara. Now this is a longstanding issue with Steven Moffat's Doctors and companions, but with the twelfth Doctor and Clara, Moffat nicely circumvented the creepiness of the eleventh Doctor and Amy and gave us a rather charming love story. Clara, who is smitten with the eleventh Doctor, kind of hates the twelfth Doctor and even dates another guy until she realizes she not only loves the twelfth Doctor, they both fulfill the other's needs. And those needs are dangerous. It's a relationship that's self-destructive and amazing at the same time, as Clara takes more and more risks and the Doctor will stop at nothing to save her.

I'm not sure if the Hybrid as a plot thread works, but confronting the Doctor and Clara's relationship does. Only I become more frustrated with this, not less, because the Doctor's grief over Clara is leading to more harm than good and the solution is . . . to forget Clara. I have real problems with this because it both cheapens the grief process and even "Heaven Sent," which is about coming to terms with bereavement, not about forgetting it.

But I'm equally not wild about what Clara does here. In deciding to go explore the universe in a TARDIS seconds from death, we're back to the consequence-free world of *Doctor Who* that annoyed me so in the days of Amy and Rory. I can't help but feel, as downbeat as it might have been, Clara returning to the bravery of the moment of her death would have been a more truthful way to end things for her. Though I do have to concede that she's demonstrated her agency throughout; her choosing to be, like the Doctor, the one who ran away, makes a lot of sense.

The one thing I will say that could potentially undo all I've said above is this: preparing for this book was the first time I've watched "Face the Raven," "Heaven Sent" and "Hell Bent" together and, in some ways, "Hell Bent" is far better for seeing these linked stories as one continuous experience because a lot of the Doctor's brokenness, harshness and desperation lands better when you have what he's gone through immediately in mind.

And yet, while it makes the Doctor losing his Doctor-ness all the more real, it still doesn't help that the Gallifrey setting adds nothing to the story or that the Hybrid is a lame story arc or that the ending's goal is to make the viewer happy, rather than to give the characters the endings they deserve.

**Second Opinion (RS?)** I've been saying for years that they shouldn't bring Gallifrey back, because it would be boring. It's too bad I was proven all too right here. My co-author has detailed the manifold problems with this episode quite well. The only thing I want to add is that I'm deeply, deeply uncomfortable with the scene where the Doctor shoots the General.

My co-author makes the argument that this illustrates the Doctor's brokenness. It's an excellent argument. It's too bad that Graeme actually does a better job at making this argument than Steven Moffat did.

As it sits, the scene doesn't scream "This is the Doctor gone off the rails!" Rather, it says, "This is the Doctor shooting someone and making a joke about it afterwards, so everything's basically okay." What message are kids going to take from this? That violence is okay if the person isn't permanently dead afterwards? That if you really need something, it's okay to hurt someone who's in your way?

That's just not *Doctor Who* to me.

What's more, this undercuts pretty much every episode of *Doctor Who*. Worried that the Doctor might die? Never mind about tension or thrills, it's all just man flu to him. Remember that time he heroically sacrificed himself on Androzani to save his companion? Not actually that big a deal, it turns out. It undoes the stakes of every regeneration story, both past and future.

Bringing back Gallifrey is an idea that could have worked, but it needed to be done with great care and skill and sensitivity. Instead, it's a mess that actively ruins other episodes. Much like this story, in fact.

## The Psychic Papers: Gallifrey

Probably the most important change to *Doctor Who* since it came back in 2005 was not bringing the Doctor's home planet of Gallifrey back from extinction but instead defining why it needed to come back in the first place.

The funny thing about the Doctor's home planet is that, for the first 11 seasons of the Classic Series and the first two seasons of the modern one, it went unnamed. Viewers finally learn it when the Doctor mentions it in casual conversation during 1973's "The Time Warrior." It was originally written in the script as "Galfrey" but attained an extra syllable during production. When the Doctor finally visits Gallifrey in 1976's "The Deadly Assassin," the viewer learns that the planet is not as previously advertised: the Time Lords aren't godlike beings but are mostly cynical and devious academics whose non-interference policy probably existed for no more noble reason than to consolidate their power.

Time Lord civilization is also a strictly indoors one. It wasn't until 1978's "The Invasion of Time" that we learn that outside of the Time Lord citadel is a desert-like wasteland. There are Time Lords who dropped out of that society, called "outsiders" in this story, who live a primitive lifestyle. The two remaining Gallifrey stories of the Classic Series (1983's "Arc of Infinity" and "The Five Doctors") are set within an interior structure not unlike an airport lounge from the early 1980s decorated by IKEA. This underscored a perennial problem of visiting Gallifrey on television: for a mythic society, they're kind of mundane. It's a law of diminishing returns, as what makes them awe-inspiring is suggestion, not seeing them close-up.

Much of what we understand about Gallifrey in the Modern Series is in fact defined by other sources. The Time Lords living in a domed citadel came from the *Doctor Who Magazine* comic strip. Until "The Day of the Doctor," the Gallifrey seen onscreen was fleeting and in flashback, because the Modern Series backstory is that the Doctor blew up Gallifrey when ending the great Time War between the Time Lords and the Daleks.

Showrunner Russell T Davies did this because he was keen to make the Time Lords less figures of continuity and more figures of mythology. If the Doctor is the last of the Time Lords, it adds some pathos to the Doctor, and it ensures that Time Lords can't disappoint because they would never be directly involved. Davies squared away the Doctor's involvement in destroying Gallifrey by making it clear in 2009's "The End of Time" that the Time Lords had become deranged because of the Time War and were prepared to destroy time itself as a final sanction, aiming to evolve into creatures of pure thought.

Steven Moffat was prepared to let this stand during Matt Smith's tenure as the Doctor. Indeed, he added a layer of complexity by giving us the Warrior, the incarnation who committed genocide and is disowned by his future selves. But with the fiftieth-anniversary special came the biggest change to *Doctor Who* since its return.

"The Day of the Doctor" starts by asking one of the bravest questions that had been skirted since 2005: when Gallifrey was destroyed, were all its people Time Lords who were embroiled in the Time War? The answer one inferred from "The End of Time" was *yes*. The answer given in "The Day of the Doctor" was *no*. There were innocent people who were killed. In fact, it goes one step further by saying there were 2.47 billion children on Gallifrey when it was destroyed. Not all Gallifreyans are Time Lords.

This meant the Doctor committed mass genocide. Not merely toppling two sides of a conflict who are as bad as each other. Which is, of course, why Gallifrey had to be saved by the end of "The Day of the Doctor."

In bringing back Gallifrey, the idea was to have one's cake and eat it too: the planet was saved, but it was lost in another dimension. The Doctor was still the last of the Time Lords, but now he hadn't committed genocide.

In the one major appearance Gallifrey has had since "The Day of the Doctor," in "Hell Bent," we see the Doctor protected by (presumably) ordinary Gallifreyans who had been saved by the Doctor previously. The brief vignette of the Doctor's past on Gallifrey in "Listen" also reinforces the notion that only a few Gallifreyans become Time Lords.

In spite of it being established that Gallifrey now exists in the same dimension as the Doctor, only in the very far future, the thirteenth Doctor has not returned home. Perhaps she may yet. However, given that, in the thirteenth Doctor's first season, she doesn't even identify herself as a Time Lord (or Time Lady), that visit may be a long time in coming.

## 9.13 The Husbands of River Song

**Written by** Steven Moffat **Directed by** Douglas Mackinnon

**Original airdate** December 25, 2015

**The Big Idea** A surgeon is required to save the life of King Hydroflax, a despotic ruler who also happens to be married to River Song. If only River knew the surgeon is actually her other husband . . .

**Roots and References** Audrey Niffenegger's novel *The Time Traveler's Wife*, an oft-cited work by Steven Moffat (the out-of-order romance culminating in a perfect moment at the very end); the Japanese anime franchise *Gundam* (the design of Hydroflax's robot body); the James Bond film franchise (the Doctor's quip after destroying the robot half of Hydroflax, "He had a bad day on the market," is very Bondian); the 1951 film *The Day the Earth Stood Still* (Hydroflax's ship is a 1950s-styled flying saucer). "Hark the Herald Angels Sing" is played on Mendorax Dellora, while "The First Noel" is played in the Darillium restaurant. Wagner's *Seigfried Idyll* can be heard in the ship's dining room.

**Adventures in Time and Space** The episode is premised on River believing she knows all the Doctor's incarnations and not knowing that the Time Lords granted the Doctor more regenerations in "The Time of the Doctor." Fleming reads from River's diary, referencing "The Pandorica Opens" (2010), the crash of the Byzantium (2010's "The Time of Angels"), Manhattan ("The Angels Take Manhattan"), Jim the Fish (mentioned in 2011's "The Impossible Astronaut") and a picnic at Asgard (mentioned in 2008's "Silence in the Library").

The Doctor says that every Christmas is last Christmas, a quote from Danny Pink in a dreamscape in "Last Christmas." River mentions the Doctor marrying Elizabeth I ("The Day of the Doctor") and Marilyn Monroe (2010's "A Christmas Carol"). The Doctor gives her a sonic screwdriver and takes her to dinner at the singing towers of Darillium for one final night, as mentioned in "Silence in the Library"/"The Forest of the Dead." River owns a fez.

River has a fold-out wallet with faces of all twelve Doctors, including the Warrior. The faces hail from, in order, 1966's "The Smugglers," 1985's "The Two Doctors" (interestingly not actually from the second Doctor's era, although it does mean we get a colour photo), 1972's "Carnival of Monsters," 1976's "The Hand of Fear," 1984's "Resurrection of the Daleks," 1986's "Mindwarp," 1989's "Survival," the 1996 TV Movie "The Day of the Doctor," 2005's "The Parting of the Ways," 2006's "The Runaway Bride" and "The Bells of Saint John."

**Who Is the Doctor?** He's not a qualified surgeon. He's known for the fact that he doesn't go around falling in love with people — and yet here he is with River. He once married Cleopatra.

**The Doctor and River** She often steals his TARDIS for extended periods of time and returns it a second later. He gave her the diary knowing how long she'd need it for, and she knows it's all coming to an end. In spite of loudly proclaiming the Doctor isn't in love with her, he's there with her, and they spend a final night together on Darillium, which lasts 24 years.

**Monster of the Week** King Hydroflax is a cyborg, with an organic head and mechanical body that can exist separately. The body has an on-board computer for the cybernetic component. New organic bodies can be added (as Nardole and Ramone are), while the neck can interface with other objects, such as a money ball.

**Stand Up and Cheer** Having mistaken the Doctor for someone else, River invites him into the TARDIS but warns him that it isn't as snug as it looks. Whereupon the Doctor pumps himself up and announces that he finally gets to have "my go." Peter Capaldi's subsequent overacting, where he proclaims that his knowledge of Euclidean geometry has been torn up and snogged to death, is hilarious.

**Roll Your Eyes** Did we really need the "hai" and "chi" noises made by the kung-fu-style assassins who guard King Hydroflax? Haven't we moved beyond that sort of thing by now?

**You're Not Making Any Sense** The interior of the TARDIS is in its own pocket dimension, something essentially confirmed by this episode when stating that the door seals the "real-time envelope" when it closes. So when the starship crashes, why does the TARDIS interior explode and toss its occupants about?

**Interesting Trivia** "All the time we've been together, you knew I was coming here. The last time I saw you, the real you, the future you, I mean, you turned up on my doorstep, with a new haircut and a suit. You took me to Darillium to see the Singing Towers. What a night that was. The Towers sang, and you cried. [ . . . ] You even gave me your screwdriver. That should have been a clue." No, this isn't a plot summary of this episode, it's a line of dialogue from "The Forest of the Dead," way back in 2008. This episode closes the loop on River's story, with a lot of details seen here that have been seeded in the past. Flemming even reads out sections of her diary to show that she's met Jim the Fish, which was the same clue used to show that the Doctor in "The Impossible Astronaut" was near the end of his life. The twelfth Doctor even discreetly scans River with her sonic screwdriver, in order to upload her into the neural relay that his tenth self will use to save her in the library. As the tenth Doctor says back then, his future self has had hundreds of years to think up a way to save her. Either that, or he simply remembered what happened earlier.

This story was to have been Steven Moffat's last as executive producer of *Doctor Who*. By this point he had done five seasons (plus some specials) of *Doctor Who*, a year more than his predecessor, Russell T Davies. Moffat planned to end his tenure on *Doctor Who* on his own terms — less grandiose than Davies in "The End of Time," with the Doctor finally closing the loop on his adventures with River Song. Moffat's last words to the show were supposed to be "And they lived happily." It didn't turn out that way. More on this later . . .

**The TARDIS Chronometer** Mendorax Dellora, December 25, 5343. On board the starship *Harmony & Redemption* in the Andromeda galaxy. Darillium in several time zones.

**Don't Be Stupid? (RS?)** The one thing you have to appreciate about the Christmas episodes is that they like to think big. Last time, we had Santa Claus meets *Inception*. The time before that, the Doctor aged to death while battling all the races of the galaxy. Here, we see River Song, perhaps the biggest in-house guest star of the Modern Series, teaming up with the twelfth Doctor in a screwball comedy that transforms into a heartbreaking romantic tragedy.

One of the big criticisms of River's character has always been that she only exists in relation to the Doctor. That's addressed beautifully here, with a glimpse into what she gets up to when the Doctor isn't around: she marries multiple times, works as a con artist and has a history of transporting dragon eggs on a starship. These details give her a life of her own and add depth to the character while also providing laughs.

Unlike, say, "Let's Kill Hitler," the previous River story with a massive tonal shift, both aspects of the story work remarkably well. The comedy is genuinely funny, from the title on down. River having two husbands is amusing, but adding Ramone to the mix sends it gloriously over the edge (and there's mention of her having at least two wives). Hydroflax's head in a bag shouting insults and muffled threats of retribution is laugh-out-loud funny. The Doctor's irritable bowel works better than it has any right to. And the idea that she regularly steals the TARDIS for side jaunts without the Doctor noticing is sublime.

The running joke of River not recognizing the Doctor threatens to wear thin until we hit pay dirt: it's good that she has a reason not to recognize him, making use of the Doctor's changed circumstances since "The Time of the Doctor"; it's great that this is used as the centrepiece of her confrontation with Hydroflax and Flemming. Alex Kingston is in top form as she professes her love for a monolith that can't love her back, while the Doctor is awkwardly standing right next to her.

It's here that the episode pivots from hilarious comedy to tear-jerking romance. Being *Doctor Who*, it's of course done by way of a crashing spaceship, a couple's argument about who married whom and jumping through time to make restaurant reservations. By the time the Doctor has rewarded a brave rescuer with a diamond in order to build the restaurant he knows he's destined to take River to, we've moved from wacky hijinks to time-traveller's tragedy.

Indeed, this only works as well as it does because we've known River the way we have. Having seen her in almost every season for the past seven years, we've been given lots of clues to piece together her timeline. That makes this ending feel inevitable, in a way that's almost unique.

One of the things that Steven Moffat does best is explore the consequences of being a time traveller. River is easily the most successful example of this. If you can't rely on linear time, how do you have a romance? One thing is clear: there's no possessiveness here. Yes, the Doctor and River fight about all the people they each married, but it's a playful fight that's primarily about making fun of each other's bad judgment. The fact that many of these marriages happened during their own romance proves that this is a partnership based on freedom and acceptance, not on jealousy. That's a depiction of romantic love almost entirely absent from TV.

As someone who doesn't ascribe to monogamy, I think their relationship is the perfect illustration of how you can have deep feelings for someone even when they're not your only partner. River genuinely cares about Ramone, even at the end of the story when he has a metal body, but it doesn't change how she feels about the Doctor. The two aren't in competition for her; they each bring different things to the table. (Literally so, in the waiter's case.)

Twenty-four years is a long time on Darillium. River ends the story spending the night with not one but two husbands, with the second one in the body of a third. It's assumed that she spends the entire time with the Doctor, but there's actually nothing to specify that this is the case. I'll leave any further speculation to the realm of fanfic . . .

After he lost Clara forever just a single story ago, having the Doctor spend a final night with River before losing her forever could have been a bridge too far. But the reason this works is because it's not all tears and sad farewells; that this story is two-thirds comedy is a massive point in its favour. The fact that the Doctor has known River even longer and more intimately than Clara makes up for the rest. And, quite simply, we were overdue for a comedic episode. Everything about this episode is perfect, as all my partners would also agree.

**Second Opinion (GB)** This was supposed to have been Steven Moffat's final *Doctor Who* story. As such, it's an elegy to what was, by then, ten years of working on the show as writer and then showrunner. And here he does what he does best: gives us a comedy about relationships and time travel with a giant robot thrown in for good measure.

As someone who has never really liked Moffat's Christmas specials, this one left me delighted. The first time I watched it, I was called away 20 minutes in to have Christmas dinner and was on tenterhooks waiting to get back to it — not because I wanted to see what would happen to River or the Doctor, but because I was having a really great time watching it. It's amazingly funny. I had been so busy enjoying Alex Kingston perform derring-do as River over the years, I never realized what a brilliant comic actress she is on top of everything.

When I came back to it, I wasn't disappointed: it got amazing mileage out of the gag that River doesn't understand that the man with her is the Doctor, and the Doctor is too pompous to just come out and say it; he wants the ego boost of River figuring it out. The payoff for this is one of the best scenes in the twelfth Doctor's era, and Capaldi is smart enough to underplay it, relying on a knowing smile to sell it all.

The ending is a brilliant summation of everything about Steven Moffat's tenure on *Doctor Who*. In spite of the fairy tale that is his era of *Who*, people can't live happily ever after . . . but they can live happily. Because happily ever after doesn't mean forever. It just means time — a little time. That is a wonderful sentiment to close a decade's worth of writing the Doctor.

And then Steven Moffat came back for another year — which will be, in many ways, great for the viewer. Alas, it took away from an ending that, as my co-author said, was perfect in every way.

## The Psychic Papers: What's the River Song Timeline?

"The trouble is, it's all back to front. My past is his future. We're travelling in opposite directions. Every time we meet, I know him more, he knows me less. I live for the days when I see him, but I know that every time I do, he'll be one step further away."

— River Song, "The Impossible Astronaut"

What a load of old cobblers! The youngest we see River is when she's born in "A Good Man Goes to War." This is clearly not the last time the Doctor sees her. The baby Melody is placed in the Graystark orphanage in New York, escapes as a child and calls Richard Nixon for help ("The Impossible Astronaut"). After escaping the spacesuit, she regenerates into an infant ("Day of the Moon").

She eventually makes her way to Leadworth, regenerating at least once more, and grows up as Mels, being inadvertently raised by her parents ("Let's Kill Hitler"). She uses the TARDIS to travel back to Nazi Germany, where she regenerates for a final time into the River Song we all know. This is where the Doctor gives her a TARDIS-shaped diary, and she enrols in Luna University, where she receives her degree in archaeology ("Let's Kill Hitler").

Notice that, at this point, we've already lost the reverse-order thing, since the screening order of these stories is "The Impossible Astronaut"/"Day of the Moon," "A Good Man Goes to War" and then "Let's Kill Hitler." But it's about to get even more jumbled.

Shortly afterwards, she's kidnapped by the Silence and forced into the Apollo spacesuit ("Closing Time"). In an alternate timeline, she and a replica of the eleventh Doctor get married ("The Wedding of River Song"). In the regular timeline, she shoots the replica Doctor ("The Impossible Astronaut"), for which she is sentenced to the Stormcage Facility ("Flesh and Stone"). During this time, she makes several side trips. The first involves acquiring a vortex manipulator from Dorium so that she can meet the Doctor at Stonehenge ("The Pandorica Opens").

At some point, she and the Doctor have a picnic at Asgard (mentioned in her diary in "Silence of the Library"). They visit the Bone Meadows (mentioned in "The Time of Angels"), which is possibly where she meets King Hydroflax ("The Husbands of River Song" mentions that he's the butcher of Bone Meadows).

Subsequently, she's recruited by Father Octavian for a mission to track down a Weeping Angel, with the promise of a pardon ("The Time of Angels"). Immediately after this, she visits her parents to tell them that the Doctor survived Lake Silencio ("The Wedding of River Song"). At some point, they go to Easter Island and meet Jim the Fish (both mentioned in "The Impossible Astronaut").

An older River is invited to a picnic at Lake Silencio ("The Impossible Astronaut"), where she witnesses her younger self shooting the Doctor. As she returns to the Stormcage, she kisses the Doctor for what she believes will be her last time ("Day of the Moon"). Almost immediately afterwards — she's wearing the same outfit — she goes to the Battle of Demons Run and tells the Doctor her true identity (the end of "A Good Man Goes to War"). She returns to the Stormcage after a trip to the Winter Frost Fair and rejects Rory's invitation to join the Doctor's battle to free Amy from the Church of the Silence (the beginning of "A Good Man Goes to War").

After the Doctor erases all record of himself from the universe ("The Wedding of River Song"), River is pardoned, since the man she killed apparently no longer exists. She travels to Manhattan and spends a month investigating the Weeping Angels in 1938 under the alias Melody Malone before meeting the Doctor and Amy ("The Angels Take Manhattan").

Shortly afterwards, she marries Ramone and King Hydroflax in order to steal the Halassi Androvar diamond. She and the Doctor spend a night on Darillium that lasts 24 years, and he gives her his sonic screwdriver ("The Husbands of River Song"). She's then recruited by the Felman Lux Corporation to investigate the library, where she meets the tenth Doctor ("Silence in the Library"). She sacrifices herself to save the people trapped there, but the Doctor uses the memory of her from his sonic screwdriver to upload a copy to the library's database ("Forest of the Dead"). River's final appearance is as a data ghost summoned to a seance, where she appears to Clara and has a final goodbye kiss with the eleventh Doctor ("The Name of the Doctor").

Happily for all the romantics out there, River is completely and utterly wrong in her quote above. Clearly, all these meetings aren't happening in strict reverse order, and neither is her first kiss with the Doctor his last, given how they finally leave things. Instead, like all relationships, it's far more complicated than that. Okay, most relationships don't have the couple meeting out of order, a wedding in an alternate reality with a robot replica of the groom nor the bride shooting the husband shortly afterwards, but you can't have everything when you're a 200-year-old psychopath archaeologist who's married to a Time Lord.

# SERIES TEN (2017)

**Starring**
Peter Capaldi as the Doctor
Pearl Mackie as Bill Potts
Matt Lucas as Nardole

**Executive Producers**
Steven Moffat
Brian Minchin

**Producers**
Peter Bennett (10.x, 10.00–10.02,
10.06–10.07, 10.11–10.13)
Nikki Wilson (10.03–10.05, 10.08–10.10)

# 10.X Friend from the Future

**Written by** Steven Moffat **Directed by** Lawrence Gough

**Original airdate** April 23, 2016

**The Big Idea** The Doctor and future companion Bill are under attack from a Dalek.

**Monster of the Week** A Dalek. A fat Dalek, with a gun and a sucker.

**Stand Up and Cheer** Bill pointing out that the Dalek is fat after being told that it's the deadliest war machine ever devised is just hilarious.

**Roll Your Eyes** The credits listed Pearl Mackie "asBill" leading many to initially believe that this new companion was named asBill. Kerning, people.

**You're Not Making Any Sense** The final moment of the story sees the Doctor and Bill trapped in a dead end. But when the equivalent scene was shown in "The Pilot," the dead end suddenly wasn't there.

**Interesting Trivia** This was a short preview of the new companion, who wouldn't be debuting for another year. Unlike the other prequels you can find in this book's appendix, it was shown on BBC1 (during the hugely popular sports program *Match of the Day* of all things; nerds really do rule the world!), so we're including it as a proper story.

The scene was originally written as Pearl Mackie's audition piece, but the producers decided to film it and use it as a promo for her character. It was later decided that the scene would be inserted into "The Pilot," but Steven Moffat has admitted that this didn't quite work, as Bill had already been introduced by this point, so he cut much of it from that episode. Annoyingly, you won't find it anywhere on the DVD boxset for no reason that we can understand (though it's easily found on YouTube).

All the Dalek footage is taken from "Into the Dalek." Look carefully and you can see the Aristotle medical base logo in the background at one point.

**The TARDIS Chronometer** An alien spaceship, sometime in the past.

**Don't Be Stupid? (RS?)** It's only two minutes long . . . but it's absolutely superb!

One of the great things about Modern Series *Doctor Who* is that they play it straight when it comes to the Daleks. Yes, we all get that they're trundling machines with balls on the outside, an egg whisk and a sucker, but ever since "Dalek" so effectively reintroduced them as terrifying killing machines, pretty much everyone has been willing to suspend their disbelief and go along with the notion that this ridiculous-looking contraption is the deadliest creature in the universe.

I think this is why the New Paradigm Daleks were so poorly received. All the hard work that went into selling the steampunk-like bronze Daleks was thrown out the window when they were replaced with a multicoloured brand that was meant to be bigger and scarier than the old Daleks . . . but it wasn't earned. The scariest New Paradigm Dalek was the one in "The Big Bang," and that was a fossil.

Consequently, the show plays a dangerous game when it comes to poking fun at the Daleks. When Rose Tyler laughs at them not being able to climb stairs, it works because the Dalek immediately starts hovering.

Why then does Bill break all these rules and get away with it? Part of it is that her comments are mostly so out of left field. It's easy to point out that the Daleks have a plunger or can't climb stairs, but this is the first time anyone's criticized them for being too wide. This hilarious moment immediately endears us to Bill. Or asBill. She's smart and lively, and her constant questions are just outstanding. It's helped by Peter Capaldi playing it absolutely straight, which keeps the fear level high.

However, this is Pearl Mackie's moment in the sun. It's not easy to have the audience fall in love with a new companion right from the outset. But that's exactly what we get here, and it's fantastic. All that in just two minutes.

**Second Opinion (GB)** It's obviously an audition piece: it's a short scene to show the character's smart-ass ways that's also designed to showcase the actor's skills with comedy. And it obviously worked, because Pearl Mackie got the part. The real genius move here was redoing it in studio for the viewers so we could all see what we would be getting in a year or so. And, of course, within 30 seconds of her riffing on the Daleks being "a bit fat," I loved her too.

# 10.00 The Return of Doctor Mysterio

**Written by** Steven Moffat **Directed by** Ed Bazalgette
**Original airdate** December 25, 2016

**The Big Idea** The Doctor accidentally creates a real-life superhero. Meanwhile, a group of insidious brains are planning to take over the world.

**Roots and References** Many parts of the Superman legend, but mostly 1978's *Superman: The Movie* (several lines of dialogue, the portrayal of Grant echoing Christopher Reeve's Clark Kent and the rooftop date) and the 1993–97 TV series *Lois & Clark: The New Adventures of Superman* (the mixture of romantic comedy and comic book; Lucy's patter is very much like Teri Hatcher's Lois Lane); other parts of the *Superman* comic are referenced, including the secret identity (Grant), *Daily Planet* (the Harmony Shoals building has a globe on top), Lois Lane (Lucy is a reporter, and her professional/married name is Lombard, which gives us the famous "L.L." initials that so many characters have in the *Superman* mythos), and there's a shout-out to Superman's creators, Jerry Siegel and Joe Shuster (though they're Miss Siegel and Miss Shuster here); the various post-1989 film versions of Batman (the Ghost's costume is body armour, and Justin Chatwin takes on the vocal affect of Michael Keaton or Christian Bale when he plays the Ghost; Lucy even mentions the Bat-signal). Spider-Man is frequently mocked ("He was bitten by a radioactive spider, and guess what happened?" "Radiation poisoning, I should think") and referenced (not only does the Doctor use "With great power comes great responsibility," but the zoom-in on Lucy saying "Go get 'em" pays homage to an iconic shot from 2005's *Spider-Man 2*). Young Grant's bedroom has posters of many 1970s and 1980s comics (including *The Incredible Hulk* #181, the debut of Wolverine), and the Doctor is looking at a *Superman* comic book that has pages from two different issues from 1987 and 1988 (#7 and #19). The Doctor uses *Pokémon Go* to empty Harmony Shoal's Tokyo office. The local cinema in Grant's neighbourhood is showing a film called *The Mind of Evil*, which is also the title of a 1971 Jon Pertwee *Doctor Who* story. During the flashback to Grant's adolescence, Primal Scream's "Loaded" plays.

**Adventures in Time and Space** Harmony Shoal sees a return of the aliens from the Shoal of the Winter Harmony that bedevilled the Doctor and River in "The Husbands of River Song." Nardole has also been reconstituted after being inside Hydroflax at the end of that story, and River's death (in 2008's "Forest of the Dead") and its impact on the Doctor is mentioned. The Doctor is in New York on the roof of young Grant's apartment trying to build a machine to deal with the time distortion created as result of the events of "The Angels Take Manhattan." UNIT briefly shows up at the end, and Osgood gets a mention by one of the soldiers securing Harmony Shoal's New York office.

**Who Is the Doctor?** While he hides it well, he's still mourning the death of River (Nardole says of him, "For a time, he's going to be very sad"). He's put Nardole back together to have someone to travel with (either the Doctor or River must have taught Nardole to fly the TARDIS). The Doctor seems to have improved in his ability to interact with people since we last saw him: he's lovely and considerate to young Grant, is concerned enough to check in on him as a teenager and takes Lucy quite seriously. He also jokes when seeing Grant's awkwardness with Lucy that he's thrilled to find someone more inept at romance than him. He's taken to snacking while working.

**Monster of the Week** Harmony Shoal is populated by an alien race that look like brains with eyes. They can be surgically implanted into human heads and take over the central nervous system of the host body, making them stronger.

**Stand Up and Cheer** Lucy's interrogation of the Doctor is delightful: she's smart enough to make all the necessary connections in what the Doctor is saying (and is even capable of admitting when her assumptions are wrong) and intuitive enough to know that squeezing a toy that sounds like a screaming baby is enough to make the Doctor answer her questions. Plus, the banter between her and the Doctor is charming. In any other circumstance, we would have suggested the Doctor take her on board the TARDIS.

**Roll Your Eyes** The date between the Ghost and Lucy starts out well enough. Unfortunately, by the time Lucy has spun out into defending Grant and realizing her feelings about him, we've moved on from contrived to some form of agony.

**You're Not Making Any Sense** The Ghost is super-strong and moves fast. Why, then, is he so easily overpowered by the surgeons? And if he can so easily break free, why doesn't he just fly Lucy and Jennifer to safety?

**Interesting Trivia** Steven Moffat's last words on *Doctor Who* were supposed to be "They lived happily" at the end of "The Husbands of River Song." And then . . . things got complicated. The BBC wanted Chris Chibnall, who had become a hugely successful showrunner on the ITV crime drama *Broadchurch*, to replace Moffat as *Doctor Who*'s executive producer and head writer. But Chibnall was committed to producing a third and final season of *Broadchurch* for broadcast in 2017. This meant there would be no showrunner to take over *Doctor Who* for its tenth season in autumn 2016. With the 2016 Olympics making the autumn schedule even tougher for *Doctor Who*, the BBC decided to simply not air *Doctor Who* until spring 2017. But that season still had no producer lined up. There were rumours that the BBC was looking for a temporary showrunner to handle a single season. In the end, Steven Moffat agreed to come back for a final season.

During the year-long wait for *Doctor Who* in 2016, the only thing fans had to hold onto was *Class*, a BBC3 spinoff about a group of teenagers at the Coal Hill School fighting the monstrous, created by Patrick Ness, an author of young adult novels. Peter Capaldi appeared as the Doctor in the first episode, but — aside from that, the setting and a brief appearance by the Weeping Angels — there was little connection to *Doctor Who*, and the series was cancelled after just one season.

The title of this story dates back to the 2014 *Doctor Who* World Tour, where the stars and showrunner went to eight cities around the world. When they got to Mexico City, both Peter Capaldi and Steven Moffat were delighted to learn that when *Doctor Who* first aired there in the 1960s, the Spanish title was *El Doctor Misterio*. (The title kept being used off and on for decades.) Steven Moffat loved the comic-book flavour of it and thought it also would be a nice reference to the show returning after 12 months.

**The TARDIS Chronometer** New York City (and, briefly, Toyko), 24 years ago, 16 years ago and the present day.

**Don't Be Stupid? (GB)** Here's the thing with most *Doctor Who* Christmas specials: whatever I think about them while I watch them, I'll have forgotten most of their content by the time I'm midway through the next season. That's not to say there aren't some exceptions to this rule —

Oh, wait. I said that exact same thing about "The Doctor, the Widow and the Wardrobe," didn't I?

I had thought that "Last Christmas" and "The Husbands of River Song" had achieved escape velocity from the curse of the Moffat Christmas special. Alas, no. "The Return of Doctor Mysterio" is unbelievably forgettable. Worse, I think it takes all the flaws of a typical Moffat-era Christmas special — the bland, almost soulless, whimsy; the small-scale stakes; the utterly forgettable nature of it — and simply regurgitates them.

My biggest problem is the Ghost. I actually enjoyed a lot of Steven Moffat's deconstruction of Superman, and I thought Justin Chatwin and Charity Wakefield's riff on *Lois & Clark: The New Adventures of Superman* was really funny and charming. I know *Doctor Who* genre-filches like sentient species breathe, but superheroes are a genre too far. I like pizza. I like ice cream. I don't like them together. The fact that I have to come up with a bland metaphor like that is a sign of how frustrated I am about having a superhero in the *Doctor Who* universe. It doesn't work. Mostly because superheroes and *Doctor Who* do two totally different things. Superheroes are about direct action, all brawn and power fantasies. I think superheroes and *Doctor Who* can both be wonderful in their own right. Combined, it gets messy.

And that's the big problem here. The Ghost stuff pushes the *Doctor Who* stuff to the background, to the point where the Doctor is a supporting character in his own show. Which thankfully is less irritating now that everything is surrendered to the retrospect of Blu-ray and streaming, but when it was *the only story in 365 days*, it really stood out. That said, it's still pretty disastrous upon rewatch: the Doctor's sole contribution to the story is to crash a spaceship. Everything else is down to the Ghost. In fact, it all feels like a backdoor pilot for *Lucy & Grant: The New Adventures of the Ghost*. While I'd almost certainly prefer that as a spinoff to *Class*, I'm not sure it could sustain more than what we see here.

Nardole offers some light relief; I love Matt Lucas's delivery of the line "We could ask you the same question. But it's your apartment, so we probably won't." And his speech at the end is fabulous, turning a comic-relief character into someone with more depth. But Nardole is such an oddball character that you don't really relate to him, which basically means all the relatable characters are in the comic-book adaptation. The same is true for the villains, who are so generic they don't merit an onscreen name.

I honestly think the next story we see, "The Pilot," should have been the 2017 Christmas special: you could have extended it to an hour, maybe built up the relationship between Bill and Heather a bit more, and it would have established the new team and the premise for the new season, introduced the very relatable primary companion and done something exciting and fun that made the Doctor the lead in his own show. As it is, we have something that would rather wallow in its whimsy, and in a few episodes, it . . .

Oh, sorry. What were we talking about? Oh darn. I used the ending from my review of "The Doctor, the Widow and the Wardrobe."

**Second Opinion (RS?)** I hate superhero stories.

There, I said it. My co-author may never speak to me again, but it's true. The great thing about *Doctor Who* is that it's fundamentally about a guy whose only special power is that he's smarter than everyone else around him. I can aspire to that. Superman is a guy who can see through walls, fly and hold up fire trucks with a single hand. No matter how many times I throw myself off the roof, I'll never be that.

Worse, it sucks all the drama out of pretty much every story. To have any kind of tension, you need to raise the stakes so high that they're no longer relatable.

Which brings me to the train wreck that is "The Return of Doctor Mysterio." Let's get this straight. By swallowing a crystal, a small boy can now fly, rescue children from buildings and hold up a nuclear-armed spaceship in front of everyone in one of the world's biggest cities. Okay, let's go with that. This is never deleted from the public consciousness, and Grant's powers aren't revoked, so he's still out there, ready to be called upon any time anything bad happens.

This should fundamentally change the fabric of society within the *Doctor Who* universe. The Ghost has been filmed, on the news and on people's cellphones. This should be a major factor in every subsequent *Doctor Who* story set on 21st-century Earth. Why aren't villains hatching audacious plans to use the Ghost in future schemes? Why isn't the Doctor using him as a resource whenever things get tricky?

Every present-day *Doctor Who* story from this point forward should either incorporate the Ghost or raise the stakes so high that the scheme is undefeatable by a flying strongman with X-ray vision. No human should die in New York ever again. This is a giant sea change for the entire future history of *Doctor Who*. The only thing that can possibly negate it would be if everyone on Earth somehow contrived to mysteriously forget the whole boring . . .

Wait, sorry. What were we talking about again?

# 10.01 The Pilot

**Written by** Steven Moffat **Directed by** Lawrence Gough

**Original airdate** April 15, 2017

**The Big Idea** Now a university professor, the Doctor agrees to privately tutor Bill Potts. Good thing, because the girl Bill has a crush on has become a monster.

**Roots and References** The 1989 film *The Abyss* (the water creature); the 1960 film version of *Psycho* (pulling back the shower curtain). Joy Division's 1980 song "Love Will Tear Us Apart" is playing in the pub where Heather and Bill meet. Bill mentions a number of sci-fi tropes (based on her Netflix viewing) including possession, lizards in people's brains and mindwipes. We suspect she's been watching *Star Trek*, mostly.

**Adventures in Time and Space** The Doctor's desk has pictures of River Song and his granddaughter, Susan, and a pencil holder with just about every version of the sonic screwdriver since the Pertwee era. The TARDIS has the Out of Order sign the first Doctor placed on it in 1966's "The War Machines" (it's the same font and everything; some graphic designer in the production office was working overtime!). The Doctor plays a bit of Beethoven's Fifth on his guitar ("Under the Lake"/"Before the Flood"). The basement where the Vault is located has a piece of the *Mary Celeste*, the ghost ship whose crew was exterminated by Daleks in 1965's "The Chase." The Doctor talks about the TARDIS's police box shape as a "cloaking device," the explanation he gave in the 1996 TV Movie (and a million fans cried, "It's a *chameleon circuit*!" in protest). We're given the context for the scene with the Daleks in "Friend from the Future," and we realize that the Daleks are fighting Movellans, their enemy from 1979's "Destiny of the Daleks." The Doctor attempts to wipe Bill's mind the same way he did Donna's in 2008's "The Stolen Earth"/"Journey's End." There's an oblique reference to the Doctor's mindwipe in "Hell Bent."

**The Vault Effect** The Doctor is now living incognito as a professor at St. Luke's University in Bristol and has been teaching for decades, with the TARDIS in drydock. It's all tied in with a vault hidden away in a basement on campus. Who or what is in the Vault is unknown, but the Doctor is now there to protect it and he's not supposed to travel off-world as a result.

**Who Is the Doctor?** Whether it's because of his decades of teaching, his grief over River or even the mindwipe Clara performed on him, there's no sign of the irritability the Doctor had in previous seasons. When Bill is in trouble, he's willing to listen and help. As a lecturer, he seems to have an arrangement with the institution to just talk about whatever he likes. He wants to wipe Bill's mind and go back to what he's been doing, but his experience with Bill has reminded him he likes travelling, or as he says to Bill, "Time and Relative Dimension in Space . . . it means 'What the hell!'"

**The Doctor and Bill** The Doctor notices Bill Potts attending his lectures and likes the fact that she doesn't frown when there's a problem; she smiles. When Bill asks why he's chosen her, the Doctor looks at the picture of his granddaughter, implying that Bill reminds him of Susan. He's touched by Bill's Christmas gift of a rug, enough to put it under the TARDIS and to go to the past to take pictures of Bill's mum as a present for her. He's so moved by Bill's request for empathy when he attempts to mindwipe her that he reconsiders travelling in time and space again.

**Monster of the Week** The semi-sentient residue of a space vessel has chosen Bill's friend Heather to be its pilot and has taken her over. Heather has become liquid but can reconstitute herself in humanoid (or Dalek) form. She can create torrents of water as a defensive measure. While Heather is bonded to the vessel, she mostly mimics the phrases of others, but her consciousness can still be reached.

**Stand Up and Cheer** We've seen new companions get introduced to the TARDIS in all kinds of ways over the years, but none quite so stylishly as here, as Bill, not realizing where she is, talks at the police box doors as the camera tracks back to reveal the vastness of space around her in darkness before the TARDIS lights gradually come back on. It's followed up by a scene of pure delight as the Doctor tries to explain the wonder enveloping them (to an amped-up score no less) . . . and Bill continues to think it's some kind of a knock-through room, possibly a kitchen or a lift. And could she use the toilet?

**Roll Your Eyes** We really wanted to put the opening scene where the Doctor interviews Bill in the section above, but that whole speech where Bill runs on about how she's fattened up a girl she fancies . . . just, no.

**You're Not Making Any Sense** Why doesn't Heather tell Bill what's wrong with the puddle the first time? Why does Bill wait six months before talking to her again about it? We get that crushes are weird and irrational — we're with Nardole on this one — but clear communication is the foundation of a good relationship. And just walking off is a jerk move.

**Interesting Trivia** If you're wondering where to fit "Friend from the Future," this is going to be tricky, because while the scenes with the Daleks in the mini-episode and here use the same sets (more or less), the action doesn't completely line up. But, for the sake of argument, it's probably immediately after the Doctor has left Heather to confront a Dalek around when the action cuts to Nardole trying not to get exterminated himself. All you have to do is pretend that the final moment of "Friend from the Future," when the Doctor and Bill turn, doesn't have a dead end behind them anymore. Voilà!

The one way "The Pilot" keeps fidelity with "Friend from the Future" is explaining why the psychic paper has a message to come back to 2017 — there was a presumed incursion to the Vault (it was actually a student throwing up) — but it leaves more questions than it answers, because it claims the Daleks are exterminating Movellans in the past. The thing is the Dalek–Movellan war took place in the future, according to 1984's "Resurrection of the Daleks." That said, the fact that the Movellans are screaming and reacting like humans suggests that this could be an early stage of that war. Or it could be a moment in the Time War, now that it seemingly isn't time locked after the events of "The Day of the Doctor" and "Listen." If it seems like a ridiculous headache just to get in a cute line about watching Bill in *Doctor Who* next year . . . that's because it is.

The opening scene suggests that Nardole is now partially robotic (his body makes servo noises, and he even drops a mechanical part while showing Bill in). It would be typical of the Doctor to build his own semi-robotic butler, and yet it's the only time this season that such a detail comes up. The behind-the-scenes reasons are more convivial: Matt Lucas and Peter Capaldi had a delightful time working together on "The Husbands of River Song" and there was a desire on the part of both of them to work together some more.

If you pause at the right moment, you can see the titles of some of the papers Bill has done for the Doctor including "The cosmic far-ultraviolet background" (she got 97% on this!), "Quantum statistics of light" (88%) and "Laser cooling of ions: atomic clocks and quantum jumps" (92%). The Doctor's tutoring is . . . a little intense.

When the TARDIS materializes in Sydney in 2017, it's supposedly at a pavilion directly across the harbour from the Opera House. Unfortunately, there's no pavilion there. That's Kirribilli, and the Opera House faces some fancy apartment buildings and the prime minister's Sydney residence. One of us actually rented one of these apartments for an evening in 2017. The view is as spectacular as it looks from the TARDIS.

**The TARDIS Chronometer** St. Luke's University, Bristol, and Sydney, Australia, the present day; a far-flung alien planet 23 million years in the future; and an unnamed place sometime in the past where there are Daleks.

**Don't Be Stupid? (GB)** I have to give full credit to Steven Moffat. He was done with *Doctor Who* and was probably either halfway to writing *Sherlock* and *Dracula* and God knows what else. (Or was halfway to Cabo.) And then he came back for one, this-time-for-reals, final season. In doing so, he decided to reinvent the whole show.

Suddenly *Doctor Who* is about Bill Potts, the bright girl who caught the attention of a mad, long-tenured professor who once taught poetry instead of quantum physics because they both rhyme. He's secretly an alien with a time machine protecting something in a vault with his very strange butler. Well, that's a bit of a shift.

But why not?

And that's part of the fun of "The Pilot." It's the exhilaration of saying *why the hell not?* Let's make *Doctor Who* something else. The opening scene, where the Doctor essentially auditions Bill Potts as a new student and probably, though he wouldn't admit it, as a new companion, is effortlessly charming. The Doctor is kindly; Nardole is odd; Bill is filter-less but whip-smart (as if to punctuate the point, Moffat has her say, "Doctor . . . what?" at the end of the cold open). It's beautifully shot, and Pearl Mackie makes an instant impression. Then it goes from there into this utterly mad TED Talk where the Doctor explains temporal physics. Or something. And I don't care because it's beautifully conceived and executed, and Peter Capaldi can sell something that delightfully bonkers.

I adore Bill. I love the way she questions just about everything. (The bit where she says TARDIS shouldn't work as a name because it's an English acronym is hilarious.) You can definitely see the throughline from Shona in "Last Christmas" to Bill here: like Shona, Bill's an everywoman who undercuts the Doctor's more aristocratic airs and in so doing makes him more relatable. It's refreshingly different than Clara (who wanted to emulate the Doctor and be the smartest person in the room). And it gives Capaldi a chance to play the Doctor in a more paternal fashion, which is lovely. The Christmas sequence is delightful, as the Doctor's initially awkward about not giving her a gift and then we smash cut to the Doctor with a cracker hat and a little Christmas spread without any of the crankiness or awkwardness we're used to. It's not as intense a relationship as it was with Clara, but the second we see the box of photos of Bill's mum, the affection the Doctor has for Bill is clear.

Nardole, I still don't know about. I love the idea that Nardole is acting as the Doctor's butler (sort of). And I love Matt Lucas as an actor, but I do fear that the quirkiness and the Shaggy-like cowardice will become irritating. That said, his relationship with the Doctor is great (I love the way they shake hands when Bill finally gets what the TARDIS is), so I'm quietly confident.

The actual plot, as in "Smith and Jones," "Partners in Crime" and "The Bells of Saint John," is slight enough that we can get to know the new central characters and their relationship, but it's still great fun. I do wonder if Bill's interactions with Heather should have been more substantial. I love the idea that a crush would be that powerful, but there doesn't seem to be a lot to hang a crush on here.

There was a lot of talk when "The Pilot" aired that it could serve as a jumping-on point for fans new to *Doctor Who*, and it does that — but it doesn't. On the one hand, you have a new premise for the show (though for how long?) and a great new companion, and the Doctor has finally abandoned being an anti-hero. On the other hand, there are more easter eggs than a chocolate factory in the opening scene (including a prop not seen since 1966!) and the Doctor's motivations for helping Bill are explained by a close-up of Susan's photo.

But why the hell not? I have a feeling this is going to be a lot of fun.

**Second Opinion (RS?)** What on earth are you on about? Easter eggs don't put newbies off. That's why they're called easter eggs. No casual viewer is going to think, "If only I knew who was in that black-and-white photograph, then I'd understand the Doctor's motivation. Without that, it's a total mystery, better abandon the show." (Side note: I myself missed his glance at the photo of Susan the first time round and yet was astonishingly not up in arms about the Doctor's motivation for helping Bill.)

My co-author is dead wrong on this point: "The Pilot" is unquestionably the *perfect* jumping-on point. It's kind of too bad this turned out to be Peter Capaldi's final season, because this set-up would have been perfect for a new Doctor when you actually had a lot of viewers interested in stepping on board. Instead, like Matt Smith's final half season, they entirely reboot the show just before it's going to be rebooted again.

But what a reboot it is! In fact, it's so brilliant, I wish they'd kept it and actually had the Doctor commit to staying on Earth investigating alien incursions at the university. Bringing Bill on board doesn't mean he suddenly needs to leave the planet, as he does at the end of the story. After all the good work put into this set-up, it's a shame that they abandon it as soon as it's up and running.

Everything else Graeme mentions is quite true, but I'd like to say that I absolutely love Nardole. He's such a refreshingly oddball character and happily stays in the background so much of the time that it's a delight when he steps up. The jokes he gets are almost always genuinely funny, and he's unlike any companion we've ever had. I'm in.

However, as my co-author indicates, this is Bill's show. She's immediately magnetic, being exactly the sort of everyperson with a personality that the companion should be but so often isn't. I love the fact that so little is made of her being into women. She's the first lesbian companion, but it's not a big deal. As it shouldn't be.

In a way that no other Doctor's era has managed, all three of Peter Capaldi's seasons manage to be startlingly different, with very distinct tones. All three are, by and large, excellent, but that variation is quite impressive. This season picks a style and runs with it, creating its own sub-version of *Doctor Who*. And it's thanks to the excellent work done in "The Pilot" that we get immediate depth and likeability with Bill, who's already punching above her weight. More like this, please.

### Pearl Mackie

Back in 2016, Pearl Mackie was enjoying an acclaimed run in the National Theatre's West End production of *The Curious Incident of the Dog in the Night-Time* when it was announced — in a special scene broadcast on the BBC no less — that she would be playing Bill in *Doctor Who's* tenth season. It was a complete shock to her theatrical castmates, as the casting (and filming of the scene) was done in complete secrecy.

Born in 1987, Mackie grew up in Brixton. (Her grandfather, Philip Mackie, wrote the 1975 film *The Naked Civil Servant*.) She studied at the Bristol Old Vic Theatre School and rose in the ranks of the theatre, while performing a few small film and TV roles as well. *The Curious Incident of the Dog in the Night-Time* was considered her breakout performance — at least until she was cast in *Doctor Who*. Following her run as Bill, Mackie returned to the West End to perform in a revival of Harold Pinter's *The Birthday Party* for an acclaimed run. She continues to do film and TV, including the series *Forest 404* and *Adulting*.

## 10.02 Smile

**Written by** Frank Cottrell-Boyce **Directed by** Lawrence Gough
**Original airdate** April 22, 2017

**The Big Idea** The Doctor and Bill travel to a deserted human colony run by emoji-bots that monitor your mood. Which is all fine, as long as nobody gets sad.

**Roots and References** *Erewhon; or Over the Range* by Samuel Butler (the space-ship, as well as the story's themes about a utopia that has harsh punishments for minor offences); the Russian fairy tale *The Tale of the Fisherman and the Fish* (the Magic Haddock story that the Doctor tells is a corruption of this tale); the Bible, specifically the book of Genesis (the colonists are said to be expecting the Garden of Eden). The Doctor quotes from the David Bowie song "Ashes to Ashes," saying, "I'm happy, hope you're happy too." Harry Campion's "Any Old Iron" is also referenced.

**Adventures in Time and Space** This story takes place during the time Earth was evacuated (1975's "The Ark in Space"). Steadfast is MedTech 1, the same designation as Vira in that story, who was also the first to be revived. The Doctor mentions having bumped into some of the ships over the years, all escaping the same great disaster (including 1966's "The Ark" and 2010's "The Beast Below"). The latter story is referenced directly when the Doctor says that there are many Scotlands in space, all striving for independence.

Bill references her "Penguin with his arse on fire" description of the Doctor running (from "The Pilot") and also mentions her first TARDIS trip in that story. She finds a bust of Queen Nefertiti in the spaceship ("Dinosaurs on a Spaceship").

**The Vault Effect** Nardole reminds the Doctor that he swore an oath to guard the Vault, part of which includes that he doesn't leave Earth unless it's an emergency.

**Who Is the Doctor?** Having escaped the Vardies, the Doctor decides to go back because he considers it a moral imperative to destroy evil. Two hearts apparently give him really high blood pressure. He's not fond of fish except socially, which can complicate meals. He once met an emperor made of algae who fancied him. He claims he always wins at chess because he has a secret move: he kicks over the board.

**The Doctor and Bill** She realizes that he keeps the TARDIS the way it is because he provides the assistance mentioned on the door panel. The Doctor couldn't leave Bill to simply serve chips, so as a result she's not leaving him. After he works out how the city was built and explains it to her, she tells him that he's an awesome tutor.

**Monster of the Week** Vardies are tiny robots that work in swarms and have built the city by becoming the infrastructure. They interface with emojibots, which can detect your mood and will preserve happiness by killing anyone who shows grief.

**Stand Up and Cheer** "Can't you phone the police?" yells Bill while standing in front of a police box. "Isn't there a helpline or something?" she says, while the camera edges the Advice and Assistance Obtainable Immediately panel into shot. This may be one of the wittiest delayed-reaction jokes ever made in *Doctor Who*. It's made a bit more explicit later on, with Bill tracing her finger over the words and then raising it with the Doctor, but that doesn't undercut the sheer glory of this staging.

**Roll Your Eyes (RS?)** Bill's finger on the map in the spaceship is quite inconsistent. When she indicates the Doctor goes down, she's pointing south of where she's standing. When she finds the ladder to do so moments later, she's pointing some distance east from the previous location.

**Roll Your Eyes (GB)** I'm just going to point out that no one, unless they're a university professor, thinks that the opposite of a massacre is a lecture.

**You're Not Making Any Sense** If the grinder chews up people for mineral fertilizer, why are all the skulls intact in the cabinet beneath it?

**Interesting Trivia** While she was working on the show, Jenna Coleman would send emoji-laden texts to Peter Capaldi and Steven Moffat, who complained that they didn't really understand them. This led to the idea of robots who communicate by emoji. It's said to be the only remnant of human language surviving into the future, but the writing on the spaceship is in English. So either the Doctor was wrong or the TARDIS is translating for us. Interestingly, the TARDIS doesn't translate emoji, so maybe it has the same problem as Moffat and Capaldi!

The Vardy were named after Andrew Vardy, a professor of swarm robotics in Newfoundland, Canada. Professor Vardy had previously worked with writer Frank Cottrell-Boyce on a short story involving robots that was related to his research.

The Doctor says that, physiologically, smiles have a measurable effect on your mood. He's right. Smiling activates the release of neuropeptides, which fight off stress by allowing neurons to communicate good feelings to the rest of the body. Dopamine, endorphins and serotonin (the feel-good neurotransmitters) are all released when we smile. Endorphins also serve as a natural pain reliever, while serotonin acts as an antidepressant. Smiling is also contagious, as studies have shown we unconsciously mimic them. Smiling also makes you better-looking; seeing a smiling face activates your orbitofrontal cortex, the part of your brain that processes sensory rewards. So the Vardy are really on to something!

In case you missed it, the spaceship is called *Erehwon*, which is "Nowhere" spelled backwards. The colony, however, is actually the City of Arts and Sciences in Valencia, Spain. One presumes the colony was eventually named the Secneics dna Stra fo Ytic.

**The TARDIS Chronometer** One of the first human colonies, thousands of years in the future. The colony isn't named onscreen, but it's stated on the BBC *Doctor Who* website to be Gleise 581d (a real extrasolar planet that is potentially habitable). Also, St. Luke's campus in the present-day and London in the past.

**Don't Be Stupid? (RS?)** They say that the second episode of every new Doctor could be a William Hartnell story. That is, these stories are often limited in their scale and provide a degree of exploration and investigation not usually seen in more action-packed episodes, often with a more explicit science-fiction bent. Peter Davison's second story was "Four to Doomsday," which featured a lengthy investigation of an initially deserted spaceship. Matt Smith's second story was "The Beast Below," showing the wonders of the universe and the future of humanity. And now Peter Capaldi's second story sees an exploration of a deserted world in a very science-fiction-y story that —

Hang on.

Okay, so it's not the second story of a new Doctor. But it sure feels like one. It's a good half hour before the TARDIS crew meet another living person. Shortly afterwards, they discover the survivors of the human race cryogenically frozen in one room. And the revitalization process that's now underway was triggered by the Doctor's arrival. But that's enough about "The Ark in Space"; let's talk about "Smile."

In some ways, this is Bill's story, as she gets to explore a new planet, learn the Doctor has two hearts and so forth. She's also key to discovering that the colonists are already present and that it's the death of the old woman that sparked the emojibot crisis. But, in so many other ways, it's the Doctor's story. He's the one identified as an intergalactic policeman, flying around and sorting things out. He's explicitly identified with the helpful TARDIS exterior. His anarchist strain is on clear display, as he not only wants to blow up the city, he very nearly succeeds. When Bill questions why he's allowed to do this sort of thing, he overrides the legality of the issue with an ethical argument: it's a moral imperative that he destroy a murder machine.

There's also a running theme of consumption happening here. The skeleton crew are consumed by the garden; the spaceship is partially consumed by the city; and the Vardy are absorbed into the infrastructure.

For the second week in a row, the Doctor espouses a vegetarian argument. Last week, he asked if Bill's bacon sandwich loved her back. Here he contrasts a fish dinner with the fish he's fond of in social situations. Personally, I love this. I think the Doctor's worldview most definitely should extend to all living creatures. I don't even mind that it goes beyond simple vegetarianism here: Bill likes the futurism of eating algae instead of livestock, while the Doctor responds that he once met an emperor made of algae. Indeed, given that everything else in the city is made of Vardy, it's very likely that the blue food cubes Bill ate were probably tiny robots designed for digestion.

So what's the answer? Should we conclude that it's impossible to find an ethical answer and simply eat whatever? Clearly not, as the horror of consuming the colonists illustrates. Doubtless the Doctor's fish friends would feel the same about a fish dinner, as would the algae emperor. Instead, I think the answer is in the opening scene: the wheat fields outside the city are never complicated in this way yet are clearly meant for consumption. The answer, I believe, lies in the idea of sentience. Although the humans (probably) aren't eating the Vardy, it's the moment when the robots are identified as self-aware that the Doctor proclaims them to be alive. Wheat clearly isn't self-aware, whereas fish with social skills and sentient algae are. Erring on the side of not eating intelligent creatures is not a bad strategy.

In the end, the consumption theme takes a different turn: the colonists become economic consumers rather than literal ones, determining an equitable arrangement with the Vardy for sharing the city and hence paying rent. This turns exploitation into trade, which is a decent exchange. It may not be perfect, and the story is clear that whether this works or not is up to the two groups — but it's a definite improvement.

As the second story of what is essentially a brand new era, "Smile" starts with the same premise as a previous second story of a brand new era but goes in several different directions. Whereas "The Ark in Space" dealt with the theme of possession and what it meant to be human, "Smile" deals with consumption and our ethical obligations to other species. The result is a rich text, complete with excellent characterization for the two leads, set against a stunning visual backdrop, an exploration of the wonder of futurism and cute but terrifying robots. That's pretty much everything you could want from a science-fiction story. It shows that *Doctor Who* can mine just as many great things from its (sometimes neglected) sci-fi side as it can from its characters. Every time I think about this astonishing episode, all I can do is smile.

**Second Opinion (GB)** Look, Robert, there are easter eggs and there are easter eggs. And I would argue that if you show enough of them in sequence, they stand out. You would have deplored the amount of fan service going on in the Capaldi era ten years ago. You've been boiled like a lobster.

Ahem. Sorry. Needed to deal with that piece of irritation from question-mark boy's review of "The Pilot." Not that it matters, because "Smile" is rancid.

Like "In the Forest of the Night," this is all about the ideas the story is about rather than the story. The beats of the script are so heinous no writer in 1963 or 2017 in their right mind would have ever structured a story this way. Except . . . Frank Cottrell-Boyce did. See the supporting cast killed in the cold open. The Doctor and Bill arrive, meet horror, escape horror, then decide to go back into horror. Suddenly throw in a group of people we've never met 35 minutes into a story so we can have a final battle, which the Doctor solves by . . . comedy.

I'd rather argue with Dr. Smith? about the use of easter eggs in *Doctor Who* than watch "Smile." I'd rather do my taxes than watch "Smile." I'd rather discuss Jodie Whittaker with a bunch of internet trolls than watch "Smile."

In short: 💩

# 10.03 Thin Ice

**Written by** Sarah Dollard **Directed by** Bill Anderson

**Original airdate** April 29, 2017

**The Big Idea** The Doctor takes Bill to the last great Frost Fair in 1814, only to discover a giant creature is chained underneath the Thames.

**Roots and References** The works of Jane Austen, particularly her 1814 novel *Mansfield Park* (the ways that slavery motivated the upper classes); Jules Verne's 1870 novel *20,000 Leagues Under the Sea* and its 1954 film adaptation (the Doctor's 19th-century deep-sea diving gear); the 2013–15 series *Hannibal* (writer Sarah Dollard has admitted the character of Sutcliffe is named after a similar character in the episode "Buffet Froid"); the 2008 *Torchwood* episode "Meat" (exploiting a massive alien creature for sustenance). Bill refers to the Ray Bradbury short story "A Sound of Thunder" when she goes on about the effects of stepping on a butterfly while time travelling. The Doctor reads aloud "The Story of Tom Suck-a-Thumb" from the 1840 children's book *Struwwelpeter*.

**Adventures in Time and Space** The Doctor talks about having been at the Frost Fair before, which River Song mentions in 2011's "A Good Man Goes to War." (A cut scene in the script makes the connection more explicit, with the Doctor talking about the difficulties of getting a piano onto the ice because he wanted a nice place to take his wife to a Stevie Wonder concert. Bill responds, "You have a wife?") He previously mentioned the possibility of taking Clara to one of the Frost Fairs in "The Caretaker." The Doctor is back to using his "Doctor Disco" alias (from "The Zygon Invasion"/"The Zygon Inversion").

**The Vault Effect** Nardole is outraged to find that the Doctor has travelled in the TARDIS and is breaking his oath. The Doctor offers to flip a coin to determine if he can continue doing so (of course he's learned how to cheat at it). Later, Nardole is at the Vault, telling its occupant he's still going to guard it even if the Doctor isn't . . . while whatever is in the Vault is banging on the door. For all his bluster, Nardole is clearly scared by whatever is in there.

**Who Is the Doctor?** The Doctor continues to be sweet and avuncular, particularly with the children he encounters, but when the urchin Spider is killed, the Doctor is once again dispassionate about the deaths of others. He tells Bill the only thing he can do when such loss happens is move on, because when he doesn't, more people die. The Doctor still asserts, as he does in "Kill the Moon," that humanity needs to make decisions about important events that will affect it, such as freeing the creature. However, perhaps as a sign of how much he's changed, he doesn't disappear but rather asks Bill for orders, saying, "I serve at the pleasure of the human race."

**The Doctor and Bill** Upset at Spider's death, Bill demands to know how many people the Doctor has watched die — and how many people the Doctor has killed. The Doctor is remarkably patient (for this incarnation), reminding her that her rage is misdirected before finally telling her, "I'm two thousand years old, and I've never found the time for the luxury of outrage." Of course, several scenes later, the Doctor punches Sutcliffe the moment he says something racist about Bill.

**Monster of the Week** A giant sea creature chained under the Thames. Aided by parasitic fish that can create temporary holes in the ice, the creature is eating people who come to the Frost Fair. This is deliberately engineered by Lord Sutcliffe, who is harvesting the creature's feces as a fuel source that burns hotter — and longer — than coal.

**Stand Up and Cheer** Sutcliffe is right about how moving and compassionate the Doctor's speech is: "Human progress isn't measured by industry; it's measured by the value you place on a life. An 'unimportant' life. A life without privilege. That boy's value is your value. That is what defines an age. That is what defines a species."

**Roll Your Eyes** Nardole's Buzz Killington act is becoming a bit much.

**You're Not Making Any Sense** Just how did the creature end up in chains? While it is true there was technology in 1814 for sustaining air under the water in a diving bell, the early diving suits were quite primitive and didn't allow for a lot of movement. For that matter, how did the Doctor (who magically put his diving suit on lickety-split) manage to get the bombs distributed in such a way as to free the creature in no time whatsoever?

**Interesting Trivia** Bill says slavery "is still a thing" in 1814. Well . . . yes and no. Slavery was, in fact, generally prohibited in England following the decision made in what's known as the Somersett case of 1772. Also, the Slave Trade Act 1807 prohibited the slave trade in the British Empire. However, that act was around the practice of trading slaves, not slavery itself. (And even then, it wasn't exactly effective, as all it did was fine people.) It wasn't until the Slavery Abolition Act 1833 that slavery was completely abolished everywhere in the British Empire. Bill had good reason to still be cautious.

The onscreen depiction of the Frost Fair is pretty accurate within the limitations of something being shot in a TV studio. The River Thames froze around 23 times between 1309 and 1814. During five of those occurrences (1683–84, 1716, 1739–40, 1789 and 1814), the ice was thick enough to withstand the weight of an actual fair. Frost Fairs were a sort of street carnival with, yes, lots of day drinking. It was a way for the watermen, who moved people up and down the Thames, and the lightmen, who moved goods, to make a few bob while the river was frozen, by charging people to come onto the ice. The 1814 Frost Fair was mostly between Blackfriars Bridge and London Bridge, and at one point an elephant did indeed walk on the frozen river. After 1814, a new construction of London Bridge, with bigger archways, prevented the water from pooling and freezing as it did in previous years, which signalled the end of the Frost Fairs.

With "Thin Ice," Sarah Dollard became the second woman to write more than one *Doctor Who* story on TV solo — and the first since 2008. Steven Moffat had repeatedly tried to bring on women writers throughout his tenure. (Like the men, he also tried for some big names, like Shonda Rhimes and Jane Goldman.) Scheduling and other problems got in the way. Not that this is an excuse, and Moffat admits the lack of women writing was a definite problem during his tenure.

**The TARDIS Chronometer** London, 1814, and St. Luke's University, the present day.

**Don't Be Stupid? (GB)** The day after "Thin Ice" first aired, I had multiple texts from two groups of people. I had texts from friends of colour, who were saying things like, "Isn't this amazing that there was a story where *Doctor Who* talked about slavery and being Black in a historical setting?!" And I had texts from friends who were middle-aged white dudes, like me, saying things like, "This story is inaccurate. Slavery was repealed in England by 1814."

Both groups of my friends are correct, in their own way. But my support goes to the former group. All *Doctor Who* historicals are faulty by nature. (Check the Interesting Trivia for any historical in our books. Spoiler alert: we never say, "This a correct and totally factual account.") What "Thin Ice" does is too damn important.

It's hard to believe this is the same television show — indeed, the same executive producer — that gave us "Journey to the Centre of the TARDIS" only four years prior. Because here we have almost its exact opposite. "Thin Ice" is a story that talks about issues of race in both metaphorical and very real terms. It's a morality play for the world of 1814 and of today.

The morality play simply boils down to "What kind of people do we want to be?" Do we want to be people who enslave others and don't care about the lives of those considered lesser? Do we want to participate in something for the material benefit of the very rich that sees human beings as chattel? (Sarah Dollard adds a delightful element of Swiftian satire by making the object of wealth *literally* shit.) Or do we want to be better than that, even though that entails risk?

And then, wonderfully, the Doctor gives the decision over to Bill.

I also love that it gives us the same gambit of "Kill the Moon" but has the Doctor at a place where he doesn't behave like an asshole anymore. Even though he's forgotten her, he's taken on-board Clara's observation that he breathes our air and walks on our ground. But the Doctor still sees this as an important human decision and tells Bill he'll do her will. It's a glorious scene, because when the Doctor says, "I serve at the pleasure of the human race," you see how much the character has evolved over the past three series. But it's also beautiful because the Doctor collaborating helps Bill see past the short-sightedness of her own fears. Everybody gets character development.

And it's a *Doctor Who* story that talks about slavery. Yes, to the point of my other friends, abolitionism was all the rage in Britain by 1814, but slavery was still an issue. You can see it in works like Austen's *Mansfield Park*. But to me that misses the point. The last time we had a scene where a woman of colour landed in the past with the Doctor was "The Shakespeare Code," where the Doctor's advice to Martha was "act as if you own the place." Which was outrageously bizarre and unbelievably unhelpful. To actually talk about race and slavery and to acknowledge that people of colour are a part of society who do not necessarily face an easy time (to put it mildly), particularly in the past, is something the Modern Series should have done ages ago.

There are a few problematic bits: the Black background artists dressed as military officers are 100 years too early (and that casting ignores the struggle real people like Walter Tull had to go through to get a commission during World War I). The Doctor punching Sutcliffe feels wonderful because, for all the Doctor's appeal to being dispassionate, retribution for watching his friend denigrated like that feels just; others might feel it's an instance of the Doctor succumbing to violence. (I dunno; I cheered.) Even so, what it does right is so important.

Here's the thing though: I talk about all these broad-minded issues of race, but this is also an unbelievably fun story. The set for the Frost Fair is astoundingly good. The Doctor and Bill arguing about the deaths the Doctor has seen (or contributed to) is a meaty scene, which two great actors perform exceptionally. It uses kids and doesn't engage in jeopardy-bending or make them seem out of place (the first time this has happened in ten seasons!). The Doctor and Bill bamboozling the foreman at the workhouse is really funny, particularly Bill's realization of what the fuel source actually is. The climax feels like there's a scene or two missing, but Bill has already made her decision so most of the hard work is done.

"Thin Ice" aired not long after the start of the Trump presidency, and it felt remarkably prescient at the time. It feels even more so now. At the end of the day, it's a *Doctor Who* story that reminds people about the value of a life and, in some small ways, helps make others in the audience feel seen. I'd like to have more *Doctor Who* stories that result in texts the next morning.

**Second Opinion (RS?)** My co-author is flat-out wrong. In today's pop-culture literate world, new viewers aren't bothered by the existence of even multiple easter eggs, so long as they don't get in the way of the story. WHICH THE ONES IN "THE PILOT" BLATANTLY DON'T! Ahem.

Oh yes, let's talk about "Thin Ice." Because I'd like to address the issue of the Doctor punching a racist.

The scene as written is pretty funny. The Doctor gives Bill a big speech about how reason and diplomacy are the keys to winning an argument, then immediately punches Sutcliffe for being a racist. That's funny, and, as my co-author says, it also kind of makes you want to cheer.

But how valid is it to have the Doctor committing violence? After the discussion of how many people he's killed, it may seem churlish to quibble over a punch. But the Doctor's also right to point out that there were extenuating circumstances with those deaths. There are here as well. So what's the difference?

A key factor, I think, is the context. The Doctor has always reacted, not instigated. He kills people, yes, but he gives them a chance first or does so in self-defence or to save lives. He doesn't initiate violence. What's more, the Doctor rewiring explosives with a magic wand can't be imitated on the playground; punching someone in the face most certainly can.

One of the best lessons I ever learned from *Doctor Who* is that reason and intelligence and romance outclass violence. Every time. The Doctor is a shining example of a hero who uses his brain to outwit his enemies, not his fists. Even as a child, I followed this model, using my smarts to avoid getting into fights or talking my way out of them when I had to. As an adult, well, I'm writing this from Cameroon, where I'm using my smarts to help people fight infectious diseases. There's a direct link between the Doctor's compassion and my own. I want kids everywhere to adopt that same model of gentleness and intelligence over violence.

I won't deny that there's a huge thrill in watching the Doctor punch someone so deplorable. There's also a thrill in watching porn. But I'd rather have flirting and seduction and intimacy than the cheap fix. Likewise, I think they erred by having the Doctor descend to the level of physical violence. It sets a bad precedent (if the Doctor goes around punching everyone who deserves it, we'll be here for a very long time) and fundamentally undermines what the series is all about. As much as I also felt the urge to cheer, I want *Doctor Who* to be better than this for the very good reason that we humans can also strive to be better, using the Doctor's morality as a guiding light.

Then again, that racist did have it coming.

## 10.04 Knock Knock

**Written by** Mike Bartlett **Directed by** Bill Anderson
**Original airdate** May 6, 2017

**The Big Idea** Bill and her friends rent a spooky house, with something living inside the walls.

**Roots and References** The haunted house trope generally, but we'll go with Shirley Jackson's 1959 novel *The Haunting of Hill House* (the noises in the house and the decidedly creepy caretaker); *The Empire Strikes Back* (Pavel is trapped in the wall in almost exactly the same pose as Han Solo in the carbonite); *Indiana Jones* (the hidden room behind the bookcase). *I'm a Celebrity Get Me Out of Here* is mentioned, while the house is called a "freaky *Scooby-Doo* house." The song "Black Magic" by Little Mix plays on Bill's phone, while "Weird People" by the same group plays over the search for accommodation at the beginning. Beethoven's "Fur Elise" is played on the piano inside the Vault.

**Adventures in Time and Space** The Doctor says, "Sleep is for tortoises," just as he did in 1977's "The Talons of Weng-Chiang." Bill mentions living puddles ("The Pilot"), weird robots ("Smile") and big fish ("Thin Ice"). There's a reference to Harriet Jones, prime minister (2005's "The Christmas Invasion"). The house-mates joke about potential spooky causes such as a doll that's come to life or a giant freaky spider. *Doctor Who* has seen both in the third Doctor's era: 1971's "Terror of the Autons" and 1974's "Planet of the Spiders."

**The Vault Effect** The Doctor has put a piano inside the Vault, which Nardole thinks is a terrible idea. The Doctor tells stories and shares dinner with its occu-pant, who seems to particularly relish the part about young people being eaten by space lice.

**Who Is the Doctor?** He says he gave up being a Time Lord and ran away because it was too posh. He once played bass for Quincy Jones. He finds insects fas-cinating and loves Chinese food. He mentions regeneration to Bill but then changes the subject to avoid talking about it.

**The Doctor and Bill** They're close enough that Bill enlists the Doctor to move her stuff to her new house. Even so, she's embarrassed to have the Doctor around when she's with her friends, saying that this is the part of her life that he isn't in, but he persists — wilfully, in fact. She pretends that he's her grandfather, although he doesn't think he looks old enough.

**Monster of the Week** The Dryads are a swarm of alien insects that live inside walls. They interact with the wood on a cellular level, actually becoming the wood itself. High-pitched sounds attract them.

**Stand Up and Cheer** The effect of the Dryads devouring the housemates is very well done. Having them surrounded by the insects is quite horrific, but it's when the pile collapses, leaving only the swarming creatures, that the horror of this really hits home.

**Roll Your Eyes** The housemates all being restored at the end is ridiculous. We're even told that the housemates are "food," so how exactly are they all still intact? (Not to mention wearing their clothes!) It would be one thing if the Doctor and Bill actually do anything to make this happen, but it's just authorial fiat. Worse, it undercuts the spookiness of the rest of the episode by giving it such a pat, unearned ending.

**You're Not Making Any Sense** The Doctor asks the landlord exactly how the insects keep Eliza alive. The scene cuts away at this point, but, actually, we'd quite like to know as well.

**Interesting Trivia** If you feel this house looks familiar, that's because it is. Filming took place in Fields House in Newport, which is the house that was used for Wester Drumlins in 2007's "Blink." (Then also called a "*Scooby-Doo* house"!) In fact, David Suchet and his family had rented this very property for his Christmas holiday the year before — though he didn't realize it until he had a horrifying revelation three days into filming!

Bill's housemate Harry was originally going to be the grandson of Harry Sullivan, the fourth Doctor's companion. Sadly, this scene was dropped from the final script. There's a reference to young Harry's grandfather having a boyfriend, which may be a reference to a joke from "The Ark in Space" that "Harry is only qualified to work on sailors." Or it may not (and, indeed, it may not even be the same grandfather).

If you have this episode on Blu-ray, try the "binaural audio" special feature and listen on headphones. The feature gives an enhanced stereophonic experience — almost like "listening in 3-D," which is really spooky in a story like this.

**The TARDIS Chronometer** Present-day Bristol.

**Don't Be Stupid? (RS?)** This is a pretty poor effort, isn't it?

It probably looked a lot better on paper. Having an Earth-based story following an outer-space one and a historical was a good idea. A spooky haunted house with a creepy landlord should have been just the ticket. CGI insects that swarm out of the walls and devour people is a great image. Cleverly, with all the wood around, the sonic screwdriver is only used to light a passageway and scan the (entirely human) landlord.

To be fair, the first half delivers the scares pretty well. But it's all undercut by the pat ending, which actively damages the threat from earlier on. Unfortunately, David Suchet overacts his menace, which is a real shame, as he has to carry so much of the episode. He's fine when he keeps it understated and quite good when he starts acting like a child, but his outbursts are too on the nose when they should have been creepily underplayed.

Unfortunately, there's not a lot of *there* there. Haunted house? Check. Creepy landlord? Check. Supporting cast picked off one by one? Check. Terrifying insects? Check. Okay, can we all go home now? (Hopefully, to a non-haunted one.)

The one thing that elevates this from a bog-standard haunted-house story is the revelation surrounding Eliza. The landlord expends enormous effort protecting his daughter . . . only for us to discover that she's in fact his mother. This is an excellent twist, the only part of the episode that isn't being fuelled by cliché. The double flashbacks, featuring first David Suchet and then the young boy, make this very effective.

The revelation brings up a very clever question: namely, who has responsibility? Is it the parent's role to look after the child or the child's role to look after the parent? Well, it depends on the circumstances. The Doctor is explicitly a father figure to Bill here, being overprotective, even when she makes it clear he isn't wanted. The scene with Bill showing her mother her room (by way of a photo) is quite heartbreaking. Bill's clearly missing a parent in her life, a role the Doctor only partially fulfills.

Her rejection of the Doctor in her daily life is almost as painful as the Doctor's refusal to accept said rejection. His attempts to bond with the housemates only show the age gap further, as he blusters his way around knowing their music and commits the faux pas of revealing Bill's playlist to her new friends. However, as difficult as it is not to be wanted by someone you care about, that's no excuse for not respecting their wishes. He flat-out says no when she asks him to leave. In his mind, he's staying to protect her, but he's committing the same error that the landlord did: not moving on.

Every parent has to let their child go at some point. And every child needs to stop being dependent on their parents. Doing so isn't easy for either party, as the confrontation in the bedroom illustrates. What's more, over time, these roles can shift, so that the child becomes the caretaker. However, as painful as it is, the same rules apply: the child eventually needs to let the parent go.

For all its flaws, "Knock Knock" illustrates this dynamic perfectly. If you hold on to the parent–child relationship too strongly, you suffocate it. As the

Doctor says, life should be new friends and fireworks, not the same old, same old. It's very tempting to spend your whole life in the safety of the childhood cocoon, but there's more to life than being safe.

This, I think, is where the ending fails so badly. By magically restoring the housemates, it shows that there was not only no true menace here (a huge disservice to an episode whose raison d'être is to provide scares), but it also plays safe, immediately after teaching us the folly of doing exactly that. That's a real shame; had the episode gone for a darker ending — with perhaps only one housemate saved with, you know, actual cost or effort or challenge — we'd have been left with something a lot stronger and more powerful.

"Knock Knock" is, at best, a mediocre failure with a curdled theme. Without the courage to pursue its own premise to conclusion, it ends up being a lot worse than it should have been. The parenting issue it raises is a good one, but the appalling ending attempts patricide even against that. Still, at least no one makes the *Doctor Who* knock-knock joke. Let's be thankful for small mercies.

**Second Opinion (GB)** When I watched "Knock Knock" in preparation for this volume, I immediately tweeted, "Why doesn't anyone talk about 'Knock Knock'? It's an amazing *Doctor Who* story."

To which I immediately had the response: "Because it's not that good? I think the issue for me is that *Who* can be scary when it wants, something about hiding behind sofas. And this story promised that but kind of chickened out from being that."

I sort of shrugged that off at the time, but now I have my co-author coming with the extra-strength version of that.

All I've got is "Well, I liked it." I probably would have preferred the more far-gone characters like Pavel to have not survived, but here's the thing . . . if people die in a contemporary story, suddenly Bill and everyone else is in for a police investigation, and the whole story becomes complicated through real-life repercussions. That's not going to happen.

The other thing I'm not bothered by is the ending. I was in this for the ghost-train ride where scary things happen in the moment, and then a scarier thing happens, and things get progressively scarier . . . and then you're out and you're safe in the daylight. Yes, I get this is undramatic, blah blah blah, but I actually find it tremendously fun. Not every foray into horror has to end like "The Waters of Mars."

And "Knock Knock" is terribly fun. I really enjoyed the Doctor/Bill interaction a lot. I didn't find it dysfunctional. The reason the Doctor doesn't leave is because he immediately gleans there's something wrong with the house when he sees the trees swaying with no wind. I enjoyed the progression of Bill and the

Doctor's relationship as Bill looks for boundaries and the Doctor looks to protect her, but both trust each other. And, frankly, dear co-author, had the Doctor "moved on," Bill would have been dead.

I even liked the twist at the end that the landlord daughter is actually his mother. David Suchet is really great through all this, going from creepy to sinister to pathetic. It's a lovely performance.

I think "Knock Knock" is a hell of a lot of fun. I'm sorry that my co-author and the denizens of Twitter are such glum people that they want darkness and misery and dead people all over. The Doctor continues to be a delight (though revealing Bill's playlist was hugely insensitive), and there were some great laughs and great scares. I guess I'm just easy.

# 10.05 Oxygen

**Written by** Jamie Mathieson **Directed by** Charles Palmer
**Original airdate** May 13, 2017

**The Big Idea** People at a mining station in deep space wear artificially intelligent spacesuits that deliver expensive amounts of oxygen — until corporate office determines it's cheaper to simply deactivate the organic content of the suits . . .

**Roots and References** The *Alien* film franchise (corporate owners jeopardizing its human workforce for profit, the exo-suits); the 1996 film *Star Trek: First Contact* (the walk around the space station using magnetic boots, battling a zombie enemy horde). *Star Trek* is referenced a couple of times, with the Doctor and Nardole debating that "space doors" should open and close quickly with a "shuk-shuk" noise and the Doctor's parody of the opening narration. ("Space: the final frontier. Final because it wants to kill us.") The Doctor quotes 1 Corinthians 15:55: "Death, where is thy sting?"

**Adventures in Time and Space** Nardole thinks he's grounded the TARDIS by pulling out a fluid link, a trick the first Doctor used to keep the TARDIS on Skaro in 1963's "The Daleks." (Nardole is wrong, but he seems to be reliant on what the Doctor claims to be a fluid link!) When Bill thinks she's dying, she thinks of a picture of her dead mother that the Doctor found for her in "The Pilot" and that she hung on the wall of her room in "Knock Knock."

**The Vault Effect** Once the Doctor is back on Earth, Nardole is furious with him, saying "You need to be here, and you need to be ready if that door ever opens . . . What if you came back injured or sick? You really think our friend down there won't know that? Won't sense it?" The inference is that whatever is in the Vault is catastrophically dangerous.

**Who Is the Doctor?** The Doctor is clearly being worn down while stuck on Earth. He keeps mentioning space travel in his lectures and missing the opportunity to be in space. He picks *Chasm Forge* as a place to travel because they have a distress signal, quipping that a distress call is his theme song. He expands on this, telling Bill and Nardole, who want to leave the space station, "The universe shows its true face when it asks for help. We show ours by how we respond."

**The Doctor and Bill** The Doctor uses Bill's vote to go back to the TARDIS as a teachable moment, to explain why they do what they do. When Bill's helmet fails, the Doctor gives her his helmet, which results in him blinding himself. He is forced to gamble that Bill's damaged suit won't kill her when the zombies advance on her to burn out her nervous system, but he keeps assuring her that he'll be there on the other side of all the pain she'll experience.

**Monster of the Week** The Smartsuits are artificially intelligent exo-suits. They can move independently and calculate the number of breaths an occupant has left. When a corporate algorithm determines that the humans in *Chasm Forge* use too much expensive oxygen, they terminate the life of the humans, allowing the suits to continue to operate with their hosts dead inside.

**Stand Up and Cheer** The opening scene is one of the most beautiful to set up the jeopardy to come in the history of *Doctor Who*. It works by focusing on Ellie as she tells Ivan she wants to have a baby with him . . . only he can't hear her because her radio is dead. With the audience now instantly connected to the couple, the camera cuts to Ivan, who can't see or hear her . . . until he sees Ellie's helmet float by, and he discovers the Smartsuit zombies, including a now-dead Ellie, moving towards him. Cue electronic sting and opening credits. It's amazingly scary, but it also pays off at the end when the Smartsuit with the dead Ellie hugs Ivan and gives him oxygen.

**Roll Your Eyes** Bill's and Nardole's awkwardness around the blue-skinned Dahh-Ren is meant to be this hilarious example of how the goalposts of perceived racism change in the future, but it just comes off like a really dull joke made by a white, middle-aged dad.

**You're Not Making Any Sense** The Doctor seems really, really confident that Bill's Smartsuit is so broken it will only put her in a coma, as opposed to burn out her nervous system. And not alert others that she's not actually dead. And sustain her vital signs, including pumping expensive oxygen to her. And the Doctor does this assessment *while blind*. There are probably a couple more points we could include here if we were pressed, but this should suffice.

**Interesting Trivia** Writer Jamie Mathieson intended the episode to connect to "Mummy on the Orient Express" by actually showing us a representative from corporate head office, whose voice sounds familiar to the blind Doctor.

Realizing it's a trap, the Doctor gets the survivors into the TARDIS and the station blows up. The Doctor then explains the representative would be eventually fired . . . but his voice would become that of Gus, the artificial intelligence in "Mummy." Steven Moffat felt that, with the threat resolved, this ending was simply stalling, and Mathieson agreed.

Nardole was a late addition to the development of Series Ten. In fact, "Oxygen" was the first script outside of "The Pilot" that was developed with Nardole being fully integrated in the story, as opposed to a scene dropped in here or there. This story also began a running gag about the tall tales Nardole tells about himself, which here includes him having another face prior to the one he has now, as well as dating the woman who became the artificial intelligence voice in the Smartsuits.

The Doctor's blindness was an innovation Jamie Mathieson made to give the Doctor an obstacle to overcome (and to demonstrate the horrors of space). It was supposed to have been resolved at the end of the story (in the final TARDIS scene). But Steven Moffat was quite taken by the story potential the Doctor's blindness had and undid the cure in the tag scene to use it in the next episode.

*Chasm Forge* is supposed to be mining copper . . . *how* precisely? There are no planetary bodies, no way to scoop meteorites, and the monetary value of what they mine isn't enough to merit piracy. Never mind deactivating the organic components; it seems like keeping *Chasm Forge* open in the first place is a bad corporate decision.

**The TARDIS Chronometer** The space station *Chasm Forge* in the far future.

**Don't Be Stupid? (GB)** "Oxygen" has pretty much everything I love about *Doctor Who* in one really amazing package.

First of all, it has a stunning cold open that starts out with a savage parody of *Star Trek* before going terrifically sentimental and then cutting that sentiment off at the knees to reveal the walking dead in spacesuits. That sequence is a masterclass in writing and how to misdirect the viewer by mainlining pure emotion. And that great writing continues throughout.

This story also demonstrates *Doctor Who*'s variety of ideas. During "Knock Knock," my co-author (and, apparently, Twitter) thought the characters being restored ruined the stakes; I felt it was simply a different, more temporal, use of horror. Here, my co-author gets what he wanted with a crew that's gradually murdered with no use of the reset button. And this is where you need such a story: in a place far away with no escape. That we can have a ghost-train version of horror in one story and a full-on horror story with suspense and real stakes is not a bug but a feature: the glorious variety that is *Doctor Who*.

A more than fair share of why "Oxygen" succeeds is the direction by Charles

Palmer, who previously directed "Smith and Jones" and "Human Nature"/"The Family of Blood" during the David Tennant era. "Oxygen" again shows what an inventive, wonderfully visual director Palmer is. The opening sequence is a testament to his skills, as is the space walk shown from Bill's point of view.

Palmer is also capable of getting the best out of his actors. Case in point: Nardole is amazing here. Matt Lucas gets a few light moments, but during the final scene when he's full of fury with the Doctor, we see the many hidden depths Lucas has. "Oxygen" is exceptionally well acted, whether that be with regulars like Lucas or Pearl Mackie (who is wonderful in the scene where the Doctor abandons her to the Smartsuits) or with a day player like Katie Braben, as we develop utter sympathy with Ellie in a single scene. As Dr. Smith? says, *Doctor Who* is always about the acting. The horror of what happens at *Chasm Forge* is made real by its characters.

"Oxygen" is so damn smart. It prizes the viewer's intelligence from the start of the episode, where the Doctor outlines all the ways that space is ultimately out to kill you, to the end, where the Doctor — while blind — comes up with a simple yet elegant way to stop the Smartsuits. Let's talk about that for a minute. The Doctor stops the threat by turning the mentality of it back on itself: if the humans are being killed to improve efficiency, then tie the humans' survival to the efficiency of the ship. This adroit solution is easily my favourite in a *Doctor Who* story in ages.

It's not only smart, it connects with the overall theme of the story. Like so many great *Doctor Who* stories, "Oxygen" has a moral element to it. And like so many great *Doctor Who* stories, "Oxygen" creates a funhouse distortion of modern life: here we have a reality where survival is monetized. Your breaths are counted and you have to pay for them . . . and eventually some algorithm determines your existence isn't needed at all. "Thin Ice" posited that a society that doesn't value human life is wrong. "Oxygen" shows us what a society is like that ignores all that, at its peril. It would be simplistic to call this "anti-capitalist"; it's a critique of 21st-century living itself.

Good writing. Good direction. Good acting. Being smart. Having something to say. These are all the things I love in *Doctor Who*. These are all the things I love in "Oxygen."

**Second Opinion (RS?)** Here's the problem with zombies: they make no sense.

Okay, I should back up here a little. In my day job, I'm actually a world-leading researcher on the topic of zombies. Yes, really. I fell into this because I was working on showing how mathematics can explain infectious diseases, but my students and I used zombies as a fun example of how that might work. This went viral in the media, so now I'm "that zombie math guy."

As much as I've thought deeply about zombies over the years, the one thing that always bugs me isn't the fact that the dead come back to life (that's just the magical handwaving to get the stories started) — it's the question of energy. How do zombies sustain themselves? Humans need food, water and sleep to recharge, but zombies have none of these things. Okay, sure, they eat our braaaiiinnnsss occasionally, but not to survive. Without replenishment, surely the cadaver would eventually keel over and collapse, unable to maintain itself. In short, how do the walking dead actually walk?

This is where "Oxygen" is brilliant. Unlike the bad-science zombies back in "New Earth," here we have a simple but marvellous solution: technology does the walking.

The genius of this is that you still get the scare factor with corpses coming after you in darkened corridors, but now it makes sense. Having our loved ones both dead and trying to kill us, as with Ellie and Ivan here, is terrifying, on a deeply psychological level. You can try to rationalize it away, but your higher brain is going to shut down in favour of your lizard brain. However, if there's no good reason for it to be happening other than magic, then the threat is dissipated.

"Oxygen" is one of the scariest *Doctor Who* stories in years, in part because it seems so plausible. The face of the threat is the distended human bodies, but the actual threat is the machine that's powering them — which could so easily cut off the air supply for everyone else.

Being unable to breathe, while trapped in a corridor by the reanimated corpse of someone you love? Those are some fundamental fears that we can all relate to. In both our higher and our lizard brains. Or should that be braaaiiinnnsss?

## 10.06 Extremis

**Written by** Steven Moffat **Directed by** Daniel Nettheim
**Original airdate** May 20, 2017

**The Big Idea** The pope travels to England to ask for the Doctor's help in translating a book. Only . . . everyone who has ever read it immediately killed themselves.
**Roots and References** Dan Brown's 2003 book *The Da Vinci Code* and its 2006 film adaptation (a conspiracy thriller set in the heart of the Vatican); cyberpunk works such as the 1982 film *Blade Runner*, William Gibson's 1984 novel *Neuromancer* and *The Matrix* series (a simulation that appears to be real life, with copies of people). *Monty Python's Flying Circus* (the Veritas is similar to the world's funniest joke, which is cut into pieces to keep people from dying laughing at it). Bill mentions Harry Potter when viewing the library of blasphemy (amusingly, the Doctor

admonishes her with "Language!" which is itself a reference to the 1980s Ronnie Corbett sitcom *Sorry!*), while the Doctor mentions *Super Mario* and *Moby-Dick*. Nardole compares the projection to *Star Trek*'s holodeck and *Grand Theft Auto*.

**Adventures in Time and Space** Nardole reads aloud from, and gives the Doctor, River's diary. Missy refers to the Doctor experiencing domestic bliss on Darillium ("The Husbands of River Song"). She also mentions the Daleks (she was last seen trying to strike up an alliance in "The Magician's Apprentice"/"The Witch's Familiar"). The Doctor swears an oath on his Prydonian credentials, the chapter of the Time Lords he was a member of, as established in 1976's "The Deadly Assassin." Bill's moving troubles in "Knock Knock" are mentioned.

**The Vault Effect** The occupant of the Vault is revealed to be Missy, who was sentenced to execution. She promised to be good in exchange for her life if the Doctor would teach her. He rewired the execution chamber to save her, but he pledged to guard her for 1,000 years.

**Who Is the Doctor?** In her diary, River states that the Doctor believes that "goodness is not goodness that seeks advantage. Good is good in the final hour, in the deepest pit without hope, without witness, without reward. Virtue is only virtue in extremis." (It's a line he repeats to a Monk in the White House.) He saves Missy in part because he acknowledges that Missy is his friend. He doesn't like people worrying about him, because when they're with him, they should be worried about themselves. Even when he realizes he's not real, he defines being the Doctor as not giving up and as tricking the bad guys into their own traps.

**The Doctor and Bill** He hides his blindness from Bill, because the moment he tells her, that's when it will become real. When he intuits that something bad is coming, he pushes her to ask out her crush Penny, incidentally noting that Penny isn't out of her league.

**Monster of the Week** The Monks have blueish skin, pointed ears and long fingers. They look like misshapen corpses, wearing red robes. They open their mouths but don't move them in order to speak, suggesting that they're telepathic. They have created a simulation of human history in order to plan an invasion.

**Stand Up and Cheer** Bill brings home a girl who's feeling unsure about being a lesbian. Bill comforts her, saying that what they're doing is nothing to feel guilty about. Whereupon the pope walks out of the next room, ranting in Italian (presumably about having just travelled in the TARDIS). It's an absolutely hilarious scene . . .

**Roll Your Eyes** . . . but also quite problematic, as the joke hinges upon the idea that there's something to feel guilty about. At least Bill wasn't the one infused with guilt, but it still seems like we should have moved past this a long time ago.

**You're Not Making Any Sense** It's a great conclusion (fake), but how exactly can the simulation of the Doctor (it's all fake) email his counterpart in the real world (Graeme and Robert, it's a fake!). It's not like avatars (listen, you have to) in *Second Life* can contact us (run!).

**Interesting Trivia** Rafando reveals that Time Lords have three brain stems, the first we've heard of this, despite once journeying into the Doctor's brain (1977's "The Invisible Enemy") and the clockwork waiter in "Deep Breath" using the singular when talking about harvesting the Doctor and Clara. (He uses "eyes" plural but "spleen" and "liver" singular; then again, he's talking about two individuals, so there are presumably at least two brain stems on offer.) This suggests Missy was lying in "The Magician's Apprentice" when she implied that Time Lords only had the one — though she was recommending a sniper aim for it at the time, so perhaps it's understandable if she wasn't telling the whole truth.

Cardinal Angelo mentions the decree signed by Pope Benedict IX in 1045. There's actually a lot to unpack here. Benedict IX was the only person to become pope more than once . . . and, in fact, he became pope three (possibly four) times. He's also the only person to sell the papacy. After his election in 1032, he was forced out in 1044 due to multiple adulteries (!) and murders (!!). He returned in April 1045 with enough soldiers to expel his replacement, but his second term lasted only two months. Deciding he wanted to marry his cousin (!!!), he abdicated in favour of his godfather, but demanded to be reimbursed for expenses. Subsequently, he regretted his decision and took Rome from his godfather, who was later annulled as pope on account of having paid for it, although the godfather was still considered to be the true pope at the time. A new pope was appointed, but after he died, Benedict seized the papal residence and remained pope for the next eight months until German forces drove him out. He was the first pope rumoured to be primarily homosexual, although "Extremis" puts a new spin on it: that Benedict was actually a woman. Interestingly, the period in which she supposedly signed this decree would have been during the two-month middle papacy before she abdicated to marry her (female) cousin. No wonder the Doctor says she was trouble!

The *Veritas* test is to name a string of numbers at random and see whether other people do the same thing. This idea comes from the fact that computers are deterministic, not random, and any apparent randomness is just a disguise. For example, a computer might run an algorithm based on the last digit of the current time — as measured in nanoseconds. So if you and your friend both pull the lever on a poker machine, there's no way you can pull it at precisely the same time, down to the nanosecond, so the resulting outcomes will be different. "Extremis" postulates that the simulation is entirely deterministic, so these fluctuations all line up. That's certainly possible for a simulation . . . but if it were, then it's a bad simulation. Presumably the Monks entered the initial data as the entirety of human history and then ran the simulation forward from there, but it still means that any chance events would likely not occur. This means the simulation would start to diverge from reality in short order. What's more, the Monks mention having killed the virtual Doctor many times, but why do they need to run multiple simulations if the outcome is entirely deterministic? The virtual Doctor says that the simulation is too good, but he's wrong: the lack of randomness is actually a pretty big flaw, and one that would be easy to overcome.

How did Nardole get River's diary? The tenth Doctor left it in the library with her sonic screwdriver, but that was after she died. As far as we know, she didn't realize she was going to die when she arrived at the library, so how did she instruct Nardole? There's a fan video to be made of Nardole peeking behind a pillar while the Doctor talks to Donna in "Forest of the Dead" . . .

**The TARDIS Chronometer** Execution planet, a long time ago; present-day Bristol; simulations of Bristol, London, the Vatican, the Pentagon, CERN (in Geneva, Switzerland) and the Oval Office, Washington D.C.

**Don't Be Stupid? (RS?)** What an excellent episode! Too bad it does so much damage to the season around it.

First, the Vault. It's been a thoroughly effective mystery all season, building up to a mysterious occupant of a prison under the university. Theories run thick and fast. Who could it possibly be?! Well, colour me surprised, it's the flipping Master.

Seriously, could there be a more obvious choice than Missy? I had a great theory at the time: I thought it was going to be Bill's mother. Think about it: she's mentioned or shown in every episode thus far, cleverly seeding the idea into the season but in a way that's still going to be surprising. We know the Doctor has had contact with her in the past, thanks to the photos he took of her. And it would give an emotional punch to the viewer if the occupant turned out to have a personal connection to Bill. Instead, it's the flipping Master.

Sadly, the outcome we got is a lot more prosaic than my idea — and, I'll wager, just about everyone else's ideas too, assuming they weren't just reaching for the most obvious one. Okay, I will admit that the flashback scenes on the execution planet are great. But that's "Extremis" in a nutshell: fantastic episode, far too damaging to everything around it.

The set-up is excellent. A "practice run" of a simulation before an invasion is a fantastic idea. Sadly, however, where this will ultimately go turns out to be somewhat less fantastic. The simulation is a way of having an "It was all a dream!" ending without it feeling like a cop-out; the episode kills off both companions, with the Doctor facing certain death at the end — not to mention destroying CERN, killing the president and so forth. However, the genius of it is that it links back to the real world, thanks to the framing device of the Doctor watching the recording while sitting outside the Vault. That both anchors it to our universe and also gives the story meaning.

The Monks are appropriately creepy, basically being walking corpses. But the key point, the one thing that dooms them here, is that they're *old*. They're the ones who grab a book when the Doctor runs off with a laptop. They're the ones who overlook the value of email. They're the ones who, despite running a giant simulation of the universe, entirely miss the wonders of modern communication.

What's clever is that, in an episode predicated around the stuffy old Vatican turning up to ask for help with a text that predates even the church, the story is genuinely thoughtful about the ways that modern communication has changed our lives. It's entirely natural that a library of blasphemy — a place very few people even know exists — would have wifi, because that's what libraries offer nowadays. Technology is used to overcome disability, both in the Doctor's "reading aid" from the TARDIS as a temporary solution and then more permanently when the Doctor uses software that reads the *Veritas* translation aloud to him.

However, the biggest effect is the ability to copy. With a text like the *Veritas*, owning the physical media was all-important. But an electronic translation can easily be sent to multiple groups at once, as happens here (as well as all the CERN scientists, Father Piero has emailed any number of people; freeze-framing reveals that most of them are related to the *Veritas*). That ties into the nature of simulation, which is to copy. And, of course, the episode is resolved by the virtual Doctor emailing a copy to his real self. ("There's always one thing you can do from inside a computer. [. . .] You can always email.")

This is great. As is the rest of the episode, which has thrills and scares and action. Nardole is particularly awesome, with a badass speech about his role as protector and his deductions about the nature of the reality they're in, hitting every note perfectly . . . right before he pixelates into oblivion. The various locations give us very different moods: the Vatican library is spooky; the CERN cafeteria is intriguing, with a high-octane countdown; the white projector room is suitably off-kilter; and the Oval Office is the perfect location for the final confrontation. Oh, and the virtual Doctor's last line is utterly perfect: "I'm doing what everybody does when the world is in danger: I'm calling the Doctor."

Final score? Excellent episode, but it tanks the next several and much of the season overall. And I still think that it should have been Bill's mum in the Vault. Was it worth it? Only in extremis.

**Second Opinion (GB)** For reasons you'll soon see, I have other things on my mind when it comes to Steven Moffat's final two *Doctor Who* stories. Consequently, I'm offering my appreciation of Steven Moffat's work on *Doctor Who* on his antepenultimate solo-written episode. "Extremis" is a great story to do that with, because it has so many of the things I love about Steven Moffat's writing.

For one thing, his *Doctor Who* stories value life above all. For a show obsessed with horror and death, Steven Moffat is remarkably sparing in who he kills off. There are some fans who despise this. I've loved this aspect of his work and his belief that because there are so many things in *Doctor Who* to be in awe of, not everyone has to die — life is important and should be cherished. And so here we have flashbacks to the Doctor preventing Missy's execution, saving her because he believes everyone should have hope and he believes in the person he once considered — and may still consider — to be his friend.

Mostly, though, I love Steven Moffat for the cleverness. At his best, Steven Moffat writes *Doctor Who* that's smart. It gets harder after 12 years (seven of them showrunning) to stay one step ahead of one's audience — and yet "Extremis" does it by starting out as a *Da Vinci Code* pastiche (all secret Vatican libraries and hidden texts) and then takes a hard left turn into *The Matrix*. But here's the nifty trick about "Extremis": the twist is not done in the M. Night Shyamalan style of "They weren't real at all!" Moffat builds the twist organically, through the trip to CERN and the discovery of what the *Veritas* means. In short, it plays fair. Hell, the visuals even glitch coming out of the opening credits.

And then there are the women. Moffat's reign on *Doctor Who* was full of smart, sassy, flirty women who are unbelievably intelligent and self-aware. The genius of the later Moffat years was that he took *Doctor Who*'s premier super-villain and made her female. And let's be clear: Missy is wonderful. The scenes with Missy in "Extremis" give the episode its heart, as the Doctor's actions with Missy's execution define him. Yes, my co-author is right that putting Missy in the Vault was the laziest possible option. (I wish I could have had Robert's genius and thought of Bill's mum, but I watched the "Coming Up" trailer at the end of "The Pilot" and figured it would turn out to be John Simms's Master.) And yet . . . it feels right that it is her. Because what would Moffat's *Doctor Who* be without the Doctor flirting with a woman smarter than him in every important respect?

But . . . that also exposes the flaws in Moffat's tenure, flaws that mostly concern his time as showrunner: his story arcs veer from the madly ambitious to the risible to the humdrum, which we now have here. And for all the amazing women who traipse through Moffat's *Who*, setting up the same flirty relationship with the Doctor again and again can get a bit forced. I think the success of Missy's execution confession is more down to the brilliance of Michelle Gomez than it actually making sense for the Master to do it. And there's a tone-deafness at times, like the implications of the joke with Penny seeing the pope. On the other hand, that joke is very funny.

I think good television writing is defined by taking small risks, like that joke, and big ones, like trusting the viewer will appreciate an episode of *Doctor Who* that is entirely unreal. Steven Moffat spent seven years as showrunner and another five as a writer, giving us *Doctor Who* that was always funny, always delightful and never safe. I'm going to miss him.

. . . . . . . . . . . . . . . . . . . . . . . . . . . . . . . . . . . . . . . . . . . . . . . . . . . . . . . . .

## Matt Lucas

Rather like Catherine Tate ten years previously, Matt Lucas comes to his role as a companion already quite famous. Lucas was best known for his work with David Walliams on the sketch-comedy series *Little Britain* and its follow-ups *Little Britain USA* and *Come Fly with Me*.

Born in 1974, Lucas first came to prominence on television through his association with alternative comedians Vic Reeves and Jim Mortimer, appearing in the sketch-comedy series *The Smell of Reeves and Mortimer* (1993–95) and the game show spoof *Shooting Stars* (which he did intermittently from 1993 to 2009); the latter gave Lucas attention for his portrayal of George Dawes, the drum-playing scorekeeper who wore a baby's onesie.

Lucas went on to develop *Little Britain* with David Walliams, first for BBC Radio (2000–02) and then for television (2003–07). It made him a star, and Lucas did a variety of film and TV projects ranging from dramatic roles in Russell T Davies's 2005 series *Casanova* to playing Tweedledee and Tweedledum in Tim Burton's 2010 *Alice in Wonderland* to a memorable appearance in the 2011 film *Bridesmaids*, as well as the sitcom *Pompidou* (2015), guest appearances on American TV series like *Community* and starring in the Damien Hirst–directed video of Blur's song "Country House."

A lifelong *Doctor Who* fan — Tom Baker was the narrator in *Little Britain!* — Lucas was also happy to star in "The Husbands of River Song" for another reason: his partner Kevin McGee, who died in 2009, was a massive fan of the series (the couple owned a TARDIS used in Series Two in their home). Lucas had so much fun with Peter Capaldi during that episode that he was asked to reprise the role of Nardole when it came time to film the following season. Since *Doctor Who*, Lucas has gone on to publish his autobiography, *Little Me*.

. . . . . . . . . . . . . . . . . . . . . . . . . . . . . . . . . . . . . . . . . . . . . . . . . . . . . . . . .

# 10.07 The Pyramid at the End of the World

**Written by** Peter Harness and Steven Moffat **Directed by** Daniel Nettheim

**Original airdate** May 27, 2017

**The Big Idea** When an ancient pyramid appears in the middle of a crisis in Turmezistan, the Doctor is called in, only to find the Monks claiming that Armageddon looms — unless humanity submits to them.

**Roots and References** The 1986 graphic novel *Watchmen* (the Doctor being locked in a room with no escape echoes Dr. Manhattan's origin, and the Doomsday Clock is a huge motif); the 1970s BBC drama *Survivors* (the Earth being destroyed by a lab accident). Bill, ever the nerd, compares the Monks to vampires, with their need for their victims to let them in. The generals all decide to "give peace a chance" invoking John Lennon's 1970 song of the same name. The Doctor gives the sign-off from the ITV game show *The Pyramid Game* (which was an adaptation of the U.S. game show *The $64,000 Pyramid*).

**Adventures in Time and Space** We're back in the fictional country of Turmezistan, last seen in "The Zygon Invasion"/"The Zygon Inversion." The Doctor is seen playing his guitar for the first time since "Hell Bent," and he's double-locked the TARDIS door (as he did way back in 1964's "The Dalek Invasion of Earth"). The United Nations protocols making him president of Earth are once again invoked (as it was in "Dark Water"/"Death in Heaven"; for once, the presidential plane doesn't crash as it did there and in "The Zygon Invasion"/"The Zygon Inversion").

**Who Is the Doctor?** The Doctor is still reluctant to discuss his blindness and still relies on Nardole to surreptitiously guide him. He seems to have stopped acting derisively towards military personnel. He possibly asks out Erica, either on a date or to join him as a companion (although he uses the word "assistant," harking back to the Classic Series).

**The Doctor and Bill** The Doctor is gloriously awkward when asking Bill how her date went, responding, "Awesome," despite being unsure if what she was saying was a metaphor or not. The Monks succeed in their plan to find a human willing to submit to them because Bill won't see the Doctor killed, though she does this because she trusts the Doctor will save them all. Her consent is pure because she offers it out of love (for the Doctor).

**Monster of the Week** The Monks return and seem to have the ability to interfere with reality: planes attacking in the air and submarines attacking from the sea both find themselves buried in the ground. They claim to require humanity to submit without fear or guile in order to save Earth from impending disaster, though they also seem to be equally reliant on technology.

**Stand Up and Cheer** The Doctor swooping in and saving the day is pretty much standard procedure, but the way the Doctor does it here — flirting shamelessly with Erica (who contributes as much to the solution as he does) and being funny and charming all the while — set our hearts aflutter.

**Roll Your Eyes** Given how loaded the term "consent" is in terms of gender politics and issues around sexual violence (even when this was made, just slightly before the #MeToo era), why did they choose that particular word to . . . Oh, wait. This story is literally produced by the same people who signed off on "Kill the Moon."

**You're Not Making Any Sense** This episode is premised on the idea that the military forces of not one, not two, but three major superpowers would abandon their chains of command. Given that the chain of command is the very basis of every army, ever, this seems . . . unlikely.

**Interesting Trivia** Peter Harness's original script had stand-ins for real-world figures of Kim Jong-un, Donald Trump and Jeremy Corbyn. (When it was written in 2016, Trump had not become president, and Harness was making a satirical point!) Harness was inspired by watching Brexit and the 2016 U.S. election campaign unfold and asking how it was that people would choose solutions that are clearly advertising themselves as dangerous or working against the best interests of voters — and was this based in fear or a twisted version of love? The situation the leaders would face was more darkly satirical, like a twisted version of *Charlie and the Chocolate Factory*, and the Monks were extra-dimensional beings. All of this was changed substantially in rewrites, including Steven Moffat's own pass through the script.

The potential life-destroying contagion was also inspired by real-world events. Harness based that on an alleged incident in the 1990s where the bacterium *Klebsiella planticola* was used in genetically modified plants in a lab experiment to destroy crop residue and help produce ethanol. The ethanol-producing bacteria quickly spread through the root system and killed all plant life. Had it been released outside the lab, it could have been disastrous.

The Doomsday Clock was created in 1947 by the Chicago Atomic Scientists, an organization of scientists who had participated in the Manhattan Project and were concerned about the effect that technological advances could have on global security and on science. The clock originally measured how close to nuclear war humanity was, but in time it took into account other concerns such as climate change. The original setting in 1947 was at seven minutes to midnight. It has changed 23 times since then (moving both forward and backwards) and, at the time of writing, is set at two minutes to midnight.

**The TARDIS Chronometer** Bristol and Turmezistan, the present day.

**Don't Be Stupid? (GB)** On the podcast I co-produce, *Reality Bomb*, there's a regular segment called "Gallery of the Underrated" where we have people on to talk about *Doctor Who* stories that have been overlooked, ignored or generally derided. I mention this because I would place this story in that pantheon in a heartbeat. "The Pyramid at the End of the World" is overlooked, ignored *and* generally derided. And it really shouldn't be.

For one thing, I think it has the best-defined scenario for Armageddon ever shown on television. For me, there's nothing scarier than the idea that the end of the world won't come about due to geopolitical clashes or what we've already done to harm the Earth but . . . someone breaking their glasses in the rush to get to work and someone else being hungover. The idea that the world will end for such humdrum reasons terrifies me. In fact, a lot of my favourite sequences in "The Pyramid at the End of the World" are in the lab with Erica and Douglas. Rachel Denning radiates charm, and I liked the idea that the end of the world was being brought about by two work chums with a friendship that feels lived-in.

On the other hand, that's more than I can say for the remaining supporting characters. I do wish that Peter Harness's original idea of using world leaders (even fictionalized ones) was used instead of generals who have no individual character other than to mutiny against their acting commander-in-chief, because they're ciphers.

I also really love the way the Monks present themselves in this story. I mean, I don't quite get how the Monks can be both reality-bending pros and also just conning people through advanced technology. (Also how can they adjust every single clock or watch in the world — including analog ones?) Even so, I think they're quite chilling as villains. I like the heightened mystery that surrounds them, from the pyramid showing up in the middle of nowhere to how they dispatch threats to the ultimately creepy way they try to elicit obedience out of people.

On the other hand, there are definitely things that *don't* work here. The tone-deafness that has previously made us scream, "Why aren't there more women working on this show?!" is back in full force with the climax premised around a woman being pressured into giving consent. The scene is trying to riff off vampire lore, where a person has to give permission to let a vampire into their dwelling . . . but the problematic use of the word "consent" adds layers of complexity to something that didn't require it.

I really love the ending. I'm not wild about solutions using the TARDIS, but the idea of blinding every camera to flush out the Monks was a great idea, and I really enjoyed the Doctor solving the problem with Erica, just as I was unsettled by the bottom dropping out with the Doctor's blindness and Bill agreeing to the Monks' proposal. As climaxes go, it really delivered the goods.

I haven't even talked about how much I loved the opening, where they incorporate the "previously" recap into the actual cold open and then repeat the punchline but with another global body. (And, like last time, they kind of didn't think it through completely, because having people with guns storm a room with two people of colour is poor optics.) Personally, I would be happy for that to have repeated again and again, with Penny and Bill being interrupted by MI-6 and, I don't know, the World Bank coming out of Bill's bedroom.

*Doctor Who* doesn't do trilogies very often, and "The Pyramid at the End of the World" sits in that awkward position of being the second part. But I think it fulfills that role by increasing the mystery of what's going on, giving some good moments for Bill and Nardole and making the Monks as strange as possible. I wish it wasn't quite so underrated, because it's one of the most enjoyable episodes of the season.

**Second Opinion (RS?)** Meh.

Sign me up to the "overlooked, ignored and generally derided" camp. Unlike my co-author, I don't see much to like about this episode. The Doctor's blindness now feels contrived, rather than tense. Not once but twice do we get an "I'm on the verge of confessing why I've been lying when — oh look, a distraction!" scene. The tumblers at the end being analogue rather than digital seem hilariously out of place in such a hi-tech™ lab.

The one thing I did like was the theme of camera surveillance that we see early on. Everyone is watching everyone else through cameras, which is a very 21st-century thing to be doing. The Doctor's later camera hack is excellent . . . but then they drop the ball at the end, because cameras could have easily solved the problem. The Doctor couldn't send a photo to Bill's phone and ask her how many clicks to rotate through for each number? Or FaceTime her? That would have solved the problem in about ten seconds. As I say, contrived.

Indeed, the whole episode is one big contrivance. Whereas previous Peter Harness efforts were interested in looking at deeply complex questions facing society, this one is just a delaying tactic to get all the pieces into one place for the cliffhanger at the end. (And, as Graeme notes, it's all undone by inadvertently painting a giant target on its back for no reason, *just like the previous two Harness stories*.) Love them or hate them, both "Kill the Moon" and the Zygon two-parter had important, passionate things to say. The message here? War is bad, and mistakes might kill you. Well, that controversy will have us all debating the issues deep into the night, won't it? Me, I don't find the idea of humdrum accidents to be particularly scary. Tune in next week when a scientist stubs her toe and her co-worker gets a bad haircut, leading to the end of the world! Ooh.

The Monk trilogy started with considerable style last week, but "The Pyramid at the End of the World" is a massive nosedive in quality. Overlooked? Thankfully so. Derided? With good reason. Ignored? Please continue to do so.

## 10.08 The Lie of the Land

**Written by** Toby Whithouse **Directed by** Wayne Yip
**Original airdate** June 3, 2017

**The Big Idea** The Monks are in charge of the Earth. In fact, the Monks have always been in charge of the Earth . . .

**Roots and References** George Orwell's 1948 novel *Nineteen Eighty-Four* and the various film and TV adaptations (the assertion that the Monks have always been here is very much like, "We have always been at war with Eastasia"; the Thought Police–esque Memory Police and the pyramid in the centre of London are just like the Ministry of Truth in the novel; the posters of the Monks are very much like the Big Brother ones in the 1984 film; the boiler suits the citizens wear are very reminiscent of costumes from the 1953 BBC TV adaptation); Thomas Harris's Hannibal novels, particularly 1981's *Red Dragon* (the Doctor's interrogation of Missy); Richard Attenborough's various nature documentaries, particularly *Blue Planet* (the opening sequence); the Doctor calls the Monks' inner sanctum "fake-news central." Missy refers to the ITV reality series *Celebrity Love Island* (now called *Love Island*) and plays a few bars of Scott Joplin's "The Entertainer" on the piano.

**Adventures in Time and Space** The photos the Doctor gave Bill of her mum in "The Pilot" become essential to the Monks' defeat. The Doctor mentions that the Monks allegedly helped stop the Daleks, Cybermen and Weeping Angels. When Bill quizzes Nardole about their past connection, she asks about the trip to Australia ("The Pilot") and the "shuk-shuk" noises space doors are supposed to make ("Oxygen"). She tests the Doctor's control by talking about the monster in "Thin Ice." We see the piano the Doctor mentions giving to Missy in the Vault back in "Knock Knock." People are watching the TVs at a Magpie Electrical outlet (2006's "The Idiot's Lantern").

**The Vault Effect** The Doctor finally opens the Vault, and we discover Missy is kept in a Plexiglas cage (so she was able to bang on the door in "Thin Ice" *how* exactly?). She insists that she could break out at any time and that she is "engaging" in the process of (as the Doctor puts it) "going cold turkey from being bad." Missy is willing to assist the Doctor (though she does so on her own terms). After everything is concluded, Missy admits that she's allowing herself to remember all the people she has killed and is experiencing remorse as a result.

**Who Is the Doctor?** The Monks have employed the Doctor as their chief propagandist (though he's imprisoned on a boat out at sea). As ever, he's not only actively opposing the Monks, but he's managed to bring everyone guarding him onto his side.

**The Doctor and Bill** The Doctor pushes Bill to the absolute limit to make sure she hasn't been brainwashed (oddly, she takes out her anger about this on Nardole). She is willing to sacrifice herself to stop the Monks and even restrains the Doctor to make this happen. After the Monks are defeated, Bill asks the Doctor why he puts up with humanity. He says, "In amongst seven billion, there's someone like you. That's why I put up with the rest of them."

**Monster of the Week** We finally learn how the Monks work: they enslave a planet through a psychic link with someone who has entered into it willingly. Using that psychic link, they are able to brainwash nearly all of the populace into believing they have always been there and that there are more Monks than there actually are.

**Stand Up and Cheer** It seems like such an odd thing to cheer, but the Doctor's stark admission of real-world politics in 2017 was something of a revelation: "History was saying to you, look, I've got some examples of fascism here for you to look at. No? Fundamentalism? No? Oh, okay, you carry on . . . the guns were getting bigger, the stakes were getting higher, and any minute now it was going to be goodnight, Vienna." Okay, it's in the context of why the Doctor allegedly let an alien race subjugate Earth, but it's an important reminder from our favourite TV character that the human race needs to sort themselves out.

**Roll Your Eyes** We understand the Doctor playing along in order to test Bill to make sure she wasn't sent by the Monks and wasn't really brainwashed. We could tolerate that to the point where she pulled a gun on him. But allowing it to go on to the point where Bill shoots the Doctor and he fakes regenerating . . . for the benefit of who exactly? (He avoided talking about regeneration with her in "Knock Knock.") We presume he did it so it could be used in the trailers. That seems like dickish gaslighting of both Bill and the audience.

**You're Not Making Any Sense** The more the Monks are explained, the less their achievements in previous episodes make any sense. The Doctor says the Monks have erased themselves . . . how? There are still monuments to them all over (enough that the "some sort of film" excuse wouldn't wash). What about the people who suddenly discover their loved ones have been in a labour camp for the past six months? What about all the Memory Police vehicles and all the boiler suits? What about the visual record of the Monks on TV, social media and in photographs? Various characters talk about the Monks "manipulating history," so perhaps they have some small amount of ability to reshape reality beyond altering memories. If so, it might have been helpful if that had been explained. How did they restore the Doctor's eyesight in "The Pyramid at the End of the World"?

**Interesting Trivia** There was a scene cut where the family watching TV in the opening were watching an episode of the popular BBC series *Casualty* (which aired after *Doctor Who* on Saturday nights) with two characters discussing the latest medical crisis: "It's lucky that Monk was passing. He literally tore the door off and pulled her out before the car exploded." To which another character replies, "Praise be to the benevolence of the Monks." The scene was shot (conveniently, *Casualty* is shot in the same studio complex at Roath Lock in Cardiff as *Doctor Who*), but it was cut from broadcast.

**The TARDIS Chronometer** Bristol, in a ship on the high seas, and London, the present day.

**Don't Be Stupid? (GB)** As season finales of *Doctor Who* go, this is much more like it.

After "Hell Bent," I was genuinely fearful that we had lost our way with writing season finales. The decision to bring in Toby Whithouse was a great way to solve that problem through fresh blood. Whithouse is great at finales (it was always one of the best things about *Being Human*), so it makes abundant sense to use his talent here.

The result is an episode that deftly weaves in elements from past stories, as the photos the Doctor took of Bill's mum in a moment of compassion in "The Pilot" have huge implications here. And we see all the references to Bill's mum — who was something of a totemic figure in "Knock Knock" and "Oxygen" — pay off, as a source of strength for Bill to overcome the change in her memories and to find the means to stop the Monks once and for all.

And, make no mistake, as this season has been all about Bill and her development as a character and her relationship with the Doctor

THIS IS NOT WHAT REALLY HAPPENED

it's only appropriate

that the season finale centres on Bill, as we see the growth of her character come to its natural conclusion. The awkward, smart, garrulous person we meet in "The Pilot" has become even smarter — able to take on a Time Lord and the Monks — and ultimately willing to sacrifice herself. The growth over these eight episodes, as Bill learns from the Doctor and then does what he would do, is astonishing and delightful. And it's appropriate that at the season's end, this is the very centre of the finale.

The interactions between Michelle Gomez's and Pearl Mackie's characters are charming and hilarious. (I love how Missy talks down to Bill at every opportunity, as though she's jealous of Bill in a way she wasn't with Clara.) I'm thrilled that the only person to write for Missy outside of Moffat is Whithouse because Missy is funnier than ever here, from her game of hot and cold with the Doctor to the way she says "awwwwkward" when Bill admits she's the link. It's nice to see the ongoing Missy-in-the-Vault arc servicing the broader shape of the season.

Like all *Doctor Who* season finales, there's a lot that's rushed in execution, especially a finale that's also the third episode

*THIS IS NOT REAL*

with the same monsters and its own arc. My main problem with the Monks is that they seem to have different powers in different episodes. In "Extremis," they're master planners who have created a virtual simulation of Earth's history. In "The Pyramid at the End of the World," they have godlike powers and can seemingly change and bend reality. Here, they're just intergalactic con artists who subjugate planets by conning them into thinking they've always been their rulers. If you squint hard enough, all these things could connect (and probably would explain why the human populace don't seem all that fussed once the Monks are gone), but more effort was required to make it work. Then again, there was a lot to resolve in a packed eight-episode season.

But the climax for this is great. The pitched battle, which we don't hear because we're listening to Bill's affirmations about reality instead, is well done, and the Monks' removal seems earned because it uses a character arc that's built up over the season.

As finales go, even for all its flaws (and I wish the Doctor was used better as well), I'd rank "The Lie of the Land" with "Dark Water"/"Death in Heaven" and "The Pandorica Opens"/"The Big Bang" for great Moffat-era finales. It does what

*THIS*

*IS*

*A*

*LIE*

Wait. What was I talking about?!

There are still *four episodes left* this season.

What are they going to do . . . ?

**Second Opinion (RS?)** Pay no attention to the man with the podcast. The Monks, in their benevolence, have always been the harbingers of poor quality *Doctor Who*.

Beautiful, finely honed trash, such as "Genesis of the Monks" or "The Talons of Monks," established the Monk stories as complete and total bollocks, remembered by generations for their dedication to tripe. *Doctor Who* has always been horrendous, and we have the kindness of the Monks to thank for it. Of course, sometimes this failed, with blips of quality like "The Horns of Monk," "The Monk Dilemma" or "Extremis," but those are isolated cases.

Even back to the very first story, "An Unearthly Monk," we saw rubbish propagated on our screens by the Monks, who had the same loving, gentle and thoroughly godawful effect on almost every *Doctor Who* story they touched. More recent examples include "Monk Nature"/"The Family of Monks" and "The Day of the Monk," which were celebrated by millions for their firm, guiding hand, leading us inexorably towards a stinking pile of crap.

Praise be to the Monks, for "The Lie of the Land" is but no exception, failing resolutely at drama, employing cheap tricks to gaslight the audience and the characters and entirely failing to develop its attempt at satire, content to excrete the "fake news" line, untouched, in the centre of the room, alongside a picture of Donald Trump. Blessed be.

*Doctor Who* under the Monks is awful, and it has always been awful. Two concepts, sharing a lack of quality as happily as they share our TV screens. *Doctor Who* and the Monks are a blissful and perfect catastrophe together, just as they always have been.

# 10.09 Empress of Mars

**Written by** Mark Gatiss **Directed by** Wayne Yip
**Original airdate** June 10, 2017

**The Big Idea** A mission to Mars by Victorian soldiers uncovers the tomb of an Ice Queen. Only she isn't quite dead . . .

**Roots and References** The works of Rudyard Kipling, particularly the 1975 film adaptation of his novella *The Man Who Would Be King* (the British imperialism, Catchlove's avarice and the journey to Mars echoes Dravot's journey to Kafristan; Godscacre is very Kipling-esque); the 1954 film adaptation of Jules Verne's *20,000 Leagues Under the Sea* (the steampunk aesthetic of the Victorian spacesuit); Daniel Defoe's 1719 novel *Robinson Crusoe* (the servile Ice Warrior is named Friday). Bill mentions the 1958 Kirk Douglas/Tony Curtis film *The Vikings*. The *Terminator* movies and John Carpenter's 1982 remake of *The Thing* are both referenced. The Doctor quotes from *Star Wars* ("I have a bad feeling about this") and from the 2013 film *Frozen*. Jackdaw sings "She Was Poor But Honest."

**Adventures in Time and Space** 1976's "Pyramids of Mars" had a lead villain described as the Tythonian Beast, something the Doctor references here when he mentions being an honorary guardian of the Tythonian Hive. The Doctor complains about the sonic screwdriver still having no setting for wood, a complaint that dates back to 2008's "Silence in the Library." He greets Friday the same way he greeted the Ice Warrior in "Cold War." The picture of Queen Victoria is an image of Pauline Collins, who played the role in 2006's "Tooth and Claw." Events here are a precursor to the Ice Warriors joining the Galactic Federation in 1972's "The Curse of Peladon," complete with an appearance by Alpha Centauri from that story.

**The Vault Effect** When the TARDIS acts up, Nardole goes to the Vault to ask Missy for help. He not only lets her out, she flies the TARDIS to Mars to rescue the Doctor and Bill, even seeming to care if the Doctor is all right. She's happy to go back into the Vault afterwards.

**Who Is the Doctor?** He's never seen the *Terminator* movies or *The Thing* but likes the idea of killer robots. He has seen *Frozen*, however. He admits that he thinks like a warrior.

**The Doctor and Bill** Nope, we've got nothing.

**Monster of the Week** The Empress of Mars is the first female Ice Warrior we've seen. She's the key to reviving the whole nest. Despite their armour, Martian skin is clearly not tough enough to resist a blade to the throat. Their sonic guns can crunch someone up into a ball in seconds.

**Stand Up and Cheer** The opening scene at NASA, with the Doctor, Bill and Nardole ingratiating themselves into the operations, is charming, with a great punchline when the message on Mars is revealed.

**Roll Your Eyes** When Vincey goes to look for Jackdaw, he entirely fails to notice that the gold-coloured prize that brought them all there is missing, despite walking around the dais several times.

**You're Not Making Any Sense** Why does the TARDIS randomly dematerialize for no reason whatsoever? Other than "utter plot contrivance"? No really, why? We'd genuinely like to know.

**Interesting Trivia** We've previously seen Ice Warriors frozen on Earth, invading a station on the moon, as ambassadors in a galactic federation (twice) and revived on board a submarine. However, this is the first time we've ever seen Ice Warriors on their home planet of Mars. That's a surprisingly long wait, given that this was the fiftieth anniversary of seeing the creatures in the show.

The alien race that the Doctor contacts at the end is from Alpha Centauri, seen in 1972's "The Curse of Peladon" and 1974's "The Monster of Peladon." This was a genderless race of aliens with a nervous disposition, six arms branching off from a shaftlike body and a single, enormous eye. Yes, exactly like you're imagining. Although we see the alien's face only on a monitor here, the full appearance was rather visually alarming if you were anyone who had reached puberty. No, seriously, search for a picture online, so long as you're not at work or don't mind your boss finding out that you're googling pictures of an enormous green phallus in a cloak (hey, we've all done it). What's even more impressive is that the actress who provides the voice of everybody's favourite hermaphrodite hexapod, Ysanne Churchman, was the same one who last voiced the role in 1974. That's 43 years between appearances, a record in *Doctor Who* — and indeed any BBC drama — for the longest gap between the first and last appearance of an actor playing the same role. But most impressive of all is that Churchman, although long since officially retired, was 92 at the time, making her the oldest actor to play a role in the New Series.

**The TARDIS Chronometer** NASA headquarters in Florida and St Luke's University, present day; Mars, 1881.

**Don't Be Stupid? (RS?)**

<u>New telly reviewed — the *Dr Who* newsletter, June 19, 1973</u>

Tally ho, pip pip and hooray! It's another stunning victory for *Dr Who*, Britain's best show on the idiot box.

Bringing the Ice Warriors back just a few months after we saw them on Peladon could have been a mistake, but fortunately they undid all that complicated guff about them being allies and went right back to the bally crocodiles as villains again, where they should be. Thank goodness for that, or I shall be forced to compose another letter to the BBC, and they don't want that! None of this character complexity stuff. This is 1973, not wartime, you know.

Dr Who and his pretty assistant make their way to Mars in 1881, where they meet a battalion of the Queen's soldiers, determined to use British pluck and a fighting spirit to colonize Mars! I, for one, was thrilled. Now *these* soldiers I can get behind. Strong fighting men, with British ingenuity and a taste for the magnificent in the invention of the Gargantuan. Yes, they have dissent in the ranks, and the colonel turns out to be a bally coward, which I didn't see coming, but thankfully Captain Catchglove takes charge and locks the yellow blighter away.

That said, I wish Dr Who wouldn't criticize the military all the time. They're just doing their jobs, upholding the proud British Empire for Queen and country. Then again, he's always teasing Brigadier Lethbridge-Stewart as well, so I suppose it's just his way. But calling the humans invaders? Really. What next, will he be telling our men in Zaire or Rhodesia they shouldn't be there? Yes, yes, I'm exaggerating for comic effect, but Dr Who does spout some nonsense sometimes, doesn't he?

At least we can all get behind the idea that the Martians need to be taught a lesson. The story might be set almost a hundred years ago, but some things never change. How I laughed watching Man Friday, the one-eyed docile Ice Warrior, carry tea for the soldiers all the time, despite its clunky body and weird hands. Thankfully *Dr Who* hasn't forgotten how to do comedy, and mocking funny-looking natives will never get old, you mark my words.

That empress of theirs had spunk, I'll grant you, but at the end of the day she was no match for Catchglove and his blade. It's a shame that traitor Godsacre had to ruin everything. Why he was given so much screentime I'll never know, but we saw his true colours in the end when he sold out himself and his men to the monsters. I know it's a lesson that my children will learn well: nothing good comes of thinking too much.

Dr Who's assistant does her usual thing here, tripping and falling down a hole, making friends with the other girl in the episode, looking pretty. Business as usual, really. I mean, what else can a girl assistant do?

She and Dr Who were able to escape from that cell only because Man Friday changed sides suddenly, without even hinting at this twist. Which just makes it so much better in my eyes, because any buildup or dialogue would have ruined the surprise. Now *that's* how to write a *Dr Who* story!

"Empress of Mars" is another fine story from the BBC that fits perfectly into the schedule. We've all been on tenterhooks since seeing the Galactic Federation a few months back, wondering just how the Ice Warriors got involved and when we'd see Alpha Centauri again, so I for one am immensely pleased at how timely this is.

Monsters that are monsters, British fighting men who are determined to teach the natives a lesson, Dr Who trying to keep everyone alive, and his pretty assistant tripping and falling. Yes, the story has everything you could possibly want. All's right with the world. Hurrah!

**Second Opinion (GB)** When I was a teenager, I wrote fan fiction. In fact, I wrote a lot of it. Most of it is embarrassing to read now but I'm still fond of it. I wrote the adventures of a future twelfth (!) and a thirteenth (!!) Doctor who had the likenesses of my best friend and myself. Just move along . . .

One story was set on Mars, where the thirteenth Doctor ("played" by me, wearing a natty costume of an argyle sweater, a bomber jacket and striped trousers that looked very 1930s cool) settled a dispute with the Ice Warriors as we finally met the Martians on their home planet. Another story was set in a Jules Verne–esque airship whose Victorian crew rescued the crash-landed TARDIS crew before going on a journey under the polar icecap and discovering an Edgar Rice Burroughs–esque inner world with a new breed of Silurians.

All this is to say, from one kid who wrote fanfic in the 1980s to another, Mark Gatiss has one-upped me because he first of all managed to combine Verne-esque Victorian adventurers with a story set on Mars. More importantly, he managed to convince the showrunner of *Doctor Who* and the entire establishment of the BBC to put his adolescent fan fiction on millions of screens. And was probably egged on by the person playing the Doctor at the time.

Personally, I think the evolved Silurian with hair who dwells in the core of the Earth that I created when I was 17 would have been a great addition. I'm disappointed I wasn't asked to contribute.

# 10.10 The Eaters of Light

**Written by** Rona Munro **Directed by** Charles Palmer
**Original airdate** June 17, 2017

**The Big Idea** The Doctor and Bill settle a dispute between them about the disappearance of the Ninth Legion of the Roman Army by travelling back to 2nd-century Scotland . . . only to discover the real cause was an extra-dimensional, light-devouring creature.

**Roots and References** The 1995 movie *Braveheart* (the Picts' face tattoos and their refusal to back down); popular depictions of the disappearance of the Ninth Legion dating back to Rosemary Sutcliff's 1954 novel *The Eagle of the Ninth* (which sides with the Doctor's theory that the Legion was wiped out by the Caledonians).

**Adventures in Time and Space** Bill figures out the TARDIS's ability to telepathically translate ("It even does lip-synch!"), first established in the Modern Series in 2005's "The End of the World" and in the Classic Series in 1976's "The Masque of Mandragora."

**The Vault Effect** To Nardole's and Bill's surprise, the Doctor has let Missy out of the Vault to perform maintenance on the TARDIS engines, believing that she can be trusted (though he has rigged the TARDIS to prevent her from leaving). Despite the Doctor's claims that Missy has never learned "to hear the music" and appreciate humanity's heroism, she seems quite moved when she later hears the Picts' music. The Doctor is becoming convinced Missy's change in attitude might be in earnest and it may be soon time for him and Missy to be friends again — which pleases Missy — though he cautions, "That's the trouble with hope. It's hard to resist."

**Who Is the Doctor?** He claims to have lived, governed and even farmed in Roman Britain and that he was a Vestal Virgin, second class — despite the Vestal Virgins only being female. (He tells Nardole the second-class part is a "long story.") He's initially sharp with Kar and her band but gradually softens towards her and encourages her to face her demons. He's arrogant enough to think that he alone needs to sacrifice himself to secure the Gate and is reluctant to let the Picts and the Romans do the job.

**The Doctor and Bill** He forgives her for overruling him and permitting the Picts and Romans to guard the Gate — and even admits that he was wrong about the Ninth Legion. When Bill sees the TARDIS translating the Picts and the Romans, she asks the Doctor, "Is this what happens when you understand what everyone in the universe is saying? Everybody just sounds like children?" The Doctor wryly replies, "There are exceptions."

**Monster of the Week** The eponymous Eaters of Light, which the Doctor describes as being locusts, even though they're more like aardvarks with tendrils. They live in a void between dimensions (a portal to which is in a Pict cairn). The Picts have for years had people guard the entrance to prevent the Eaters of Light from entering our universe.

**Stand Up and Cheer** When Kar tells the Doctor she's mourning those who died as a result of her, the Doctor says, "You know, every moment you waste wallowing about in that happy thought means more of the living are going to join them. When you want to win a war, remember this: it's not about you. Believe me, I know. Time to grow up, Kar. Time to fight your fight." It's a speech that starts out savage and brittle and ends with incredible tenderness. Ladies and gentlemen, Peter Capaldi.

**Roll Your Eyes** It would have been so nice if, when noting the Roman soldiers' hiding spot was connected to the Picts' camp by an underground tunnel, someone said in the campiest way possible, "*Howwww con-veeeen-iennnt.*" Because it really would save us the trouble.

**You're Not Making Any Sense** Just how did the Bronze and Iron Age Picts figure out that the portal led to nasty light-eating creatures that were kept out by routinely sacrificing the lives within their tribe without, you know, destroying the sun in the process?

**Interesting Trivia** Rona Munro wrote the final story of the Classic Series, "Survival," in 1989. After that, Munro went on to a celebrated career writing films (particularly 1994's acclaimed *Ladybird, Ladybird* for Ken Loach) and plays. Her friend Mark Gatiss introduced her to Steven Moffat. Consequently, Munro is the only writer from the Classic Series to write for the Modern Series as well. The gap between her episodes spans 27 years — longer than the original run of the Classic Series!

The Ninth Roman Legion, or *Legio IX Hispana* (Ninth Legion Spanish), has been a source of controversy for decades. After being stationed in Britain in the middle of the 1st century CE, the Legion disappeared from surviving Roman records early in the 2nd century. It had been theorized that the Ninth Legion was wiped out around 108 CE after a war with the Picts — a confederation of Celtic tribes in what was then called Caledonia (and is now called Scotland). However, archaeological finds in Nijmegen, the Netherlands, suggest that the Ninth Legion might have gone there as late as 120 CE. (Though this could have been a detachment, not the whole army.) Short of time travel, this is a mystery that likely won't be solved.

Nardole tells the Picts that the passengers on the fabled ghost ship the *Mary Celeste* disappeared because they encountered the Enzomodons, who unfortunately communicated with people by digesting them. Either Nardole is making up the story or this is what happened to the poor souls on board after they jumped overboard (or were exterminated) facing the Daleks in the 1965 story "The Chase."

**The TARDIS Chronometer** Scotland in the 2nd century and the present day.

**Don't Be Stupid? (GB)** When I do panels reviewing eras or seasons of *Doctor Who* at conventions or on my podcast, I often ask people to use one word to describe something. For "The Eaters of Light," my one word is *inert*.

"The Eaters of Light" is inert in every sense of the word. It's lacking in the strength to move, and it lacks any reaction in terms of chemistry.

To be honest, I'm still scratching my head trying to figure out why that is. Rona Munro is a writer I have tremendous respect for both in *Doctor Who* (you can read about my love of "Survival" in *Who's 50*) and outside of it. In "The Eaters of Light," she's written a tale that, like "Survival," has so much to admire. It's a story with lots of good ideas (the crows; the remnants of two armies, both of which are made up of children; Bill facing people with a more fluid sense of sexuality than her "modern" one). There are some delightful comedic lines ("I'm ingratiating myself"; "Death by Scotland"). There's some brilliant acting from Peter Capaldi, Matt Lucas (who is actually never better than here) and Rebecca Benson as Kar. And my respect for director Charles Palmer is on record back in my review of "Oxygen."

There are so many things to like, and yet . . . nothing really happens. The monster is scary, but not scary enough. The direction is surprisingly bland. The good ideas, like the crows, seem a smidge too whimsically earnest, like the sort of bad poetic lyrics found in the music of a "Celtic" pub band. For all the good scenes with Capaldi, Lucas and Benson, there isn't quite enough excitement.

Part of the problem is that it's so reliant on tropes. Bill is hurt, but *luckily* not quite enough. The monster is advancing on the remaining Legionnaires, but *luckily* there's a tunnel underneath that leads to the Picts . . . I would complain about all this luck, but then the story ends with the Doctor offering to sacrifice himself before being taken out of contention by people who want to do it more. By the time this episode was made, *Doctor Who* had been in existence for 53 years — that particular trope wasn't just tired, it was comatose with a do-not-resuscitate order.

But the bigger problem is . . . it's inert. It should fizz like vinegar on baking soda, and instead it's water on flour. The result is 42 minutes pleasantly spent and not 42 minutes being dazzled and excited.

I don't really know why that is. Sometimes you can have all the right people doing all the right things . . . and nothing happens. "The Eaters of Light" is the greatest example I can think of that.

**Second Opinion (RS?)** I love the way Bill figures out the TARDIS translation from scratch and what it means for the peace negotiations and also the Doctor's view of the world. That's really cool, even if you then realize that she must have thought the Daleks or the Ice Warriors were speaking English. Wait, what?

I wish poor logic was the only problem with this story.

My co-author is right that this story is inert (I prefer "boring"), but not about why. The right people are not doing the right things at all here. What we have isn't a story, it's an epilogue. The battle between the Ninth Legion and the monster — released because of a terrible decision by a child wanting to hold off a powerful invasion force — now that's a story! "The Eaters of Light" is just a coda.

If this were part two and we'd witnessed part one, it might have worked. Unfortunately, when all you can do is default to "There are thousands of them, just offstage!" — especially in today's era when that's perfectly possible thanks to CGI — then all the moralizing that happens is useless because it hasn't been earned.

This could have been "The Zygon Inversion," with everything coming to a head because of the hard work done during the set-up. But without "The Zygon Invasion," it's just a speech. Sadly, this story didn't even have that. I can live with *Doctor Who* being bad, like it was in the Monk trilogy. That happens — and sometimes it's so bad, it's good (see the previous episode, for example). But when *Doctor Who* is boring, it really suffers.

Had we seen the deaths of thousands, the Doctor's attempt at sacrifice might have made sense, rather than feeling tacked on. Had the two armies faced each other across a battlefield, the peace negotiation by the children might have rung more powerfully. Had we seen the monster do anything, anything at all, it might have been scary. But we didn't, they didn't and it didn't. Instead, there's too much talking and not enough showing.

I wish being inert was the only problem with this story.

# 10.11–10.12 World Enough and Time / The Doctor Falls

**Written by** Steven Moffat **Directed by** Rachel Talalay
**Original airdate** June 24, 2017

**The Big Idea** A 400-mile-long spaceship is trying to escape from a black hole, causing time at one end to move faster than the other. And anyone human is taken for conversion. But into what?

**Roots and References** *The Twilight Zone* episode "Eye of the Beholder" (the aesthetic of the hospital and the patients covered with bandages); J.D. Bernal's 1929 essay "The World, the Flesh & the Devil" (the generational starship); the 1972 film *Silent Running* (farms on board a spaceship); the 1986 film *Flight of the Navigator* and the 2014 film *Interstellar* (time dilation causing characters to age differently); the 1955 film *Night of the Hunter* (the Doctor sitting outside the house in a rocking chair holding a rifle, protecting the children inside); Ken Kesey's novel *One Flew Over the Cuckoo's Nest* and the 1975 film adaptation (the nurse is very much like Nurse Ratched); siege dramas such as 1960's *The Alamo* (which Nardole mentions). The title comes from the 17th-century poem "His Coy Mistress" by Andrew Marvell.

**Adventures in Time and Space** The Mondasian Cybermen originally appeared in 1966's "The Tenth Planet," which is also the snowscape setting in which the twelfth Doctor meets the first at the end of the story. Many other forms of Cybermen have been seen since, but this is the second appearance of the Mondasian Cybermen. The Doctor mentions that the Cybermen always happen, such as on Marinus. That planet appeared in 1964's "The Keys of Marinus," which wasn't a Cybermen story per se, but the *Doctor Who Magazine* comic strip later posited that the Voord from that story evolved into Cybermen. The Doctor mentions sealing the Cybermen in ice tombs on Telos (1967's "Tomb of the Cybermen"), Voga (1975's "Revenge of the Cybermen"), Canary Wharf (2006's "Army of Ghosts"/"Doomsday"), Planet 14 (mentioned in 1968's "The Invasion") and the moon (1967's "The Moonbase").

The third Doctor regularly indulged in Venusian aikido (1970's "Inferno"). Missy makes reference to the Doctor having regenerated after falling (which he did from a radio tower, as a result of the Master's interference in 1981's "Logopolis"). The John Simm Master mentions being a former prime minister, which occurred in 2007's "The Sound of Drums"/"Last of the Time Lords"; he was last seen driving Rassilon and the Time Lords back to Gallifrey in 2009's "The End of Time," which he and the Doctor discuss here. Missy gives the Master a TARDIS dematerialization circuit that looks like the one used throughout the Jon Pertwee era (only slightly smaller).

The Doctor carries jelly babies, just as his fourth incarnation did. "Sontarans perverting the course of human history" was the fourth Doctor's first line. The twelfth Doctor also says, "I don't want to go" and "When the Doctor was me," the tenth and eleventh Doctor's last lines, respectively. (Peter Capaldi does a particularly good impression of Matt Smith, right down to the way the Doctor was standing at that moment in "The Time of the Doctor.") He quotes River's "without hope, without witness, without reward" line from "Extremis" as he faces the Cybermen. The Doctor attributes Bill's ability to resist cyber-conditioning to her time living under the Monks in "The Lie of the Land."

Both the first and twelfth Doctors say, "I am not a Doctor. I am *the* Doctor. The original, you might say." This is a line from 1983's "The Five Doctors" (interestingly, made by another actor replacing William Hartnell). There's a montage of Modern Series companions, featuring Rose, Martha, Donna, Jack, Vastra, Jenny, Sarah Jane, Amy, Clara and River all saying "Doctor" — echoing the montage of companions saying the same thing during the fourth Doctor's final moments in 1981's "Logopolis."

**The Vault Effect** The Doctor tests Missy by sending her to answer a distress call. He desperately wants to see if she can become good. However, she runs off with the Master when the going gets tough but then has a change of heart and intends to stand with the Doctor . . . until the Master shoots her.

**Who Is the Doctor?** He wants to believe in Missy because she was his first friend and because she's the only person even remotely like him. When the Master asks if the future is going to be all girl, he says, "We can only hope." When he is dying, he wishes he could see stars.

**The Doctor and Bill** Saturday is their usual day for adventuring together. She disapproves of the Doctor's plan to test Missy in the field. It ends up getting her shot and then stuck at the other end of the ship for ten years, where she gets converted into a Cyberman. When they part, she notes that he's aware that she's into women and people her own age, a symbolic thanks for accepting her for who she is. She leaves thinking he's dead but can't quite bring herself to believe it.

**Monster of the Week** The Mondasian Cybermen convert humans from all over the ship in order to make them stronger and build an invasion force. The head-piece that all Cybermen wear is revealed to be an emotional inhibitor, designed so the wearer won't care about the pain they're in. They keep upgrading and evolve into a form that resembles the Cybus Cybermen.

**Stand Up and Cheer** The Doctor's speech about being kind and not acting out of hate is just perfect: "I do what I do because it's right. Because it's decent. And above all, because it's kind." He makes the point that it isn't easy and that it hardly ever works, but that's not a reason not to do it.

**Roll Your Eyes** Heather, the pilot, comes out of nowhere. Yes, she made a promise back in the first episode of the season, but why didn't we see her show up elsewhere this season to remind us she was still around?

**You're Not Making Any Sense** It's said that time moves faster at the bottom of the ship (where the Master landed), which is technically true . . . except that it's time at the top that's actually slowed down; the bottom is relatively unaffected by the black hole and is thus moving at a similar speed to the rest of the universe. Which means this story actually takes place over thousands of years, as far as the outside universe (and the bottom of the ship) is concerned. So why, in all that time, did no one else answer the distress call?

**Interesting Trivia** Peter Capaldi had long been calling for the return of the Mondasian Cybermen, so Steven Moffat finally gave in and wrote them in as a going-away present for him. The actor was slightly disappointed to find that the costume design now included latex gloves; Capaldi had preferred the originals, which used actual human hands. However, director Rachel Talalay explained that the gloves were needed to avoid giving away that Bill was inside a Cyberman.

The time-dilation idea was suggested by Moffat's son Joshua, who was studying physics at school. Gravity warping time was originally predicted by Einstein: his theory of relativity said that the larger a body is, the more it warped space-time, slowing down time around large bodies; this has since been confirmed by testing. However, we should note that this is true for any large body, not just black holes; indeed, the Earth's mass affects time in satellite navigation — admittedly by a tiny fraction of a second, but it's enough that the navigation has to compensate every time you use Google Maps.

We've seen many multi-Doctor team-ups (and are about to see another!), but the appearance of the Master and Missy here is the first time we've seen multiple incarnations of any other Time Lord together.

**The TARDIS Chronometer** On board a 400-mile long Mondasian ship, as well as flashbacks to St. Luke's University in the present.

**Don't Be Stupid? (RS?)** This may be the perfect Steven Moffat story. It has it all: brilliant ideas, witty flashbacks, clever structure, spooky atmosphere . . . and poor treatment of women. I'll let my co-author deal with the problems because I want to focus on the good. Of which there is an enormous amount.

For starters, the design is fantastic, with clean, well-lit, ultra-futuristic gracefulness at the top and dirty, dark, olde-worlde claustrophobia at the bottom — and pastoral farms in the middle. Rachel Talalay's direction is excellent — the Bill/Cybermen scenes are simply stunning. Every back and forth between Bill and her Cyberself is clever, and each is done differently. The scene where Bill picks up a mirror and sees her Cyberface is amazing, as is the one where she sees her Cyberhand and the camera pans around to show her Cyberself where a moment ago we saw Bill. Or the shadow of the Cyberhelmet on the wall. I could go on for some time.

However, it's the writing that I'm really here to praise. After seven years at the helm, Steven Moffat is finally on the way out. For many people, this couldn't have come soon enough, and I'll admit that he probably overstayed his welcome somewhat, but I also think we're really going to miss him. While he had his problems, he also brought a level of genius to *Doctor Who* that it probably should have always had but so rarely did. His scripts were usually powered by remarkable ideas, but they also contained their share of rich characters, genuinely funny jokes and an insistence on subverting our complacency again and again, keeping the show constantly fresh.

Never is this clearer than in this stunning two-parter. The theme here is transformation, especially after death. The three Time Lords die, Bill becomes a Cyberman, and Nardole is already a biomechanoid. The Mondasians transform into Cybermen (to cure illness) and then into an army. But there's also rebirth as well: Bill becomes a pilot, Nardole becomes a farmer, and at least two of the Time Lords will regenerate (eventually). Even the cameo at the end features a transformed first Doctor.

And yet, part of this transformation is the inherent unfairness of it all. After an amazing arc, the twelfth Doctor is killed by . . . Mondasian Cyberman #46. Not tragically by a converted Bill or heroically; just shot in the back, randomly. Likewise, Bill is shot in the chest by a terrified janitor for no reason other than because she's human. Previously, Nardole was decapitated by a biomechanoid simply for information. Yes, the Bill stuff brings up lots of issues, which probably should have been thought through more carefully, but it does allow for a stunning performance by Pearl Mackie, who has been an absolute highlight of the season.

A clever aspect of the unfair tragedy is that everyone's fate is unknown to everyone else. The Master and Missy kill each other but don't know the final result. The Doctor sends Nardole to an uncertain future, while the last he sees of Bill, she's a Cyberman. Bill, in turn, thinks the Doctor's dead and leaves him in the TARDIS to become a Space Lesbian™.

Nardole's fate is easily the best of the three. He refuses to look after children and spend his days protecting innocents until the Doctor asks which of them is stronger. It's left unsaid, but the clear implication is that it's Nardole who is stronger than the Doctor. Their final parting makes me cry every time. ("You're wrong, you know. Quite wrong. I never will be able to find the words.")

Meanwhile, despite the issues along the way, Bill not only survives the story, she thrives. The biggest problem here is that the ending is too similar to Clara's a year before. And while that one was seeded for a whole season, the salvation here comes out of left field. Well, almost. There is a premonition, but it's so subtle I missed it the first time around. When CyberBill cries real tears, the Doctor says that shouldn't be possible, and that's for a very good reason: because they're Heather's tears. The contrast between Bill as a crying Cyberman and Heather as a dripping Dalek in "The Pilot" is excellent.

Then there's the Doctor's fate. It's mostly deferred to the next story, but it does give us a new take on a regeneration story and also the stunning cameo by David Bradley at the story's conclusion. I absolutely did not see that coming, but it's an amazing moment when you realize who it is that's stepping out of the snow.

It's not perfect, of course. In "The Tenth Planet," we learned that the Mondasians were getting weak and their lifespans shrinking, so they devised spare parts for their bodies. We see something very similar in action here . . . except that this isn't the motivation to create the Cybermen at all, as it turns out. No, there was an expedition to Floor 507 that never returned, which could have happened for a million reasons. Best to break out the Cybermen and invade everyone then. This feels contrived: there are perfectly good reasons for the Mondasians to become Cybermen (the polluted floor is another), but the awkward Floor 507 away-team explanation undercuts the superb hospital set-up.

Meanwhile, after setting events in motion, the Master and Missy have almost no intersection with the rest of the plot. This matters not one whit, partly because they're so entertaining, but mostly because they're here for one reason only: to be the recipients of the Doctor's kindness speech. That speech is so magnificent and so achingly real that it might just qualify for the second-best speech in all of *Doctor Who*. (Let's be honest, nothing will ever beat the one in "The Zygon Invasion"/"The Zygon Inversion.") The fact that it almost never works is the real clincher for me, because I spend my days attempting to combat diseases across the world, which almost never works either . . . and yet a) you still do it because it's the right thing to do — the kind thing to do — and b) sometimes, when the stars align, it actually does work, and that makes everything worth it. I particularly like the hints that, despite her protests, Missy remembers everything. This suggests that she knew the Master would shoot her in the back and hence prepared for it. I can't believe I'm cheering for the Doctor's arch-nemesis to survive. That's how amazing this is.

I'm not blind to the story's problematic treatment of Bill, and I understand why that ruins it for many people. For me, however, the rest of it worked so well and was so clever and touching that I adore it nonetheless. So just like every other Steven Moffat story, then.

**Second Opinion (GB)** I thought the spaceship was very clever and the Master killing Missy was genius (even if it ultimately renders the season's arc useless). The Doctor's speech about kindness was everything I want *Doctor Who* to be. Nardole gets a great ending. The last two minutes were fanboy heaven. I love the Alamo/ *Magnificent Seven*/Battle of Helm's Deep siege-against-massive-odds vibe.

I even loved, initially, what happened to Bill. The idea of a typical *Doctor Who* situation going south and ending in Bill being made into a Cyberman has unbelievable impact, both for the body horror and the implication that the Doctor was too late to save her.

But . . . it went too bleak.

Here's the thing. At its heart, *Doctor Who* is a promise to the viewer that whatever terrors happens, everything ultimately will be okay. Here, that promise is horribly broken. And every time I rewatch this story, I struggle to understand why.

I mean it. Why? The whole thing doesn't even make sense in terms of bringing back the Mondasian Cybermen. The costume itself does not support the idea that the Mondasian Cybermen would do away with the human hosts. These are creatures with enhancements like an exoskeleton covered in cloth. That's why Bill's human face is behind the mask. The idea that her whole body is disposed of is ridiculous, and it takes away the obvious fix that the Doctor somehow uses the pent-up regeneration energy to restore Bill. But the Doctor has all but abdicated himself from saving her.

Again, why? I guess the biggest reason I keep asking is that I don't think anyone, including Steven Moffat, really thought through how much Bill might take off as an audience-identification figure — and how significant an actress of colour playing a companion for the first time in a decade might be. Rose wouldn't be written out as body-horror victim. Amy wouldn't be stripped of her humanity only to have it restored in a perfunctory manner. The Doctor wouldn't walk back a promise to save Clara. I wish they had given that same care to Bill.

But tone-deafness is one of the pervasive problems in the Moffat era. In spite of lots of positive elements, it was occasionally tone-deaf to gender dynamics, and it was tone-deaf to racial dynamics. Matt Smith's tenure looked as white as

*Midsomer Murders.* Here, the Doctor tells a Black woman to control her anger after she becomes the only companion unlucky enough to get shot in ten seasons. That's not a good look. (And let's not even get started on the fact that fans have long fought against the whole "kill off the lesbian" trope that's been rampant in television, only for this to happen to Bill.)

And, unfortunately, that's not the only problem. Missy becomes the focus of the season after "The Lie of the Land," and she even gets as an added bonus, the first multi-Master story, in the deal. Bill, on the other hand, gets two episodes where she has hardly anything to do and then they blow a hole in her. The result is that we don't have an ending that's worthy of the character. Even without other considerations, you don't make something like "The Pilot" that totally creates a back-to-basics new POV character, get a great actress to play her, only to have her final appearance be so . . . unintegral to the story. *Nardole* gets more to do than Bill. She even spends the final battle out of view, having done nothing. If she had been the one who detonated everything, at least she might have had actual agency. But, nah. Let's go for full fan service instead with the Doctor naming off continuity references.

That Bill is saved by a *deus ex machina* is offensive. Heather coming back was ridiculous. If we had callbacks to her throughout the season, if she had even showed up at critical junctures, it could have had dramatic weight. But in the end, Bill is rescued by someone she had a few chance encounters with — in fact, Bill and Heather have their longest conversation ever *in this very story* — and it's portrayed as fulfilment of some kind of romance because . . . again, why?

The problem is every time I say "Why?" I keep thinking the answer is "because LOLZ." It's cool to have a companion be a victim of body horror. And if that's the answer, then . . . that's not good enough. Not for *Doctor Who.* Cool ideas should not be more important than honouring your characters and your audience.

I really would like to be my co-author, celebrating this story as the perfect Steven Moffat tale. Unfortunately, it also has all the flaws we've seen in Steven Moffat's work as well.

## 10.13 Twice Upon a Time

**Written by** Steven Moffat **Directed by** Rachel Talalay
**Original airdate** December 25, 2017

**The Big Idea** When the first and twelfth Doctors both refuse to regenerate in the same place, time gets unstuck. Meanwhile, an alien ship is harvesting something from people shortly before they die — and Bill Potts appears to be one of them.

**Roots and References** The *Alien* franchise (the Dalek facehugger); *Dad's Army* ("Up and at 'em, Corporal Jones"); the writings of Bertrand Russell ("hate is always foolish, and love is always wise"); the 1989 film *The Abyss* (the glass aliens). The twelfth Doctor describes the first as Mr. Pastry. This was a doddery old character played by Richard Hearne — who was initially offered the role of the fourth Doctor, except that he wanted to play it as Mr. Pastry. Continuing the food theme, the first Doctor is also called Mary Berry, after the elderly British food critic best known for *The Great British Bake Off*.

**Adventures in Time and Space** We have black-and-white flashbacks to 1966's "The Tenth Planet" starring William Hartnell as the first Doctor . . . that morphs into a colour recreation starring David Bradley (the aspect ratio also changes). At the end of the story, just before the first regeneration, we morph back to the black-and-white footage. The first Doctor's TARDIS looks as it did back in its day, shorter and thinner than the current Doctor's (the twelfth Doctor adds a flippant explanation for this). The final scene from "The Doctor Falls" is presented here, but from the first Doctor's point of view. Archibald is the grandfather of Brigadier Alistair Gordon Lethbridge-Stewart (and great-grandfather of Kate Stewart). Rusty the Dalek was last seen in "Into the Dalek." Bill refers to the Doctor serving at the pleasure of the human race ("Thin Ice"), while the weapons factories at Villengard were first mentioned all the way back in Steven Moffat's first story, 2005's "The Empty Child"/"The Doctor Dances."

Images of past Doctors and Davros (from 2008's "Journey's End") are briefly shown, while some of the names that Testimony offers for the Doctor include the Imp of the Pandorica (2010's "The Pandorica Opens"), the Shadow of the Valeyard (1986's "The Trial of a Time Lord"), the Beast of Trenzalore ("The Name of the Doctor"), the Butcher of Skull Moon ("Hell Bent"), the Destroyer of Skaro (1988's "Remembrance of the Daleks") and the Doctor of War ("Hell Bent"). The first Doctor previously threatened someone with a jolly good smacked bottom in 1964's "The Dalek Invasion of Earth." Testimony's creator is from New Earth in the year 5 billion and 12, which the Doctor visited in 2006's "New Earth" and 2007's "Gridlock." The Doctor gets his memories of Clara restored (after the events of "Hell Bent") and sees her as she was in her final appearance in "Face the Raven." The Cloister Bell goes off (1981's "Logopolis"), signalling disaster during the twelfth Doctor's final speech. After regenerating, the twelfth Doctor's ring drops to the floor much the same way that the first Doctor's ring did in 1966's "Power of the Daleks."

**Who Is the Doctor?** Both the first and the twelfth Doctor have doubts about their impending regenerations, holding back the change in order to decide their fates. The first Doctor wants to prevent the change, because he wants to have autonomy over who he is. The twelfth Doctor is tired and thinks that if all things should end, why should he be denied his final rest? However, he changes his mind saying, "I suppose one more lifetime wouldn't kill anyone. Well, except me." The Doctor doesn't usually admit that he's afraid to anyone else (and since it's the first admitting it to the twelfth, technically he still hasn't). The first Doctor admits to Bill that he ran away from Gallifrey to look for a reason that goodness in the universe endured, despite not being a practical survival strategy; he's still looking, all these years later. For the first time ever, he gives advice to his next incarnation, saying, "Run fast, laugh hard, be kind."

**The Doctor and Bill** He's torn between wanting to trust her and doubting she can be real, but he also clings to the hope that she might be alive. For her part, she realizes his quest is solved by his very existence and hopes for the possibility that they spend years laughing together. She says that the hardest thing about knowing the Doctor was letting go of him.

**Monster of the Week** The Testimony Foundation is an alien ship full of souls. They take memory imprints just before the moment of death in order to preserve them. Testimony's interface appears as an impossibly thin glass avatar that they use to let the dead walk among the living.

**Stand Up and Cheer** The portrayal of the human miracle that is the World War I Christmas Armistice is simply magnificent. It's incredibly touching to hear "Silent Night" sung in German from the trenches, followed by the English joining in, and then to watch the soldiers shaking hands with each other, tending to the wounded and playing soccer. ("Everybody was just kind.") This is also possibly the best-ever link to Christmas in a *Doctor Who* Christmas Special.

**Roll Your Eyes** Yes, the first Doctor threatened his granddaughter with a jolly good smacked bottom back in 1964. Yes, the episode is using his casual sexism to show how far we've come. Yes, the aftermath, with Bill wanting to laugh about it for years, is well done. But did we really need to go there? Really?

**You're Not Making Any Sense** Are we seriously supposed to believe that the elderly first Doctor leaps onto a moving chain, slides down with his bare hands and then jumps from a great height — without shattering every bone in his frail body?

**Interesting Trivia** Once again, Steven Moffat had his plans for leaving *Doctor Who* thwarted. His intention was to end with "World Enough and Time"/"The Doctor Falls" and hand off to his successor Chris Chibnall (and the new Doctor) for the 2017 Christmas special. However, Moffat learned that Chibnall didn't want to start with a Christmas special (understandably so, given that it would be ten months before a new season would begin) and Moffat worried that *Doctor Who* would lose the Christmas special in the future if there wasn't one in 2017, so he decided to write — and convinced Peter Capaldi to stick around for — one more episode.

Moffat alighted on an idea that had come up a year or so earlier at New York Comic Con when he was asked which Doctors contrasted most. Moffat said that he'd always liked the idea of contrasting the current Doctor with the first but that this was impossible because William Hartnell was dead. However, Peter Capaldi, who was on the same panel, suggested that they could use David Bradley, who had played Hartnell in the fiftieth-anniversary docudrama *An Adventure in Space and Time*.

More "Previously on *Doctor Who*" scenes were filmed than shown; these recreated several key moments in episode four of "The Tenth Planet" (which is missing from the BBC archives), including a pitched battle in the control room and the melting of Mondas and the Cybermen. They're easily found on YouTube and well worth a watch if you're a Classic Series fan.

Mark Gatiss isn't the only *Doctor Who* writer who was also an actor. Toby Whithouse is as well — and he speaks German. Whithouse was thus employed in this story to play the German soldier pointing a gun at Gatiss's Archibald.

Everything about the 1914 Christmas Armistice more or less happened as it's depicted here, with carol singing escalating into a cease of hostilities, where small gifts were exchanged, arrangements for the recovery and burial of the dead were made and, in some instances, even some friendly soccer matches occurred in no man's land. Such fraternization with the enemy was subsequently highly discouraged.

During the 20th century, almost all Classic Series stories were novelized. These books were a way of reliving the story before the advent of VHS and also filled in little nuggets to smooth over plot holes, add characterization, and so on. Sometimes the books patched up problems, and sometimes they provided additions that would have slowed down the action on TV but worked in print. They were immensely popular, selling widely across the world for decades. On April 5, 2018, four novelizations of the Modern Series were released, covering all the modern Doctors and with throwback covers. The four episodes adapted were "Rose" (by Russell T Davies), "The Christmas Invasion" (by Jenny T. Colgan), "The Day of the Doctor" (by Steven Moffat) and "Twice Upon a Time" (by Paul Cornell). Just like their antecedents, these novelizations threw in extra details. Paul Cornell's adaptation included unused material from Steven Moffat's script to fill in Bill and Heather's fate (Bill returned to being human, and they lived together on Earth until Bill died of old age), Nardole's fate (he remained on the colony ship, dealt with the Cybermen, had six wives — two of them simultaneously — and lived until he was 728) and had Testimony ultimately restore Bill's

memory of Heather. It also explains the critical continuity point of how the first Doctor — who could barely pilot the TARDIS — managed to get his ship back to Antarctica. (He employed the Fast Return switch, which was last used in 1964's "The Edge of Destruction"!)

The first Doctor's TARDIS was mostly a recreation. By 1966, the TARDIS control room set was vastly smaller than it was originally, and one wall was a photographic blow-up. Steven Moffat justified the change saying it was "what 1960s *Doctor Who* looks like when you point an HD camera at it" (which also explains why the first Doctor's hands now have the regenerative "glow"). Originally, the police box exterior was to look more like a Modern Series box, but they found a fan-made version of the original design (though it's adapted from the version used for the Jon Pertwee era, and it's slightly taller than it was in 1966). There was one element in the TARDIS set that wasn't created for this episode: the two standalone brass pillars beside the doors are in fact the original ones from the 1963 set, found while they were making *An Adventure in Space and Time*. This wasn't the only original prop to feature in the episode: Mark Gatiss brought in Jon Pertwee's original jacket from 1973's "Planet of the Daleks" (which he owns) and hung it in the twelfth Doctor's TARDIS during the regeneration scene.

As with the regeneration scene in "The End of Time," the new production crew supervised the first scenes featuring the new Doctor. The thirteenth Doctor's first scene was written (and produced) by Chris Chibnall. The actual final scene of the Steven Moffat era was shot a few weeks later: Jenna Coleman couldn't come on location to shoot her scene with the Doctor because of her commitments to *Victoria*. Coleman's scene was shot against a green screen in the BBC's London offices of *Top Gear*!

**The TARDIS Chronometer** The South Pole, 1986; Ypres, 1914; the Weapon Forges of Villengard in the future.

**Don't Be Stupid? (RS?)** "Twice Upon a Time" is all about perspectives.

The episode starts by showing us the final scene from "The Doctor Falls" but from a different perspective than the previous episode. Archibald's approach in the snow is initially shown from the Doctors' POVs and then again from his. Testimony appears to be carrying out an evil plan but turns out not to be once seen the right way. That's courtesy of a good Dalek — something previously unimaginable — who in turn is persuaded to help by changing its perspective: namely, that helping the Doctor will annoy the other Daleks.

Time and again, the episode is telling us that things are not what you think, that every situation has multiple points of view and resolution can be reached simply by understanding them.

The twelfth Doctor's future perspective leads him to give away spoilers in calling the Great War "World War One," which gives Archibald a viewpoint he'd never imagined. The first Doctor's reaction to the TARDIS interior ("hideous!") is contrasted with Archibald's sheer wonder at what he's seeing. Our own understanding of what's happening when the action shifts from the modern TARDIS to the classic one is contrasted with Archibald's assumption that this is simply what police boxes are.

What this does is show us multiple views of the same situation, allowing us to turn the possibilities around in our minds until we understand all sides of the problem and then update our thinking. This is precisely how the process of learning works: not by didactically telling the student what to think, but by showing them multiple points of view so that they can come to their own conclusions. That's the only way the lesson will stick.

Even the German soldier plays his part. The TARDIS usually translates for us, but here the point is made that both Archibald and the soldier cannot understand each other. This is even clearer when you translate the soldier's German into English. His line at the beginning is "Just leave me here. I don't want you dead. Please go." And his line at the end is "That's crazy. I don't want to hurt you." However, it turns out that the two opposing forces actually do have a language in common: music. That's the genius of the human miracle: it shows that these soldiers have far more in common than not; it just requires the right way to view it for them to see.

The first Doctor's and Archibald's sexist viewpoints are brilliantly counterpointed by Bill challenging their assumptions, once again showing them a perspective they simply couldn't have imagined. The central debate over whether Bill is real or fake is also a matter of looking at things in the right way. She's both Bill Potts and a glass avatar, with the issue resolved at the end of the story when she points out that, regardless of her form, everyone is just a bunch of memories. Indeed, Testimony's entire raison d'être is to hear the dead speak again and gain wisdom from a perspective that would have previously been unthinkable.

It's this foray into the previously unknowable that really brings this episode's theme to life. Not only do we see multiple views but, when this is done right, we can see into the darkness and think thoughts we never imagined possible. The Doctor is right: this is the very opposite of an evil plan.

The idea is even played for comedy when the first Doctor wears a monocle and the twelfth wears the sonic sunglasses. They're both taking an altered view of the situation, using technology to look at something from another perspective, yet we also see the contrast across the centuries, with one an Edwardian gentleman and the other an ageing hipster. It's the first Doctor who figures out that the Testimony interface was a real person, as opposed to the simulation that the twelfth assumes, simply because he looks at her. We even see two views on the decanter of brandy, while the Doctor saves Archibald on the grounds that "everybody's important to somebody" — we subsequently discover that somebody is in fact him, given who Archibald turns out to be. The pun on the Doctor of War also depends on where you're standing: it sounds horrific at first, because we immediately draw a parallel with the War Doctor and the terrible things we know the Doctor sometimes has to do — and yet the ending shows *Doctor Who* at its most magnificent, turning a battlefield into kindness.

Finally, the twelfth Doctor alters his perspective from someone who wants to lie down and die to someone who offers not only new life but actual advice to his successor. And then we, the viewers, are offered our own altered viewpoint, as the Doctor we've always known as a man regenerates into a woman. What might have once been as unthinkable to fans as Bill's sexuality is to Archibald has been transformed into something that simply is, which it achieves by taking the theory and applying it. So now we update our own point of view and accept that the Doctor can be a woman, because the fact of her becoming so means that of course it's possible. What was once unimaginable has proven to be enlightening because we looked at it in the right way.

And now for an entirely different perspective . . .

**Second Opinion (GB)** Here's my perspective. Why did we even need this story in the first place?

There is literally no need for it. You could cut "The Doctor Falls" at the point where the Doctor wakes up and put in the Doctor's final speech and regeneration from this story and not miss a beat. "Twice Upon a Time" is a massive stall, created by production fiat that there be a 2017 *Doctor Who* Christmas special. It's utterly inconsequential.

And it makes no sense. The Doctor suddenly, from out of nowhere, doesn't want to regenerate anymore. What. The. Fuck?! Five episodes earlier, he was gaslighting Bill (and the viewer) about regenerating. He has shown no desire to stop changing or come to an end up until this point.

Oh, and the first Doctor shows up feeling the same way. We're back to WTF territory. Everything we know about the final episode of "The Tenth Planet" shows a Doctor in his final moments who is infirm and resigned to his fate. But then again, everything about the first Doctor here is wrong. It's a cute trick to have David Bradley play the first Doctor after having played William Hartnell, but as much as I enjoyed him in *An Adventure in Space and Time*, I find him far less convincing as the Doctor than I did him playing Hartnell. Bradley adds

Shatner-length pauses to everything and plods through every scene he's in. It doesn't help that Moffat has decided, since this Doctor was created in the 1960s, he should be written as though he's wandered off the set of *Mad Men*, making casually sexist remarks the actual first Doctor would never make and little Englander jokes about the French. I'm amazed he doesn't have the first Doctor smoking cigarettes too. It would be just about as accurate as what we see here.

And here's the thing: the whole episode is a giant chase, which results in nothing. I agree the Christmas Armistice scenes are deeply moving, but I would almost have preferred to have a whole story set during that moment rather than using it so perfunctorily. (Also, did they keep Toby Whithouse's German solider frozen in time for the whole time the Doctor delayed? And why didn't the Testimony spot that?) Mark Gatiss offers some relief — Archibald gets some of the best lines, and I like the scene where the character reflects on returning to the scene of his death — but even this could have been used to better effect. Worse, the one thing that could have made this better — Bill coming back and the prospect of giving her a better, more deserved ending with agency — is neutralized, because it's a Testimony copy of Bill and everything is surrendered to retrospect. Like just about everything else here.

The final scene is a slam-dunk though. It's a little weird when you consider that the Doctor is effectively mansplaining what being the Doctor is like to his future, female self, but Capaldi makes it effortlessly charming. (It's also a shame the Doctor didn't pause to notice the Cloister Bell was going off, so maybe the TARDIS blowing up wouldn't have been a surprise.) And Jodie Whittaker's look when realizing what's happened is, as she says, brilliant. I love that it doesn't try to otherwise establish her character and it goes straight into a massive cliffhanger.

I've had a few friends suggest that "Twice Upon a Time" might be just a fever dream on the part of the Doctor in the moments before he regenerates. That makes a lot of sense given that we could effectively go from the ending of "The Doctor Falls" to the regeneration here without missing anything. Now there's a perspective I could get behind.

. . . . . . . . . . . . . . . . . . . . . . . . . . . . . . . . . . . . . . . . . . . . . . . . . . . . . . .

## Steven Moffat

Born in 1961 in Paisley, Scotland, Steven Moffat began his career as a teacher, although he also wrote plays performed at the Edinburgh Festival Fringe. His big break as a writer happened when his father recommended him to some film producers as someone who could write a series about a school newspaper. That led to the ITV children's series *Press Gang* (1989–93), for which Moffat wrote all five seasons.

From there, Moffat moved to writing comedy for adults, beginning with *Joking Apart* (1993–95) and *Chalk* (1997). In 2000, Moffat created his best-known comedy series, *Coupling*, which lasted four seasons and a number of international remakes including a failed U.S. version, which only lasted a few episodes but proved to be quite lucrative for Moffat and his wife, producer Sue Vertue.

Moffat has been a fan of *Doctor Who* since childhood. He wrote a short story, "Continuity Errors," for Virgin Publishing's 1996 *Doctor Who* anthology *Decalog 3* (the central idea of which was adapted for his 2010 *Doctor Who* episode "A Christmas Carol"). In 1999, he wrote a Comic Relief *Doctor Who* parody episode, "The Curse of Fatal Death," which starred Rowan Atkinson, Richard E. Grant, Hugh Grant, Jim Broadbent and Joanna Lumley as the Doctor. Moffat was one of the first writers Russell T Davies engaged on the revival of the series in 2004; his first story, "The Empty Child"/"The Doctor Dances," was so popular that he became the only writer other than Davies to write for all four seasons of Davies's tenure as executive producer.

At the time, Moffat was already moving from comedy into drama with the 2007 series *Jekyll*, a modern adaptation of (and sequel, of sorts, to) Robert Louis Stevenson's novella *Strange Case of Dr. Jekyll and Mr. Hyde*. Moffat followed this up by developing a modern-day version of Sherlock Holmes with fellow *Doctor Who* writer Mark Gatiss. After a false start with its first pilot episode, *Sherlock* debuted to critical acclaim and high ratings in 2010 and continued for four seasons until 2017.

In 2008, Moffat was approached by Russell T Davies to succeed him as executive producer and head writer of *Doctor Who*. Moffat became showrunner with Series Five in 2010 and stayed eight years, becoming the longest-serving showrunner on modern *Doctor Who*. Additionally, Moffat has written more scripts for *Doctor Who* than any other writer in the Classic or Modern Series.

Following *Doctor Who*, Moffat adapted "The Day of the Doctor" as a novelization for the revived Target Books range. He is now at work on an adaptation of Bram Stoker's *Dracula* with *Sherlock* co-creator Mark Gatiss, which will air on BBC1.

. . . . . . . . . . . . . . . . . . . . . . . . . . . . . . . . . . . . . . . . . . . . . . . . . . . . . . . . . . .

## SERIES ELEVEN (2018)

**Starring**
Jodie Whittaker as the Doctor
Bradley Walsh as Graham O'Brien
Tosin Cole as Ryan Sinclair
Mandip Gill as Yasmin Kahn

**Executive Producers**
Chris Chibnall
Matt Strevens
Sam Hoyle

**Producers**
Nikki Wilson (11.01–11.03, 11.05, 11.07,
11.09, 11.11)
Alex Mercer (11.04, 11.06, 11.08, 11.10)

# 11.01 The Woman Who Fell to Earth

**Written by** Chris Chibnall **Directed by** Jamie Childs

**Original airdate** October 7, 2018

**The Big Idea** An alien hunt has come to Sheffield at the same time that the new Doctor has fallen from the sky.

**Roots and References** The 1987 film *Predator* (Tim Shaw's basic look); the 2011 film *Attack the Block* (fighting aliens in urban Britain) featuring Jodie Whittaker; *MacGyver* (the montage building the sonic screwdriver). The title is borrowed from the 1976 Nicholas Roeg film *The Man Who Fell to Earth*, starring David Bowie.

**Adventures in Time and Space** The energy that the Doctor tracks to locate the TARDIS is likely Artron energy (1976's "The Deadly Assassin"). Her discussion of carrying her family with her echoes the "They sleep in my mind" scene from 1967's "Tomb of the Cybermen." She emits the same post-regenerative energy that the tenth Doctor did in 2005's "The Christmas Invasion."

**Unfinished Business** Ryan has dyspraxia, a coordination disorder, making it hard for him to ride a bike or climb a ladder. He refuses to call Graham "Granddad," even when prompted to by his nan, Grace. Graham met Grace, a nurse, while he was being treated for cancer (he's now in remission). Yaz is a junior police officer on probation who went to primary school with Ryan. Grace is very much into the lifestyle of hunting aliens, far more than Graham.

**Who Is the Doctor?** This new Doctor immediately distinguishes herself from her previous incarnation with her decency and openness: she incorporates people's first names in conversation, apologizes when her friends see things they shouldn't (like Rahul's mutilated corpse) and stays around for Grace's funeral. She immediately establishes authority with Yaz, partly from experience (she has no knowledge of the tentacle creature, but she's asking the right questions) and partly out of sheer charm ("I'm calling you Yaz now, 'cause we're friends"). Her childlike enthusiasm bubbles over as she asks Yaz to turn on the police car's lights and siren. She builds her own sonic screwdriver from scratch. As she processes the after-effects of her regeneration, the one constant she holds onto is that when people need help, she never refuses. She eventually comes to remember who she is: the Doctor, sorting out fair play throughout the universe.

**The Doctor and Team TARDIS** The Doctor immediately connects with Graham, Grace, Ryan and Yasmin, who not only believe her about aliens but actively help her. She sympathizes with Ryan touching an alien shape, saying that she would have done the same. Consoling Ryan on the loss of his nan, she tells him that she lost her family a long time ago but carries them with her and makes them a part of who she is.

**Monster of the Week** Tim Shaw (really Tzim-Sha) is a member of the Stenza. They're a warrior race who participate in a human hunt in order to determine the next leader. They live in extremely cold temperatures and wear the teeth of their conquests embedded in their faces.

**Stand Up and Cheer** Karl repeating life lessons such as "I am valued" and "Somebody out there wants me" just after it's been revealed that he's the focus of an alien hunt is hilarious.

**Roll Your Eyes** The drunk guy throwing salad at Tim Shaw is a bit on the nose.

**You're Not Making Any Sense** How did Tim Shaw fit inside his chrysalis? Even crouched down, he's way too big to have been inside it.

**Interesting Trivia** For the first time in the Modern Series, *Doctor Who* was moved to a Sunday timeslot. The move was a huge success: this episode garnered the highest ratings for a series premiere in *Doctor Who* history and the highest ratings since the end of the Matt Smith era, with 10.96 million viewers tuning in. That wasn't the only change: almost all the behind-the-scenes personnel were new, including Segun Akinola taking on responsibility for the music and theme tune; he replaced Murray Gold, who had been the most prominent person continually associated with *Doctor Who* since its return in 2005.

Back in 1981's "Logopolis," the fourth Doctor fell off a 70-foot-high radio telescope and died. In 2010's "The End of Time," the tenth Doctor fell 200 feet and (barely) survived. Here, the thirteenth Doctor plummets from the stratosphere and is absolutely fine. Is that because she's still regenerating, à la the tenth Doctor having his hand cut off in 2005's "The Christmas Invasion" or River Song surviving being shot in 2011's "Let's Kill Hitler"? Or is it because Time Lords gradually become Wile E. Coyote as they get older?

Dyspraxia is an actual condition, although it's not an official diagnosis. It refers to trouble with motor skills or coordination and is often paired with other conditions, such as ADHD, dysgraphia or autism. The official diagnosis is development coordination disorder (DCD), defined as an impairment in the learning of coordination and motor skills. The term "dyspraxia" is in more common use in the U.K. than the U.S. (it also became more widely known when actor Daniel Radcliffe revealed he had it). New showrunner Chris Chibnall felt that, as many children live with this condition, it was important for the young audience to see someone like Ryan coping with it.

The actual script for "The Woman Who Fell to Earth" treats everything up to the Doctor crashing into the train as a pre-credits sequence. However, Chris Chibnall made the unusual decision to keep the action continuous and do the episode without any opening titles. There is a brief snatch of the title music when the Doctor arrives, indicating where the titles would have gone, one of the only instances of the *Doctor Who* theme being used in the actual score of an episode since the Modern Series began in 2005.

**The TARDIS Chronometer** Sheffield, present day.

**Aw, Brilliant? (RS?)** The miracle has happened again.

Back when the fiftieth-anniversary celebrations were happening, I was often asked what I thought was the secret to *Doctor Who*'s longevity. My answer then is the same as my answer now: its ability to regenerate.

Not just the main character, although that's useful too, of course. But in truth the best thing about *Doctor Who* is that it finds itself for a while, continues along in a house style . . . and then throws it all away, often while the going is still good. Of course, this can be traumatic to many fans, who often love the show because of what it is. So throwing that aside for something entirely different seems foolhardy and guaranteed to put at least some people on the back foot. But it's also a very necessary part of *Doctor Who*'s long-term survival.

Here we see perhaps the second-biggest change in *Doctor Who*'s history, after its 2005 return. It's not just a female Doctor, which is a relatively minor change by this point, having been trialled in various ways throughout the Capaldi era with a lot of groundwork preparing the way. Sensibly, they briefly acknowledge this change and then simply move on, allowing Jodie Whittaker to slide into the role of the Doctor with consummate ease.

No, it's far more than that. This looks unlike any previous *Doctor Who*. There are no opening credits, no continuity to past episodes, the aspect ratio is different, the camera lenses are different, and the grim Sheffield setting is a far cry from the previous Earthbound settings. The theme tune appears only at the end of the story. Even the "Coming Soon" trailer simply shows the guest stars for the season, with almost no giveaways. The Doctor is a member of a team, with a procedural approach to problem-solving and minimal outright heroics.

All of these aspects are marvellous. I say that as an unabashed fan of the Moffat era and its cleverness, its continuity and its heroism. As much as I loved all that, I also want to be challenged by *Doctor Who* and for the show to take me places it's never gone before. With "The Woman Who Fell to Earth," it most certainly does that.

I confess that I don't watch much other TV. I only care about *Doctor Who*. So maybe this looks just like every other show out there (I'll never know), but Series Eleven looks nothing like what's come before in *Doctor Who*, which I think is stupendous. The weakest aspect is the writing, as the plot is light and misses some obvious tricks. That probably should bother me more than it does, and I get why it may be difficult for people familiar with the Davies and Moffat eras to make the transition, but I was so swept away by the charm, the likeability and the visuals that it simply didn't bother me.

The new team is resolutely ordinary. When confronted with the possibility of aliens, they consult bus drivers, nurses and social media. The person with the most standout success in life is a junior police officer on probation. And the Doctor is fairly ordinary as well. She's bereft of all the accoutrements of her predecessors: no TARDIS, no sonic screwdriver; even her pockets are empty. And so she has to rebuild both her character and her accessories from scratch: she gets down and dirty in a workshop to make a new screwdriver, steadily grows to accept who she is and creates a portal to the next planet where her TARDIS supposedly is.

And yet, despite this ordinariness, Whittaker is utterly fantastic. The thirteenth Doctor is immediately likeable, bouncing into her friends' lives and walking them through every situation. She's not condescending, openly admits when she's wrong and makes space for her friends. Oh, and the new outfit just adds to the charm: she's a big kid. Just like all the other Doctors.

I also like the diversity of the new cast. It's the first time we've seen multiple companions of colour, which is long overdue and helps to redress some of the faults in the previous eras. It also means that killing Grace is less loaded than it otherwise would be. It's still a tricky thing — a woman of colour is killed off so that the men who are left behind can bond — but it's at least tempered by the fact that she's not the only prominent one. (Part of it may simply be that Sharon Clarke delivers such a likeable performance, so it hits harder that she isn't joining the fam.) And the reveal that Ryan's YouTube video is about Grace rather than the Doctor is just beautiful.

"The Woman Who Fell to Earth" is a simple and fresh episode, perfect to grab new viewers, as it clearly did. It's a great showcase for both the new Doctor and the new style, stamping its mark on the landscape in a bold new fashion. That's the true miracle of *Doctor Who*: not the changing face in front of the camera, but all the changing faces behind it. *Doctor Who* is dead. Long live *Doctor Who*.

**Second Opinion (GB)** You know what I really love about "The Woman Who Fell to Earth"? That I really liked it a lot more on rewatch.

Don't get me wrong, on first viewing I enjoyed it and was struck by many of the same things my co-author was — though it must be said I watch far more TV and film than he does. That said, his instincts are right: *Doctor Who* looks and feels more of the moment than it has in a while. As exceptionally well made as it has been, the revised house style has been in effect since 2010 or so; by this point, *Doctor Who* kind of looked and sounded like its own thing. It was shocking — in a good way — to see scenes largely set to silence during the first ten minutes. As much as I love Murray Gold, the show had become overreliant on using music to tell the viewer how to feel. I love this shift in aesthetic, and Segun Akinola's score is pleasingly different to Gold's work on the show. The shift to a slightly more cinematic look feels more like television in 2018 generally.

But . . . for all that's great about the look of it and Jodie Whittaker's supernova of a debut, there was a part of me that was left cold by "The Woman Who Fell to Earth" on broadcast. That was not my feeling on rewatch. I found it delightful, fast-paced and engrossing. *Doctor Who* is back to being a straight-ahead adventure series with a soapy ensemble. I'm on board for that. My shift in appreciation is a reminder that this story had the burden of a lot of expectations on it. Too many expectations, perhaps. If you leave behind those expectations, this episode is great. It's hugely exciting, and the introduction of a full-on ensemble as well as a new Doctor works surprisingly well.

Perhaps too well: Grace's death is meant to have impact, to impart that there's danger in travelling with the Doctor and to pull the rug out from under the viewer. That the person who is most enthusiastic about adventuring gets killed is meant to sound a cautionary note. But it doesn't for the reason my co-author sets out above. It doesn't help that Grace is the most interesting and compelling character in the ensemble of new friends (and, as Robert says, she's amazingly portrayed by Sharon Clarke). Nor does it help that three-quarters of the people killed in this story are people of colour. I do sort of wish that Grace had simply broken her leg and become a recurring character like Jackie Tyler was back in the day. That said, the one thing I did love about the story is that the new Doctor stayed for the funeral.

That for me is a radical signal of who she is. She's someone who stays for the funeral of a friend. She's someone who watches over Ryan when he's back on the bike. She's someone who makes sure that Karl didn't have a DNA bomb on him and gives Tim Shaw fair warning before he detonates the bomb. She's *kind*, basically. In a radical way. She's also funny, smart, unselfconsciously brave and charming too.

She's the Doctor.

The great thing about "The Woman Who Fell to Earth" is how it feels new even though in some ways it's *Doctor Who* gone back to basics: a straight-ahead adventure with lots of huge dramatic moments (the Doctor jumping from crane to freaking crane and declaring who she is!), stunning direction, a great new ensemble cast and a lead who is fantastic from the word go. More, please.

## Jodie Whittaker

By the time Jodie Whittaker took on the role of the thirteenth Doctor, she had developed an impressive resumé on television, most notably chalking up three seasons playing Beth Latimer, one of the central characters in Chris Chibnall's crime drama *Broadchurch* (2013–17).

Whittaker was born in 1982 and grew up in Skelmanthorpe, West Yorkshire. She graduated from the Guildhall School of Music and Drama in 2005 with its highest prize. Her first major role was a year later opposite Peter O'Toole in the 2006 film *Venus*. Film and TV work continued from there, most notably the BBC adaptation of *The Night Watch* (2010), the cult film *Attack the Block* (2012) and the 2016 film *Adult Life Skills*, which she executive-produced (the 2014 short film it was based on, *Emotional Fuse Box*, which Whittaker also produced, was nominated for a BAFTA).

It was on a train journey with Chris Chibnall where Whittaker talked with him about making *Emotional Fuse Box* (and convinced him to watch it), that Chibnall first had an inkling that Whittaker would be ideal for the part of the Doctor. When Chibnall became showrunner in 2017, he invited Whittaker out for coffee. Whittaker went hoping she could land a guest spot as a villain or monster, but Chibnall told her he was interested in her playing the Doctor. Whittaker auditioned as part of a secretive (even by modern *Doctor Who* standards) casting process — her code name for the role at home and with her agent was "the Clooney," on the grounds that George Clooney also played an iconic doctor! — and the short video that announced her casting that aired on BBC during the Wimbledon final on July 16, 2017, was assembled by a tiny crew.

She said of playing the part of the Doctor, "There's the chiselled superhero that we're used to seeing and we've all grown up with. But *Doctor Who* has never been that, which is wonderful. It's attainable in so many ways."

## Chris Chibnall

Born in 1970, Chris Chibnall grew up in Liverpool before moving to Sheffield. A *Doctor Who* fan from an early age, he appeared on the BBC discussion series *Open Air* in 1986 as a member of the *Doctor Who* Appreciation Society and criticized the current season of *Doctor Who* being broadcast at the time!

Chibnall studied theatre and film and initially started as a playwright before a monologue he wrote, "Stormin' Norman," was shown by ITV. This eventually led to Chibnall being approached to develop the 2001–05 series *Born and Bred*, for which he was head writer and eventually showrunner.

On the strength of this success, Chibnall was hired — at the eleventh hour — to become the showrunner of the new *Doctor Who* spinoff *Torchwood*. Chibnall was head writer for the first two seasons and wrote eight episodes of the series, as well as three episodes of *Doctor Who* under showrunners Russell T Davies and Steven Moffat. Chibnall went directly from *Torchwood* to act as showrunner on ITV's *Law & Order* franchise, *Law & Order: U.K.*, which he did for two seasons. Chibnall also produced and wrote a few more series and TV movies (including *United* with David Tennant) before he finally managed to get a passion project he had been working on since 2003 greenlit.

That series — built around the mystery of child murdered in a Dorset town — was *Broadchurch*, which became an overnight sensation and was one of the most popular series ITV had broadcast in recent years, peaking at over ten million viewers. It made Olivia Colman a household name in Britain, cemented David Tennant's reputation as an actor after *Doctor Who* and was the first major television role for Jodie Whittaker. (It also featured *Doctor Who* and *Torchwood* alumni David Bradley, Eve Miles and Arthur Darvill.) The show ran for three seasons from 2013 to 2017 (and even sparked an American remake, *Gracepoint*, which also starred Tennant). On the strength of *Broadchurch*'s popular appeal, the BBC approached Chibnall in 2016 to succeed Steven Moffat on *Doctor Who* in 2018.

· · · · · · · · · · · · · · · · · · · · · · · · · · · · · · · · · · · · · · · · · · · · · ·

# 11.02 The Ghost Monument

**Written by** Chris Chibnall **Directed by** Marc Tonderai
**Original airdate** October 14, 2018

**The Big Idea** The Doctor and her friends are rescued by the finalists in a space-faring rally. Only now they must cross the deadly planet Desolation to get to the end of the race — and to the TARDIS.

**Roots and References** Globetrotting reality shows like *The Amazing Race* (the Rally of the Twelve Galaxies, with its various "bonuses" and "snake traps" and ultimate prize); the 1942 film *Casablanca* (Ilin seems very much like Sidney Greenstreet's Ferrari). Graham compares the race to the Paris–Dakar car rally. The Doctor says Epzo's ship should be on *Antiques Roadshow*. Ryan cites his time playing *Call of Duty* as legitimate experience fighting SniperBots with a gun. (It wasn't.)

**Adventures in Time and Space** The Doctor uses Venusian aikido, the form of hand-to-hand (to-hand-to-hand) combat that was a staple of the third Doctor's era. Specifically, she paralyses Epzo with one finger — a trick the Doctor demonstrated way back in 1970's "Inferno." The Stenza (from "The Woman Who Fell to Earth") have conquered much of the sector.

**Unfinished Business** Ryan's dyspraxia becomes an issue more than once (though Yaz, Graham and the Doctor all look out for him). Ryan still doesn't trust Graham, and Graham's encouragement seems to fall on deaf ears. He continues to refuse to call Graham "Granddad"; both are still mourning Grace's death. Yaz admits she has a father who annoys her and a sister trying to get her to move out so she can have Yaz's room. The Remnants tell the Doctor of a "timeless child," something that is hidden even from her — "the outcast, abandoned and unknown."

**Who Is the Doctor?** This new Doctor strongly asserts her belief in "brains over bullets" and is against using guns. She's become an inveterate name-dropper, much like some of her previous incarnations. She repeatedly rejects Epzo's self-centred philosophy and is proud to point out that teamwork saved them.

**The Doctor and Team TARDIS** The Doctor is terribly apologetic about transporting all of them into the vacuum of space and grateful they don't give her a hard time. They still trust her, based on the exploits they've already seen. While the Doctor is angry at Ryan for trying to use a gun to stop the SniperBots, she also encourages him (perhaps seeing that Ryan is not receptive to Graham), saying, "Think of what you've gone through to be here, and you're still going. I'm proper impressed."

**Monster of the Week** The Remnants are creatures that look like pieces of cloth. They are dormant during the day and are capable of independent movement (either slithering or floating). They were created to clear the wounded and now kill the living by smothering them. They develop a psychic link with their victims and can see their memories — possibly including, in the case of the Doctor, memories that are suppressed.

**Stand Up and Cheer** The Doctor finally being reunited with her ship is quite an emotional scene. It's even more impressive when you realize it's just Jodie Whittaker talking to a box. It's so touching the way the Doctor speaks so tenderly to the TARDIS ("Oh you've done yourself up!") and awkwardly mentions she doesn't have a key. Particularly so when you consider that more recent incarnations snapped their fingers to open the TARDIS doors! The TARDIS responding by opening the door is just lovely.

**Roll Your Eyes** Ever heard of Anton Chekov's axiom that if you're shown a self-lighting cigar in act one of a play, it must go off in act three?

**You're Not Making Any Sense** For robots with presumably a computer brain and complete precision movements, the SniperBots are actually really terrible at being snipers.

**Interesting Trivia** This story and the next one were shot in South Africa. The conditions weren't ideal; the region was in a severe drought, and there were water restrictions in effect. Tosin Cole suffered heatstroke while on set, though in interviews he said he wasn't that bothered, as the January filming was better than freezing on a roof in Britain, as he did while filming the episode prior.

During the shoot in South Africa, actor Shawn Dooley (who played Epzo) took a picture of Jodie Whittaker at the location of the Ghost Monument where she was silhouetted against the sunset with the TARDIS in the background. If this picture sounds familiar to you, it should: it was the iconic photo that promoted Series Eleven. Everyone loved it so much that it was rushed to become a part of the show's marketing collateral when *Doctor Who*'s new logo debuted in February 2018. Not bad for a picture snapped on an iPhone 6!

For the fourth time in the Modern Series, the TARDIS control room has been redesigned. After a very spaceship-like control room and console late in the eleventh Doctor's years and in the twelfth's, the new interior resembles the early eras of the Modern Series, with various bric-a-brac festooning the console and organic-looking crystal plinths surrounding it. Production designer Arwel Wyn Jones previously asked Jodie Whittaker what her favourite biscuit was; when it came time to unveil the new console, it was a complete surprise to Whittaker when she touched the foot pedal and a custard cream appeared!

**The TARDIS Chronometer** The planet Desolation, presumably the present day.

**Aw, Brilliant? (GB)** I'm not going to lie. By the end of my first viewing of "The Ghost Monument," I was jumping on my feet and dancing around as though my favourite team had scored a perfect goal. And I still feel they did.

First of all, the first scene with the Doctor on Epzo's ship is fantastic. She gets in the face of the alpha-male Epzo, talks him into doing things her way, takes charge and then proceeds to successfully crash-land a spaceship. It's amazingly shot (all hand-held and mostly in one continuous take, which is really impressive when you consider there's green screen in the mix when they blow the rear section of the ship), and Jodie Whittaker throws in these lovely touches such as the face she makes to Yaz. And the dialogue is superb. I love the Doctor's retort to Epzo's claim that people have written songs about his ship: "They'll be writing operas about our pointless deaths if we don't take drastic action right now."

In fact, the dialogue is great throughout. Who doesn't love "Are you confused?" "Pretty confused." "Proper confused." "I'm way beyond confused." This caught me off guard, because Chris Chibnall is not exactly known for being particularly funny, but "The Ghost Monument" had some great bits, like Epzo and Angstrom trying to explain currency with equivalents that were even more obscure. Or the way Ryan's videogame-fuelled macho swagger completely evaporates when the SniperBots get back up. (Tosin Cole is going to be an asset to this show.) Or Ilin's complete indifference to the Doctor and her friends. (Art

Malik is so good.) It was so important to me that Chibnall didn't forget that *Doctor Who* is funny.

The story is relentlessly linear, and I feel, at this point, that this is a good thing. A race from point A to point B with a lot of exciting diversions along the way is not a bad idea for a second story when you need to consolidate the team you've created. The episode has lots of great scenes that develop not only Ryan and Graham (Yaz gets short shrift; that's not the first time you're going to hear this complaint this season) but also Angstrom and Epzo, whose chilling speech about how he learned to not trust anyone courtesy of his sociopathic mother ultimately sets the backdrop for how the Doctor proves that teamwork is important and that people can rely on each other.

And the Doctor's radical take on kindness is still wonderful. I appreciate the decency of apologizing for nearly killing her friends and how she tries to help Ryan stay focused on climbing the ladder. Here's the thing: some would say this is a deliberate "feminization" of the Doctor. I think it's welcome. I spent far too many years with a character who kept preaching kindness but acting like a total arse. I think decency, kindness and respect are things lacking in the world's leadership. Thank you *Doctor Who* for reminding us that it's vital. Also, the Doctor is not afraid to use her authority. The way she steps up with Epzo (Shawn Dooley, by the way, is totally channelling Russell Crowe here), the way she challenges the Remnants, even the way she rebukes Ryan for getting gun-happy, shows that Jodie Whittaker can show real steeliness in the Doctor when it's demanded.

I don't come away from this story without frustrations. I feel like there's a bit too much telling and not enough showing. I really would have loved a scene where they *discover* the water has flesh-eating microbes, if by risking one of the cast or finding a way to demonstrate it with a piece of meat or something. Epzo's capitulation makes sense — he really was fighting a losing battle at that point — but I feel that it could have been landed on in the scene before they went in the tent. I also would have welcomed more encounters with the Remnants, to be honest.

But "The Ghost Monument" does far more right than wrong. The TARDIS rediscovery scene has a real emotional weight to it. Using the "it's not here after all" trick is a dicey proposition, particularly when the TARDIS appears a second later, but Whittaker sells the emotion of having the bottom drop out of her world. The reunion with the TARDIS is surprisingly emotional, as the Doctor has a conversation with a blue box like it's her very best friend, and you believe it's true.

That whole scene excited me, as I realized that this new version of *Doctor Who* has layers: it can be emotionally powerful, it can be funny, and it can be thoughtful. That's one beautiful bit of goal scoring as far as I'm concerned.

**Second Opinion (RS?)** This episode has only two problems: the beginning and the end. Oh, and the self-lighting cigar.

In *The Hitchhiker's Guide to the Galaxy*, Douglas Adams famously got stuck when he realized that the probability of two people being rescued from deep space within 30 seconds was so unlikely that he was forced to turn the problem around entirely and invent the infinite improbability drive. In "The Ghost Monument," this infinitely improbable event happens not once, but twice.

It's this kind of sloppy plot logic that hampers an otherwise lovely story. The water is said to be teeming with flesh-eating microbes . . . so the entire group spend the next several hours relaxing on a boat, not at all worried about the deadly creatures underneath them. Likewise, they stroll across the beach with the waves coming rather close, and nobody seems too worried. Wouldn't there be microbes in the wet sand under their feet? This team must be made of sterner stuff than I am.

But my co-author is mostly right that this is a pretty charming story, lack of thought aside. I'm fine with the linear storytelling, even if Chekhov's self-lighting cigar is pretty telegraphed and the digging into the sand doesn't achieve much.

However, where this really falls down for me is actually the TARDIS rediscovery. Not the scene itself, which is lovely, but why did we need to find the TARDIS in the second story? Had it actually not been there, forcing the Doctor to innovate her way to a new planet, we'd have continued a thread started in the previous episode and used the buildup to generate actual excitement. I'd have loved to have seen four or five episodes — or even a whole season — with a TARDIS-less Doctor, chasing it across the universe using other methods. That would have held the season together really nicely and provided a triumphant note when it was finally located. Oh well.

I'm being way harsher on this story than it deserves. The flaws and the missed opportunities are all there, but Graeme is right that there's a charm and energy to it that does still make you want to dance. Time to click my fingers and activate that self-lighting cigar I told you about in the first paragraph.

## The Psychic Papers: The *Doctor Who* Title Sequence

Over the years, your humble co-authors have been at dinner parties, barbecues, social events and axe-throwing nights where the subject of *Doctor Who* has come up. For years, we were often greeted by five words said by non-fans about their experience watching *Doctor Who* as a kid.

"The opening titles scared me."

There's a reason for this. Back in 1963, when the original title sequence was made, it was using technology no one had ever used before. To be more specific, it was using technology in a way it wasn't designed to be used.

The principle was, basically, the same as when you point a microphone at a speaker: the mic picks up the speaker's ambient noise and amplifies it, making it louder and louder. This is known as feedback. The visual version of this is when you point a camera at its own monitor and shine a light or put shapes in front of the camera. The camera and monitor create a sort of visual feedback, repeating the image onscreen again and again in a ghostly fashion.

The boffins at the BBC called this "electronic howlround," though nowadays it's called "video feedback." The BBC used it on the 1958 production of the Christmas operetta *Amahl and the Night Visitors* as an inventive visual for the heavenly host but not much else. It wasn't until 1963 when a new science-fiction series was in production featuring an entirely electronic theme song that the process was definitively used.

It was BBC graphic designer Bernard Lodge who created shapes in the howlround by shining a flashlight at the camera, as well as using shapes like the *Doctor Who* logo. All of this was recorded on film and edited to the music. Surprisingly, all the film elements survive, including footage using the face of a production assistant in the howlround, which distorted his face satanically. The sight of this repulsed the producers, leading them to pass on using William Hartnell's face in the opening credits.

The result was something like the theme tune: it was spooky and ethereal and impressionistic. And no one had experienced anything like it.

In 1967, the titles were revised. It was cut to a more up-tempo version of the theme song and used a new typeface for the logo. This time, *Doctor Who*'s producers were amenable to the idea of incorporating Patrick Troughton's face, so the Doctor's face became an integral part of the credits for the rest of the Classic Series.

The arrival of Jon Pertwee brought a colour version to the title sequence. Since howlround worked better with black-and-white cameras, Lodge did the sequence in black and white and then filmed the finished result with coloured gels on top.

In 1973, it was decided to revise the title sequence for what became Pertwee's final season. This time, a new process called slitscan was used. Slitscan was a technique perfected for the starfield sequence at the end of the 1968 film *2001: A Space Odyssey*. Put simply, a "slit" in a black card, cut in a particular shape, is filmed moving towards the camera with a moving backdrop (in this case, several sheets of coloured plastic film on a motorized reel) behind it. When shot at high speed, it looked as though you were travelling up or down a vortex-like tunnel (which was just the coloured plastic film creating interesting patterns while combined). Shapes like the TARDIS or the Doctor or the logo were superimposed over this. This version of the title sequence (with a refreshment for Tom Baker a year later) was used for eight years and became hugely popular with fans, as it conveyed travelling through the time vortex.

In 1980, John Nathan-Turner became producer of *Doctor Who*, and he wanted to put his stamp on the series by commissioning a new arrangement of the theme song and new titles. The title sequence was done by designer Sid Sutton, with traditional animation techniques using painted cells of a starfield forming into the outline of the Doctor's face and then the new neon version of the *Doctor Who* logo. This was used for Tom Baker's final season, through Peter Davison's tenure and, with a few changes, for the entirety of Colin Baker's era as well.

When Sylvester McCoy debuted in 1987, Nathan-Turner invested in the still-new frontier of computer animation for the opening titles. A firm called CAL Video spent almost a month rendering the one-minute sequence where a big bang coalesces into a galaxy, orbited by the TARDIS (in a clear globe, to make it distinct). The only elements overlaid into it were animated photos of Sylvester McCoy's face winking. (This was an effect tested for Colin Baker, which didn't quite work three years earlier. The sixth Doctor smiled instead.)

By the time of the 1996 TV Movie and then the 2005 revival, CGI titles were *de rigueur*. *Doctor Who*'s own special effects house The Mill designed the first Modern Series titles, which featured the time-vortex effect (blue for past, red for future) used in the series. Matt Smith's debut in 2010 refined this by making the vortex more menacing, while a version created for the latter half of Smith's final season added the Doctor's face for the first time.

When it came time for Peter Capaldi's Doctor, fans were getting in on the act, designing their own titles and putting them on YouTube. One such fan was Billy Hanshaw, who made a title sequence that used the motif of a deconstructed pocket watch: gears and the hours on the clockface peeling in a spiral. Steven Moffat saw it and loved it, so the BBC bought the concept from Hanshaw and made their own version (mostly using the gears and the clockface; Hanshaw's use of the Prydonian seal from "The Deadly Assassin" was nixed from the final version). It was probably the most literal version of the titles yet, given the prominence of the number 12 for the twelfth Doctor!

For Jodie Whittaker, the producers went directly to a fan visual-effects artist. Ben Pickles, from Vancouver, had designed a popular YouTube *Doctor Who–Sherlock* mash-up called *WhoLock*. Pickles knew director Rachel Talalay, who found him work doing VFX for *Doctor Who*'s social media and specific shots on the TV series (including working on the spaceship in "World Enough and Time"/"The Doctor Falls"). On the strength of this, Pickles was commissioned to do the latest version of the title sequence, which went back to first principles: a moody, impressionistic sequence made of different shapes before moving into space — almost a 3-D version of Bernard Lodge's howlround effect of the 1960s.

In this way, *Doctor Who* has come full circle with its title sequence. Hopefully, it will continue to scare a new generation of viewers and one day become the topic of conversation at futuristic dinner parties, virtual barbecues, cyber social events and holographic axe-throwing nights.

# 11.03 Rosa

**Written by** Malorie Blackman and Chris Chibnall **Directed by** Mark Tonderai
**Original airdate** October 21, 2018

**The Big Idea** The TARDIS lands in Montgomery, Alabama, in 1955, days before Rosa Parks is due to make her historic protest on the bus. But someone else has come through from the future, determined to stop it.

**Roots and References** The 1989 film *Mississippi Burning* (the depiction of life in the segregated South); *Quantum Leap* (the mission to stop Krasko; it's also cited by Malorie Blackman as an influence). Ryan paraphrases Muhammad Ali's "Good, because I don't eat them" (a line Ali said in 1971). The Doctor references the invisible-theatre artist Banksy. Andra Day's "Rise Up" is played over the closing credits, while "Woke Up This Morning" by the Freedom Singers plays at the beginning (despite not being released until 1964).

**Adventures in Time and Space** Krasko was in a Stormcage prison (like River Song in various stories starting with 2010's "The Pandorica Opens"/"The Big Bang") and uses a vortex manipulator (first seen in 2005's "The Empty Child"/"The Doctor Dances"), just like Captain Jack and River Song. Krasko's weapon leaves traces of Artron energy, which has been mentioned in connection with time travel and Time Lords since 1976's "The Deadly Assassin."

**Unfinished Business** Graham wishes Grace were there to meet Rosa Parks, but Ryan's glad she isn't, as she would have started a riot.

**Who Is the Doctor?** On the bus, the Doctor's forced to do nothing, which goes against her very grain, but she does it. She's on friendly terms with Elvis and hints that she might be Banksy. She doesn't seem to mind being called "Doc," in contrast to earlier incarnations, although she's still not used to being called "ma'am."

**The Doctor and Team TARDIS** When Graham puts an arm around the Doctor's shoulders to pretend they're a couple, she gives a hilariously bewildered look. Realizing how dangerous Montgomery is in 1955, she suggests that Ryan and

Yaz go back to the TARDIS — but both refuse on the grounds that if Rosa Parks can live here, then they can stay a little while.

**Monster of the Week** No monsters, just racism. And human monsters.

**Stand Up and Cheer** It's hard to stand up and cheer the bus scene, because it's so painful to watch. Everybody's put in a difficult position: Rosa being screamed at and arrested; the Doctor powerless; Graham the unwilling catalyst. But the recreation is nonetheless incredibly powerful.

**Roll Your Eyes** Saying that Rosa changed the universe because she had an asteroid named after her does not make it so. Worse, it takes a great episode and makes it trite. Rosa Parks isn't special because somebody named a rock after her, and the implication that her ultimate achievement is somebody else's action is actually pretty offensive.

**You're Not Making Any Sense** Krasko is literally incapable of being dangerous towards the Doctor and her friends. The Doctor, fully knowing this, *walks away from him multiple times*. Instead of, you know, locking him up so he can't actively thwart their plans to undo what he has put into motion. This is particularly galling since the Doctor takes all of his weapons as well.

**Interesting Trivia** The day that Rosa Parks refused to give up her seat, December 1, 1955, was a Thursday. The following Monday, the Montgomery Bus Boycott began. What the episode fudges is that this wasn't a simple situation where Rosa's civil disobedience sparked everything. The NAACP had been considering an action like this for a while, and there had been several other incidents of Black people refusing to give up their seats, but none were deemed suitable as the central figure of the movement. Rosa Parks's case, however, was different, as she presented a more "wholesome" image.

The Montgomery boycott lasted over a year but was successful: racial segregation on Montgomery buses helped to usher in the Civil Rights movement. The specific law was overturned on June 5, 1956, as unconstitutional under the Equal Protection Clause of the 14th Amendment. The city and state appealed, but it was upheld by the U.S. Supreme Court in December 1956.

This story was shot on location in Cape Town, South Africa (which does not look much like Montgomery!). Getting a bus that resembled the one Rosa Parks rode in was a challenge, and the bus used had its fair share of problems while filming, as its interior filled with gasoline fumes from the engine.

Not only is this the first *Doctor Who* story written by a woman of colour (acclaimed author Malorie Blackman, no less, which is quite a get for *Doctor Who*), it's also the first story both written and directed by people of colour (and bonus points for the musical score). All we can say is: about bloody time!

Mark Tonderai isn't the first non-white director; there was also Wayne Yip, who directed two stories in Series Ten and will be back later this season. But before that you have to go all the way back to 1963 to Waris Hussein, one of the original directors to work on *Doctor Who*.

The ending of the story is the first time a song is played over the end credits, a common occurrence in most television these days. "Rise Up" was suggested by Mark Tonderai, who had no trouble getting permission — because he just called his friend Andra Day!

**The TARDIS Chronometer** Montgomery, Alabama, 1943 and 1955.

**Aw, Brilliant? (RS?)** This is indeed brilliant. Especially given the fact that it could have gone so badly.

Previous TARDIS forays into the past, with the exception of pure historicals, have usually had the Doctor and company becoming key players in the events in question, often in heroic roles. When I first found out they were doing a Rosa Parks episode, I feared the worst: that the Doctor (or Yaz, I guess) would somehow have to become Rosa, who had never existed or something. Almost every iteration of this idea went somewhere pretty awful.

Fortunately, the story we get is absolutely fantastic. Key to its success is that nobody tries to take away Rosa's agency. This is the closest the Modern Series has come to presenting a pure historical, with the TARDIS team mostly observing and learning about the time they're in. The sci-fi elements are introduced but quickly disposed of: the suitcase is destroyed, the vortex manipulator crushed, the weapon's power pack disconnected. Even the villain is removed from the story relatively early on, leaving events to unfold as they should.

This also showcases the benefits of having diversity both behind and in front of the camera. This is an episode that's thankfully (co-)written by a woman of colour; I'm fine with having a more experienced writer assisting to get the demands of television (and *Doctor Who* in particular) straight, while neverthe-less keeping the focus on the historical details. This is utterly unlike any other Chibnall script, which suggests that he was concerned with making sure his co-writer's themes came through.

It's also a positive boon to have multiple companions of colour. The con-versation behind the bin is far stronger for being between two people we care about, rather than (say) a companion and a guest star — and the conversation only works because it's two modern perspectives. I also particularly like that we don't get a friendly white saviour anywhere in 1955. All the contempora-neous white people are uniformly awful, either through direct confrontation or by sitting silently and glowering at the mere existence of Ryan and Yaz. That's probably how it should be; yes, it's an exaggeration, in a #notallwhitepeople kind of a way, but we don't need to see it, because — for once — it's not actually about white people.

The two sympathetic white characters we do get are both pushed into uncomfortable roles once they're on the bus. These events force the Doctor into the two things she's railed against her entire life: 1) not standing up for the oppressed and 2) being a Time Lord, compelled to simply observe history and not interfere. Jodie Whittaker sells this beautifully, with an absolutely haunting expression. Likewise, Graham has to face some uncomfortable things himself: he's usually a textbook white ally, but here he has to be the catalyst, and it's pretty terrible for him. And yet, as much of an ally as he is, he very likely hasn't experienced too many awful things in his life. That's almost certainly not true of his grandson and definitely not true of Rosa Parks. The moment with Graham hurts because it stands in contrast to the fact that he has a fairly smooth life, all up. That's a luxury only the white characters in this story have.

There's a problem with *Doctor Who* historicals in the Modern Series when it comes to race, but it isn't the obvious one. In the modern show's well-meaning attempt to provide onscreen diversity, there's a tendency to populate the past with people of colour in ways that aren't true to history. We see background extras in "The Shakespeare Code" or the relative racial harmony of "Thin Ice," and it looks like a stand-up-and-cheer moment. The trouble is, by making the past look basically like the present, it erases the fact that getting beyond said past was a struggle. Companions of colour have slotted into adventures through entirely unlikely means: "Just walk about like you own the place," says a white male Doctor in "The Shakespeare Code," who can get away with that sort of thing and who, in the same breath, claims that the (fictional) state of not being human is somehow more likely to have him be the victim of oppression than the (actually real) state of being Black in 1599. Tellingly, those lines were written by a white dude. You don't *have* to be a member of a minority to get the details right . . . but it sure does help.

"Rosa" makes none of these mistakes. That the episode is co-written by a woman of colour automatically avoids so many of the well-meaning-but-actually-terrible ideas that get thrown into these sorts of stories. Ryan and Yaz aren't just casual tourists to 1950s Alabama, they're actively caught up in the world, unsure of the rules and unable to brazen it out for the simple reason that the rules make no objective sense. (Yaz's confusion about how she's viewed is an excellent example.) But the best part of all is that by not trying to sketch 1955 as though it were 2018 with the serial numbers filed off, the episode gives credit to Rosa Parks and others like her who did the hard work of making society better, one struggle at a time.

It's also just a really exciting episode. The scene with Ryan fanboying over Martin Luther King and Rosa Parks is delightful, while the screwball comedy of trying to get everybody into their right historical places works very nicely. I also enjoyed the fact that they have to work with the tools at hand, like the very thin, old-style phone books or looking through newspaper ads.

I love this story to bits. It's gripping, achingly real, fun and touching, all at once. I showed it to one of my partners, who'd never seen so much as a frame of *Doctor Who* before. She was blown away not only by how good it was but also by the fact that, whatever she'd been expecting from this *Doctor Who* thing, this wasn't it. Thankfully, so was I.

**Second Opinion (GB)** Here's the thing — and it's not only about "Rosa" but about *Doctor Who* this season generally — this is a 7/10 episode, but it has 11/10 moments.

Everything said by my co-author is true. The individual moments in this story make it utterly gripping, from Ryan getting slapped to Ryan and Yaz talking about their experiences of bias and casual racism to the astonishing ending that is predicated on the Doctor and her friends being complicit in Rosa Parks's arrest.

There's so much that makes "Rosa" special. One of those things is Vinette Robinson's stunning portrayal of Rosa Parks. (It's hard to believe this was the same actress who played a forgettable medical officer in "42" 11 years earlier!) Everything Robinson does is so thoughtful and measured; you believe that Rosa is someone who carries herself with absolute dignity and demands that of everyone.

The problem is the rest of it is derivative, bland, humdrum and poorly plotted.

Krasko is the most easily defeated *Doctor Who* villain of all time. If the Doctor returned him to Stormcage — as she could have easily — this episode would have ended at the 20-minute mark. While I do think Krasko's racism is a fascinating place to go (particularly since I'm curious how this might play out with someone from the 47th century), in the end it's there only to set up the punchline for Ryan's heroism. (Although is sending someone back in time who nudges history really a good idea? It would have been nice if they had shown Krasko running away from a dinosaur or something.) In the end, Krasko is a cipher who provides absolutely no threat (I'd have been happy for him to even displace the TARDIS). He's a paper tiger who looks bad, and that's all.

And there's so much poor writing on top of it. Ryan holds up Krasko's time-displacing gun, is told by the Doctor not to use it . . . who then shows him how to use it — so he does. James Blake finds no sit-in protests, but there's a weird guy (who has a Black grandson) who drives his bus to him after he's been told the route's been cancelled . . . so he drives anyway. This is the kind of writing we'd roll our eyes at if it had been in any other story.

But this isn't every other story.

"Rosa" uses a rather simple (and at times dull — in all senses of the word) story format as a backdrop for some great moments that say some meaningful things about race and racism and history and show a lot of complex — and sad — things about the world. And so everything in "Rosa" becomes about those incredible moments. The Doctor is there to (literally) keep the bus running on time.

Those moments on their own are so extraordinary, I feel churlish for criticizing it. Because, at its best, "Rosa" is magnificent and deeply important television. The ending is, once again, one of the most incredible scenes in *Doctor Who*, ever. I just wish the rest of it was as good.

. . . . . . . . . . . . . . . . . . . . . . . . . . . . . . . . . . . . . . . . . . . . . . . . . . . . . . . . . . . . . . . .

## Tosin Cole

At the age of 17, Tosin Cole began his acting career in a stage production of *Julius Caesar* set in the modern day. A year later, in 2009, Cole made his TV debut in the BBC young adult series *The Cut*. This was followed by a role in the *EastEnders* online spinoff *EastEnders: E20*, a two-year stint on the Channel 4 soap opera *Hollyoaks* and various guest-starring roles and small parts (including a role in the 2015 film *Star Wars: The Force Awakens* as an X-Wing fighter pilot). Outside his role as Ryan on *Doctor Who*, Cole was a lead in the 2019 film *The Souvenir*.

. . . . . . . . . . . . . . . . . . . . . . . . . . . . . . . . . . . . . . . . . . . . . . . . . . . . . . . . . . . . . . . .

# 11.04 Arachnids in the U.K.

**Written by** Chris Chibnall **Directed by** Sallie Aprahamian

**Original airdate** October 28, 2018

**The Big Idea** The Doctor gets her friends back home, but Sheffield is experiencing an outbreak of spiders of unusual size — which lead back to the new hotel where Yaz's mum works.

**Roots and References** The 1990 film *Arachnophobia* (the giant spiders); *Teenage Mutant Ninja Turtles* (the toxic waste enlarging the spiders); the career of Donald J. Trump (Robertson is clearly modelled after him, even though he says he despises him). Ed Sheeran is mentioned, but the Doctor doesn't know who he is. Ryan listens to grime music and plays Stormzy's "Know Me From" to drive the spiders to the panic room. The title is a shout-out to the Sex Pistols' 1976 song "Anarchy in the U.K."

**Adventures in Time and Space** The Doctor uses her psychic paper. Usually we wouldn't mention this, but it's the first time the thirteenth Doctor has used it and the first time it's been seen since "The Empress of Mars." Hilariously, she simply waves it in Robertson's face for a fraction of a second.

**Unfinished Business** The Doctor returns everyone to Sheffield, and Graham has to confront his grief for Grace, imagining her talking to him when he visits his house. Ryan receives a letter from his father, offering an apology for not being at Grace's funeral and telling Ryan he can live with him. (Ryan is offended that his father calls himself his "proper family.") We also meet Yaz's family, which includes her annoying sister, Sonya; her conspiracy-obsessed dad, Hakim; and her formidable mother, Najia. Ryan is thrilled when Yaz tells him that of course the invitation to tea extends to him.

**Who Is the Doctor?** She acknowledges she's socially awkward, though she mostly manifests this by nervously talking too much. She requests permission from Jade before breaking into Anna's apartment and is resorting once more to name-dropping (this time she was friends with Amelia Earhart). She notes that she now calls people "dude." She also insists on calling Najia "Yaz's mum" and is instantly loyal to her. This latest incarnation is definitely into hugging.

**The Doctor and Team TARDIS** The Doctor is (adorably) horribly awkward at the idea of saying goodbye to her new friends and is visibly relieved when Yaz invites her to tea. When Najia wants to know the Doctor's relationship with Yaz, she asks, "Are you two seeing each other?" The Doctor responds, bewildered, "I don't think so. Are we?" (The Doctor seems nonplussed by Yaz's answer that "We're friends.") When it comes time to say goodbye for real, Graham, Yaz and Ryan ask to continue travelling with the Doctor, and Yaz speaks for all of them when she says she wants "more of the universe. More time with you. You're like the best person I've ever met." The Doctor is blunt in response, telling them she can't guarantee their safety and that travelling with her could change them completely. They accept this, and seeing that "fam" isn't going to work as a term, she calls them "Team TARDIS" instead.

**Monster of the Week** Spiders. Big Spiders. Gigantic Spiders. Huge Freaking Spiders.

**Stand Up and Cheer** The Doctor's newfound obsession with Ed Sheeran is unbelievably funny. Especially when she confuses Robertson for him.

**Roll Your Eyes** Robertson's bodyguard Kevin pulls a gun on Yaz and Najia, and, for reasons of apparent and sudden stupidity, Yaz does not pull out her warrant card, identify herself as a *police officer* and immediately arrest both Kevin and Robertson for threatening them with a firearm.

**You're Not Making Any Sense** How is Graham the only other person in Sheffield who has a giant spider in his house? And how is it dead? And why isn't anyone else talking about gigantic spiders in the media or social media? The presumption of this story is that these outsized spiders can't survive and will ultimately die out. But have there been any other people in the Park Hill estate (and elsewhere) killed by giant spiders? While we're at it, was Anna's death a coincidence or not? And . . . we could be quite a while.

**Interesting Trivia** Just a note if you ever come across an invasion of giant spiders: there's no proof that vinegar and garlic would act as a deterrent, especially to a creature that size. They do have what is called chemotactile senses, which means they sense through the hairs of their legs — though "smelling" using their feet isn't quite accurate. The bit about the tensile strength of spider web is true enough however.

**The TARDIS Chronometer** Sheffield, the present day.

**Aw, Brilliant? (GB)** There are things this story does really, really right. There are things this story does really, really wrong. I think the right just about overtakes the wrong — but if this were a sporting match, we'd have two referees arguing over a video replay.

Let's talk about what went wrong, which boils down to plot — or indeed anything that requires any sort of judgment. In some ways, I'm almost prepared to let this off, because a toxic waste dump under a golf course and a hotel creating giant spiders is the sort of nonsense that we used to have in *Doctor Who* when it first came back. It's the sort of thing that's done with a wink and a nod and quite a bit of handwaving, so we can just get on with the monsters and the fun. And I would be quite happy to let any deficiencies off and just be scared by giant spiders. But . . . this story doesn't play fair.

There are far too many coincidences: Anna, who just happens to be a lab assistant at the university, *just happens* to be one of the victims of the spider and *just happens* to be sought after by the chief scientist by said lab while Graham — and no one else — *just happens* to find a dead giant spider carcass. And, of course, the Doctor *just happens* to figure out that it all originates from the hotel where Najia *just happens* to work where a Donald Trump stand-in *just happens* to be covering up a massive problem that's taken place in a toxic waste dump under his hotel. One or two *just happens* is careless; more than that is utter desperation.

So much of this could have been fixed simply by setting all of it in the hotel. You cut down the — pardon the pun — web of coincidences by starting with Najia and Robertson having to deal with the outbreak of giant spiders there. (The Doctor and crew could even track down Jade for her part of the story.) That could be classic base-under-siege *Doctor Who*. But instead they elect for a ridiculous amount of *just happens*. And then double down with lots of general stupidity. Why does no one call, I don't know, the military or even the police for help? Or actively find out if Anna is the only actual victim outside the hotel? Why does everyone act like everything's okay because they locked a bunch of spiders up in a panic room without determining whether that's all of them? Why did no one ask if they laid eggs?! The only thing that makes sense is why Robertson is so stupid that he doesn't realize the cobwebs in the room isn't a sign of poor housekeeping; it's because he's based on a very real president of the United States.

Which brings me to what's good about this story. I think a lot of this nonsense goes down better because Robertson really is that stupid and that arrogant — and, moreover, he's there as a satirical stand-in for someone stupid and arrogant. Why on earth would there be a toxic waste dump put in a disused colliery under a golf course? Because Robertson believes he can get away with it. The fact that Chris Noth is clearly having a ball playing Robertson helps this immensely. ("Oh, my God. It got Kevin. I have no more Kevin. I'm compromised.")

It's also really funny. A lot of that is down to Jodie Whittaker, who gets many of the best lines, whether that be the Doctor musing on what kind of sofa she would own if she were to get a flat (purple) or thinking that Robertson is Ed Sheeran. She plays the Doctor as a total dork who has zero sense of self-reflection (I love the costuming choice here of giving her a fanny pack), but you can't help but love her. And even when they're in the background, the rest of the ensemble are trying in their own way to outdo her; watching Ryan make shadow puppets on the overhead projector is hilarious.

I really adore the character beats in this story. Each member of Team TARDIS gets their own thing to deal with: Yaz, with her slightly controlling (and yet not outrageously so) mum; Ryan, with the letter from his dad; Graham, with the reminders of his grief for Grace (Bradley Walsh continues to bring it). I like that everyone is sussing out everyone else still, with Ryan being insecure about being invited for tea and yet calling out Yaz for her lack of street cred in not knowing the local grime FM station. But, in the end, in spite of it all, they choose to create a family (don't call it a fam, though) with the Doctor. The character growth here feels both organic and earned. Even some of the seemingly stupid moments, like Ryan and Graham being too engrossed in an emotional discussion to look at the ceiling, checks out as something ordinary people would do.

But mostly . . . what really, really works is that the spiders are scary. On the one hand, making them just ordinary — but enlarged — spiders fits with *Doctor Who*'s new remit as a procedural series (though it does kind of soften the climax, which is to let them die with dignity and give Robertson a supremely asshole-ish moment). On the other hand, that makes them all the more terrifying, as they can't be reasoned with, and you have to deal with them as you would actual spiders. If you're an arachnophobe, as I am, that's surprisingly creepy.

It's a tough call, but in the end I really like "Arachnids in the U.K." What works triumphs over what doesn't. If there were fewer elements that worked — less emphasis on character, fewer scary spiders, less of Jodie Whittaker being charming — this review might have been quite different.

Plus it has the *best* title of a *Doctor Who* story in a long time.

**Second Opinion (RS?)** Never mind the bollocks, here's "Arachnids in the U.K." I think I'm in a better mood than my co-author, because I pretty much loved this from start to almost-the-end. Or maybe it's because I grew up in a deadly-spider-infested house in Australia; we basically don't have the luxury of being arachnophobes there . . .

In fact, I loved it so much, my only problem is the morality of the ending. Everyone agrees that the spiders must die (though how much more interesting would it have been for the Doctor to be the one arguing otherwise?). The only debate is in how to achieve that. Robertson favours shooting them, while Team TARDIS prefers to lure them into a panic room and let them starve to death.

Only . . . as obnoxious as he is, Robertson's right here. Shooting them is far more humane than letting them starve or suffocate to death. He calls it a mercy killing, and he's correct. If the dilemma were phrased as the Doctor being so blind to her hatred of guns that she couldn't see that, this would be fine. But the episode simply hammers home its blind criticism of ~~Trump~~ Robertson, without pausing to think that the drama would be stronger if he was actually right.

I'm no fan of guns, and I'm no fan of authoritarians. And, big left-wing vegan softie that I am, I'd have preferred them to find (or at least try to find) a solution that kept the spiders alive. Why not use the grime music to drive them towards the TARDIS and take them to somewhere they can live out their days? Or lure them into that clearly-not-very-stinky-because-no-one-is-covering-their-mouths-or-noses mine and trap them there? The extent to which they attempt to save the spiders is so half-hearted that they might as well not have bothered. But if we're going with the idea of a mercy killing, then we should at least pause to consider what that mercy actually looks like.

I sorely wish the episode had developed its premise more and dealt with some of the issues it brings up. But I guess that's not really why anyone comes to this story. Like Chibnall's "Dinosaurs on a Spaceship," the entire appeal of this episode is in its title. It's just too bad they didn't go with a different Sex Pistols song and called it "God Save the Spiders."

## Bradley Walsh

By the time Series Eleven aired, Bradley Walsh was 58, making him the oldest actor to play a regular companion in *Doctor Who*. Walsh is another actor who came to *Doctor Who* already famous for other roles, including hosting game shows and starring in a number of respectable dramas.

Born in 1960, Walsh tried his hand first as a professional footballer in the late 1970s. He never made the first team, but he played for four years in various leagues. Ankle fractures put an end to his career in 1982, and he eventually wound up in television where he appeared first as a presenter of the National Lottery on the BBC before hosting several game shows for ITV. Walsh moved from this into acting, eventually becoming a regular on *Coronation Street* (2004–06). Following his tenure there, Walsh appeared as the villain in a 2008 *Sarah Jane Adventures* serial "Day of the Clown."

His breakthrough acting role came in 2009 when he was cast by Chris Chibnall as DS Ronnie Brooks in *Law & Order: U.K.* (playing what was essentially the Lenny Briscoe role in the U.S. version). He played the role until the series' cancellation in 2014. Around the same time, Walsh became the presenter of *The Chase*, a popular British game show, since it began in 2009. Walsh was such a fan favourite, he even released a number of celebrity crossover albums, the first of which became the biggest-selling debut album by a British artist in 2016!

A supporter of Arsenal, Chris Chibnall added insult to injury by making Walsh's character on *Doctor Who* a supporter of West Ham. And yet Walsh managed to secure from West Ham FC a scarf and a vintage pin from the club for Graham to wear — because Bradley Walsh is just that popular.

# 11.05 The Tsuranga Conundrum

**Written by** Chris Chibnall **Directed by** Jennifer Perrott
**Original airdate** November 4, 2018

**The Big Idea** When Team TARDIS accidentally sets off a sonic bomb, they're brought on board a medical ship. But something is eating through the ship . . .

**Roots and References** *Casualty* and other U.K. medical dramas (the various simultaneous crises in a hospital setting); *Gremlins* and *Lilo and Stitch* (the Pting is kind of a cross between both). Graham's a big fan of *Call the Midwife* (although he looks away at the squeamish bits), while the Doctor gives a shout-out to the musical *Hamilton*.

**Adventures in Time and Space** When the Doctor is looking at the hologram of the Pting, a blink-and-you'll-miss-it quickfire series of images flashes by, showing

Davros, a Cyberman, an Ood, a Weeping Angel, a Slitheen, a Sontaran, a Silent, a Silurian and a Zygon. You probably know who they are by now . . .

**Unfinished Business** Ryan's mother died of a heart attack when he was 13, and he was the one who found her. Ryan hasn't seen his father for a year, and their last conversation didn't go well. Yoss feeling unfit to raise a baby gives Ryan insight into what his dad must have been feeling when he was born. This in turns helps Ryan to encourage Yoss to accept his baby.

**Who Is the Doctor?** In contrast to previous Doctors, this one is prepared to apologize and admit when she's wrong, as she does here when attempting to bully Astos into turning the ship around. She maintains a sense of optimism, looking at life as a series of problems to be solved, with solutions that will turn up eventually. She's mentioned in the Tsuranga Book of Celebrants, has an ecto-spleen and carries a stethoscope in her coat pocket (as the tenth Doctor sometimes did). She's a big fan of the musical *Hamilton* (she's seen all 900 casts). She describes herself as a doctor of medicine, science, engineering, candy floss, LEGO, philosophy, music, problems and people — but mostly hope. She willingly participates in the quasi-religious incantation ceremony in Eve Cicero's honour.

**The Doctor and Team TARDIS** While everyone is knocked out for several days by the sonic mine, the Doctor is affected much more strongly than the humans, either by the mine itself or the medication. She tells Yaz she's keeping score for all of them (as she gives Yaz ten points for realizing there's a bomb in the room they're in).

**Monster of the Week** The Pting is a short but deadly creature with an outsized head and huge mouth. It can survive in space without oxygen, moves with impressive speed and can digest any and all non-organic material. Thankfully, it's not carnivorous, but it seeks out energy. It can be stunned but is impossible to wound or kill, and its skin is poisonous.

**Stand Up and Cheer** Ryan's line to Yoss — "Mate, you're growing a person; I couldn't do that" — is hilarious.

**Roll Your Eyes** Call us old-fashioned, but that whizzy CG opening on the junk planet could have been done on location, and the money it saved could have been used to show General Cicero flying the ship through the asteroids.

**You're Not Making Any Sense** If something goes wrong with the escape pods on one of their medical ships, Resus One doesn't have the option of sending out rescue craft or talking to the medical personnel to see what happens? They just blow up the ship? Worse, the bomb is *pre-installed* by these trigger-happy medics. Is this a make-work project?

**Interesting Trivia** If you read the end credits, you'll see that the Pting was created by Tim Price. Usually such credits are to previous writers or producers for returning monsters, but this is the Pting's first appearance. So you might be wondering who Tim Price is and why he's credited with creating an alien we've never seen before. The answer goes back to the set-up of the season. Chris Chibnall proposed a writer's room, similar to how American TV shows like *Buffy* or *Lost* are constructed. Price, a Cardiff-based screenwriter and playwright whose credits include Billie Piper's *Secret Diary of a Call Girl*, was one of the early members, but the writers' room concept didn't work out, and Price didn't end up writing for the show.

The Doctor sets the bomb to explode in 51 seconds. Let's see how that works out. From the moment she sonics it, the scene lasts another 25 seconds, where they discuss *Hamilton*. The next Doctor and Yaz scene (where she draws the analogy to the mouse and the cheese) runs for 17 seconds. The one after that, where the Pting eventually arrives and hisses at them, is a long one: 37 seconds. Finally, the next scene ("Get a shift on!") runs for 20 seconds until the bomb explodes. Even assuming no time at all passed during the cutaways, that's 99 seconds from activation to explosion. If it really had been set for 51 seconds, the bomb should have exploded about the time the Pting was walking down the corridor, killing the Doctor and Yaz outright. (Presumably the Doctor was just messing with Yaz when she told her to pick a number between one and 100 and was always going to set the timer for 99 seconds. What if Yaz had chosen seven?)

**The TARDIS Chronometer** Seffilun 27 and the Tsuranga medical ship, the 67th century.

**Aw, Brilliant? (RS?)** There's a conundrum here, but it isn't the one involving a cute monster eating through my review versus my editor threatening to blow up my laptop remotely. Instead, it's the question of whether this story is any good or not.

Here's my problem with this season: the episodes are too long. Sometimes that can really work ("Rosa" doesn't drag in the slightest, for example), but I think they would have been better going the *Star Trek: Discovery* route and making the episodes as long as they needed to be, rather than forcing them all into the same structure. "The Tsuranga Conundrum" is a case in point. This would be a really gripping 42-minute episode, but, with ten extra minutes, it drags interminably, despite the attempt at frenetic pacing.

The death of Astos is an exciting sequence, the Pting is a great menace, and events move fast enough that you aren't thinking too deeply about them . . . until they don't. Somewhere around the point where the sibling rivalry results in two characters we don't particularly care about hugging, the episode's powers have completely failed it. Which is too bad, because there's a lot of exciting stuff here. There's a monster on board. And a ticking bomb. And a pregnant dude. And the only pilot is at death's door. And the qualified medic is dead. And the escape pods are gone. And . . .

It's all too much, with almost no time to breathe, until you hit your saturation point and the fifteenth crisis seems like another day at the Tsuranga office. Getting the Pting to eat the bomb is the perfect resolution, so why didn't the story end there?

Worse, the Tsuranga conundrum itself is incredibly contrived. The built-in bomb is just laughable (I'm not sure I'd ever dial 9-1-1 if every ambulance was laced with C4) and the danger from the asteroid belt almost nonexistent, because we don't see it. There's an attempt to raise the stakes *even more yet further and still all the more higher*! by having the Doctor incapacitated from the medical treatment, but it doesn't sit well, because her symptoms vanish for long periods, then return whenever it's mildly inconvenient.

The Ciceros piloting the ship is dull and even more clichéd than the hackneyed birth-in-a-crisis TV trope. Sibling rivalry is a fine topic . . . for children. But adult siblings with unresolved issues who've never said "I love you" until the last second? Please. This looks absolutely hilarious when it's a couple of middle-aged people. What next, will they go skateboarding together while licking lollipops and whining about their lack of pocket money?

Okay, so that's the bad half of my conundrum. But there's also a lot of good here too. In particular, the gender roles are absolutely outstanding.

The mechanics of the pregnancy crisis may play out precisely according to TV stereotype #47, but the fact that it's a man giving birth helps alleviate that. It's a great joke when it first appears, but the follow-through has a massive effect on the plot structure, because it forces the two male regulars to be sidelined from the main plot, as they're shunted into caretaker roles the way Rose or Donna have been in the past. Astos is introduced as a likeable, trustworthy, caring man . . . who's promptly killed in order to illustrate how dangerous the monster is. Durkas and Ronin are both subservient to the alpha female in their lives, both explicitly marked as holding roles that are less valued.

Meanwhile, the women are scientists and heroes. Mabli steps up to take Astos's place, while Eve is already established as a Hard-Bitten Hero With A Secret. In the meantime, we have the first proper female Doctor/female companion combination, as Yaz effectively functions as a solo companion for the bulk of the story, defending the antimatter drive, helping to trap the Pting and even heroically soccer-kicking it down a corridor, in exactly the way a male companion might have. I really like this, and I'd be perfectly fine with having a single female companion going forward.

However, it's the Doctor who comes across best of all in this traditional gender role inversion. She starts off by bullying her way through the ship's system, just the way any of her predecessors might have but pulls back once she's called on it and immediately proceeds to build bridges with Astos. That's a rejection of the male Doctor philosophy, but she's also resolutely an old-school Doctor-as-scientist here, fixing things and learning about creatures she's never encountered before. Her fangirling over the antimatter converter ("I love it . . . conceptually and actually") is fantastic, the perfect example for inspiring girls to love science in the way Tom Baker inspired boys, myself included.

So I'm stuck with trying to assess an episode that's 50% clichéd and dull, but 50% innovative and progressive. I think I'll just swallow the whole thing in one gulp and let it explode inside me, a dreamy look on my face as I drift away . . .

**Second Opinion (GB)** I think I like this episode a lot more than my co-author does. In particular, I really liked the relationship between the Ciceros. I thought the resolution was a lot more emotionally satisfying than grumpy question-mark boy did. In fact it was one of my favourite parts.

But that's not really what I want to talk about with "The Tsuranga Conundrum." I want to talk about how it's the best example of how *Doctor Who* has radically changed this season. Because *Doctor Who* . . . is now a procedural.

A procedural TV show is one in which, in each episode, a problem is introduced, investigated and solved. We know it best thanks to cop shows like *Law & Order* and *CSI* and *The Rookie*, but shows like *ER*, *House* and now *New Amsterdam* demonstrate that it also works in the medical realm. The procedural is a staple of TV. They're dramas that, no matter how good they are, have a straightforward formula. It's nicely self-contained while the cast's relationships and character arcs add a more serialized element. There are a lot of procedurals within genre television ranging from *Supernatural* to *The Flash* to *Arrow*.

*Doctor Who* was never like this. Under the previous two showrunners, *Doctor Who* was — and this is acknowledging it's never the same genre two weeks in a row — more of a fantasy show in terms of its construction. Once upon a time, there was a monster or a menace that terrorized people in a faraway land or somewhere close by, and the Doctor rid the world of that monster. The trappings of fantasy were quite clear: the emphasis was on a singular menace that the larger-than-life hero defeats, with lots of comedy and romance swirling around.

This season, *Doctor Who* stopped being that kind of a show, where a great evil is stopped each week by someone who makes giant soliloquies while doing it. Case in point is "The Tsuranga Conundrum."

If the Pting had been in Series Nine and not Series Eleven, it would be treated like some kind of a witty dragon-like monster that needed to be slayed or timey-wimeyed somewhere or somewhen. Now . . . it's an obstacle. It's incidental. The real problem is getting a space ambulance to safety while helping the people on board. The Pting isn't a dragon; it's a problem to be solved. And, honestly, one of my favourite parts of the episode is the Doctor figuring out a solution to the Pting.

However, as a procedural, *Doctor Who* is now going to live and die by the incidental character material. And some of it really works (like Astos's death and I would argue the Cicero family), and some of it really doesn't (like Yoss's pregnancy, which I did not find nearly as hilarious as my co-author did). Robert is totally right that the pacing is off as well. And I'm not so sure if portraying the Pting as such an adorable creature worked in its favour, either.

In the end, I came out liking "The Tsuranga Conundrum" more than I disliked it. But it's clear that *Doctor Who* is now an ensemble procedural. I don't mind that in the same way I didn't mind it being a fairy tale, a gothic horror or any number of different genres it has been over 55 years. Just do it well.

# 11.06 Demons of the Punjab

**Written by** Vinay Patel **Directed by** Jamie Childs
**Original airdate** November 11, 2018

**The Big Idea** When Yaz is given a broken old watch by her grandmother, she asks the Doctor to solve the mystery behind it — and discovers her Muslim grandmother married a Hindu during the Partition of India in 1947.

**Roots and References** Usually, we list things we've extrapolated from the episode in question. However, writer Vinay Patel recommended on Twitter several works he used for research for this story, including historian Yasmin Khan's 2008 history *The Great Partition*, Irfan Master's 2011 novel *A Beautiful Lie* and the short fiction of Pakistani writer Saadat Hasan Manto (1912–55).

**Adventures in Time and Space** The Doctor uses the TARDIS telepathic circuits to take the TARDIS to the watch's point of origin, a technique used in "Listen" and "Dark Water"/"Death in Heaven." The Doctor is all set to award Ryan a gold star when she realizes she previously was awarding points to her friends ("The Tsuranga Conundrum"). She mentions her past incarnations. It's also the first time this season the TARDIS's translation faculty is shown to work.

**Unfinished Business** We briefly see Yaz's family again and meet Yaz's grandmother, Umbreen.

**Who Is the Doctor?** At some point the Doctor officiated Einstein's wedding (presumably with Einstein's first wife; that marriage didn't go so well, by the way).

The Doctor speaks of love as something she believes in, saying, "Love, in all its forms, is the most powerful weapon we have, because love is a form of hope and, like hope, love abides in the face of everything."

**The Doctor and Team TARDIS** The Doctor takes Yaz back to find out about the watch, and once Yaz discovers the existence of Prem, the Doctor instantly regrets it, saying she's too nice. And yet she sticks with her friends and even officiates the doomed marriage of Prem and Umbreen. The Doctor asserts they can't change history, mostly because she can't countenance a world without Yaz.

**Monster of the Week** The Thijarians were once the deadliest of assassins but now have chosen to read the timewaves and become witnesses to those who die unacknowledged or alone. They have transmat technology and collect remembrances to make up for the loss of their own people, who died unwitnessed.

**Stand Up and Cheer** In a deeply emotional moment, the Thijarians mourn the death of Prem. The music is beautiful, as is the imagery as a hologram of Prem's head rises up to join the constellation of others who have died, or will soon die, in the Partition. It's hard to see this and not weep.

**Roll Your Eyes** The Thijarians' new mission is laudable, but they might want to learn to tone down being so threatening for no reason whatsoever. How about simply saying to people, "We're just here to mourn the dead"?

**You're Not Making Any Sense** How did no one realize that Bhakti the holy man was killed by a gunshot wound? Surely there would have been a hard-to-miss massive, bloody hole when they examined his body or prepared him for burial.

**Interesting Trivia** By 1947, Britain — which was suffering crippling debt after World War II — wanted to cease its rule of India, which was demanding sovereignty. Complicating matters was that the centuries-long coexistence of Hindus, Muslims and Sikhs had begun to dissolve into sectarian violence. Britain decided to split India into two independent nations: Hindu-majority India and Muslim-majority Pakistan. But the implementation was rushed by the new (and final) viceroy of India, Lord Mountbatten, who declared the border between the two new countries would be decided within five weeks. A British lawyer, Cyril Radcliffe, who had never been east of Paris, was appointed to determine how to split the territory. The result of the Partition was 14 million people — roughly half on each side — who found themselves in the "wrong" country, causing a mass migration that erupted into terrible sectarian violence. The reported number is that 200,000 people died, but the number of people killed could be as high as two million.

Both writer Vinay Patel and showrunner Chris Chibnall were keen to use the Partition as a backdrop for a story, but there were limitations in the portrayal due to *Doctor Who*'s family audience. The story fudges historical accuracy for the sake of a clearer story: there were many more Hindus like Prem who were against Partition (indeed, Mahatma Gandhi was one of them). The issue of borders at the time would not have been a concern for radicalized Hindus like Manish — and, given that the government of India didn't receive a copy of the plan for the borders until two days after the country was granted independence, it's doubtful that Manish could have seen even a preliminary version quite so soon.

While making this story, composer Segun Akinola decided to write music for traditional Indian instruments including the tabla and shehnai (all performed by South Asian artists). Akinola arranged for the *Doctor Who* theme to be played using those instruments as well, making it the first time that acoustic instruments were used to play the theme tune on television.

Before "Demons of the Punjab" was broadcast, Vinay Patel went home to visit his grandmother. Without knowing anything about this episode, she gave Patel a gift: his dead grandfather's broken old watch!

**The TARDIS Chronometer** On the newly defined India-Pakistan border in the Punjab region, August 17–18, 1947, with flashbacks to Singapore during World War II and a framing device set in present-day Sheffield.

**Aw, Brilliant? (GB)** Let me say this from the outset: "Demons of the Punjab" is a breathtaking story that takes *Doctor Who* to a place and time it's never been before and explores a deeply unsettling chapter in history to powerful effect.

But, let's be honest, this is not a factual portrayal of the Partition, any more than, say, "The Shakespeare Code" is a factual portrayal of life during the Elizabethan era. The Partition was a big, ugly, messy thing, and I recommend Vinay Patel's reading list to you to learn more about it. The more I've learned about the Partition, the more I think "Demons" does what it can, given its limitations, as opposed to capturing the full horror of it. But I think this speaks to how we deal with history nowadays — or rather how *television* deals with history nowadays.

The Partition was a difficult time in history, and television drama isn't a truth and reconciliation commission. Television has to make the stakes personal and relatable in order to make such an event understandable. Especially if you're producing *Doctor Who*, where you face the dilemma of having 50 minutes to convey to a family audience a historical event that ended in a massive tidal wave of sectarian violence where former neighbours literally killed the other, horrifically and violently . . . and most of the money you'll spend on the episode will be on the location (which is in Spain by the way, because going to India is prohibitively expensive) and a tiny cast.

In the face of this, "Demons of the Punjab" makes a virtue of going small. The emotional beats to do it are an intercultural wedding and two brothers:

one on the side of a multicultural India and one not. Is it perfect? No. For one thing, it picks a side in the conflict by focusing on Hindu sectarianism, while I think it could have pointed out that Prem would have been equally unsafe in Pakistan.

But does the episode carry the emotional weight to paint so compelling a picture that you'll go read about the actual Partition? The answer to that is: hell, yes!

Because that's what modern television is good at: conveying the emotional truth of a situation. Prem facing down his brother and a band of marauders that includes a fellow soldier is one of the most heartbreaking scenes on television, let alone *Doctor Who*, in 2018, because it speaks to the horror of historical violence as well as the violence we experience in today's world. Beautifully so.

But there is a cost to doing this in *Doctor Who*. The problem with "Demons of the Punjab" is that the boundary devised by (presumably) the writer and showrunner to make the Doctor and friends purely observers also renders the Doctor ineffective. And while I agree that an intergalactic superwoman has no place interceding in the real-life horror of the Partition, the problem is that the whole story is predicated around her being totally wrong about the Thijarians too, which I don't think needed to happen. Indeed, the Doctor's role could have been in ensuring that the Thijarians succeed in their mission, rather than effectively using the Thijarians only to stall the plot by making the Doctor (and the viewer) think they're a threat, when they're far from it.

What bothers me more is that this should be more of a personal story for Yaz . . . but it studiously avoids making the story Yaz's in any way. Look at how the scene is shot when Prem is killed: it's a medium shot with the Doctor in the foreground. Yaz is an afterthought, in the background. Graham gets the genuine emotional moment with Prem where he grapples with the foreknowledge of Prem's impending death as he tells him he's a good man moments before his doomed wedding — and the scene is utterly electric — but there isn't a similar emotional moment for Yaz to process that with Umbreen. (Instead, Yaz gets a plot dump where she learns why her nani picked Sheffield to live.) I find these choices completely frustrating. Yaz is the most underserved character this season; as this is a story about her family, this should be all about her. However, she gets a great scene with Graham where she's forced to come to terms with her grandmother's secrets, and that's it. I look at all the great scenes in this story — Graham with Prem, the Doctor challenging Manish, the Doctor walking away from Prem's murder — and all of them might have benefitted by using Yaz instead of (or with) the Doctor or Graham.

However, I want to praise "Demons of the Punjab," because there are things here that are unbelievably powerful. The wedding is beautiful, as is the Doctor's speech about love and Prem and Umbreen being, at that moment, the most powerful people in the universe — especially given that the Doctor knows Prem won't last past the next few hours. Jodie Whittaker is amazing in the scene where she faces Manish. (The way she steps in front of his rifle is gloriously un-self-conscious: this isn't heroism, this is just her way of being.) And the cast is amazing, particularly Shane Zaza and Amita Shuman, who vividly depict Prem and Umbreen as a perfect couple — a war-weary dreamer and someone who will work to make dreams come true — and a complicated couple as well. That's hard to do in 50 minutes (especially for Shuman, who has to somehow make her performance congruent with Leena Dhingra's portrayal of an older Umbreen, but she nails it).

And the ending is beautiful. On the one hand, we could have done this story without the Thijarians (particularly since their presence is to mislead everyone), but without them we wouldn't have the scene where we see Prem, who has been discarded by even his brother, remembered with all those dying in this genocide. And the tag scene finally gives Mandip Gill something to do as Yaz, as she tries to speak of this with Nani — and she lets her have her secrets.

That's a lovely moment that really gets to the heart of "Demons of the Punjab": history is the story of people. It's the story of your nan and the private things she never tells. That's beautiful. And tragic. And all too real.

**Second Opinion (RS?)** In 2013, Timothy Morton identified certain phenomena, such as global warming, as what he called hyperobjects: entities of such vast temporal and spatial dimensions that they defeat traditional ideas about what a thing is in the first place. These hyperobjects are such enormous tears in the structure of our world that they effectively mean the world — at least as we know it — has already ended. Depressingly, this is what we're up against these days, in everything from climate change to Trumpism to incels. Massive tidal waves that are ripping through our society, destroying it forever — and it's already too late.

Watching "Demons of the Punjab," I couldn't help but think that the Partition is a clear example of a hyperobject.

What do you do when something so massive overtakes society, pitting brother against brother, neighbour against neighbour? The bulk of this story is a holding pattern, as the Doctor and company deal with the distraction that is the Thijarians and celebrate a wedding. But the framing pattern is the massive societal shift that's underway around them, one that the Doctor — or anyone else — is entirely powerless to stop. "Nothing worse than when normal people lose their minds," says Prem, and he's right.

He was right then, and he's right now. What do you do when faced with a hyperobject? What anyone would do: run away. The only solution here is to flee, as both the Doctor's and Umbreen's parties (separately) do. Those who don't are either killed (like Prem) or converted (like Manish). The Doctor has a magic box that can take her away, but Umbreen takes on a different challenge: becoming an immigrant.

I'm sure being an immigrant in 1947 was no picnic. And it's no different now, with hyperobjects like ISIS destroying societies, and the only solution being to flee and hope that the new destination offers the same stability that Umbreen found in Sheffield. Unfortunately, this crashes head-on with the rise of the far right, itself another hyperobject.

And yet . . . in among all this, the story takes the time to celebrate the moments. The Doctor's wedding speech is lovely, and I guarantee nerd couples will be using this as their vows for years to come. The fact that everyone comes together to celebrate the happiness of a man they know is doomed is quite amazing and very human. We may not be able to fight the hyperobjects, but we can find the joy in the small moments anyway.

"Demons of the Punjab" is an outstanding story in its own right. But for what it illustrates about today's society, by way of analogy, it may be all too depressingly accurate. It also offers the only way out of these messes: we have to act with love and hope. Let's pray that it's enough.

## The Psychic Papers: *Doctor Who* Abroad

During the Classic Series, *Doctor Who* was mostly made in the BBC's studios in London and on location throughout Britain (but mostly the Home Counties; primarily in quarries, some would joke). In 1979, production manager (and future producer) John Nathan-Turner realized that a story set in 1930s Monte Carlo could be made in Paris inexpensively if there was a small crew and they ditched the period setting. The producers agreed, and "City of Death" was *Doctor Who's* first foray outside of Britain. During each of the 1983–85 seasons, Nathan-Turner had a story shot in a foreign locale, visiting the Netherlands in 1983's "Arc of Infinity," Lanzarote in the Canary Islands in 1984's "Planet of Fire" (there it acted as both Lanzarote and an alien planet) and Spain in 1985's "The Two Doctors." A trip to Singapore for the original 1986 season was planned and then nixed when that season was cancelled.

The Modern Series has been primarily filmed in Britain, though the setting of 2008's "The Fires of Pompeii" sent the cast and crew to the Cinecittà studios in

Rome, which has a massive ancient Roman backlot. In 2009, "Planet of the Dead" was partially made in the deserts of the United Arab Emirates. It wasn't until Steven Moffat became showrunner that using foreign locations became a regular occurrence (around the same time that air travel became less expensive). Two stories in Series Five, "The Vampires of Venice" and "Vincent and the Doctor" (both from 2010), used locations in Croatia to fill in for period locations in Venice and France, respectively. The snowy mountain wastes in "Asylum of the Daleks" were shot in the Sierra Nevada National Park in Spain, while a Western backlot in Spain doubled for the titular American Old West town in "A Town Called Mercy."

For years, stories set in America were filmed in Britain (or elsewhere, including the 1996 TV Movie, which used Vancouver for San Francisco). In 2011, "The Impossible Astronaut"/"Day of the Moon" was the first *Doctor Who* story to have principal filming in the U.S., with actors travelling to Utah. A BBC production (even with co-production money from BBC America) is not flush with cash, and the American actors working on it had to sign waivers indicating they were working on a "non-union independent film" in order to avoid running afoul of the actors' unions. In 2012, this was followed up with the Modern Series' last foray (to date) in America, a three-day shoot in New York City for "The Angels Take Manhattan." An New York–style backlot in Sofia, Bulgaria, was employed for "The Return of Doctor Mysterio."

During the Peter Capaldi era, trips to various places in the Canary Islands included Lanzarote ("Kill the Moon"), Tenerife ("The Magician's Apprentice"/"The Witch's Familiar") and Fuerte Ventura ("Hell Bent"). "Smile" was largely shot on location at the City of Arts and Sciences in Valencia, Spain. With the advent of Jodie Whittaker's Doctor, South Africa (and its studio backlots) became the place to go abroad, for "The Ghost Monument" and "Rosa" (where Cape Town stood in for Montgomery, Alabama), while "Demons of the Punjab" was filmed in the Granada province of Spain. It wasn't quite the Indian subcontinent, but at least it wasn't in the Home Counties!

## Mandip Gill

Born in Leeds in 1988, Mandip Gill had her first blush of stardom in a role in the Channel 4 soap *Hollyoaks*, where she was a central member of the ensemble cast for three years from 2012 to 2015. (Ironically, she started around the same time her fellow *Doctor Who* actor Tosin Cole was leaving; they only briefly overlapped!) Guest roles in TV's *Doctors*, *Casualty* and *Love, Lies and Records* followed, before she was cast as companion Yaz. Gill was also a lead in the 2019 film *The Flood*.

# 11.07 Kerblam!

**Written by** Pete McTighe **Directed by** Jennifer Perrott

**Original airdate** November 18, 2018

**The Big Idea** Delivery for the Doctor. Kerblam is the galaxy's biggest retailer but when the Doctor's fez comes with a note for help, she and her friends go to Kerblam's headquarters to investigate.

**Roots and References** A small online concern known as Amazon.com (Kerblam); the 1990 film *Total Recall* (the Kerblam Postman resembles the JohnnyCab driver); *Toy Story 2* (the conveyer system seems inspired by the airport baggage system in that film).

**Adventures in Time and Space** The Doctor receives a fez from Kerblam, the headwear of choice of the Doctor's eleventh incarnation. ("Still me?" she asks.) The Doctor uses Venusian aikido again (used most recently in "The Ghost Monument," but it dates back to 1970's "Inferno"). As they hide in the alcove, the Doctor prepares to regale Yaz and Ryan about the events of 2008's "The Unicorn and the Wasp." The Doctor talks about robophobia (meant as an irrational terror of robots back in 1977's "The Robots of Death" but now used to describe anti-robot slurs) and mentions some of her best friends being robots (which we presume is a reference to the Doctor's robotic dog and best friend K9 but could equally apply to Handles from "The Time of the Doctor").

**Unfinished Business** Ryan's dyspraxia comes to the fore again as he talks about how he had to adjust to warehouse work and as he has to jump onto the conveyer system.

**Who Is the Doctor?** She doesn't like bullies, conspiracies or people being in danger. (Unfortunately, all three are happening around her at this point.) She means it too: she gets in Slade's face and calls him out for bullying Kira.

**The Doctor and Team TARDIS** The Doctor praises Yaz's and Ryan's skills as detectives. When Yaz asks if she could make a request of the Doctor, she tells her, "Always."

**Monster of the Week** The Kerblam Men are humanoid robots that are either TeamMates (who supervise operations) or Postmen (who deliver packages). The Postmen are beloved (by the Doctor, anyway) while the TeamMates are unctuous busybodies ("Great conversation, guys! But unnecessary talking can lead to efficiency reductions. Why not pick up the pace a little?"). Both unfortunately can be a little bit . . . murder-y.

**Stand Up and Cheer** The climax is probably the best of any story this season as the Doctor uses Twirly, the comical early version of Kerblam's delivery robots, to get all the Postmen to deliver their packages to themselves — to deadly effect. The scene has comedy (Twirly to the Doctor: "Customers with your current medical symptoms browsed blood-pressure medication") and genuine pathos as Graham and the Doctor try to get Charlie to turn back. And it ends perfectly, with the Doctor, safely teleported to the lobby, forlornly saying the Kerblam corporate slogan.

**Roll Your Eyes** Does anyone actually believe Judy — who until now has been a devoted disciple of corporate messaging — when she talks about Kerblam working towards becoming a mostly human workforce from now on?

**You're Not Making Any Sense** The twist that Kerblam's system was actually in the right might have played better had it not killed Kira for no good reason other than to try to teach a sociopathic zealot like Charlie empathy. But it's more mind-bogglingly shameful that the Doctor doesn't condemn the system for it.

**Interesting Trivia** For the second episode in a row, the entire story is predicated on the Doctor being wrong about what's going on. Kerblam's system, which knew what Charlie was doing and had brought the Doctor there, had deliberately put the Doctor on maintenance duty so she could discover what Charlie was getting up to . . . only she changed her GroupLoop because she thought she'd learn more in packing. This is leaving aside the problem of why, instead of saying "help me" to the Doctor, the system doesn't just say, "Charlie Duffy in maintenance is about to kill everyone." Presumably Charlie put restrictions on the system so it couldn't identify him, and the system had to act covertly (though sending a TeamMate to murder Charlie is pretty damn overt).

One of the interesting things this story does is in how it uses past continuity. Prior to this season, we had an easter-egg approach: objects from *Doctor Who*'s distant past would turn up randomly. Here it's more targeted and thoughtful — and more like how the Classic Series did it in the 1960s and 1970s. Back then, continuity to past *Doctor Who* was what might be remembered off-hand by a casual viewer — so the fourth Doctor would find a frilled shirt of his third incarnation in the TARDIS secondary control room in 1976's "The Masque of Mandragora," for example. Here, the Doctor receives a parcel from Kerblam containing a fez because that's what casual viewers might remember from the recent past.

**The TARDIS Chronometer** The headquarters of Kerblam, which is on a moon orbiting the planet Kandoka.

**Aw, Brilliant? (GB)** On the surface of things, "Kerblam!" feels like a throwback. It's the first story this season to have a really traditional monster, and the procedural element focuses more on the *Doctor Who*–friendly idea of a murder mystery. To no one's surprise, Jodie Whittaker's Doctor and her friends thrive in a format where there's murder and mayhem every five minutes or so. The Kerblam Men are perfect monsters in part because of the design but mostly the voices by Matthew Gravelle and the amazing decision to make them sound cheery, like an automated voicemail system from Hell.

Getting away from the trappings, there are things that aren't working here, and some of them are things that haven't been working for a while. The Doctor for one. Don't get me wrong, Jodie Whittaker is stupendous here — her banter with Slade as she defends Kira from his bullying is amazing. But . . . she's wrong about what's really happening at Kerblam at every turn. This is something that really sticks out once you have the whole picture, because the Doctor actively thwarted the system's attempt to put her on the right track by assigning her to maintenance. She's wrong about Slade, she's wrong about Judy, she forgets she has her GroupLoop on, which means she can be tracked . . . and she doesn't even guess that Charlie has anything to do with it, even though all the clues are easily in front of her.

All that might be okay, except she was wrong about the Thijarians last episode, and she was wrong about wanting to take Tsuranga back to the TARDIS the week before that, and it goes all the way back to her thinking the hunt in "The Woman Who Fell to Earth" was an invasion. The Doctor is wrong *a lot* this season. On the one hand, I think we should commend Chris Chibnall and his writers for making the Doctor more fallible (it was only a season and a half ago that the Doctor was a Sherlockian superhuman who calculated a successful dive from a high tower into a moat in mere seconds) but . . . at some point the Doctor needs to be right about something important. Having her not put the pieces together to see that Charlie's behind it all the second Kira is abducted (or shortly after) diminishes her as a character, especially given her most recent (male) predecessors were portrayed as big brains who were capable of figuring out the big picture instantly. The reason the Doctor is a hero is because the Doctor is smarter than everyone. It's time the thirteenth Doctor showed this.

There are things this story really gets right, though — indeed, more than many episodes this season. For one thing, it shows and doesn't tell at *almost* every opportunity. (I do think we could have stood seeing another victim before the action started, even seen Slade come upon the scene of the disappearance, but compared to "The Ghost Monument" or "The Tsuranga Conundrum," that's pretty minor.) Here it spends the VFX budget wisely, on the climax. Ryan, Yaz and Charlie on the system conveyer belts is one of the best CG-generated sequences *Doctor Who* has done in recent memory. Ryan's dyspraxia adds some interesting stakes to it, but it's the comedy touch of Ryan accidentally knocking

Charlie off the belt that adds jeopardy and some great laughs to the mix. Pete McTighe brings a really deft comedic touch to "Kerblam!"; Twirly in particular is an inspired creation. I really enjoyed the satire on Amazon and its culture. It's also shrewdly cast. Lee Mack, who plays Dan, isn't really known outside the U.K., but he's arguably the most famous U.K. TV star on *Doctor Who* in about a decade. And rather like casting Janet Leigh in *Psycho*, he's the character you feel immediate sympathy for . . . so it's a shock when he's killed off only a third of the way in.

All that said, it's a shame it scores an own goal this late in the game.

"Kerblam!" is the latest victim of a problem endemic to current *Doctor Who*: it's forgotten that the devil is in the details. This story attempts the bravura idea that the artificial intelligence isn't behind the killings at all but is trying to prevent them. (Furthermore, it doubles down by having the killer turn out to be a woke pro-human terrorist.) But it fails to stick the landing. Killing Kira is, on the one hand, one of those brave storytelling choices where you elicit real sympathy for a character (and, boy howdy, Claudia Jessie plays the hapless innocent like she's in a 1920s silent melodrama) so that you can see the horror of what's going on. Only, it's the side of the conflict we're supposed to care about that kills her. And the wrongheadedness is confounded further because at no point does the Doctor — who was moved by Kira's plight enough to get in the face of a bully over it — do anything more than provide exposition about why they might have done it. Details like this ruin what was, until then, a clever twist. And details like this get missed again and again this season.

But there's something in "Kerblam!" we've seen only rarely this season that I hope paves the way forward: the climax is clever, with huge stakes (the Kerblam Men filling a hangar is great), and the Doctor gets to improvise her way out of a huge jam in a credible and fun way. It's an amazing, traditional, big-flourish moment for the Doctor, the likes of which we haven't seen a lot of lately. Plus it redeems the Doctor's dumb streak, slightly. I'm thrilled to see it return, and I think, as good as the ensemble is, the Doctor is our hero and she needs more moments to shine. I hope we don't forget the lesson of this.

For a story that on the surface seems like a throwback, "Kerblam!" is a perfect summing up of everything that's right and wrong about *Doctor Who* right now — and a perfect summing up of the potential it has to be so much better.

**Second Opinion (RS?)** Steven Moffat recently made the point that *Doctor Who* is not just for pinko lefties like him (or me). Instead, the genius of *Doctor Who* is that it's a show that everyone can watch, from the apolitical (e.g., children) to readers of the *Daily Mail*. As an unabashed liberal myself, I agree entirely.

But of course, politically speaking, it usually isn't. The very nature of the show means the Doctor is usually on the side of the underdog and not too concerned with tax breaks for the rich or dismantling the welfare state or policing gay marriage. The Doctor's pretty resolutely small-L liberal, and the show largely stays away from politics, which is mostly as it should be.

"Kerblam!" doesn't do that. Like "Kill the Moon" or the Zygon two-parter, here we have a very strong episode that's putting its nose into a political debate and making a stand. However, it goes to some strange places to do so.

I don't agree at all with the Doctor when she says that the system isn't the problem. Especially not when the system is literally murdering people but everyone turns a blind eye, as my co-author ably illustrates. Yes, Charlie is in the wrong, but one fanatical nutjob is actually a lot less capable of inflicting damage than an entire system designed to oppress people and provide only the merest of opportunities, as it's already done before the episode starts.

But fair enough if that's where the episode wants to go. *Doctor Who* doesn't always need to share my politics, so if the Doctor wants to perpetuate a system that oppresses workers, I guess that's up to her. Where this looks weird, however, is in having a middle-aged writer railing against those woke millennials who want to make a better life. The message here: accept your lot and let the system eat away at your rights. It's what the Doctor would do — at least in this episode. No, the problem here is that it's punching down, not up. It's very easy to make fun of those whiny millennials for wanting a better life, but it's a cheap shot made by someone who never had to cope with crippling debt or wage stagnation freezing them out of home ownership or global warming destroying their future. Much better to keep things as they are, with happy consumers buying a bunch of junk and nobody questioning the human toll.

Worse, it's a cheat. At the beginning of the story, Judy says that 10% of Kerblam's employees are people. But Charlie's justification at the end of the story is that only 10% of the humans have jobs. These are not the same things at all.

Also, I disagree with my co-author that the Doctor being wrong is a problem. I don't think it is. Part of the problem these days is that too many people are afraid to admit they're wrong, about anything. We're all wrong sometimes. What matters is what you do about it. To me, this is a Doctor who doesn't come in with all the answers, the way her predecessors would have, but rather someone who tries out ideas and is willing to admit fault and update her thinking if she's mistaken. That's actually pretty heroic.

I personally wish she'd realize that her views on the Kerblam system also fall into this category and update accordingly. But that's just me.

# 11.08 The Witchfinders

**Written by** Joy Wilkinson **Directed by** Sallie Aprahamian

**Original airdate** November 25, 2018

**The Big Idea** The Bilehurst Cragg witch trials have killed 35 people. The Doctor tries to intervene, but the arrival of King James means she herself is accused of being a witch.

**Roots and References** Arthur Miller's 1953 play *The Crucible* (the witch trials); the 1968 film *Night of the Living Dead* (the zombie women). Graham quotes from the 1994 film *Pulp Fiction*, which itself quotes from Ezekiel in the Bible. The Doctor quotes Clarke's law when she says that any sufficiently advanced technology is indistinguishable from magic.

**Adventures in Time and Space** Team TARDIS were aiming for the coronation of Elizabeth I (odd given how things turned out for the Doctor after the events of "The Day of the Doctor" and 2007's "The Shakespeare Code"). The Doctor once spent a wet weekend with Houdini (first mentioned in 1974's "Planet of the Spiders"), learning how to escape from chains underwater.

**Unfinished Business** Yaz was bullied at school by Izzy Flint, who turned the whole class against her for a year. She told herself she'd eventually stand up to the Izzy Flints of this world.

**Who Is the Doctor?** She identifies with other women for the first time, railing against being patronized. She likes Willa's gran's philosophy that there's enough wonder in nature without making things up.

**The Doctor and Team TARDIS** Both the Doctor and Graham take pains to point out that they have a very flat team structure (though Graham does give the Doctor his Witchfinder General's hat). The Doctor once again tries out "gang," "fam" and "team," but seems to settle on the latter.

**Monster of the Week** The Morax were an alien army who were imprisoned under Pendle Hill for war crimes. They initially manifest as living mud that takes the form of tendrils under the ground. However, they can also reanimate the dead, filling them, and can infect living people.

**Stand Up and Cheer** The Doctor's impassioned speech to King James is stirring and moving: "We want certainty, security, to believe that people are evil or heroic. But that's not how people are." She plays on psychology to try to get through to him, mentioning his mother and the hurt inside him. The speech doesn't directly work, because he immediately sentences her to be dunked. However, it clearly affects him and sows enough seeds that he comes on board later. It's also pretty powerful in its own right, despite the Doctor being tied to a tree at the time.

**Roll Your Eyes** The enormous, long, wet, uh, tentacle that shoots out of the stump when it gets, erm, excited, aiming to — ahem — "fill" the king . . . might . . . and we're only suggesting this . . . be a little bit rude.

**You're Not Making Any Sense** As Graham points out, a lock that can be broken by anyone with an axe isn't much of a security system for a deadly army. Yes, the Doctor points out that it's old . . . but does this mean anyone who dislikes the tree on Pendle Hill will release an army of living mud determined to fill everyone on the planet? What happens when the Lancashire council decides to build condos there?

**Interesting Trivia** Despite dying at age 58, King James was king of Scotland for over 57 years, the longest reign of any Scottish king at that time. He wasn't king of England until later in life, however, as the two countries had separate crowns until they were united in 1603, upon the death of Elizabeth I, whereupon James became king of England and Ireland as well. As well as being responsible for the translation of the Bible that's still in use today, his obsession with witchcraft led him to write *Daemonologie*, the book that the Doctor and Graham find on Becka's bedside table — which informed the background of Shakespeare's *Macbeth*. Oh, and one of the things begun during his era was the English colonization of a little place called North America. James's sexuality has been subject to speculation by historians: he had very intimate relationships with his male advisors, but he also decried sodomy. Given his active flirtation with Ryan, we know where "The Witchfinders" lands on this debate. After all the (quite justified) fears he had of assassination, not least of which was the Gunpowder Plot engineered by one Guy Fawkes, he ultimately died of natural causes.

King James's interest in witch hunts sprang from a visit to Denmark, which led to the Witchcraft Act of 1563, where witchcraft was made a capital crime. Several people were convicted of using witchcraft to send storms against James's ship in a trial where James played both victim and investigator. Several thousand people were tried for witchcraft, of whom three-quarters were women, although James himself became sceptical in later years and sought to limit prosecutions. The trials outlasted King James by some time, with the last execution in 1706, the last trial in 1727 and the Witchcraft Act being repealed in 1736. The Salem witch trials of the late 1600s overlapped with this later period, with the new colony inheriting many of the fears from its motherland. Scholarly estimates claim that between 40,000 and 60,000 people, mostly women, were executed as witches during this time.

Graham might also want to go on a better walking tour of Pendle: the most famous of the witch trials happened in Pendle in 1612 when 12 people (eight women and four men) from two families were charged and executed for witch-craft. Both families were, like Old Mother Twiston, acting as local healers (or making money off it and pretending to be witches).

King James mentions the necromancer Dr. Dee. This is John Dee, who was a mathematician, occultist and advisor to Queen Elizabeth I during the late 16th century. He died early in the 17th century, about the time this story is set. He was in favour of imperial expansion, and his expertise in navigation meant that he not only trained many of England's captains but is also credited with coining the term "British Empire."

**The TARDIS Chronometer** Bilehurst Cragg, Lancashire, early 17th century.

**Aw, Brilliant? (RS?)** I love *Doctor Who* deeply and passionately, but it is a bit ridiculous.

One of the conceits of the series is that certain things kind of get taken for granted. People are introduced to someone called "the Doctor" and rarely question that as a name. Credentials aren't double-checked, and nobody comments on the wildly out-of-date fashions or impossible clothing. Historical episodes see future technology being used with handwaving explanations. An eccentric scientist turns up and blags her way through the local situation, often knowing way more than she possibly could, but everybody just rolls with it.

Usually, this makes perfect sense, because having episodes full of people repeatedly saying, "Yes, but Doctor WHO?" or forcing Team TARDIS to wait in line until verification documents can turn up would be the height of boredom. But every so often, the rules get broken.

"The Witchfinders" is a perfect example of this. The first part of the story sees the Doctor and company bluster through, with jokey explanations and the usual impetus to get on with the plot. However, all the markers come back to haunt them here, as things like the Doctor's name or the sonic screwdriver become cause for suspicion, while the friendly guest star of the week is the one who betrays them. Even the psychic paper fails in the face of the societal sexism.

When Jodie Whittaker took on the role of the Doctor, one of the smartest things they did was to have a light touch around the fact that the Doctor was now a woman. Thus far this season, there have been a few references here and there, but it barely had any effect on the story. Surrounding her with a team of people who defer to her was a good move, as it means she comes in with ready-made authority (Robertson being shouted down by Team TARDIS when he questions her in "Arachnids in the U.K." is a great example of this). I think this is a case where actions were better than words: rather than having a big speech, simply show her being competent and already having the authority.

However, it's now far enough into the season that it's good to deal with the fact that a woman during most of history was always going to face an uphill battle. Setting the story amid the witch trials of the 17th century was a stroke of genius, because it brings this into focus. And it makes the story reflect the season in microcosm: first it builds her up, then it tears her down, in order to see what she's really made of.

The arrival of King James in the plot means that every piece of the Doctor's established authority is challenged, both explicitly and implicitly, with a stream of microaggressions and a flat-out refusal to believe she could know what she's talking about. Even when complimenting her, James assumes that women are only good for snooping and gossip and must of course be subservient to men.

The Doctor herself makes an excellent point, that if she were still a bloke she could simply get on with the job and not waste time defending herself. It's the kind of problem that didn't exist for the Peter Capaldi or Matt Smith Doctors, yet it stymies her enormously here, leading to a whole new plot direction as the Doctor is arrested and tied up, her only remaining power the force of her words.

In this, she's ably balanced by Alan Cumming's bravura performance as King James. Every word out of his mouth in the first half is hilarious, from his overt flirting with Ryan to his pride in his implements of torture or the way that attempts to keep him "safe" are met with diatribes about nowhere being safe and Satan being everywhere. When he turns on the Doctor, Cumming transforms that comedy into deadly menace, the single-minded focus on witches proving to be terrifying rather than comedic. The fact that the Doctor almost gets through to him while tied up but then loses the hold she has on him is perfectly conveyed through Cumming's facial expressions. A lesser actor would have played that scene straight. Then, at the end, he goes back to his amusing former self, his eyes lighting up at Ryan's "protector" role and his witchcraft/Satan obsession returning to the realm of the comedic.

If it weren't for dealing with the sexism head-on, "The Witchfinders" would be a pretty generic story. Instead, it takes the fundamentals of *Doctor Who* and breaks them down, adding in layers of deeply uncomfortable realism to the situation. Many people watch *Doctor Who* for the escapism, but, as the foundering of the psychic paper illustrates, sometimes there's no escaping the overwhelming nature of society's prejudices. It's important that they dealt with it, even though you wouldn't want every episode to be like this. Hopefully next week *Doctor Who* can go back to being pleasingly ridiculous . . .

**Second Opinion (GB)** Back in the mists of time, I took a Women's Studies class in university, and they showed a documentary about the witch trials called *The Burning Time*. While most scholars dispute the documentary's claim around the number of women killed in the trials, it was a stark depiction of a large-scale massacre of women like Willa's gran, who had a point of view or knowledge that made her a little bit different.

"The Witchfinders" neatly circumvents some of the less palatable aspects of the witch killings by having a female antagonist behind those in Bilehurst Cragg, thanks to Becka Savage (more on her in a minute) and by having Becka turn into a *Doctor Who* monster for the story's final act. But in other ways it gets it chillingly right, like the way the Doctor and friends enter a village that's having a party right before Old Mother Twiston is executed on a ducking stool.

I agree with my co-author that the setting made "The Witchfinders" the perfect story to confront that our favourite program has changed the lead's gender. What I love about it is that it builds an amazing *Doctor Who* story around all that business. Alan Cumming is all that's been said and more. Fun fact: I rewatched "The Witchfinders" on Boxing Day with my goddaughter, and I can confirm that Cumming's portrayal of King James is officially camper than Christmas.

Cumming isn't the only intriguing character on the scene here. Becka Savage is monstrous even before the Morax take her over — and yet she isn't a cipher, either. She's motivated by mundane pettiness (the fact that this whole thing started because she cut down a tree that obstructed her view is brilliant) and desperation to not be exposed as a witch herself. Siobhan Finneran is amazing in the scene where Becka comes clean about everything. It's haunting, because you want to hate her for all the women she's killed out of a lie, but you pity her as well. At the same time, I especially love the journey Willa Twiston takes in this story, as she's told to stand up to bullies, fails to do so and eventually then finds the strength to. The added bonus is Yaz finally getting something to do, which is welcome.

Even more than "Kerblam!" this is a story that could not have been made by any previous regime in *Doctor Who*: the procedural mandate is temporarily lifted to give us a third-act reveal of an alien invasion (one that's fairly easily dispatched, but, hey, it's fun to see it defeated by James's ridiculous flouncing). The Doctor, in spite of the hostility she experiences towards her new gender, is really heroic (and has some of her best scenes this season here as well). What makes this the best story of the season, though, is the very human failings, and evil, at the heart of things.

# 11.09 It Takes You Away

**Written by** Ed Hime **Directed by** Jamie Childs

**Original airdate** December 2, 2018

**The Big Idea** The Doctor and Team TARDIS find a cottage in Norway that's barricaded, the sounds of monsters outside and a portal in a mirror upstairs. But it's about to get a whole lot stranger than that . . .

**Roots and References** *Stranger Things* (the anti-zone, while the mirror world is basically a cleaned-up version of the Upside Down); *The Girl with the Dragon Tattoo* (a damaged young girl in Scandinavia); Lewis Carroll's 1871 novel, *Through the Looking-Glass, and What Alice Found There* (the mirror as a portal to a world that's mad and backwards); the 1972 Soviet science-fiction film *Solaris* (alien intelligences manifesting themselves as dead people); the 2004 film *The Village* (the faked monsters); the TV series *Angel* (the conduit to the senior partners is a strange little girl sitting in a white room). Erik wears a T-shirt featuring the logo from the American thrash metal band Slayer, while Hanne and Yaz bond over the Arctic Monkeys, a Sheffield-based rock band.

**Adventures in Time and Space** Granny Five told the young Doctor that Granny Two was a secret agent for the Zygons. Graham tells Grace about meeting Rosa Parks and going to an alien planet ("Rosa" and "The Ghost Monument"). Yaz suggests reversing the polarity of the sonic screwdriver, which was something the third Doctor liked doing a lot (1972's "The Sea Devils"). The Doctor has remarkable taste buds that can identify where she is with ridiculous specificity (which follows from the Doctor's sense of smell doing the same in stories like in 2008's "The Unicorn and the Wasp").

**Unfinished Business** Graham always comes prepared for the fact that their adventures can go a long time without food and now carries sandwiches in his pocket (it's odd that this preparation didn't extend to including a Ziploc bag, though). Ryan's first assumption about Hanne's dad, based on his own life experience, is that he's run away . . . which turns out to be essentially correct. Graham finds Grace in the mirror world, but she turns out to be a fake, as the real one would never leave Ryan in danger. Grace loved frogs, and once both Graham and Ryan got her a frog necklace for the same Christmas. Sensing his pain over having seen Grace again, Ryan finally calls Graham "Granddad."

**Who Is the Doctor?** She deceives Hanne outright, writing a note about her father's presumed death on a wall so she can't see it. She had seven grandmothers, but Granny Five was her favourite and used to tell her bedtime stories. She easily admits to being scared, in contrast to her predecessors (see "Hide" or

"Heaven Sent" for how difficult this was in the past). She offers herself to the Solitract on the grounds that she's seen more, lived longer, loved more and lost more than anyone else.

**The Doctor and Team TARDIS** The Doctor and Graham go head to head over his feelings for Grace. He wants to stay in the mirror world with Grace, but the Doctor has to convince him that the real world is more important, telling him that what he's seeing is merely furniture with a pulse and that he has to reject the Solitract version of Grace.

**Monster of the Week** The Solitract is an energy from before time that's incompatible with our own universe, ruining all its basic ideas. It's a separate universe that's also a consciousness, and it just wants to be connected to our world. Rejecting it gets you thrown through the mirror into the anti-zone.

**Stand Up and Cheer** The episode's final confrontation goes against every expectation from *Doctor Who*, television drama — or indeed life. First, it's with a talking frog. Second, it's in a white void with one actor, pouring her heart out. Third, it's about friendship. Fourth, it's with a *talking frog*. Did we mention the talking frog?! This is gloriously mad.

**Roll Your Eyes** Instead of barricading the house and recording imaginary monster noises, why didn't Erik just bring his daughter into the mirror world so they could all be together? (Yes, it would have failed, but he didn't know this.)

**You're Not Making Any Sense** The entire reason the Doctor is suspicious of the cottage is because it's in Norway and it has no smoke coming out. Except . . . Hanne is living there, in Norway, so why isn't smoke coming out?

**Interesting Trivia** Ellie Wallwork, who played Hanne, is the first blind actress to appear in *Doctor Who*. Although blind characters have featured in the show before, this was the first time the actor shared the condition. Wallwork has been blind since birth, although — as you can imagine — it didn't stop people complaining on Twitter that she couldn't act blind. Wallwork is on Twitter herself and found this hilarious.

Erik's T-shirt is an adept touch. The logo for the band Slayer is reversed when we meet him in the mirror world, only to be righted once he returns home. In fact, if you look carefully, you'll notice that many more details are reversed, such as the Doctor's and Graham's hair parts. This only applies to the mirror world: they're all back to normal in the anti-zone.

Before the episode aired, Paul Sturgess, the tallest basketball player in the world, posted a photo of himself from the anti-zone, dressed as an alien with a blank face, long tubular snout and clawed fingers, towering over the Doctor, Yaz and Ribbons. It wasn't a spoiler, however, because he'd already been informed that all his scenes as this creature had been cut. At seven-foot-eight, Sturgess is currently the tallest man in Britain, having inherited the title after the death of Neil Fingleton, who played the Fisher King in "Before the Flood" and sadly only lived to age 36.

**The TARDIS Chronometer** Norway, 2018.

**Aw, Brilliant? (RS?)** I love *Doctor Who* deeply and passionately, but it is a bit ridiculous. And thank goodness for that.

Whether it's a show featuring farting aliens faking an invasion with a space pig or Edvard Munch–esque creatures that no one can remember manipulating Richard Nixon or emoji robots controlled by a building enforcing happiness on a deserted colony, one of the best things about *Doctor Who* is its willingness to grab the ridiculous and run with it. Sometimes they approach it completely po-faced, treating a hospital on the moon being inspected by rhino police as the most serious thing ever, but sometimes the show is in on the joke and laughs along with us at a giant spider using a bride to bring her eggs back from the centre of the Earth or the Doctor's wife stealing her new husband's head for the diamond inside it.

What's great about this is that it appeals to the child in all of us and makes the point that sometimes you just need to step back and have a bit of a laugh. I think we can all use that, these days more than ever. The latter part of the Tom Baker era was predicated upon the Doctor being wittier than the villains and pointing out that people with no sense of humour were the worst. Any time we hark back to that is fine by me.

As you might be able to guess by now, I absolutely adore "It Takes You Away." Don't get me wrong, I really love the serious stories too, when they're done well. The three historicals this season have been excellent. But *Doctor Who* sorely needs a dose of the ludicrous every so often, and this one is just loopy.

Okay, so Erik barricading his disabled daughter in her house and trauma-tizing her with recorded noises is pretty awful, as is the fact that the Doctor doesn't condemn him at the end, with the episode instead reuniting them as a happy family, which is extremely . . .

. . . hey, you know what? I kind of don't mind, just this once, because it's such a bonkers thing to do. A fake monster outside is such a bizarre way to discipline a teenager that you almost want to give points for effort. On the (somewhat) bright side, Erik believes utterly in Hanne's ability to take care of herself, which is weirdly touching, while she makes the point that he's not well, which goes a long way to soften the blow. And they do it while wearing their clothes backwards.

But what I really want to talk about is the Solitract. It's an amazingly out-there idea, an entire universe that is incompatible with our own but — and this is the kicker — just wants to be friends. And, best of all, it's represented by a talking frog. *On a white chair.* Oh. Em. Gee.

Yes, yes, this is really an excuse to bring Grace back in a way that honours the character and furthers Graham's grief, something that the season has been tackling remarkably well. The fact that both Grace and Trine are so authentic and remember their deaths is clever: it's a step beyond Bill's appearance in "Twice Upon a Time," where questions of what happened to her kept being sidestepped. Here they're dealt with head-on, and Grace feels more authentic here than Bill did then, despite the fact that this one is definitely fake. Interestingly, merely a season later, the "memories are who we are" concept has been entirely reversed. Surely if Grace remembers everything, including dying, then she functionally is Grace. Even if it's a trap, it's one that the Grace we see here shouldn't know about. That she willingly engages with Graham's test of her memories is good, while the fact that this sows the seeds for the appearance of the frog at the end is just divine.

The episode also throws in the scares, thanks to the anti-zone, with its flesh-eating moths and cannibalistic traders. My one criticism of the episode is that it doesn't follow through on its promise. A few fleshmoths devour Ribbons in seconds, but a whole swarm of them chase after Ryan . . . so he successfully hides in a corner *from creatures that live in the dark*. Wait, what? And the fleshmoths, despite gathering right outside the portal, resolutely fail to attack anyone else. This is the problem with raising the bar so high on a monster: if you don't follow through and have them eat Erik, then it's fundamentally a cheat.

But let's go back to the talking frog. I want to put my cards on the solitary white chair right now: I love the talking frog. Upon encountering it, the Doctor marvels at how bizarre things can be, saying that she thought she had no more surprises left and that the Solitract is the maddest, most beautiful thing she's ever experienced. I pretty much agree. This celebration of the utterly gonzo is just fabulous. People have complained about the frog as embarrassing or whatever, but they're flat-out wrong. It makes perfect sense that an entirely incompatible universe would choose as its mouthpiece something entirely incompatible with our sense of drama. Grace loved frogs, so the universe becomes a frog. Why the hell not? And it's a friendly, adorable frog too, just wanting to be friends and giving a cute wave of its leg when it sends its new BFF into the anti-zone. No, I have no problem with the talking frog, and, dammit, I'll defend it — and everything else ridiculous about *Doctor Who* — until the day I croak. Or else my name isn't Ribbet Smith?

**Second Opinion (GB)** I don't give a rat's arse about the frog, but the idea that Erik would not only abandon his blind child but actually gaslight her and terrify her to keep her in the house is appalling. What's worse is *nobody does anything about it* once they're back home. That's not bonkers. That's dangerous and irresponsible.

That aside, "It Takes You Away" doesn't really do anything for me. The frog stuff at the end is probably my favourite part, so that's not my issue. I think the anti-zone stuff is really dark and funny, though having Hanne navigate through it so easily stretches credibility. But credibility in this story is not so much stretched as pulled completely out of shape.

I like the idea of a bottle episode set in a remote location. The first third, as they try to piece together what's going on, is really engrossing. Hanne is a great character and sparks off the cast really well. I really liked it up until they arrived in the mirror world version of the cabin, at which point you knew the second Grace appeared that none of this was real. And Graham would have to make a terrible decision. And the Doctor would have some ridiculous universe-origin-involving explanation. And the whole thing would become very, very contrived and predictable. I was bored. Horrible Father (that the Doctor doesn't seem to be too concerned about) only made it worse.

Thank goodness Bonkers Frog showed up.

I wish "It Takes You Away" had showed the promise that the first half and its ending showed. It could have been something special, instead of just the story with the frog at the end.

## 11.10 The Battle of Ranskoor Av Kolos

**Written by** Chris Chibnall **Directed by** Jamie Childs

**Original airdate** November 18, 2018

**The Big Idea** The Doctor and friends investigate multiple distress calls on a battle-scarred planet, only to find a pair of godlike beings taking their orders from Tim Shaw.

**Roots and References** The 1978 *Doctor Who* story "The Pirate Planet" (the shrunken planets). Graham steals a line from *Die Hard* ("Yippee-ki-yay, robots").

**Adventures in Time and Space** We find out what happened to Tim Shaw after the events of "The Woman Who Fell to Earth," which provokes discussion of Grace's death, also from that story. The Stenza's proclivity for putting people in suspended animation is demonstrated once more, as is other Stenza technology, including the SniperBots from "The Ghost Monument." The comm-dots from "The Tsuranga Conundrum" are mentioned. The Doctor recalls using the TARDIS to tow Earth across the universe (2008's "The Stolen Earth"/"Journey's End") and the heart of the TARDIS reverting Margaret the Slitheen back into an egg (2005's "Boom

Town"). The TARDIS telepathic circuits are employed, and the Doctor mentions when they were used with Yaz's grandmother's watch ("Demons of the Punjab"). The explanation for the TARDIS being dimensionally transcendental is a line of technobabble dating back to 1970's "Spearhead from Space."

**Unfinished Business** Graham wants to kill Tim Shaw for his role in killing Grace. This creates a lot of tension between the Doctor and Graham and between Graham and Ryan. Ryan not only reiterates that Graham is his granddad, he admits that he loves him. In the end, Graham merely disables Tim Shaw, and both Ryan and Graham put him in suspended animation in memory of Grace.

**Who Is the Doctor?** The Doctor admits her attitude towards weapons is a lot more flexible than she claimed in "The Ghost Monument": "Doors, locks, walls, buildings, fair game. If it can be rebuilt, I'll allow it." She can summon the TARDIS with the sonic screwdriver now. Her advice to Andinio, Delph and Paltraki is "Keep your faith. Travel hopefully. The universe'll surprise you . . . constantly."

**The Doctor and Team TARDIS** The Doctor bitterly disagrees with Graham about his stated goal to kill Tim Shaw. To make matters worse, a few minutes later, Ryan calls the Doctor out about her letting them use weapons. (She tells them that during the events of "The Ghost Monument," she didn't know them and had to lay down the law.) When Graham admits he didn't kill Tim Shaw, she calls him one of the strongest people she knows (and then adds, "Well, one of a few"). She calls her friends "fam" and decides she likes it (and Yaz agrees).

**Monster of the Week** Tim Shaw is back and regarded as a god by the Ux, a duo-species that can perform dimensional engineering through the power of faith.

**Stand Up and Cheer** Playing the moment where Tim Shaw confronts Graham with such comedy is surprisingly lovely, from Ryan's declaration of "Don't diss me Granddad, ever!" to Graham's protestations that he only shot Tim Shaw in the foot. ("Don't tell the Doc, she'll be livid.") But the capper is when Graham and Ryan, after multiple attempts throughout the season, finally fist bump . . . and Graham asks what happens next.

**Roll Your Eyes** The title is pretty pathetic. Not only is there a meaningless planet name, but it's called "The *Battle* of Ranskoor Av Kolos." Where's the freaking battle?

**You're Not Making Any Sense** Throughout the whole episode we're warned of deadly effects of taking off the neural balancers . . . and when the Doctor and Yaz take them off, they just seem like they're mildly hungover.

**Interesting Trivia** Back in "The Woman Who Fell to Earth," Tim Shaw stated that he put the quarries from his hunt in suspended animation at a point between life and death. Now he's putting the captured crew members of the various ships in suspended animation. It is possible he was being poetic about suspended animation, but it certainly sounded like he put them in while they were dying just for his pleasure — which makes his current behaviour a little incongruous. But not inexplicable: it may be that he's trying to keep the Ux onside and it's easier to do that if he's not murdering everyone indiscriminately.

One of the running gags this season is the fact that humanity is virtually unknown in the corner of the universe the Doctor's been travelling lately. Angstrom and Ezpo have no idea what a human being is. Yoss's understanding of human culture is so limited he thinks "Avocado Pear" is a name. And now we have Paltraki's reaction to the name of Yaz's home planet: "What kind of name is that?" Under previous production regimes, humanity and Earth had some kind of special status. We have new rules under Chris Chibnall.

Here's a curious fact . . . we're at the season finale (with a special to go), and the Doctor hasn't said onscreen that she's from Gallifrey or that she's a Time Lord. (Or Time Lady; we don't even know if the Doctor has Missy's sense of tradition!) This is the longest the Doctor has gone in the Modern Series without stating her origins. In fact, it may be the longest stretch of time for any Doctor since the second incarnation admitted who he was in 1969's "The War Games."

**The TARDIS Chronometer** The planet Ranskoor Av Kolos. Presuming Tim Shaw simply travelled across space, it's 3,407 years in the future (so the year 5425).

**Aw, Brilliant? (GB)** Wow. This is just *lame*.

There have been season finales that have disappointed me. There have been season finales that have angered me. There have even been a few that dazzled me. But this is the first time that I've been bored by a season finale in *Doctor Who*.

"Season finale" used to mean the conclusion of a story arc and the myriad details that took place during a season. This year, there was no story arc. On the one hand, that was a refreshing change (though in this era of binge-watchable television, I'm not entirely sure if making everything standalone was a great idea strategically), but, on the other, there's nothing to resolve. So we fake-resolve things instead: Tim Shaw comes back. Except . . . Tim Shaw was that placeholder villain you have at the start of a new era that doesn't take up too much foreground in order for the new Doctor and companions to have the limelight. Given a more prominent role, he doesn't actually improve at all. In fact, he flat-out bewilders. The con job he's done on the Ux seems so tenuous that all it takes is the Doctor to say, basically, "Oh he's a bloke I met in Sheffield" to break their faith in him. It's not that difficult.

That's my problem with "The Battle of Ranskoor Av Kolos": nothing in it is difficult for anyone.

Graham, who for the whole season has been the nicest grandfather we all wished we had, suddenly wants to kill Tim Shaw. But he doesn't. The argument between the Doctor and Graham is half-hearted at best (the one between Graham and Ryan is slightly better), but there's absolutely no doubt that Graham isn't going to pull the trigger on Tim Shaw. (Which is why resorting to comedy was a welcome relief.) There isn't much moral conflict for Graham. Everyone is just going through the motions.

This has been a problem for the season generally. There hasn't been a lot of conflict between the characters. Graham and Ryan had some in-built tensions, but for the most part it never got in the way of their interactions. The Doctor's disagreement brought to mind prior disagreements with Clara and Donna . . . but those had intensity and heat. These are so mild as to be barely noticeable. I find this bizarre, because on *Broadchurch* Chris Chibnall was a genius at raising the emotional temperature in a scene between characters and creating conflicts and letting them wax and wane. Why isn't he doing this in *Doctor Who*?

The climax is so easy it may well still have training wheels on. The Doctor and Yaz take off the neural balancers and . . . nothing happens. Here's a top tip: this is the point where you go nuts with weird point-of-view shots and even throw in the faces of some past monsters this season and, you know, give Mandip Gill an actual chance to act. Basically, demonstrate the threat the audience was warned about 45 minutes earlier. Nah. Let's not have stakes or make things hard.

As I've said elsewhere, I really like the move to a procedural form of *Doctor Who*. And I think it's one of the reasons there's been an uptick in interest in *Doctor Who* this year by casual viewers. But I do think it could be done better. Good procedurals test the limits of their characters and their relationships with each other. The best anyone has done this season is say to each other, "Well, I hope you don't do that." And they don't. Good procedurals know how to ramp up jeopardy and excite audiences and work with consequences. None of this can be said about "The Battle of Ranskoor Av Kolos."

Thankfully, Jodie Whittaker is great. Her scene confronting Andinio is charming and delightful. Graham Walsh struggles gamely with the unbelievable thing they've given him to pull off. Tosin Cole gets some great moments, and Mandip Gill . . . oh, was she in this?

A great season finale on *Doctor Who* makes you feel exhilarated and overjoyed as all kinds of plot elements and character bits come together. It should fizz in your brain and warm your heart. The Doctor's speech at the end aside (and even that seemed tacked on), this was just . . . a thing. Thank goodness there's a do-over coming with the New Year's special.

**Second Opinion (RS?)** Well, I didn't think it was quite that bad.

My co-author's right that it's no kind of season finale. The final brief speech by the Doctor aside, the season just sort of . . . stops. In two stories' worth of appearances, the supposedly deadly SniperBots have managed to hit precisely zero live targets. But it's reasonably well paced, and I think bringing back a monster from earlier in the season was a smart move. (Though it would have been amusing if all the villains who'd been tossed out into the void this season had turned up in the same place.) I don't even mind that the battle itself is pushed into backstory.

What made it work for me, at least to some degree, was the way they dealt with grief. In particular, Graham and Ryan at odds with each other over how to approach the aftermath of Grace's death was great. Graham's angry and wants revenge, while Ryan wants to honour the memory of the person they lost. Both are believable points of view.

Partway through this season, I lost my beloved dog, Baldwin. In fact, it happened (unbeknownst to me) while I was watching one of the episodes. My grief over this has been insurmountable, far more extreme than losing any human in my life has been. I was as torn as Graham and Ryan, half wanting revenge on the person responsible and half wanting to honour the memory of a beautiful creature. I found the theme developed throughout this season to be achingly real, with the echo of Grace that Graham sees in "Arachnids" exactly like the echo of Baldwin I've seen so often in my house or the park.

The fact that Graham is so resolutely prepared to throw his entire life away for an act of revenge felt intensely accurate to me. And the Doctor telling him that he didn't actually understand was also right. Like Graham, I fantasized about doing something stupid but didn't do it, instead finding the strength to be a better person. Until I rewatched this episode, I wasn't entirely sure that was the right decision.

Seen objectively, "The Battle of Ranskoor Av Kolos" probably is a pretty terrible episode. But it actually helped me to be more at peace and give me more insight into the grief process that I'm still going through. I'll always be grateful for that.

## 11.11 Resolution

**Written by** Chris Chibnall **Directed by** Wayne Yip
**Original airdate** January 1, 2019

**The Big Idea** An archaeological dig in Sheffield unearths a Dalek mutant that rebuilds itself and threatens to take over the world.

**Roots and References** *Game of Thrones* (the opening medieval battle scene);

*Frankenstein* (the Dalek creature coming to life); the 1989 film *Brain Damage* (the mutant on the back of a host). Lin and Mitch discuss the real-life finding of Richard III's remains in a carpark in Leicester.

**Adventures in Time and Space** Dalek-Lin logs into the Black Archive ("The Day of the Doctor"). The Doctor tries to contact Kate Stewart at UNIT ("The Power of Three"). The possessed Lin manually builds a Dalek shell in much the same way the Doctor built her sonic screwdriver in "The Woman Who Fell to Earth." The Doctor says that Earth is protected, just as she did in 2005's "The Christmas Invasion." Rels, the Dalek unit of time, was first used in the 1960s Peter Cushing Dalek movies and Dalek comics before crossing over into the TV series in 2006's "Army of Ghosts"/"Doomsday." (Oh, the Doctor didn't know, but we do: a rel is 1.2 seconds!)

**Unfinished Business** Ryan's dad, Aaron, shows up, wanting to turn over a new leaf, but Ryan isn't ready to forgive him — and, indeed, he deliberately calls Graham "Gramps" in front of Aaron. Grace saved all of Aaron's things from when he was a child, which Graham still keeps. Aaron didn't come to Grace's funeral because he didn't want to face the fact that she was gone. When the Dalek possesses Aaron, Ryan realizes he loves him and is here for him.

**Who Is the Doctor?** As ever, anything with a Dalek is personal to her. She is reminded that every time she thinks she's rid of the Daleks, she never is. She tells her friends that she learned to think like a Dalek a long time ago. That said, she still gives it a chance to leave peacefully.

Otherwise — this is a question we'll come back to in a few moments . . .

**The Doctor and Team TARDIS** She's fiercely loyal to Ryan, telling Aaron that he let Ryan down by not showing up to Grace's funeral. (She also keeps up her habit of not using the names of relatives of her friends, opting to call him "Ryan's dad.") The Doctor vacillates between calling them "team," "gang" and "extended fam," which includes Lin, Mitch and Aaron.

**Monster of the Week** A recon scout Dalek. It has capabilities beyond the normal Dalek soldier, such as being able to short out a phone trace through the TARDIS. Recon scout Daleks were the first to leave Skaro, and this one may have been the first to reach Earth. Even a third of a Dalek can be reactivated and brought back to life if exposed to ultraviolet light. It recovers a weapon and builds its own casing from spare parts in a junkyard. It installs missile launchers inside the Dalek's "bumps."

**Stand Up and Cheer** "Oh, mate. I'm the Doctor. Ring any bells?" The Doctor revealing who she is to the Dalek is a magnificent moment, with the Doctor's cocksure smile and the Dalek backing away in fear.

**Roll Your Eyes** It is a truth universally acknowledged that a single dad in possession of a microwave oven in the first act must be in want of using said oven to destroy a Dalek in the third.

**You're Not Making Any Sense** You've been a custodian of a third of a deadly weapon for your entire life, as have your direct ancestors. It suddenly starts coming to life. Is it a good idea to immediately dig it up with your hands? (Also, why were they buried so shallowly?)

**Interesting Trivia** Even when the series takes a longer-than-usual break, Christmas specials have aired every year from 2005 to 2017. Instead of a 2018 Christmas special, "Resolution" was screened as a New Year's special, incidentally making it the only new *Doctor Who* to be screened in 2019, as regular episodes would not resume until early 2020. The only previous New Year's special was "The End of Time, Part Two," nine years earlier. The hope was, rather like moving the series to Sunday nights, it could get a bigger rating on New Year's Day, the same way *Sherlock* season openers had previously. The gambit didn't quite pay off; although it scored the fourth-highest ratings of the night, with 22.4% of the overnight audience, at 7.13 million viewers it was also the lowest overnight viewership for a *Doctor Who* special.

So if UNIT is currently mothballed due to a funding dispute, what happens to the eight million Zygons currently being rehoused off their books? Would they seriously surrender their alien materials to a third party as the Black Archive is apparently now being held by MDZ Research? It's possible that MDZ has only the black-market alien tech we see here. We hope so, because at least UNIT's version was almost impregnable and didn't rely on the digits of a cheeky chappy to get in.

The Sheffield Dalek prop has the honour of being the first speaking Dalek not to have a human inside it. It was fully robotic and radio controlled, with three separate systems controlling the eyestalk, the arms and the lights. To hide the fact that there was a returning monster in this special, Nick Briggs remained uncredited in both the *Radio Times* and on BBC iPlayer, while the Dalek was codenamed "Kevin." The deception was so effective that Nikesh Patel (who played Mitch) had no idea that he was in an episode starring the Daleks until he arrived on set. It didn't help that Jodie Whittaker kept using the codename in readthroughs, saying, "I'm coming for you, KEVIN!" with gusto.

**The TARDIS Chronometer** Anuta Island, South Pacific; Siberia, Russia; and Yorkshire, England in medieval times and the present day.

**Aw, Brilliant? (GB and RS?)** We've come a long, long way together.

When we began, we couldn't have known that we would wind up where we are now. We began with the Doctor being male and in what we were sure was his eleventh incarnation. We end with the first female Doctor and the Doctor having had a few more incarnations than we previously knew about.

This book started with the 2011 Christmas special, starring a solo Doctor deliberately disguising who he was because pretty much everyone in the universe knew about him thanks to how heroic he'd been. It ends, more than seven years later, with the Doctor as part of a team, with minimal continuity to the show's past and a new remit of relatively small-scale problem-solving. The TARDIS has transformed from a cyberpunk interior to a crystalline form, the sonic screwdriver is now curved and was built in Sheffield, while the stories have switched from manic pacing and heroic speeches to procedurals with a healthy dose of kitchen-sink family drama.

And yet, some things still remain. We still have the Doctor facing off against a Dalek.

Sylvester McCoy once said that no actor could be taken seriously as the Doctor until they fought the Daleks. This is where "Resolution" cements the work done in the past season: by bringing back the Daleks, it anchors the show as faithful to *Doctor Who* as we know it, even as it moves on from the continuity-bound elements of the previous nine seasons. The Doctor and a box, fighting Daleks. There's a beautiful simplicity to that.

More than that, though, the Doctor is still the smartest person in the room, facing off against injustice and inventively taking down villains with the help of a magic box, assorted friends and a lot of luck. The show is still all about exciting stories, a gifted alien who looks like one of us and a time machine that resets the genre every week.

Indeed, the latest era takes us full circle, not back to the Matt Smith days but to those of Christopher Eccleston. Once again, the Doctor is an eccentric with a northern accent, a disposition very close to human and a regular bunch of friends. Stories are once again tied to a sense of extended family: not only the families of the human characters but the found families fashioned between the Doctor and her friends.

As for "Resolution" itself, it's a charming episode. We're particularly taken with the conceit of having the Dalek mutant controlling Lin. It's a clever twist on a Dalek story (even if it feels like the best *Torchwood* story Chris Chibnall never made!). Charlotte Ritchie puts in a virtuoso performance as a woman both possessed and simultaneously fighting said possession. Contrast this with Daniel Adegboyega's acting when he's taken over: it's exactly how you'd expect someone to act when they have a Dalek on their back. Ritchie doesn't do that, and it's magnificent, making the first half a tense thriller of an episode.

Adegboyega, however, is astounding in what turns out to be the season's longest scene, as Ryan tells Aaron what his absence has done. Tosin Cole's performance in this scene is electric. It's a beautiful, dramatic scene that gives us something that's been missing from this season: interpersonal conflict. At the same time, it gives Aaron the space to have his own motivations explained, which help overcome the soap-opera dynamics.

As good as Charlotte Richie is, we wonder if "Resolution" didn't miss a trick by having Yaz be the one possessed by the Dalek. It could have added a certain frisson within the team dynamic as the Doctor is battling an alien using her friend's knowledge (and face). And it could have given Yaz more to do. We hope there's more ahead for her. Mandip Gill is a great actress, but "Resolution" favours Ryan and Graham with great scenes and gives her nothing to do. Again.

One of the great moments here is the Doctor talking to the preternaturally calm call-centre agent. This is a great example of *Doctor Who* doing what science fiction always should: using the weird set-up to talk about issues of the day. Here, the attempt to contact Kate Stewart and UNIT simultaneously ties the episode into the recent past, removes the Doctor's support structure and makes a biting commentary on Brexit, which is glorious.

While the departure from past continuity and monsters during Series Eleven no doubt made it friendlier to new viewers, it did create the dilemma that this new Doctor hasn't faced the same menaces her male counterparts did. "Resolution" approaches that challenge head-on: the Doctor faces the Daleks with the same baggage the character has always had towards them. The result is a new way of seeing this Doctor. While the preceding season pitted the Doctor against a variety of insurmountable problems and allowed her to be fallible, which made this new Doctor a hero suited to our times, it was also nice to see her be right about what's going on. "Resolution" gives us a more heroic thirteenth Doctor by having her fight on familiar ground: it's definitely easier to battle Daleks than it is to fight racism.

Given that the episode was filmed as a regular part of the preceding season, we don't know why it wasn't billed as a season finale, as it slots in perfectly as one. More than that, "Resolution" gives us optimism for what might come next for *Doctor Who*. We would love more stories like this — with an epic sense of scale, an innovative take on a monster (whether that be old or new) and the Doctor more proactively involved — in the mix with the more ambiguous procedural episodes. "Resolution" signposts that we might be in for a great time come Series Twelve.

Seven years on, with four lead actors playing the part, multiple companions we've cared about, two producers and an almost entirely new crew, "Resolution" shows us that the magic of *Doctor Who* is bigger than who's in front of the camera or who's behind it. While the producers, writers, actors and so forth shepherd a variety of exciting and thrilling and bizarre (and, yes, sometimes even dull or cringeworthy) stories onto the screen, it's the fundamental concept of *Doctor Who*'s ability to renew itself that keeps it fresh and exciting, 56 years on. Here's to the next 56.

**Who Is the Doctor?** The Doctor is still the Doctor. Still the smartest person in the room. Still funny. Still sometimes wrong, but always heroic. Still demonstrating kindness. Still fighting evil. Still a little bit weird (well, more than a little). Still played by an infectiously likeable actor.

# Doctor Who? Yes, she is.
*Where to next? We were thinking...*
*Everywhere.*

APPENDICES

# The Night of the Doctor (2013)

**Written by** Steven Moffat **Directed by** John Hayes

**Starring** Paul McGann (the eighth Doctor)

**Original airdate** Released online November 14, 2013

**The Big Idea** The Time War is consuming the universe. The eighth Doctor refuses to be involved, until he meets a young woman on a crashing spaceship . . . and dies as a result.

**Roots and References** The Doctor quotes the Bible when he says, "Physician, heal thyself" (Luke 4:23).

**Adventures in Time and Space** The Sisterhood of Karn was previously seen in 1976's "The Brain of Morbius." They're a group of seers who are somewhat related to the Time Lords and had something to do with the science of regeneration (indeed, Ohila says that Time Lord science is elevated on Karn). They worship the Sacred Flame, which produces the Elixir of Life. Before he regenerates, the Doctor mentions companions Charley, C'Rizz, Lucie, Tamsin and Molly, who were the eighth Doctor's companions from the Big Finish audios. The list isn't complete, though: he doesn't mention Grace from the 1996 TV Movie or any of his companions from other media such as the BBC Eighth Doctor Adventures or the *Doctor Who Magazine* comic strip.

**Who Is the Doctor?** The eighth Doctor is not part of the Time War. He helps where he can, but he refuses to fight. However, the Sisterhood convinces him that the universe needs a warrior more than it needs a Doctor, so he chooses his next regeneration and changes into a young version of the man we saw in "The Name of the Doctor." The warrior gives up the name "Doctor," which the eighth Doctor had considered synonymous with being a good man.

**The Doctor and Cass** The Doctor invited Cass aboard the TARDIS because she teleported the rest of her crew off the gunship on the grounds that she was the only one who wasn't screaming. However, once she finds out he's a Time Lord, she refuses to travel with him, which results in her own death as well as his.

**Stand Up and Cheer** "I'm a Doctor," says Paul McGann, appearing as our favourite character onscreen for the first time in 17 years. "But probably not the one you were expecting." And the fans went wild.

**You're Not Making Any Sense** It whizzes by pretty quickly, but the St John Ambulance logo is clearly visible on the TARDIS when it's chasing after Cass's gunship. Not only is it not there a few minutes later, but the logo wasn't reintroduced until 2010's "The Eleventh Hour," much later in the Doctor's personal timespan.

"The Night of the Doctor" was originally intended to be released during the fiftieth-anniversary week. But somebody was about to leak it, so Steven Moffat released it a week early in order to preserve the surprise of Paul McGann's appearance. As it turned out, the release date happened to be McGann's fifty-fourth birthday, so McGann regarded it as Moffat's birthday present to him!

The body of the warrior strapping on the bandolier was actually Paul McGann's, thus making him the second actor to play two incarnations of the Doctor (after Sylvester McCoy doubled for the sixth Doctor in 1987's "Time and the Rani"). The reflection of a young John Hurt was taken from the 1979 TV series *Crime and Punishment*.

**The TARDIS Chronometer** On board a gunship and on the planet Karn, during the Time War.

**Yes, Yes, Yes? (RS?)** It was one of the best-kept secrets of the fiftieth anniversary.

The fiftieth anniversary saw releases of a variety of online mini-episodes, as well as teaser trailers and any number of retrospective documentaries about the series. There was a behind-the-scenes documentary about the making of the show in the '60s and even the insertion of a brand new Doctor, retroactively. But it was Paul McGann's return to the fold that turned some serious heads.

We just never saw this coming. Not only that, but we had the eighth Doctor in the middle of the Time War, the return of the Sisterhood of Karn — and a regeneration, to boot. All that in seven minutes.

There are many great things about this mini-episode, from the doom-laden atmosphere of the universe in peril to the Doctor's bittersweet regeneration into someone unworthy of the name Doctor to his antagonistic relationship with what should be his next companion. The fact that he regenerates into a young John Hurt was a huge surprise as well: suddenly, there were hundreds of years between this story and Hurt's appearance in "The Name of the Doctor" (and the upcoming "The Day of the Doctor"). Just how long did this guy spend fighting in the Time War?

But the greatest thing about this is the rehabilitation of Paul McGann's Doctor. After the awkward TV Movie, the eighth became the George Lazenby of Doctors, stuck with a single appearance. Bringing him back for a final story was lovely . . . but it's McGann's full-force performance that really sells it. He's not the romantic, whimsical "these shoes fit perfectly!" gentleman we saw last; instead, he's battle-hardened and weary, but still oh so Doctorish. His request for knitting and television when he has four minutes to live (in case he gets bored) is sublime. This story cements McGann's stature as a proper Doctor.

In fact, the biggest shame is that he wasn't the warrior all along. Moffat had ruled out giving the role to McGann, as there was a need for a more hardened character than the one we'd seen in the TV Movie, but "The Night of the Doctor" proves that the eighth Doctor could have easily taken on the role. How fascinating would it have been to have Paul McGann in John Hurt's role in the fiftieth anniversary?

We've included "The Night of the Doctor" as an entry in this book because, short though it is, we think it's every bit as important and worthy as the other stories we cover. It's a key moment in the Doctor's personal history, it has important information about the Time War, it reintroduces the Sisterhood of Karn, and it shows the regeneration into a much-younger-than-expected Warrior.

But even if it had done none of those things, we'd still want to include it for Paul McGann's outstanding performance alone. It's utterly superb. And the best thing of all is that nobody saw it coming.

**Second Opinion (GB)** I don't really have anything to add to this review, except to emphasize my co-author's opinion that Paul McGann could have played John Hurt's role in the fiftieth-anniversary cycle of stories brilliantly. In fact, I always assumed it was him who ended the Time War and destroyed Gallifrey anyway.

No, why I'm here today is to offer a public apology to our esteemed editor, Jennifer Hale. Back when we wrote the original volume of *Who Is The Doctor*, Jen asked the question, "I'm assuming by calling the TV Movie guy the eighth Doctor and calling Eccleston the ninth, fans automatically assume that McGann's Doctor regenerated into Eccleston's, but how do we know that there weren't three or four Doctors in between?"

It was a perfectly reasonable question. And, diva author that I am, I was an utter jerk to her in my response. I said, "You are SUCH a noob . . . The Doctor explicitly numbers himself on several occasions throughout the New Series. We document those incidents throughout in those stories."

When "The Night of the Doctor" was released online, Jen helpfully reminded us of this exchange. And pointed out that she was actually right. Which, of course, she was.

If "The Night of the Doctor" did anything, besides be a perfect showcase and ending for Paul McGann's Doctor, it helped fans like me realize that just because you know everything about a fictional world doesn't mean that fiction is immutable and can't change. And perhaps fans like me should be a little less arrogant about the knowledge they wield. That, to my mind, is a good life lesson. Sorry again, Jen . . .

# The Doctor's Meditation (2015)

**Written by** Steven Moffat, **Directed by** Ed Bazalgette

**Starring** Peter Capaldi (the twelfth Doctor)

**The Big Idea** In preparation for his final battle, the Doctor attempts to meditate in 12th-century England. It doesn't go as planned.

**Adventures in Time and Space** The twelfth Doctor wishing for a visitor's centre at a newly dug well is quite similar to the tenth Doctor wishing for a little shop at the cat-nun hospital in 2006's "New Earth." He attempts to wage a swordfight using a spoon, just as he did in "Robot of Sherwood." The Doctor's resemblance to a magician follows on from previous references including "Time Heist" and "Last Christmas," though the actual magic tricks are new; unlike 1988's "The Greatest Show in the Galaxy" and 1970's "The Ambassadors of Death," the twelfth Doctor isn't actually very good at prestidigitation.

**Who Is the Doctor?** Perhaps unsurprisingly, he can't sit still or not speak for very long at all. He's there to meditate because he is haunted by a mistake (one we'll see in the opening moments of the next story).

**Stand Up and Cheer** Watching the Doctor completely fail to sit still or focus when he's supposed to be meditating is comedy gold. But the highlight is surely him getting distracted in the middle of trying to pass off his impatience as attention deficit . . . something or other. Sorry, what were we talking about again?

**Interesting Trivia** This six-minute mini-episode was first shown in theatres in Canada, the United States, Russia and Denmark as part of a theatrical screening of "Dark Water"/"Death in Heaven." In Britain, it was eventually released on Facebook. It serves as a prologue of sorts to "The Magician's Apprentice"/"The Witch's Familiar." However, a) it's not really a prologue, as it takes place between scenes of "The Magician's Apprentice," and b) there was actually another prologue for this story, consisting of a two-minute webcast that was released four days earlier.

The Modern Series has had many visits to the past, just as the Classic Series did. However, this is the first "pure historical" in the New Series. This was a subgenre in the original *Doctor Who*, where the first two Doctors (and the fifth, for one story only) visited the past without any monsters or aliens other than the TARDIS and its crew. The Modern Series has been very careful to avoid this, for the same reason the Classic Series stopped doing them: they run the risk of being boring or simply educational, which tends to encourage viewers to reach for the remote control. Doing one as a short episode was probably the perfect way for the New Series to cross that off its bucket list without losing viewers who might not stay for 42 minutes' worth of history but could handle six.

**The TARDIS Chronometer** England, 1134 CE.

**Don't Be Stupid? (RS?)** *Aries*: You will find yourself attempting to meditate. Good luck with that, because there's no way you'll be able to sit in silence for more than about three hours. The digging of wells features prominently in your future, as does a visitor's centre. On the bright side, you've seen your last battlefield, which might come in handy. If an old friend is dying, best to pop off to a rock somewhere for a few weeks to have a bit of a think. If all else fails, spend your time practising the old "which hand holds the coin" trick. This will be in no way offensive for your forthcoming visit to your old friend, unless of course said old friend has only one hand, in which case it might seem a bit insensitive. Lucky number: 12.

*Taurus*: Some sort of donut shape, isn't it? Maybe a bagel? Either way, your future is clear: you're going to be eaten, most likely for breakfast.

*Gemini*: You are an idiot. But you already knew that. Still, you're good at magic tricks. You will find yourself drawn to a tall stranger. Serve him loyally . . . at least until you find yourself swallowing a snake and being overcome by the inner Dalek agent inside you. But until then, carry scrolls, provide distractions and generally hang around a bit, making it appear that you'll be a major character in events to come, only to have that rug ripped out from beneath everyone's feet when that Dalek eyestalk pops out and your plotline is left entirely unresolved. Presumably you'll just stand there for all eternity, much like the nearby tank and electric guitar, which will throw a bit of a wrench into archaeology, when it's finally invented. The celestial heavens move in mysterious ways.

*Cancer*: So . . . your star sign is named after a disease. I'm sure that's nothing to worry about. Nothing at all.

*Leo*: You enjoy chalices, fire and wearing red robes. Chanting will feature heavily in your future — and your past. You will be entrusted with a friend's last will and testament. You know who to give it to. (So don't go making a terrible mistake and handing it to his worst enemy or anything like that.) Remember, an enemy is just a friend you don't know yet.

*Virgo*: Mrs. Sauskind, it's under the couch!

*Libra*: Getting old sucks. Especially when you're stuck in the same chair all that time. But you can always go home. Even if that home has been bombed, destroyed, time-looped, retconned, renamed and made invisible for reasons that elude me right now. Still, you've got to laugh, haven't you? Best to send for your oldest living frenemy, because some arguments never seem to end.

*Scorpio*: You are one-twelfth of the population. You enjoy breathing, eating several times a day and sleeping. You are often found sitting, standing or lying down. You may find yourself either thinking or doing. Eat nothing except food, and drink nothing except liquids.

*Sagittarius*: You're a democracy, so vote wisely. But best to avoid the snake-oil sellers, regardless. You'll find yourself running missions to all corners of the galaxy to find a being who can travel to any place in the universe at any point in its entire history. Your primary means of accomplishing this goal is to stand in a variety of rooms, saying, "Where is the Doctor?" You might be doing this for some time.

*Capricorn*: You are the central planet of the 12 colonies of Kobol, the place where the first Cylons were created. No wait, that's Caprica. What series are we talking about anyway?

*Aquarius*: You so fine. Remember that friendship is so much better than the reproductive frenzy of the noisy little food chain. Your long-term prospects are looking good because death is for other people. On the other hand, you'll discover to your horror that you don't quite put the "arch" into arch-enemy. Probably best to avoid air travel in the near future.

*Pisces*: You are much too fat, and you insist on wearing that stupid hat.

**Second Opinion (GB)** Meh. It was . . . *okay*. It has a bigger budget than most web extras, but it's not necessarily better. This was funny, but not incredibly so. It was charming, but not spectacular. That said, my co-author's review of it is really funny, so there's that.

# Recommended Resources

*"I always rip out the last page of a book. Then it doesn't have to end."*
— The Doctor, "The Angels Take Manhattan"

At the risk of contradicting the Doctor, please don't rip out the last pages of any book. Or this one. It's not that we love endings; it's just that we love books and hope you do too. However, information about *Doctor Who* isn't only found in books anymore. We've restricted this list to things available since the first volume of *Who Is The Doctor*, on the grounds that *Doctor Who* is one of the most researched shows in existence. (Full disclosure: we mention some of our own work here because it honestly is useful!)

### The Worlds of Doctor Who
*A History of the Universe in 100 Objects* by James Goss and Steve Tribe uses a series of items — from sonic screwdrivers to glass Daleks to the first carrot grown on Mars — to tell the story of *Doctor Who* in a way that isn't just a dry recitation of story synopses. *Whographica: An Infographic Guide to Space and Time* by Ben Morris, Simon Guerrier and Steve O'Brien also breaks down the *Doctor Who* universe through a series of mind-blowing infographics. Obverse Books has been publishing short but in-depth guides called *The Black Archive*, with an entire book devoted to each individual story. And we'd be remiss if we didn't mention the first volume of this very book, as well as *Who's 50: The 50 Doctor Who Stories to Watch Before You Die* and *The Doctors Are In* by Graeme Burk and Robert Smith?, which are episode guides to the Classic and Modern Series, as well as a guide to who the Doctors are.

### The Making of the Show
*The Vault* by Marcus Hearn tells the story of the making of *Doctor Who* (up to its fiftieth anniversary, at any rate) through behind-the-scenes memos, photographed artefacts from the show's history and interviews with key cast and crew members. *Impossible Worlds: A 50-Year Treasure of Art and Design* by Stephen Nicholas and Mike Tucker is an art tour of the show, containing production sketches, design notes and an exploration of how the art department works with costumers and makeup and special effects artists. It's a celebration of the creative vision behind the show from a perspective we haven't seen, focusing

on the Modern Series. If you want to know more — a lot more — about the show's origins, Robert would like to recommend *Head of Drama*, a memoir of *Doctor Who*'s creator Sydney Newman with edits, explanations, context and a supplementary essay by one Graeme Burk that unearthed any number of new facts about the show's genesis.

### General Resources

We once again recommend *Doctor Who Magazine* on the grounds that it's still going strong. It now has an electronic version, so it's a lot cheaper than it once was. As the flagship magazine of the show, it has access to cast and crew for interviews and features, as well as in-depth analysis. All the showrunners for modern *Doctor Who*, including Chris Chibnall, have contributed a regular column about the production of the series. The *Doctor Who* News Page (doctorwhonews.net) has been providing *Doctor Who* news on the internet since the days when we used to call it, unapologetically, the World Wide Web.

### The Wilderness Years

There were a series of *Doctor Who* novels published in the '90s when the TV show was off the air. Many are sadly out of print, but *Bookwyrm* by Anthony Wilson and Robert Smith? is a guide to what you missed and how the novels influenced the Modern Series. Likewise, *Downtime: The Lost Years of Doctor Who* by Dylan Rees details the various semi-professional videos and audios made during this time that skirted the official licence. *The Comic Strip Companion* by Paul Scoones charts the weird and wonderful world of *Doctor Who* comics.

### Reviews

If you want commentary and reviews of the show, the first two *Outside In* volumes (edited by Robert Smith?) have literally hundreds of people reviewing hundreds of *Doctor Who* episodes — but with a twist. *Chicks Unravel Time* (edited by Deborah Stanish and L.M. Myles) is a journey through every season of *Doctor Who* by female writers. *Children of Time: The Companions of Doctor Who* (edited by R. Alan Siler and Drew Meyer) examines all the companions, both onscreen and off. If you'd like to write your own reviews — of pretty much anything — check out *The Doctor Who Ratings Guide* at pagefillers.com/dwrg (edited by that question-mark guy again).

### Geekery

If you want something a bit more hardcore, *AHistory: An Unauthorized History of the Doctor Who Universe* by Lance Parkin and Lars Pearson is a complete chronology of the *Doctor Who* universe, taking into account every story in every medium. There's also *Timelink: Volume 1: The Unofficial and Unauthorised Guide to Doctor Who Continuity*, a massive tome on *Doctor Who*'s byzantine continuity by Jon Preddle. *Lost in Time and Space: An Unofficial Guide to the Uncharted Journeys of Doctor Who* by Matthew J. Elliott charts the chronological events of everything in the *Doctor Who* universe that wasn't seen; it takes every mention of offscreen events and places them in sequence in an act of true fannish obsession. (We love this.)

## Podcasts

Podcasts aren't just for people to avoid human contact on public transit; they're for *Doctor Who* fans as well. The most popular *Doctor Who* podcast is *Radio Free Skaro* (radiofreeskaro.com), which features three fans who argue and discuss all things *Who* in each episode. *Verity!* (veritypodcast.com) is full of insightful commentary and conversation. We're also quite fond of *The Moment* (themomentpod.com), which features a single guest talking about a specific moment in *Doctor Who* that meant something to them. Oh, and if you would like a *Doctor Who* podcast that sounds more like public radio with multiple interview segments, spoken word, songs and comedy, give *Reality Bomb* (realitybombpodcast.com) a try. Full disclosure: one of us hosts it and the other sometimes appears. You'll be able to figure out who's who, because one has the perfect voice for radio — and the other has an Australian accent.

## Fandom

If you want to jump in the mix with other fans, check out the Gallifrey Base online forum (gallifreybase.com). Or if you prefer real-life interaction, check out a *Doctor Who* convention near you (or not so near). Our favourites are Gallifrey One in Los Angeles in February and Chicago TARDIS in November. We hope to see you there!

# Acknowledgements

A book often has multiple authors: there are the two on the front of this book, and there are all the people who contributed to it in myriad ways.

One of those people is our editor for four books and eight years, Jen Hale. We still don't know how she puts up with us, but she certainly makes us sound a lot better. Special thanks also to the ECW Press co-publisher David Caron for being pretty darn understanding, our copy editor Crissy Calhoun and all the fine people at our amazing publisher.

A few people went above and beyond in commenting on the book. We'd especially like to thank Jon Arnold, Jim Sangster, Jon Preddle and Shannon Dohar for their detailed notes and thoughtful assessment of our work. We'd also like to thank Scot Clarke and Joy Piedmont for their strategic input as well.

This guide has been eight years in the making (and only two and a half of them writing it!), and it's the product of a lot of conversations with a lot of people over the years including Ari Lipsey, Lori Steuart, Anthony Wilson, Alex Kennard, Sage Young, Kim Rogers, Petra Mayer, Lindsey Mayers, Nick Abadzis, Simon Fraser, Warren Frey, Heather Berberet, Erika Ensign, Steven Schapansky, Rachel Donner, Andy Hicks, Bill Evenson, Felicity Kuzinitz, Deborah Stanish, Lizbeth Myles, Matthew Sweet, Paul Cornell, Clayton Hickman, Graham Kibble-White, Robert Shearman, Phil Ford, Philip Hinchcliffe, Dennis, Christine and Felix Turner, Cadence Gillard, Sarah Jupp, Daniel Changer, Matthew Palmer, Damien Oliver, Jez Cartner, Jonathan Blum and Cameron Dixon (for that Clara/Me theory).

Special thanks must go to Julie Hopkins, Laura Collishaw, Jennel Recoskie, Anna Vaughn and Chris Casimiro for their love and kindness and their patience towards our hobby (ahem ... *lifestyle choice*). Thanks to our employers who must be surprised we wrote a book in our off-hours. Thanks especially to David Field, whom we're naming so he can be tickled to find himself in the acknowledgement section of a book! Thanks also to Aileen Page, Moya Teklu, Feroneh Neil, Kathleen Murphy, Janet Budgell, Randy Ellsworth, David McKillop, Mary-Ann Cocchetto, Brenna Frazer, Rachel Batty, Dorothy Zaionchkovsky, Eric Pelot, Laurine Bergeron-Hamel, Lily Mitchell, Gina Rosich, Alina Barnett, Miriam David, Catherine David, Jaymie Maley, Kate Small, Katie Moon, Zoë Tulip, Fiona Halar, Tara Gallimore, Steph Lacoste and Alison Kealey for various and sundry kindnesses that made our lives easier during the writing of this book.

Time to end the suspense: the lies are both #3. Graeme told Sophie Aldred that she was tied with Sarah Jane (not Leela) for best companion, while Robert does share a birthday with Matt Smith but is (precisely) a decade older than him — and a few years younger than David Tennant. The rest are all true. Even the pirates.

This book was written in (deep breath) Mexico, Malaysia, Australia, Germany, Czechia, Austria, Hungary, India, the Philippines, Russia, Chile, Cameroon, Namibia, the U.K., Oman, Nepal, Kazakhstan, Kyrgyzstan, the United Arab Emirates, the Dominican Republic and in Canada and the United States — in Ottawa, Toronto, Oakville, Winnipeg, Waterloo, Naples (Florida), Chicago, Long Island, Los Angeles, Seattle, Pullman, Salt Lake City, Raleigh, Baltimore, Lake Placid, Hamilton (NY) and on many a transatlantic flight. And several transpacific ones. The secret to our success is laptops, wifi, lithium batteries, cell phones and charging stations. Really.

And thanks to you, dear reader, for journeying with us in these pages. If you have comments, we always want to hear them. You can contact us at whoisthedoctor@gemgeekorrarebug.com.

We said at the start of this book that we love *Doctor Who* because of how much fun it is. We hope you had just as much fun reading this.

*Let's get a shift on!*

**GRAEME BURK** is a writer and communications professional based in Toronto. This is the fourth guide to *Doctor Who* that he has co-written with Robert Smith? for ECW Press, the others being *Who Is The Doctor* (2012) *Who's 50* (2013) and *The Doctors Are In* (2015). In 2017, he provided historical notes and a biographical essay to *Doctor Who* creator and television pioneer Sydney Newman's memoir, *Head of Drama*. He is the co-host and co-producer of the *Doctor Who* podcast *Reality Bomb* (realitybombpodcast.com) and the music podcast *Deeper Cuts* (deepercuts.com). Graeme has written for magazines, websites and small presses in Canada, the United States and the United Kingdom and currently has a screenplay in development.

**ROBERT SMITH?** is, in addition to the above list, the author of *Bookwyrm*, a guide to the original *Doctor Who* novels, as well as the slightly-less-popular-but-about-equally-studied *Modelling Disease Ecology with Mathematics*. He's also the editor extraordinaire of the *Outside In* series of pop-culture reviews with a twist, covering *Doctor Who*, *Star Trek*, *Buffy*, *Angel* and *Firefly*. In his day job, he's a professor of mathematical biology and a world leading expert on zombies. Yes, really. He also doesn't have a screenplay in development.